Beyond the Occult

COLIN WILSON
BEYOND
THE
OCCULT

BANTAM PRESS

LONDON · NEW YORK · TORONTO · SYDNEY · AUCKLAND

TRANSWORLD PUBLISHERS LTD
61–63 Uxbridge Road, London W5 5SA

TRANSWORLD PUBLISHERS (AUSTRALIA) PTY LTD
15–23 Helles Avenue, Moorebank NSW 2170

TRANSWORLD PUBLISHERS (NZ) LTD
Cnr Moselle and Waipareira Aves,
Henderson, Auckland

Published 1988 by Bantam Press,
a division of Transworld Publishers Ltd
Copyright © Colin Wilson 1988

British Library Cataloguing in Publication Data
Wilson, Colin, *1931–*
Beyond the occult.
1. Occultism
I. Title
133

ISBN 0-593-01174-0

Printed in Great Britain by
Mackays of Chatham PLC, Chatham, Kent

CONTENTS

Analytical Table of Contents

I am asked to write a book about 'the occult'. The moments of 'mystical freedom'. Muz Murray's experience in Cyprus. My own experience in Alsace. Derek Gibson sees inside the trees. Jacob Boehme's vision of 'the signature of all things'. Yuliya Vorobyeva develops X-ray vision. Jim Corbett and his 'jungle sensitiveness'. Why man has lost his 'occult faculties'. Calculating prodigies. How to gain control of our 'hidden powers'. My original scepticism about 'the occult'. Impressive consistency of reports. 'Reading' through the skin of the stomach. 'Community of sensation' under hypnosis. Buchanan and the discovery of psychometry. Peter Hurkos and precognition. My attempts to create a 'Newtonian theory' of the occult. My increasing doubts.

1 Mediums and Mystics
Lawrence LeShan studies Eileen Garrett. She 'psychometrizes' his daughter's hair. The case of the missing doctor. The case of Marmontel's memoirs. Eileen Garrett on mediumship: *'A kind of turning inward'*. Warner Allen's 'timeless moment' at the Queen's Hall. Is time an illusion? Poets as 'natural psychics'. A. L. Rowse is almost decapitated. The 'superconscious attic' of the mind. The mystical experience. Wendy Rose-Neill lies on her lawn. Claire Myers Owen and the 'golden light'. Bucke's flash of 'cosmic consciousness'. 'A brilliant shaft of light from out of the sky.' Vision of God in a cow-barn. Moyra Caldecott and the 'Timeless Reality'. Ouspensky's vision of 'connectedness'. Steppenwolf's mystical insight. Henri Bergson is converted from materialism to mysticism. The inability of thought to grasp experience. Two ways of grasping reality. The left and right brain. Peak experiences. Anne Bancroft's mystical experience. The branch of rhododendron. Douglas Harding loses his head. Is it desirable to have no head? William James's 'Suggestion about Mysticism'. Robert Graves and 'The Abominable Mr Gunn'. Another mathematical prodigy.

2 The Other Self
My dream of the amusement park. Thomson Jay Hudson watches a

hypnotic demonstration. Return of the dead philosophers. Charcot and hypnosis. Man's 'two minds' – the subjective and the objective. The power of the subjective mind: Henry Clay speaks for two hours. The artist who saw a picture before he painted it. Puysegur and 'magnetism'. Councillor Wesermann makes telepathic contact with a friend. The Verity Case. Hudson practises 'distant healing'. His success. Doctor Albert Mason performs a miracle. Why Shakespeare was not Bacon. Learning to use the right brain. The Laurel and Hardy theory of consciousness. The 'robot'. Negative feedback. The power of the Spectre. Graham Greene and the revolver in the corner cupboard. The gloominess of the great philosophers. Schopenhauer complains about life. Dylan Thomas's 'foul mousehole'. Thomas Mann's 'Disillusionment'. Schizophrenic patients 'stop seeing things'. Artsybashev's *Breaking Point*. The Master Ikkyu writes, 'Attention'. Hesse's *Journey to the East*. My experience of being caught in a snowstorm. Raising consciousness by an act of will. The journey to Northampton. Rilke's solution: 'To praise in spite of.'

3 Down the Rabbit Hole
Arnold Toynbee's vision of the battle of Pharsalus. Frank Smythe's vision of the massacre near Glen Glomach. Toynbee's 'time-slip' in Crete. His experience in the ruins of the temple at Ephesus. His vision at Monemvasía. The destruction of Mistrà. The nature of Faculty X. Doctor Johnson and the Happy Valley. Toynbee's vision of 'all history'. Proust and the madeleine dipped in tea. Other experiences of Faculty X described in Proust. 'The past was made to encroach upon the present.' G. K. Chesterton and 'Absurd good news'. Helen Keller learns to spell 'water'. Why Faculty X is so difficult to achieve. Sartre and 'nausea'. Camus and 'the Absurd'. 'Ordinary consciousness is a form of nausea.' Roquentin is 'sickened' by a tree. Maupassant and sexual failure. The 'erase key'. The demon Screwtape heads off a conversion. Physical, emotional and intellectual values. 'Upside-downness'. Sartre in the French Resistance. The parable of the emperor and the grand vizier. The mechanism of 'upsidedownness'. Arthur Koestler joins the Communist Party. Koestler's mystical experience in a Spanish jail. Einstein on science and mysticism. 'Holiday consciousness'.

4 The Information Universe
Mr Chase sees a cottage that no longer exists. 'Time-slips'. The English ladies at Versailles. Jane O'Neill and Fotheringhay Church. Falling 'down the rabbit hole'. J. B. Priestley on Faculty X. Ivan Sanderson's 'time-slip' in Haiti. Can 'time-slips' be explained scientifically. Lethbridge and the 'tape-recording' theory. The Long Gallery at Hampton Court. Buchanan and 'psychic bloodhounds'. Denton experiments with geological fragments. Hudson attacks Denton's results. 'The memory of the subjective mind seems to be practically limitless.' Sulla's villa. Pascal Forthuny psychometrizes a letter by a murderer. Pagenstecher's experiments with

10

Maria de Zierold. Walter Franklin Prince and the 'sea bean'. Maria 'shares' Pagenstecher's consciousness. Rilke's experience at Castle Duino. How to make time stand still. Bentov's *Stalking the Wild Pendulum*. Stephen Jenkins sees a phantom army in Cornwall. Joan Forman sees ghosts at Haddon Hall. 'Tape-recording' of the Battle of Edgehill. Stephen Jenkins on ley lines. Doctor Robin Baker's experiments with earth magnetism. Is dowsing a superstition? Harvalik's experiments with electrical fields. 'The human body is a magnetic detector.' Harvalik detects brainwaves. Lethbridge and the long pendulum. Tom and Mina Lethbridge throw stones. Edgar Devaux traces a missing housewife. Edison invents the gramophone record. Robert Leftwich and the underground water main. My wife investigates Bodmin gaol. Doctor Maximilien Langsner solves a murder case. Is reality 'out there'? 'The hologramatic universe.' Karl Pribram and David Bohm. Could the world be a hologram? Bohm's theory of reality as 'implicate order'. Wing Commander Goddard flies over Drem airfield and sees into the future. Eileen Garrett on clairvoyance.

5 Intrusions?
J. B. Priestley's dream of being shot. Visions seen on the edge of sleep. Wilson Van Dusen on hypnagogic images. Woman who murdered a useless husband. Her powers of prediction. The 'Feminine Aspect of the Divine' writes in Greek. Doctor Houston's patient talks to Socrates. An illiterate servant girl speaks Greek, Latin and Hebrew. 'Sleep learning.' Mavromatis and hypnagogic images. Could they be telepathy? Upton Sinclair experiments with 'mental radio'. Guy Playfair learns to induce hypnagogic states. Playfair transmits mental pictures to an audience. The powers of Marcel Vogel. The girl who woke up in bed with a male colleague. Rudolf Steiner and 'inner space'. Steiner and Faculty X. Blake on imagination. The Akashic Records. Denton's son travels to Mars. Cosmic memory. Swedenborg and the 'spirit world'. The Dutch Ambassador's wife. Jung falls 'down the rabbit hole'. Active imagination. 'Thoughts are like animals in a forest.' 'Some intelligent entity . . . .' Nelson Palmer solves the murder of Joy Aken. Jung's patient commits suicide. Ghosts dictate *Seven Sermons to the Dead*. Jung and the haunted cottage. Jung and the *I Ching*. Jung on synchronicity. Pauli's power to cause accidents. My own experiences of synchronicity. Jacques Vallee and the cult of Melchizedec. Rebecca West in the London Library. Camille Flammarion and M. Fortgibu. Helmut Schmidt's experiments in psycho-kinesis. 'As above, so below.' Can the human mind 'make things happen'?

6 Memories of the Future
Wilbur Wright's best friend foresees his own death. Wilbur Wright dreams winners. Earl Attlee dreams the winner of the Grand National. Lord Kilbracken wins £450. Peter Fairley develops second sight. Wilbur Wright's dreams of the future: the red airliner. J. W. Dunne and *An Experiment with Time*. Dunne's theory of 'serial time'. Lethbridge's

11

dreams of the future. Dunne's 'real time'. J. B. Priestley's theories of time. Ouspensky's 'three-dimensional time'. Arthur Osborne's experiences of precognition. Can the future be altered? Air Marshal Goddard and 'the night my number came up'. Is the future predetermined? G. K. Chesterton on predetermination. Premonitions about the *Titanic*. Amazing 'coincidences' of identical twins. The 'Jim twins'. Glimpses of future romance: Arthur Osborne, J. B. Priestley. Parallel time? Priestley's archives. Woman foresees her son's death. 'A dog is going to bark a long way off.' The 'super-computer' theory. Priestley's 'three selves'. Wilbur Wright's theory of time. Robert Morris is killed by a salute. Wilbur Wright's 'Fixed Time Field'. The paradoxes of quantum physics. Can a photon interfere with itself? Erratic behaviour of electrons. Einstein exclaims, 'God does not play dice.' Einstein proves to be mistaken. Bell's inequality theorem. Identical twins again. The Allans go to Wotton Hatch. Their 'time-slip' experience. Do human beings possess freedom?

7 Minds Without Bodies
Mrs McAlpine's vision of a suicide. 'Paralysis'. Robert Cracknell's experience of 'paralysis'. Sylvan Muldoon and *Projection of the Astral Body*. 'Out-of-the-body experience'. Miss Z reads a five-digit number in the next room. Robert Monroe floats out of his body. Goethe sees his *doppelgänger*. W. B. Yeats and accidental astral projection. Cases from *Phantasms of the Living*. Susie Bauer's experience of astral projection. The girl and the 'magician'. Cases cited by Camille Flammarion. Arthur Ellison's experience of 'astral projection'. Ellison's experiments in the laboratory. Jack Seale is bitten by a twelve-foot black mamba. He recovers eight days after 'dying'. Van Eeden and 'lucid dreams'. The 'dream body'. Albert Heim falls from a ledge. Caresse Crosby is almost drowned. Lyall Watson's 'out-of-the-body experience'. 'Seeing with the eyes of the spirit.' Alexis Didier and 'astral travel'. Didier solves a crime. Mesmer 'influences' a man through a brick wall. Doctor Gibert hypnotizes a woman from a distance. Is it possible to hypnotize someone against his will? The case of Thimotheus Castellan. The case of Franz Walter. Hypnosis in animals. Lady Abercrombie's ability to influence other minds. In betweenness. Robert Monroe visits Andrija Puharich. Divided consciousness. Rosalind Heywood splits into 'White Me' and 'Pink Me'. Sir Auckland Geddes leaves his body. Do we have 'a whole collection of consciousnesses'?

Part Two: Powers of Good and Evil
1 The Search for Evidence
My own involvement in the 'search for evidence'. Screwtape on how to keep human beings stupid. The inability to believe in the unfamiliar when the familiar is at hand. Rimbaud on becoming a visionary. Holidays fill us with *courage*. The Outsider problem. Can civilization survive without religion? Abraham Maslow and peak experiences. Yeats and the

'partial mind'. Multiple personality: the case of Clara Fowler. The three faces of Eve. Are multiple personalities *doppelgängers?* The Doris Fischer case. My panic attacks. 'Discouragement'. The problem of self-division. The case of Billy Milligan. Max Freedom Long and *The Secret Science Behind Miracles*. The Huna theory of the 'three selves'. Doctor Brigham and the 'death curse'. Doctor Leapsley's case of multiple personality. Could multiple personality be 'spirit possession'? Does the soul exist apart from the body? The case of Shanti Devi. The case of Jasbir Lal Jat. Case of Imad. The case of Mary Roff and Lurancy Vennur. William James's theory of multiple personality. The case of Ansel Bourne. The beginning of spiritualism. The Hydesville knockings. Why Hudson did not believe in spiritualism. Nandor Fodor and the poltergeist. The case of Esther Cox. The Rosenheim case. The Pontefract poltergeist. Guy Playfair tells me that poltergeists are spirits. My experiences in Pontefract. The story of the Black Monk.

2 The Truth About Magic
The life of Allan Kardec. Kardec questions the spirits. The success of *The Spirits' Book*. Introduction to spiritism. The spirit healers of Brazil. Arigo, surgeon of the rusty knife. Playfair investigates poltergeists in Brazil. Black magic centres. David St Clair is bewitched. The girl who was driven to suicide by a poltergeist. The story of Marcia and the statue of Yemanja. Why the 'paranormal' is always unbelievable. My reassessment of witchcraft. The North Berwick witches. Witchcraft in Africa. Was the Rosenheim poltergeist the spirit of a murdered girl? The case of the bewitched housewife. Montague Summers and his views on witchcraft. The *Shaman* Raymon Medina. Steiner and the ages of civilization. Margaret Murray and *The Witch Cult in Western Europe*. Stan Gooch on the paranormal. Martyn Pryer is attacked by an 'invisible entity'. Stan Gooch is seduced by a succubus. The case of Ruth. Gooch's 'hypnosis' theory of apparitions. Guy Playfair and the case of the Enfield poltergeist.

3 The World of Spirits
The case that convinced Jung of life after death. The case of Nils Jacobsen. Wilbur Wright sees a ghost. The ghost that shook hands. John Cowper Powys appears to Theodore Dreiser. Are ghosts mental television pictures? The case of the murdered Filipino nurse. The Eric Tombe case. Spirit 'possession' and multiple personality. The nuns of Loudun. Walter Franklin Prince's case of Phyllis Latimer. How James Hyslop came to believe in spirit possession: the case of Frederic Thompson. The cases of Doctor Titus Bull. The case of the 'possessed' Arab youth. Bill Slater fights off possession. Wilson Van Dusen and Emanuel Swedenborg. How Dusen learned to talk to 'spirits'. Philip K. Dick is possessed by a benevolent entity. Tibetan spirit possession. Adam Crabtree and the case of Anna Ecklund. Crabtree's case of Sarah Worthington. The case of the girl possessed by her father. Possession by

family spirits. The girl possessed by Elizabeth Barrett Browning. The case of Marius. Arthur Guirdham on obsession. Ralph Allison and the case of Janette. The case of Carrie Hornsby. The case of Babs. The case of Elise and Shannon. Was 'Dennis' a spirit? Allison's categories of spirit possession. Beyond rationalism.

4 Visions
Eileen Garrett and visionary consciousness. Albert Tucker – an unwilling psychic. The woman who sat on his legs. The man in the tweed overcoat. Rosalind Heywood's psychic experiences. 'The Singing'. Non-human presences. Eileen Garrett's career as a psychic. Death of her children. 'Uvani'. Her increasing dislike of spiritualism. Work in experimental psychical research. An experiment in astral projection. Failure with Zena cards. The haunting of Ash Manor. Paranormal powers among primitive people. The 'telephone' system of the Montagnais Indians. Doug Boyd and Rolling Thunder. Rolling Thunder at Leavenworth Penitentiary. Donald Wilson's story of Hadad. Was Hadad a hypnotist? Daskalos on hypnosis and the Indian rope trick. Daskalos and the Nazi spirits. Daskalos on 'elementals'. Daskalos takes on the karma of his son-in-law. How Markides was convinced. The story of the vampire. An epidemic of black magic. The demon in the bottle. Daskalos and Skylab. Daskalos on concentration. Communication with Nature. Daskalos and Steiner. Daskalos on reincarnation. The three planes of existence. The 'borderland' between two worlds.

5 Completing the Picture
Does it matter whether there is a 'psychic world'? More about mystical experience. Daly King's experience on a railway platform. Compton Mackenzie on a street corner. The leakage of energy. 'To be free is nothing; to *become* free is heavenly.' Freedom and the peak experience. Barbara Tucker's experience listening to Beethoven. Albert Tucker and the Museum of Modern Art. What prevents us from experiencing mystical awareness? Franklin Merrell-Wolff's mystical experience. 'The great Tragedy – the failure of man to realize his own Divinity.' Beethoven on the power of music. Focusing the 'me'. Sex and the peak experience. Daskalos on the two personalities. The problem of 'upside-downness'. The concept of 'completing'. Development of the 'completing' faculty. Kierkegaard: 'Take me to see the director.' The mystic and 'hidden powers'. John Heron and 'astral projection'. 'Protective entities'? Anita Gregory on 'survival'. Lodge and Conan Doyle. T. S. Eliot on Steiner.

6 Towards the Unknown Region
The weak anthropic principle. The strong anthropic principle: the universe *had* to bring life into existence. Fred Hoyle and the 'superintendent'. John Wheeler's participatory anthropic principle. The single photon experiment. Is the universe created by observers? The final anthropic principle: life will never die out. Did life come from 'outside'? The vitalism of

14

Bergson and Shaw. Human evolution. What the mystics say about the nature of the universe. The mystical experience *more real* than ordinary consciousness. R. H. Ward's experience under dental gas. The near-death experience. The 'connectedness' of everything. Ouspensky's vision of a flower. The seven levels of consciousness. What are we doing in this 'wooden world'? The problem of the 'robot'. Non-robotic consciousness. 'The spirit that negates.' Margaret Lane's experience of schizophrenia. The purpose of language. The problem of 'doubt'. The billiard balls. What is imagination? The evolution of human creativity. The 'Outsider' problem. Why Shakespeare thought life 'a tale told by an idiot'. The problem of 'upside-downness'. Grasping the mechanisms of the peak experience. 'Psychic powers' are evidence of man's evolutionary potential.

Bibliography

Index

Acknowledgements

As usual, I owe a considerable debt of gratitude to the Society for Psychical Research (particularly its librarian Nick Clark-Lowes), the College of Psychic Studies, and the London Library. Many friends have also provided me with information, pointed out cases I was unaware of, and recounted personal experiences. These include Muz Murray, Nona Coxhead, John Kennedy Melling, Lyall Watson, Lawrence LeShan, Andrija Puharich, Guy Lyon Playfair, Adam Crabtree, William Arkle, Anne Bancroft, Christopher Bird, Douglas Harding, David Peat, Bill Corliss, Bob Cracknell, J. Finley Hurley, Brian Inglis, Mina Lethbridge, Stanley Krippner, Scott Rogo, Peter Russell, John Heron, David St Clair, Ian Kimber, Joan Foreman and Joe Gaute. Wilbur Wright's kindness in allowing me to quote from his unpublished typescript on the I Ching was a major stimulus in the writing of this book. My friend Howard Dossor introduced me to Albert and Barbara Tucker, whose contribution also proved to be of immense importance. I wish to thank Sir Stephen Runciman for information that enabled me to correct Toynbee's account of his Mistrà experience. Finally, I am deeply grateful to Jim Cochrane for endless editorial suggestions and for his incredible patience.

C.W.
Gorran Haven, Spring 1988.

Prefatory Note

This book is an attempt to summarize everything I have learned about the paranormal in the past twenty years.

When the idea was first suggested to me I felt strong misgivings: it would obviously involve repeating a great many things I had already said in other books. Then I recalled similar misgivings when I had been asked to write a book about Gurdjieff in 1978 – having already discussed him extensively in three earlier books. On that occasion I had brushed aside my doubts, decided to repeat myself where necessary, and found that I gained a completely new insight into Gurdjieff in the process.

In the present case, so much new material came to light that the real problem was how to incorporate it all without making the book overlong. For what repetitions there are I make no apology: they have enabled me to discover new perspectives, and to present an overall picture that would otherwise have been impossible.

Part One
Hidden Powers

Introduction

My serious interest in the paranormal began twenty years ago, in the late 1960s, when an American publisher asked me if I would be interested in writing a book about 'the occult' – a subject that had achieved immense popularity ever since a book called *The Morning of the Magicians* by Louis Pauwels and Jacques Bergier had sold over a million copies in France in 1960. I accepted in a fairly light-hearted spirit. Like most people, I had always enjoyed reading speculations about Atlantis, the Loch Ness monster and the ghosts of Borley Rectory, and had accumulated a fairly large library of second-hand books and cheap paperbacks on such matters. But I had another reason for accepting. For many years I had been possessed by a strong conviction, amounting to a certainty, that all human beings possess 'hidden powers'.

Some of these powers came under the general heading of extra-sensory perception; I had suffered my wife's birth pangs, and on one occasion experienced her toothache. One close family friend had described how she found herself floating up above her body during a serious illness, while another had foreseen a traffic accident – a collision with another taxi – at least a minute before it happened. But it was not this type of 'hidden power' that really interested me. I was even more fascinated by those strange moments of pure joy in which we experience an almost god-like sensation of power or freedom. The following, for example, is taken from a friend's account of an 'illumination' that happened when he was hitch-hiking around the world in 1964:

I had been through a great deal of emotional turmoil and privation during my travels and arrived at the port of Limassol [in Cyprus] with great relief at having left the scenes of my suffering behind me. One evening I was sitting gazing vacantly at the sea in the afterglow of sunset, having just finished a meal in a little Greek eatery, feeling very tranquil and relaxed, when I began to feel a strange pressure in my brain. It was as if some deliciously loving hand had slipped numbingly under my skull and was pressing another brain on top of mine.

I felt a thrilling liquidity of being and an indescribable sensation, as if the whole universe was being poured into me, or perhaps rather as if the whole universe was welling up out of me from some

21

deep centre. My 'soul' thrilled and swelled and my consciousness passed out across the ocean and the land in all directions, through the sky and out into space. Within moments I was among the stars and planets and strange entities of space. Somehow I was aware of great beings, millions of miles high, moving in space, through which the stars could be seen. Wave after wave of revelation swept through my whole being, too fast for my normal mind to record other than the joy and wonder of it.*

I had never experienced anything as overwhelming as this. But ever since childhood I had been prone to drift into those moods of intense happiness and affirmation that the psychologist Abraham Maslow calls peak experiences. One of the most vivid had occurred when I was nineteen and was hitch-hiking my way across France to Strasbourg. A lorry-driver had given me a lift to a little *routier*, and I had eaten a hot meal and drunk a glass of wine. So far I had found it rather a strain being in a foreign country with very little money; but as I walked out of the *routier* and looked across the rolling countryside to the mountains in the distance, I experienced a feeling of joy that was so complete that all the problems of my life vanished into insignificance. It was like a *shift of viewpoint*, as if I had suddenly left my body and was looking down on my own life. No doubt the wine had something to do with it, but that is beside the point, for what I experienced was not just a 'feeling' but a *seeing*. Once again, as on so many other occasions, I could see that the real problem of human beings is that we live too *close up* to life, like a short-sighted painter who has to paint with his nose within an inch of the canvas, and that close-upness deprives us of meaning. We accept this as inevitable – for, after all, we are men, not birds, and modern life requires constant attention to detail. But the 'moments of vision' reveal that this assumption is a mistake. Apparently we possess a faculty that can instantly 'distance' us from present reality – just as the short-sighted painter could, if he wanted, stand back from the canvas and put on a pair of strong glasses. If we could learn to call on this faculty at will our lives would be transformed, for we waste 90 per cent of our time in coping mechanically with minor problems and vastly overestimating them. And if many people could learn to do it our earth itself would be transformed, for most of the ugliness and evil of our lives is due to stress and 'close-upness'.

Perhaps the most important aspect of these 'moments of vision' is that they suggest that there is a way of acquiring knowledge that is quite unlike the ordinary method of 'learning from experience'. When the visionary faculty is switched on the mind seems to be able to penetrate reality – rather in the manner of X-rays – and to grasp meanings that normally elude it.

In 1969 a man named Derek Gibson was travelling to work by

*Muz Murray, *Sharing the Quest* (1986).

motorcycle when he noticed that the sound of his engine had faded to a murmur:

> Then everything suddenly changed. I could clearly see everything as before with form and substance, but instead of looking *at* it all I was looking *into* everything. I saw beneath the bark of the trees and *through* the underlying trunks. I was looking *into* the grass too, and all was magnified beyond measure. To the extent that I could see moving microscopic organisms! Then, not only was I seeing all this, but I was literally *inside* it all. *At the same time* as I was looking into this mass of greenery I was aware of every single blade of grass and fold of the trees as if each had been placed before me one at a time and entered into.
>
> My world became a fairyland of vivid greens and browns, colours not seen so much as felt. Instantly also my mind was not observing but was living what it was registering. 'I' did not exist. Power and knowledge surged through my mind. The words formed in me – I can remember clearly – 'Now I know', 'There is *nothing* I could not answer. I am a part of all this.'*

A similar revelation had come to the Protestant mystic Jacob Boehme in the year 1600. This is how this biographer Bishop Hans Martensen describes it:

> Sitting one day in his room, his eye fell upon a burnished pewter dish, which reflected the sunshine with such marvellous splendour that he fell into an inward ecstasy, and it seemed to him as if he could now look into the principles and deepest foundations of things. He believed that it was only a fancy, and in order to banish it from his mind he went out into the green fields. But here he noticed that he could gaze into the very heart of things, the very herbs and grass, and that actual nature harmonised with what he had inwardly seen.†

It seems obvious that Derek Gibson and Jacob Boehme had the same basic experience, and that therefore it is some perfectly normal faculty that might be activated at any time in any one of us. It is as if the human race is colour-blind – as most animals are – and a few men suddenly develop colour vision.

It also seems clear that there is a close link between these 'mystical' experiences and the faculty labelled extra-sensory perception. For

*Quoted by Nona Coxhead in *The Relevance of Bliss* (1985).
†Hans L. Martensen, *Jacob Boehme, Studies in his Life and Teachings* (1949).

example, the Russian newspaper *Izvestia* reported in June 1987 the case of a woman named Yuliya Vorobyeva, 37, who was pronounced dead after receiving a 380-volt electric shock in March 1978. She recovered after two days in the morgue, but was unable to sleep for the next six months. Then she sank into a long sleep, and awoke to discover that she had acquired paranormal powers. 'I went shopping one morning. I got to the bus-stop and a woman was standing there. Suddenly I was struck by horror – I thought I could see right through this woman like a television screen.' When *Izvestia*'s reporter interviewed her she looked at his stomach and told him correctly what he had had for lunch. Within seconds of meeting a doctor she was able to tell him that one ear was weaker than the other, and that the same was true of his eyes.

Significantly, Vorobyeva also states that she can see ultra-violet rays from the sun. This could offer a clue to her 'X-ray vision'. The human eye is only able to see light of wavelengths of between 16 and 32-millionths of an inch (violet and red respectively). Nature has apparently decided that it would serve no purpose for the eye to detect energy of wavelengths longer than 32 millionths (heat and microwaves), or shorter than 16 millionths (ultra-violet and X-rays). But we might regard these limits as more or less arbitrary. In 1828 a youth named Caspar Hauser walked into Nuremberg with bleeding feet, and it soon became clear that he had been kept captive in a darkened room since birth. Physicians who examined him discovered that as a result he was able to read aloud from the Bible in a completely dark room and see the heat from a stove long before it had become red hot.* Vorobyeva seems to have developed the power to 'see' energy from beyond the other end of the spectrum, including ultra-violet and X-rays; one result – according to *Izvestia* – is that she can see through the asphalt surface of a road to the soil underneath.

It is easy enough to understand why human beings do not possess X-ray eyes. They would simply complicate our lives *without enhancing our power of survival*. If we are to live with maximum efficiency our lives need to be as simple as possible. If a human being could somehow get inside a frog's head he would be astounded at the crude simplicity of its world. Experiments have shown that the frog's eyes pass on only very limited information to its brain – a simplified picture of its surroundings, moving shadows which might be enemies and edible objects like flies. Everything else is ignored. Humans are more complicated because they need to be in order to survive; but anything that has no survival value is filtered out by the senses.

There is strong evidence that we have also 'filtered out' various powers that our ancestors once possessed. The tiger-hunter Jim Corbett, author of *Man Eaters of Kumaon*, explains how he has developed a faculty which he calls 'jungle sensitiveness', which has often saved his life when a tiger has been lying in wait. But such a faculty would obviously be

*See my *Encyclopedia of Unsolved Mysteries* pp. 92–8.

useless to a stockbroker. There is also much evidence – which we shall consider later – that animals and primitive peoples possess far more highly developed powers of extra-sensory perception than civilized human beings. We do not need them; therefore we have discarded them – or rather put them into cold storage, to be recovered as needed (as, for example, by Jim Corbett when stalking tigers). Caspar Hauser and Yuliya Vorobyeva seem to suggest that our brains are 'wired up' to perceive X-rays and infra-red rays but that we only rarely have to call these powers into operation.

But now we come to the most baffling part. It is easy enough to see why man has discarded 'jungle sensitiveness' and other simple forms of ESP: they are no longer essential to his survival. But 'moments of vision' like those experienced by Muz Murray and Derek Gibson are an entirely different matter. Powers like these cannot have been essential to our survival at *any* point in our evolution. In fact they seem to be a contradiction of the theory of evolution. If you think of the evolution of tiny micro-organisms into amoebas, then into fishes, then into land animals, you can see that there was *no* point in our evolution when we needed to the power to see into the heart of trees or to float out among the stars and planets in space. And the same applies to many more mundane faculties. Children known as calculating prodigies can perform incredible feats with numbers. A five-year-old boy named Benjamin Blyth asked his father what time it was and was told, 'Half past four'. A few minutes later the child said, 'In that case I have been alive . . .' and named the exact number of seconds since his birth: about 158 million. His father worked it out on a sheet of paper and said, 'No, you were wrong by 172,800 seconds.' 'No I wasn't,' said the child, 'you forgot the two leap years.'

The obvious explanation for this is that our brains are 'wired up' to calculate numbers, and some brains are better at it than others – after all, an ordinary abacus could calculate in billions and trillions if necessary. But that explanation simply fails to fit the facts. For example, there are certain numbers known as primes – numbers that cannot be exactly divided by any other, like 5, 7, 13, 17 and so on. But there is no simple method of finding out whether a number is a prime except by dividing all the smaller numbers into it. So if a number is extremely large there is no quick way of discovering whether it is a prime or not; even a modern computer would have to do it 'the hard way'. Yet there are certain calculating prodigies who can do it almost instantaneously. The Canadian 'lightning calculator' Zerah Colburn was asked whether a certain ten-digit number was a prime or not; after a moment's thought he replied that it was not, because it could be divided by 641. Yet what he did was a logical impossibility. The psychiatrist Oliver Sacks has described a pair of subnormal twins in a New York mental hospital who amuse themselves by swapping *twenty-four-figure* primes – an even greater impossibility. The brain cannot be 'wired' to perform such feats

25

instantaneously. The twins must be arriving at their results by some non-logical process akin to mystical vision. (Derek Gibson experienced the feeling: 'There is nothing I could not answer. . . .')

Once again we confront the question, how *could* such powers have developed in the normal course of our evolution? Man began as an amoeba, then turned into a fish, then became an amphibian, then developed into a kind of rodent, then into an ape, then into a human being. There is no room in this process for a power of recognizing twenty-four-digit primes. It is easy enough, of course, to explain how we might develop such a power at some *future* date. After all the very word evolution implies an extension of our powers. What is so baffling is that we already appear to possess this power in a latent form. G. K. Chesterton would probably say that it proves that man is a fallen angel rather than a 'risen ape'. Whatever the explanation, it seems to fly in the face of common sense.

Yet if we are willing to use a little imagination we can begin to see at least the outline of an answer. As you are reading these words, try to recall what it was like when you first learned to read – the misery, the exasperation, of trying to understand row upon row of squiggly little symbols; recall how you occasionally felt as though you were suffocating and your head was bursting. Yet now you read almost as naturally as you breathe. That is because you have disciplined all those bursting energies, put them into harness and tamed them as a rider tames a wild colt. Now the discipline has become quite unconscious and you do not even notice it – unless the print is too small or you are feeling tired and impatient. For thousands of years civilized man has been imposing a similar discipline on his senses, so that he no longer notices that he is wearing a saddle and harness.

In effect he has learned to look at the world through a kind of microscope which shows him the immediate present with extreme clarity, so he can handle it with remarkable precision. But since his attention only has room for a small number of things at a time, he is obliged to 'forget' 99 per cent of his experience, or at least place it in a kind of cold storage. (Sherlock Holmes told Watson that he couldn't care less whether the earth went round the sun or vice versa; he said his mind was like an attic that could only store a certain number of facts, so if he admitted some new piece of information he had to throw out an old one.) Animals almost certainly have a far wider and more interesting form of consciousness – probably something closer to the consciousness of a slightly drunken man for whom the whole world is a marvellously warm and glowing place.

The most obvious characteristic of mystical experience is that it happens to *relaxed* people. Muz Murray was relaxing outside a Cypriot café, Boehme was staring at a pewter dish, Derek Gibson was following a familiar route in the early morning. In this state it seems that the harness often slips off and allows us to experience something closer to the free, untrammelled consciousness of the animal or child with its 'glory and freshness'. So instead of being aware of just one or two things, we glimpse the whole panorama of existence. The mentally subnormal twins who can swap twenty-four-digit primes must somehow *hover* above the whole 'number field', like birds looking down on the landscape and seeing hills and lakes and villages all at a glance.

In short, our chief limitation lies in our *assumption* that our narrow, tightly-harnessed consciousness is normal and natural, whereas it is in fact highly abnormal and highly unnatural. The basic problem of human beings is simply an inability to 'get it all together'. We possess all the pieces of the jigsaw puzzle but it is so huge that we never see it as a whole. The moment we learn to *grasp* this fact we have also begun to learn how to achieve the 'moments of vision' *at will*, and how to gain control of our 'hidden powers'.

When I began systematic research for my book *The Occult*, I must admit that my attitude was basically sceptical. As a child I had been fascinated by spiritualism, ghosts and magic, and had devoured all the books in the 'occult' section of our local library, from poltergeists to voodoo. But around the age of eleven my mother presented me with a chemistry set and an uncle produced a book on astronomy, and I fell under the spell of the potent magic of science. Suddenly the 'occult' seemed absurd and slightly disgusting. Later on, when I decided I wanted to become a writer rather than a scientist, my attitude became less censorious and I began to experience a certain nostalgia for the interests of childhood – such as murder and the supernatural. At twenty-four, as the author of a successful book, I once again began to accumulate a library on the 'supernatural'. But I was inclined to treat it as light summer reading. I had no doubt whatever that most 'occultists' are indulging in pure wishful thinking.

As I began to study the subject systematically this attitude soon changed. I was struck first of all by the impressive consistency of reports of telepathy, 'second sight' and precognition. If they were really lies or delusions they ought to possess as much variety as a shelf-full of novels: in fact, they all sounded remarkably similar. The same was true of reports of magic and contact with 'spirits': you would expect to find very little in common between the beliefs of an African witch-doctor, an Eskimo shaman and a Siberian medicine-man. In fact they are practically interchangeable. Invented ghost stories – by writers like Dickens or M. R. James – are full of a most weird diversity of occurrences; real ghost stories all sound alike. It was soon obvious to me that I was not studying a subject full of imaginative inventions or impostures, but a fairly narrow range of facts, just as in astronomy or cybernetics. As a result I soon became convinced that the evidence for poltergeists, premonitions and second sight is as sound as the evidence for atoms and electrons. I wrote in *The Occult*, 'I sympathize with the philosophers and scientists who

27

regard it as emotional nonsense, because I am temperamentally on their side: but I think they are closing their eyes to evidence that would convince them if it concerned the mating habits of albino rats or the behaviour of alpha particles.'

For someone trained as a scientist, the domain of the paranormal was like travelling to a foreign country. I found myself in a strange and exciting world that was also reassuringly consistent. It could be explored exactly like a foreign country, by wandering around and studying what was to be seen. Admittedly parts of it had to be treated with suspicion, like any modern tourist trap. But in deciding what to believe and what not to believe I applied exactly the same standards that I would apply in science. If something had been observed independently by a number of trust-worthy observers, then I was inclined to accept it as fact. But some of these facts certainly left me feeling baffled. For example, a German doctor named Justinus Kerner spent three years studying a 'psychic' lady called Frieder-icke Hauffe and had no doubt whatever that she could read a book that was placed, face downwards, against her bare stomach. By any normal scien-tific standards that sounds absurd; yet it was observed many times by nineteenth-century investigators. Professor Cesare Lombroso, a con-firmed scientific 'materialist', studied a girl who could see through her ear and smell through her chin. The possibility that she was cheating vanished entirely when her sense of smell transferred itself to the back of her foot: if pleasant smells were brought close to her heel, she smiled, while unpleas-ant ones made her react with disgust. Lombroso also came across the case of a girl who developed X-ray vision and asserted that she could see worms in her intestines – she counted thirty-three. Under treatment she excreted exactly thirty-three worms.

Another curious phenomenon that I came to accept as a fact was called 'community of sensation'. When Alfred Russel Wallace – co-founder of the theory of evolution – was a young teacher he became interested in hypnotism and experimented with a number of his pupils. When one of these pupils was in a trance he could share Wallace's sense of taste and smell. When Wallace sucked a lump of sugar, the boy went through sucking motions; when Wallace tasted salt, he grimaced; when Wallace stuck a pin in himself, the boy jumped and rubbed the appropriate part of his body. Years later, when Wallace was chairman of a scientific commit-tee, he received a paper from a young Irish professor named William Barrett who had taken part in similar experiments and seen a young girl distinguish between various substances that the hypnotist put into his own mouth. So Wallace had no doubt that Barrett was telling the truth. The rest of the committee lacked Wallace's experience, and the paper was never published. But Wallace was so convinced that such matters deserved to be investigated that he became a founder member of the Society for Psychical Research. Since that time 'community of sensation' has been observed again and again by open-minded investigators. For example, Dr Gustav Pagenstecher, a German physician working in Mexico City, began to treat a patient called Maria de Zierold soon after the First World War and discovered that he could cure her insomnia with hypnosis. When in a trance Maria de Zierold's senses were apparently transferred to the hypnotist so that she could taste substances he put into his mouth, feel the burning of a match he held underneath his hand and hear the ticking of his watch. And even though her eyes were closed she could see him quite normally and describe the things he was doing, even in the next room. On the whole, then, most open-minded enquirers would agree that 'community of sensation' is a scientifically established fact. Only scientists continue to regard it as a myth.

The same applies to psychometry, the ability possessed by certain people to hold some object in their hands and 'read' its history. In 1843 an American doctor named Joseph Rodes Buchanan met Bishop Leonidas Polk, who told him that he could always distinguish brass, even in the dark, because when he touched it he felt a 'brassy' taste in his mouth. Buchanan decided to try this out on his pupils and was fascinated to discover that many of them could detect various substances with their fingertips, even when the substance had been swathed in thick brown paper. But his greatest surprise came when some of his best 'sensitives' showed themselves able to hold a sealed letter in their hands and describe the person who had written it in precise detail. They were also able to 'sense' the writer's mood. A disciple of Buchanan named William Denton, a professor of geology in Boston, began his own series of tests with geological specimens – rocks, meteorites, prehistoric bone fragments and so on – and found that his best 'sensitives' had very precise 'visions' of the place where the object originated. Both Denton and Buchanan wrote long books describing their experiments, which excited widespread interest at the time. But scientists quickly lost interest in these wonders, particularly when 'psychometry' (Buchanan's coinage, meaning 'soul-measurement') was taken up by spiritualists and occultists. Hundreds of well-documented cases* leave little doubt that psychometry is one of the commonest 'paranormal faculties'. But science continues to ignore the subject, and even serious investigators of the paranormal seem to regard it with a kind of embarrassment. (For example, Brian Inglis does not even refer to it in his comprehensive history of the paranormal, *Natural and Supernatural.*)

All this should make it clear why, when I had finished writing *The Occult* in 1971, I had no doubt whatever that I was dealing with scientific actualities and not with the delusions of muddle-headed spiritualists. Even that most baffling of all paranormal faculties, precognition – the ability to glimpse the future – was so exhaustively documented that there could be no possible doubt that it occurs again and again. So I arrived at the reasonable conclusion that human beings possess a whole range of 'hidden powers' of which they are usually unaware, and that these

*See my book *The Psychic Detectives*. Denton's major work *The Soul of Things* has now been republished by Aquarian Press.

include telepathy, 'second-sight', precognition and psychometry. It seemed fairly obvious that our ancestors possessed these faculties to a far higher degree, and that we have gradually lost them because we no longer need them. This seemed to be illustrated by the case of the Dutch 'clairvoyant' Peter Hurkos, who became aware of his powers as a result of an accident during the Second World War in which he fell off a ladder and cracked his skull. As he began to recover in hospital he found that he 'knew' things about his fellow patients simply by looking at them – for example, that the patient in the next bed had sold a gold watch left to him by his father. But this was not simply telepathy, for when Hurkos shook hands with a patient who was about to leave he suddenly 'knew' that the man was a British agent and that he would be killed shortly. This insight almost cost him his life, for the Dutch Resistance assumed that Hurkos was working for German intelligence and it was only with the utmost difficulty that he convinced them that he possessed genuine powers of clairvoyance.

But the most interesting point about the case of Hurkos is that after he left hospital he could not work at any normal job because he was unable to concentrate. It was not until he stumbled upon the idea of using his newly-discovered powers as a stage 'magician' that he was again able to start supporting himself and his family. This reveals clearly why man has suppressed his 'psychic' abilities; they involve a kind of mental receptivity, an 'openness' that would make him far less efficient at everyday living.

As I wrote *The Occult* I experienced the pleasurable excitement of someone who sees fact after fact fall neatly into place – I imagine Newton must have felt something of the sort as he wrote the *Principia*. And this was the example that was at the back of my mind in writing *The Occult* and its sequel *Mysteries*. It was breathtaking to realize that so many of the things I had regarded as superstitious absurdities had a sound basis in fact. And if they were factual then they could be incorporated into some sort of scientific framework. And since I had started life as a scientist – my first book, written at the age of thirteen, had been a seven-volume *Manual of General Science* – it seemed a reasonable assumption that I might be the right person to do it.

And indeed, when I came to re-read the book in proof, I had a satisfying sensation of having created a comprehensive theory that explained the existence of paranormal faculties from a scientific viewpoint. It was as rigorous and logical as I could make it, and I felt that no one could accuse me of being credulous or gullible. The book had considerable success, and it was pleasant to walk into a big department store in my home town and see a whole rack devoted to copies of the paperback. But even by that time I had begun to be troubled by doubts. The more I learned about the paranormal the more I saw I was being absurdly optimistic in believing that I had covered all the basic facts. It was true that the unconscious mind seemed to provide a fairly convincing explanation for telepathy, clairvoyance and psychometry. But it hardly seemed adequate to explain some of the highly convincing evidence for life after death, and even for reincarnation. And it totally failed to explain the experience of my musician friend who was travelling in a taxi along the Bayswater Road when he suddenly *knew* that another taxi would jump the traffic lights at the Queensway intersection and hit them sideways-on. The fact that it was late at night and he was exhausted after playing in a concert could help to explain why he was in the right condition to receive the message from his unconscious mind. But how could his unconscious mind know about something that was going to happen in a minute or so? Even if it could somehow 'see' the other taxi approaching the traffic light and read the mind of the driver, he could still not *know* that there would be a collision. There can be no 'scientific' explanation for precognition because it is obviously impossible to know about an event which has not yet happened. Yet my reading revealed that there are hundreds of serious, well-documented cases.

It was at this point that I found an important clue in a book that had been presented to me by its author not long after publication of *The Occult*. It bore the intimidating title *Towards a General Theory of the Paranormal* and it led me on to so many fresh clues and new insights that they will require a chapter to themselves.

1

Mediums and Mystics

In 1964 an experimental psychologist named Lawrence LeShan became increasingly interested in the way the mind can influence the body and decided – with some misgivings – to study the evidence for extra-sensory perception. This was out of sheer conscientiousness, for his training as a scientist had convinced him that it could not exist. 'I was fairly sure that I would wind up trying to figure out how it was that serious men like William James, Gardner Murphy, and half a dozen Nobel Prize winners had been deluded into believing such nonsense.'

Careful study changed his mind:

> To my intense surprise, as I began to read the scientific journals and serious books in the field, it became obvious that the material *was* valid. The standards of research were extremely high, and the evidence scientifically valid. The only alternative explanation to the hundreds of carefully studied 'spontaneous' incidents reported, and the hundreds of scientifically controlled laboratory experiments, was that the greatest conspiracy in history had been going on for more than eighty years.

LeShan heard that a medium named Eileen Garrett was highly regarded in scientific circles, and decided to work with her. His first professional encounter convinced him that she was no fraud. Previous researchers had been trying to get Mrs Garrett to 'guess' the colour of cardboard squares. That sounded dreary, so LeShan decided to try to make it more interesting. He clipped a lock of hair from the head of his twelve-year-old daughter Wendy, persuaded the next-door neighbour to give him a tuft of hair from the tail of their dog, and plucked a fresh rosebud from the garden. These were placed in three clear plastic boxes, and LeShan began the experiment by telling the medium what was in each of them. Then he retreated behind a screen with the boxes, and Mrs Garrett had to put her arm in through a narrow hole. LeShan took a box at random and placed it where she could touch it. She immediately identified it correctly as the box containing the lock of his daughter's hair, then went on to make incredibly accurate comments about the child. Her first remark was, 'I think I'll call her Hilary – she'll like that.' In fact when Wendy LeShan was four years old she had developed a crush on a

32

girl called Hilary, and had begged her parents to let her change her name to Hilary. But the incident was long forgotten – it had not even been mentioned in the family for years.

Mrs Garrett then went on to make a series of weirdly accurate comments on Wendy – for example, that she loved horses and had recently developed an unexpected interest in American history.

Her insights into the dog were equally impressive, particularly since LeShan knew nothing about dogs and the neighbours had only just moved in. Mrs Garrett announced that the dog had had a severe pain in its paw, and that it seemed to have a Sealyham companion. The neighbours verified that the animal had cut his paw so badly that it had turned septic and necessitated a six-week stay in hospital, and that although a pure-bred Welsh terrier, something about its bone structure made dog fanciers ask whether it had a touch of Sealyham. (LeShan did not even know what a Sealyham was.) As to the rose, Mrs Garrett commented that the soil was too acid for it to grow well – something LeShan had been told by expert gardeners.

But perhaps his most impressive encounter with Eileen Garrett concerned a missing doctor. The man had gone to a medical conference in a distant town and failed to return home. Knowing that he was working with Mrs Garrett, the doctor's wife sent LeShan a two-inch square from the shirt the doctor had been wearing the day before he vanished. When Leshan visited the medium he said nothing about the missing doctor. But when she was in a trance he placed the cloth in her fingers and told her that the man to whom it belonged had disappeared. Mrs Garrett replied, 'He is in La Jolla [California]. He went there due to a psychic wound he suffered when he was fourteen years old and his father disappeared.'

That evening Leshan telephoned the wife – who lived a thousand miles away – and asked her if anything had happened to her husband between the ages of thirteen and fifteen. She replied that his father had deserted the family when he was fourteen and returned home twenty-five years later. In due course the doctor reappeared of his own accord and verified that he had indeed been in La Jolla.

The more LeShan investigated mediums, the more he became convinced that they see the world from a viewpoint that differs completely from that of the ordinary person. It is as if they can put themselves into states of mind in which they cease to be subject to the ordinary limitations of space and time. LeShan cites a case involving Mrs Margaret Verrall, the wife of a Cambridge don, who was one of the most remarkable mediums in the early decades of the twentieth century. When practising 'automatic writing' Mrs Verrall recorded the following scene: 'The cold was intense and a single candle gave poor light. He was lying on the sofa or on a bed and was reading Marmontel by the light of a single candle. . . . The book was lent to him, it did not belong to him. . . .' In a script a few days later she wrote, 'Marmontel is right. It is a French book, a memoir I think. Passy may help, souvenirs de Passy, or Fleury. The book was bound and was lent – two volumes in old-fashioned binding and print.'

Some time later she met a friend, a Mr Marsh, who told her that she had accurately described something that had happened to him. He had borrowed one volume of Marmontel's memoirs from the London Library and taken it to Paris, where he had read it in bed, on a freezing cold night, by the light of a single candle. The chapter he had been reading was about the discovery of a picture painted at Passy and associated with a certain M. de Fleury.

An interesting piece of clairvoyance, one might think, but not particularly remarkable. . . . Until we learn that Mrs Verrall wrote her description on 11 December 1911 and Mr Marsh did not read the book in Paris until 21 February of the following year. Mrs Verrall had accurately foreseen something that would not happen for more than two months.

But then the episode of the vanishing doctor seems to carry the same implications. The doctor's wife sent a shirt he had worn on the day *before* he went off to the conference. And all the evidence indicates that the doctor vanished on a sudden impulse several days later. How could the shirt afford Mrs Garrett a clue to something that was to happen in the future? LeShan decided that the best way of finding out was to ask her – in fact to ask all the 'sensitives' he could find what it felt like to 'know' something that it was logically impossible to know.

'When I approached them with this question, something fascinating immediately happened. "Oh yes," they said, "when we are getting the paranormal information the world looks different than at other times." "Different?" I asked, as this clearly seemed very important. "Different how?"' Mrs Garrett explained that she somehow shifted her whole field of awareness, and that this involved a kind of *turning inward*. She did this, she said, by a sort of self-hypnosis. Asked what she meant by this she explained, 'It is a withdrawal from the conscious self into an area of the non-conscious self. And . . . within this other mind, life is being worked out on a different level.' She described the sensation as being like 'living in two worlds at once'. And she emphasized that her 'glimpses' were not something she achieved with conscious effort; they just 'happened'. 'You open a door for a moment, and are confronted with it. The door closes, as it opened, and the image is gone.'

LeShan was struck by the close similarity between what Mrs Garrett told him and various mystics' descriptions of their sudden 'illuminations'. Here, for example, is a well-known description of an 'illumination' experienced by a modern writer, Warner Allen:

It flashed up lightning-wise during a performance of Beethoven's Seventh Symphony at the Queen's Hall, in that triumphant fast movement when 'the morning stars sang together and all the sons of God shouted for joy'. The swiftly flowing continuity of the music was not interrupted, so that what Mr T. S. Eliot calls 'the intersection of the timeless moment' must have slipped into the interval between two demi-semi-quavers. When, long after, I analyzed the happening in the cold light of retrospect, it seemed to fall into three parts: first, the mysterious event itself which occurred in an infinitesimal fraction of a split second; this I learned afterwards from Santa Teresa to call the Union with God; the Illumination, a *wordless* stream of complex feelings in which the experience of Union combined with the rhythmic emotion of the music like a sunbeam striking with iridescence the spray above a waterfall – a stream that was continually swollen by tributaries of associated Experience; lastly Enlightenment, the recollection in tranquillity of the whole complex field of Experience as it were embalmed in thought-forms and words.*

Here again we have the opening of a door and a sudden brief glimpse. The comparison of many such 'illuminations' with the descriptions of 'psychics' like Eileen Garrett, Rosalind Heywood and Phoebe Payne finally convinced LeShan that both the 'medium' and the mystic experience the same abrupt shift of viewpoint so they find themselves looking into another world. It might be compared to a man sitting in a boat looking at the surface of the ocean, who suddenly plunges his head beneath the surface and sees an entirely new world down below. And for some odd reason beyond our understanding, this paranormal world below the 'sea' is *timeless*, so that events in the future or the past can be studied just as easily as the present. This is one of the most basic statements of all the mystics: that time is somehow an illusion. And this, LeShan thought, must be the ultimate solution – the *only* solution – to the mystery of precognition. Of course the statement that time is unreal strikes most of us as nonsense – the philosopher G. E. Moore thought he had disproved it by pulling out his watch – yet if there are really people who can foresee the future then our commonsense view of time as a one-way street *must* somehow be wrong.

LeShan first outlined these ideas about mystics and mediums in a small book called *Towards a General Theory of the Paranormal* (1969), and when he presented me with a copy in the early 1970s I was immediately struck by the similarity of these views to a theory I had put forward in *The Occult*: that poets seem to be natural 'psychics'. I had cited a number of cases – some of them gathered at first hand – of poets who had had experiences of 'second sight' or precognition. The poet and historian A. L. Rowse had described how he was leaning out of an old-fashioned Victorian window at Christ Church when it entered his head, 'Suppose the thing should fall?' Being in a black mood he said to himself, 'Let the damned thing fall!' As he withdrew his head a moment later the sash window fell with a crash that would probably have broken his neck if he

*Warner Allen, *The Timeless Moment*, 1946.

35

had still been leaning out. I theorized that the poet is a person who has the power to sink into moods of reflective calm in which he withdraws *into himself*, and in such moods he becomes aware of the voice of the unconscious mind. Or, as LeShan expresses it, 'The sensitive opens a channel of communication to some part of his non-conscious self which normally operates in this way.'

LeShan was also willing to entertain a notion first put forward by the psychical researcher Frederick Myers in the 1880s: that the part of the 'non-conscious self' which has paranormal powers is not the unconscious mind as described by Freud – a kind of dark basement, full of guilts and repressions – but some kind of *superconscious* mind, a kind of 'attic', as much above 'everyday awareness' as the subconscious basement is below it. And this was also the view held by Mrs Garrett:

> There are certain concentrations of consciousness in which awareness is withdrawn as far as possible from the impact of all sensory perceptions. . . . Such withdrawals of consciousness from the outer world are common to all of us in some measure . . . .
>
> What happens to us at these times is that, as we withdraw from the environing world, we relegate the activities of the five senses to the field of the subconscious, and seek to focus *awareness* (to the best of our ability) in the field of the superconscious – the timeless, spaceless field of the as-yet-unknown.

Most of us – as Mrs Garrett remarks – have some experience of this kind of thing: for example, we can occasionally become so deeply absorbed in a book that if someone slams a door it almost gives us a heart attack. We also slip into this same world of 'deep absorption' on the edge of sleep (a subject that will be explored in chapter 6). But these excursions are usually brief: we either fall asleep or quickly return to the normal world. What Mrs Garrett seems to be suggesting is that the psychic has the power to change her viewpoint so as to slip into this state at will. But once it has been attained she has no further power: the will goes to sleep. It is no use trying to obtain results: they can only be obtained by *not* trying. Eileen Garrett remarked, 'I knew from experience that conscious effort was the one thing which would produce no results that could be described as supernormal.'

In an essay called 'Mysticism and Logic' Bertrand Russell asserts that all mystics seem to agree on four basic points: (1) that there is a better way of knowing than through the senses, (2) that there is a fundamental unity or oneness in the universe, (3) that time is an illusion, (4) that evil is a mere appearance. Russell considers these statements and ends by dismissing them as nonsense – his own final conclusion being that 'scientific philosophy comes nearer to objectivity than any other human pursuit'. Most normal people will be inclined to agree with him. Yet as soon as we begin to study accounts of mystical experience one thing becomes very clear: that they are all talking about exactly the same thing. What follows are a few typical accounts, taken from Nona Coxhead's *The Relevance of Bliss*. The first is a description by a medical journalist, Wendy Rose-Neill:

I had always found gardening a relaxing activity, and on this particular day I felt in a very contemplative frame of mind. I remember that I gradually became intensely aware of my surroundings – the sound of the birds singing, the rustling of leaves, the breeze on my skin and the scent of the grass and flowers.

I had a sudden impulse to lie face down on the grass and as I did so, an energy seemed to flow through me as if I had become part of the earth underneath me. The boundary between my physical self and my surroundings seemed to dissolve and my feeling of separation vanished. In a strange way I felt blended into a total unity with the earth, as if I were made of it and it of me. I was aware of the blades of grass between my fingers and touching my face, and I was overwhelmed by a force which seemed to penetrate every fibre of my being.

I felt as if I had suddenly come alive for the first time – as if I were awakening from a long deep sleep into the real world . . . . I realized that I was surrounded by an incredible loving energy, and that everything, both living and non-living, is bound inextricably with a kind of consciousness which I cannot describe in words.

Here is an account by an American authoress, Claire Myers Owen:

One morning I was writing at my desk in the quiet writing room of our house in Connecticut. Suddenly everything within my sight vanished right away. No longer did I see my body, the furniture in the room, the white rain slanting across the windows. No longer was I aware of where I was, the day or hour. Time and space ceased to exist.

Suddenly the entire room was filled with a great golden light, the whole world was filled with nothing but light . . . .

Extraordinary intuitive insights flashed across my mind. I seemed to comprehend the nature of things. I understood that the scheme of the universe was good, not evil as our Western society had taught me as a child; all people were intrinsically good. Neither time nor space existed on this plane . . . .

This flood of light is a common feature of mystical experiences. In one of the most famous of all books on mysticism, Richard Maurice Bucke described his own experience as he was driving home in a hansom cab:

All at once, without warning of any kind, I found myself wrapped in a flame-coloured cloud. For an instant I thought of fire, an immense conflagration somewhere close by . . . the next, I knew that the fire was within myself. Directly afterwards there came upon me a sense of exultation, of immense joyousness, accompanied or immediately followed by an intellectual illumination impossible to describe. Among other things . . . I saw that the universe is not composed of dead matter, but is, on the contrary, a living Presence; I became conscious in myself of eternal life. It was not a conviction that I would have eternal life, but a consciousness that I possessed eternal life then; I saw that all men are immortal. . . . The vision lasted a few seconds and was gone.

Bucke labelled his glimpse 'cosmic consciousness' and gave his book the same title. It consists of fifty studies of mystics who have experienced 'cosmic consciousness', beginning with the Buddha and ending with the Victorian Edward Carpenter. Bucke jumped to the conclusion that such an experience is rare – and that since there are an increasing number of modern examples, mankind is probably evolving to a higher level of awareness. In fact modern surveys – such as those taken by Sir Alister Hardy's Religious Research Unit in Oxford* – show that an incredible 36 per cent of people have had some kind of religious or mystical experience.

Another basic element in accounts of mystical experience is the feeling that the light – or power – comes from *within*. Muz Murray's account of his 'illumination' in Cyprus contains the phrase, ' . . . an indescribable sensation as if the whole universe was being poured into me, or rather, more as if the whole universe was welling out of me from some deep centre.' One of Nona Coxhead's correspondents, Jim Harrison, told her how he had been wondering how God could permit his wife to remain ill when it struck him, 'Maybe it wasn't God's fault after all.'

So then I thought all right, I take it all back, and filling my heart with the tender love often reserved for my little daughter, I projected it towards him, thinking, if you exist then I give you my love.

I could feel this love being passed on and on, and then suddenly it returned, a brilliant shaft of light from out of the sky, brighter by far than the mid-morning sun, permeating me with such an intensity of happiness and Love as to halt me in my tracks with a jump for joy – and lingering for five or ten seconds before fading away. I knew intuitively that this light, plainly visible, somehow, mysteriously, stemmed from within.

*See *The Spiritual Nature of Man*, A Study of Contemporary Religious Experience, Oxford 1979.

Jim Harrison, like so many others who have experienced a flash of 'cosmic consciousness', concluded:

> So then I knew for certain that God does indeed exist, that he is love, that he is joy, that he is light, that he stems from within as much as from without, and that we alone are responsible for our own sufferings and problems in consequence of the mis-use of our free will.

C. G. Price, a farmer whose farm was on the point of bankruptcy, had a similar experience of light:

> With thoughts of self-pity such as these in my mind, one Sunday morning in February 1968 ... I set about the task of bedding my cows down with straw ... I don't even remember the feeling creeping up on me, but suddenly....
>
> I seemed to be enveloped in a cocoon of golden light that actually felt warm, and which radiated a feeling of Love so intense that it was almost tangible. One felt that one could grasp handfuls of it, and fill one's pockets.
>
> In this warm cocoon of golden light I sensed a presence which I could not actually see but knew was there. My mind became crystal clear, and in an instant of time I suddenly knew, without any doubts, that I was part of a 'Whole'. Not an isolated part, but an integral part. I felt a sense of 'One-ment'. I knew that I belonged and that nothing could change that. The loss of my farm and livelihood didn't matter any more.

In fact he *was* forced to sell the farm, but his mystical experience made this seem unimportant.

Moyra Caldecott, a South African schoolgirl, had a similar experience when kneeling at the altar rail to take Communion. As the bishop placed his hand on her head:

> I suddenly seemed to cease to be me (that is, in the sense of 'me' I had thought I was – living in a particular house, in a particular street, going to a particular school). I felt the most incredible flow of energy and power coursing through me and had what I believe to be an experience of Timeless Reality ... of consciousness that took in everything without limit ... but reacted to nothing except in the sense of 'knowing' ... and ... 'loving'.

In fact it is very tempting to say that what mystical experiences all have in common is a sudden sense of one's *real* identity, and that this 'real self' is in some sense god-like – could even be described as God.

But perhaps the most remarkable of all accounts of mystical experience

39

is to be found in P. D. Ouspensky's book *A New Model of the Universe*, in a chapter called 'Experimental Mysticism'. Ouspensky was the most important follower of the Russian philosopher and mystic G. I. Gurdjieff, but he was also a considerable thinker in his own right, as his books reveal. Ouspensky does not tell us the details of how he achieved his states of mystical consciousness, but his biographer James Webb is probably correct in assuming that he used yogic and magical methods combined with the use of some sort of drug, almost certainly nitrous oxide – 'laughing gas'.* Ouspensky states that the change took place more quickly and easily than he had expected. The account that then follows is one of the most important and detailed in the whole literature of mysticism.

'The unknown', Ouspensky notes, 'is unlike anything that we can suppose about it. The complete unexpectedness of everything that is met with in these experiences, from great to small, makes the description of them difficult.' And he goes on to make an observation of central importance:

> First of all, everything is unified, everything is linked together, everything is explained by something else and in turn explains another thing. There is nothing separate, that is, nothing that can be named or described *separately*. In order to describe the first impressions, the first sensations, it is necessary to describe *all* at once. The new world with which one comes into contact has no sides, so that it is impossible to describe first one side and then the other. All of it is visible at every point . . . .'

Here we have one of the most basic assertions that all descriptions of mystical experience have in common. *Everything is seen to be connected.* And the word 'seen' deserves to be underlined. This world of infinite relationships, in which everything is connected with everything else, is seen all at once – from a bird's-eye view, as it were. And language instantly becomes useless, because it can only pin down one thing at a time. 'A man becomes lost amidst the infinite number of totally new impressions, for the expression of which he has neither words nor forms.'

What seems equally strange is that the normal sense of the distinction between objective and subjective disappeared:

> Here I saw that the objective and the subjective could change places. The one could become the other. It is very difficult to express this. The habitual mistrust of the subjective disappeared; every thought, every feeling, every image, was immediately objectified in real substantial forms which differed in no way from the forms of objective phenomena; and at the same time objective

*James Webb, *The Harmonious Circle*, p. 112.

phenomena somehow disappeared, lost all reality, appeared entirely subjective, fictitious, invented, having no real existence. . . .

And he goes on to say that this strange world resembled more than anything else 'a world of *very complicated mathematical relations*'.

This vision of infinite meaning made it very difficult to carry on a conversation, for between each word of the sentence so many ideas occurred that it was difficult to remember what he intended to say next. He began a sentence with the words, 'I said yesterday . . .' but could simply get no further. The world 'I' raised hundreds of insights about the meaning of 'I', the word 'said' raised just as many ideas about speech and self-expression, each of which produced 'an explosion of thoughts, conjectures, comparisons and associations', and the word 'yesterday' led to endless thoughts and ideas about the nature of time, so that he was left with a feeling of breathlessness that made it impossible to continue.

Something strange also happened to his sense of time, so that when his companion spoke, there seemed to be an immense gap between each of his words. 'When he had finished a short sentence, the meaning of which did not reach me at all, I felt I had lived through so much during that time that we should never be able to understand one another again, that I had gone too far from him.'

All this, says Ouspensky, was accompanied by immensely powerful emotional states. 'I took in everything through feeling, and experienced emotions which never exist in life.' His inner world became a kaleidoscope of 'joy, wonder, rapture, horror, continually changing one into the other'. The state seemed to allow access to infinite knowledge, but when he looked for the answer to any particular question, it 'began far away and, gradually widening, included everything, so that finally the answer to the question included the answers to all possible questions'. He encountered the same problem when he looked at physical objects: an ashtray seemed to arouse an infinite succession of meanings and associations, so that he scrawled on a slip of paper, 'A man can go mad from one ashtray.' And the ashtray, like everything else, seemed to be *communicating* with him, almost as if it had a voice.

The remainder of Ouspensky's description is too long and detailed to quote here even in summary (although I shall have occasion to mention specific items elsewhere in this book). His experiments usually ended in sleep, and his awakening the next morning was a dreary and disappointing experience. The ordinary world seemed unutterably dull:

. . . this world contained something extraordinarily oppressive: it was incredibly empty, colourless and lifeless. It was as though everything in it was wooden, as if it was an enormous wooden machine with creaking wooden wheels, wooden thoughts, wooden

41

moods, wooden sensations; everything was terribly slow, scarcely moved, or moved with a melancholy wooden creaking. Everything was dead, soulless, feelingless.

They were terrible, these moments of awakening in an unreal world after a real one, in a dead world after a living, in a limited world, cut into small pieces, after an infinite and entire world.

In other words it is as if man found himself stranded on a planet whose gravity was so enormous that he was unable to stand upright – unable even to crawl on his hands and knees without immense effort. (Gurdjieff once said that our world is the cosmic equivalent of Outer Siberia.) In this iron world even thought is trapped by the tremendous gravity, so that it has to drag itself along the ground like a wounded animal. For the most part consciousness is little more than a mere reflection of the environment, and life is basically a mere succession of visual images, of being 'here and now'. *This* is why our world seems to be 'cut into small pieces', why its basic characteristic is 'separateness'. If you were utterly exhausted as you read this page it would dissolve into separate words, and even if you succeeded in grasping the meaning of an indivudal sentence the total meaning of the paragraph would still elude you. This is what our world is like. Everything stands separate and disconnected, and we have become so accustomed to this state of affairs that we assume that it is natural and inevitable. Yet it is *not* natural, any more than it is natural to fail to grasp the meaning of a sentence. And we realize this every time a spring morning fills us with a sense of the sheer *interestingness* of the world. 'Separateness' is unnatural; the true and natural state of affairs is a basic 'connectedness', just as Ouspensky realized during his mystical experiments.

In short this world, which seems to us so oppressively real, has been robbed of a dimension of reality by the feebleness of human consciousness and its inability to function efficiently in the powerful gravitational field of our universe. This is only a part of the problem. What turns a difficult situation into a dangerous one is that our mental numbness deprives us of all sense of direction, so that most human beings have given up any attempt to see things as a whole. In effect most of us waste our lives battling against the difficulties of the present moment, and when life offers us the occasional breathing space we are inclined to waste it in boredom or the search for amusement. This is why man, who is fundamentally a well-disposed and sociable creature, is capable of so much evil where his fellow creatures are concerned; the harsh Siberian environment has made him brutal and short-sighted. Yet every flash of poetic or mystical insight makes us instantly aware that such a view is, quite literally, an absurdity.

One thing seems clear: the world glimpsed in these moments of insight is *more* real than the world of everyday reality. And by this time it should also be quite clear that everyone who has experienced these glimpses has *seen* the same thing. It always involves the recognition that our usual sense of being at the mercy of circumstance, of being a slave of material reality and our own bodies, is an illusion. We possess 'hidden powers', tremendous reserves of unsuspected strength. One simple consequence of this insight is the power to heal sickness, in oneself and sometimes in others. The schoolgirl Moyra Caldecott described how, after her marriage, she developed angina, then had another mystical experience that left her healed. And Lawrence LeShan decided to test the validity of mystical experience by training himself to go into 'altered states of consciousness' through meditation, and developed the power to heal. A chapter of his book *The Medium, the Mystic and the Physicist* is devoted to a description of some of his cases, including that of a boy who broke his back on a trampoline and was diagnosed as being permanently paralysed – until a group led by LeShan tried 'distant healing' and restored feeling to his legs in just about one hour.

But the main insight of all mystical experiences is obviously a sense of *meaning* – a feeling that the universe is not just an accidental conglomeration of matter, the chance result of some unexplainable big bang, but has the same kind of overall pattern and purpose that we can perceive in living organisms. Nobody feels that a flower or a kitten are chance occurrences, like a broken bottle; they obviously are not. And the mystic feels – or rather 'sees' – that the whole universe is a gigantic pattern, like some enormous flower. Mystical experiences invariably seem to instil courage and optimism.

All this enables us to see that in spite of the mystic's insistence that they are ineffable – impossible to express in words – these experiences have a great deal in common with feelings and insights that are common to us all. Nietzsche talked about sudden feelings of overflowing vitality, 'the glorious delight which arises in man from the very depths of nature, at the shattering of the *principium individuationis* . . . the Dionysian rapture whose closest analogy is with drunkenness.' In Hermann Hesse's novel *Steppenwolf* the hero (a typical self-divided 'Outsider') spends a night with a beautiful girl and has an overwhelming feeling of affirmation about his own life:

> For moments together my heart stood still between delight and sorrow to find how rich was the gallery of my life, and how thronged the soul of the wretched Steppenwolf with high eternal stars and constellations. . . . My life had become weariness. It had wandered in a maze of unhappiness. . . . It was bitter with the salt of all human things; yet it had laid up riches, riches to be proud of. It had been, for all its wretchedness, a princely life. Let the little way to death be as it might – the kernel of this life of mine was noble. It came of high descent, and turned, not on trifles, but on the stars.

This is the authentic mystical insight, yet neither Steppenwolf nor his creator were mystics – merely romantics.

43

Mysticism can appear on still lower levels. William James even insists that the feeling we derive from alcohol (in the right circumstances) is a minor form of mystic experience. And 'Walter', the anonymous autobiographer of the sexual classic *My Secret Life*, admits that he sometimes suffers from what he calls 'erotic madness', in which he is so carried away by physical lust that he has no idea of what he says or does. All these experiences obviously have something in common with Bucke's cosmic consciousness. Which inevitably raises the central question, would it be possible to build a bridge between everyday experience and the experience of the mystic, so we could cross it at any time?

In fact the scaffolding for such a bridge has already been erected by a French philosopher, Henri Bergson. Bergson was born in 1859, in the middle of the Victorian era, and soon came to share the materialism of thinkers like Auguste Comte and Herbert Spencer. His fellow students at the Ecole Normale nicknamed him 'the atheist' because he insisted that the universe was a product of purely natural forces and that religion and morality were delusions of the human imagination. When his teacher reprimanded him for keeping his bookshelves untidy and asked, 'How can your librarian's soul stand such a mess?' the whole class shouted in chorus, 'Bergson has no soul.' It was when he became a schoolmaster in the Auvergne and began taking long walks that the peace of the countryside made him aware of the poetic side of his nature. As he looked at the woods and hills his atheistic materialism dissolved away. But it was not so much a religious conversion as a philosophical one. Bergson's great insight was that if we try to grasp reality with the mind we are bound to remain empty-handed. It passes through our fingers like a handful of water. But this does not prove that reality – or water – does not exist, or that the insights aroused in us by nature can be dismissed as 'mere feelings'.

When I draw a line with a ruler, says Bergson, my reason tells me that it consists of billions of points in space. But I know that this is not true, for it is a *continuous* line. If it really consisted of billions of points it ought to be possible to divide it into these points – or at least to imagine it divided into points. But no matter how many points I divide it into I can still imagine billions more points – in fact an infinite number – between them. In theory my pencil should take an infinite amount of time to draw it. Obviously there is something badly wrong with my reason, which tells me that a line consists of points. The same applies to time. How long does twelve o'clock last for? It doesn't last for any period of time, for you can always imagine a billionth of a second to twelve, or a billion-billionth. . . . So, according to reason, time consists of an infinite number of points, each one of which has no duration. In fact we know that time *flows*.

It is as though my rational mind suffered from some odd disability, like colour blindness. If I try to think about a sunset, I can only think about

44

rays of light vibrating in space. If I try to analyze a symphony, I can only speak of wavelengths of sound. If I look at a gramophone record through a microscope, I shall only see wavy bumps in the plastic – yet as the stylus travels over them it creates a Beethoven symphony, which in turn can induce a flash of mystical vision in a man like Warner Allen. The mind is a marvellously powerful instrument, but it is no more capable of *grasping* reality than I can eat gravy with a fork. It was not made for the job.

It seems astonishing that human beings have failed to recognize anything so obvious: *that when we try to grasp reality, we falsify it.* When I respond to a baby's laugh, to a line of poetry, to the smell of a spring morning, I am responding directly to reality. But the moment I try to think about why I respond to these things it is like trying to pick up a soft-boiled egg with a pair of fire tongs; I simply squash it out of shape.

This is not to say we should avoid thinking about reality: thought is a powerful and valuable instrument provided we do not try to use it for picking up soft-boiled eggs. What Bergson recognized as he walked in the countryside of the Auvergne was that our most valuable experiences *cannot* be thought about. But that does not mean they should be ignored or dismissed as 'mere feelings'. All we have to remember is not to try to *reduce* them to the crude simplicity of thought. Bergson had grasped that he had been *closing his senses* to the poetry around him (for the mind has an amazing capacity for ignoring things it considers unimportant), and that his soul had become shrivelled and dehydrated as a result.

In fact closing the senses to these finer shades of meaning can be extremely dangerous: it results in a sense of futility and boredom, the feeling of Ecclesiastes that all is vanity and there is nothing new under the sun. To avoid this problem we merely have to understand that we have *two* instruments for grasping the world around us, not – as we naturally tend to assume – just one. One part of the mind has the power to encounter reality as simply and directly as drinking a glass of water. The other part can only come to terms with reality by strapping it into a kind of rigid iron framework and measuring it with rulers and clocks.

Now in fact science has recently come to recognize the physical existence of these two ways of grasping reality, and that they are located in the left and right halves of the brain – the cerebral hemispheres. The science of split-brain physiology has uncovered the fact that we have two people living inside our heads: the person you call 'you', and a total stranger who lives in the other half of the brain.

Our brains are divided into two, like a walnut. The left hemisphere deals with language and logic, the right with intuition and 'recognition' – you could say that the left side is a scientist and the right an artist. The two halves are joined by a mass of nerve fibre called the commissure or *corpus callosum*. It this is severed – as it is occasionally to cure epilepsy – the patient begins to act like two separate people. One split-brain patient tried to zip up his flies with one hand and unzip them with the other.

Another tried to hit his wife with the left hand while the right held it back. (For some odd reason the right half of the brain controls the left side of the body and vice versa, so it was the intuitive side that was trying to hit her and the rational side that was holding it back.) When a female patient was shown an indecent picture the right half of her brain caused her to blush with embarrassment: when asked why she was blushing she replied, 'I don't know.' The 'I' that spoke was, of course, her left-brain self.

What this clearly demonstrates is that the person you call 'you' lives in the left cerebral hemisphere – the 'logical' half – while the 'stranger' lives in the 'intuitive' half. At first it seems difficult to account for anything so odd, until we recollect that man has been forced to develop his 'logical' aspect in order to build civilization. And this – as we observed in the case of Peter Hurkos – involves *suppressing* faculties that are not essential for survival. In fact brain physiologists call the left hemisphere – the 'you' – the dominant hemisphere and refer to the right as the non-dominant hemisphere. They could be compared to two partners in a marriage, where the husband is highly dominant and the wife unobtrusive and shy.

It is a pity that Bergson did not live long enough to see his philosophy scientifically justified – for that is what split-brain physiology has accomplished. The right brain is concerned with pattern-recognition – which means that a patient with right-brain damage might have difficulty recognizing his own mother, except by *telling* himself that she has grey hair and brown eyes. An undamaged right brain recognizes faces in a flash, without the need to analyze. And the same faculty responds to poetry and music and pretty girls and mountain scenery. And our response to these things is a valid *recognition*, not just a 'feeling'. If science insists on confining itself to those things that can be grasped by the left side of the brain, then it is ignoring a half of reality.

But it would be a mistake to blame the left brain for being too dominant. It is not really a male chauvinist bully. The problem is that in our complex modern civilization, it *has* to work hard just to survive. It can easily become exhausted and overworked, in which case we begin to experience the 'Ecclesiastes effect', the feeling that all is vanity. T. S. Eliot was complaining about his left brain when he wrote:

And I pray that I may forget
These matters that with myself I too much discuss
Too much explain,

and Yeats was speaking of the same thing when he wrote about:

. . . the old mill of the mind
Consuming its rag and bone . . .

46

But this feeling of aridity and futility is simply due to having *forgotten* that we have another faculty for grasping reality. In effect the husband has become so overworked and exhausted that he has forgotten that he has a wife – and, moreover, a wife who can offer him extremely powerful support. So when he feels abandoned and miserable, it often comes as an extremely pleasant surprise to realize that *he is not alone after all*. He collapses from sheer exhaustion and is amazed to be suddenly overwhelmed by an exquisite sensation of relaxation and pure serenity: the recognition that the world *is* a delightful place after all. The psychologist Abraham Maslow called such moments 'peak experiences' – those moments of bubbling, overwhelming happiness when we realize we had forgotten how marvellous life can be. Maslow offered as a typical example the case of a young mother who was watching her husband and children eating breakfast when it suddenly dawned on her how lucky she was, and she went into a peak experience. She had been taking them for granted, then stopped taking them for granted.

An even better example concerns a marine who had been stationed in the Pacific for a long period without seeing a woman. When he went back to base and saw a nurse, he had a peak experience – because, he said, it suddenly struck him *that women are different from men* – that they're soft and curved and gentle and as different from men as horses are from cows. Anyone who is enjoying a holiday has a similar sensation – the delighted feeling that the world is a far larger and more interesting place than we had given it credit for. It is then that we realize that our ordinary workaday awareness tell us lies. It tells us that reality is rather dull and repetitive, and that if we were somewhere else it wouldn't really be all that different from where we are now. And now we see that this is outrageously untrue: the world is full of infinite variety and strangeness. And connectedness.

The problem is that an efficient left brain is a 'workaholic'. This word – which has entered the current vocabulary since the sixties – means a person who has become so accustomed to making an effort that he can no longer enjoy relaxation. He is too tense to relax for long. In the past few thousand years of human evolution the left brain has developed into a workaholic – and this applies to *all* human beings, even the laziest. This is why we have forgotten the sheer variety and strangeness of the universe, and why it took a philosopher like Bergson to even notice that something had gone wrong.

The peak experience makes us aware of the same thing: this is why it is so important. It descends upon us as a flash of *recognition* – the same kind of recognition that made Archimedes leap out of his bath shouting, 'Eureka!' What we recognize is what Bergson put into words: that we have two modes of perception, and that they are *equally valid*. Maslow also made another important observation: that most healthy people have peak experiences every day. The reason is obvious. We have peak experiences when we are full of energy and optimism. But the peak experience is not a mere overflow of energy and optimism: it is a *perception* that comes to us when the brain is highly energized. This explains another important observation made by Maslow. He discovered that when his students began talking and thinking about having peak experiences, they began having peak experiences all the time. This is because the peak experience is a perception – something suddenly *grasped*, like Archimedes' perception of the law of floating bodies. It is not easy to grasp, because of the 'logical' limitations of the left brain. But once it has been seen, once it has become an *insight*, it can be recreated by a kind of mental flick of the wrist.

This is an exciting recognition, for it means that we are on the way to grasping how the peak experience – or even the mystical experience – can be recreated at will. We find it difficult to hold on to such experiences because our words and ideas are too crude and simplistic. (We have seen, for example, how Bergson's insight can actually enable us to understand what happens in the peak experience by providing us with a more complex set of ideas.) A person who is overwhelmed by the mystical experience could be compared to someone who is given a glimpse of a city from an aeroplane, and then told to make a drawing of it from memory. *This* is why the mystical vision is ineffable – not because it is impossible to express in language, but because our language is at present too crude. Once we have learned to make some kind of simple map of the main features of the city, we have taken a major step towards learning how to recreate the peak experience – or the mystical experience – at will.

It must be admitted that Maslow once remarked that peak experiences should not be confused with mystical experiences. But he was only pointing out that they are different in degree, not in kind. In fact it is obvious that the two have a great deal in common. Consider, for example, the following mystical experience described by Anne Bancroft, a lecturer in comparative religion:

> 'When I was young . . . I felt sure that there was a wonder and a mystery and all the world was somehow full of a meaning which I couldn't really understand and couldn't reach . . . I was sure that I truly belonged to it and that it had a great deal to do with God, whom I called the Presence because he seemed often to be present to me when I was alone in the fields and woods.
>
> 'But when I was sixteen I became afraid and stopped it all. I was afraid that I might lose myself altogether and although I had wanted this when I was younger, now the outer, everyday world had attractions for me too and I began to reject the inner, solitary quest.'

That is to say, she deliberately suppressed the right-brain mode of grasping reality in favour of a more practical approach.

When I was very young I married and started a family. The years began to trickle past but the marriage was not a happy one, we were completely unsuited to each other, and it ended with a bitter sense of guilt and failure. I kept the children and took them to America, where I remarried. But this marriage too was founded on sand and not on rock, and in a last-ditch effort to keep it going I persuaded my husband to return with us to England, hoping that a calmer and saner society might help us both. I think it did, but it was too late to save the relationship. It was when this marriage too seemed doomed to end in a wasteland of quarrels, jealousy, fear and hatred, that I suddenly woke up to the fact that something had gone badly wrong, not just with this situation but with me. Looking hard at myself I saw that I had become really futile, so much a slave to my emotions, so involved with my own feelings, so centred on myself that my life had narrowed down to the compulsive behaviour of a zombie. Where was the true? I saw clearly that something vital was missing in me. It lay there out of my reach, even beyond my imagination, because I could not see what it was: I only knew I was without it.

I then came to a time of great despair. In the middle of ordinary life – of looking after my children and sending them to school and playing with them, trying not to be inadequate for them – I saw myself as a person of no light, a person who was thick, opaque and joyless, not a real person at all. A tremendous sense of remorse came over me for the years I had messed up so badly, and an enormous depression closed down . . . .

One night I could not go to bed and I sat still all night, feeling a great repentance and sadness of mind. When the morning light came and the birds began to sing, I suddenly found myself strangely aware of them. I looked into the garden and saw a blackbird and it was as though I had never seen a blackbird before. It had a significance that was completely new to me and I suddenly felt that this blackbird was the most real thing I had ever seen, and that just to see a blackbird in this way would make life worth living. The days that followed were different from any that had passed before. I was suddenly intensely aware of sound and light and found myself more vulnerable to the impact of other people. Other things – a group of trees – would fleetingly take on the significance of the blackbird. I realized I was coming close to something, some new quality.

One evening I was looking at a branch of rhododendron which I had put in a vase. As I looked, enjoying its beauty but without any purpose in my mind, I suddenly felt a sense of communication with it, as though it and I had become one. It seemed to come from my forehead and the feeling was immeasurably happy and strong . . . that strange sense of oneness with the rhododendron seemed to have come about because I was still, and not wanting anything, and therefore somehow free to see it properly and know it as itself.

I wished I could know everything in this way, and then I found myself thinking, why not? It was only myself that was stopping me. There was no limit to the amount of love that I could give to everything that I saw. And then I realized that for most of my life I had never done this. I had thought lots of things not worth my attention because they gave me nothing in return. But now I could not imagine how I could have spent so long turning away from things or being indifferent to them . . . .

A few days later a new and somehow crowning experience came. It was in the morning and I switched on the wireless to hear a concert. As the first note of music sounded, there was an almost audible click in my mind and I found that everything was transformed. I was in a different state of consciousness altogether. It was as though the separate feeling of 'me' which we all feel had gone, clicked away, and instead there was a sense of clarity, of utter beneficent, wonderful emptiness. And in that emptiness there were no barriers. The stones on the road were exquisitively beautiful and as significant as a person. An upright, old-fashioned bicycle propped up by the road was wonderfully funny. It was as though my mind could now embrace, without reserve, all that it encountered, whether people or animals or things, because it was living in clearness and emptiness. I was in this state of the completest and greatest happiness for three days . . . .*

She goes on to tell how this experience led her to decide to investigate religion, and how reading Aldous Huxley's *The Perennial Philosophy* led her to decide that her own experience fitted in with Buddhism.

The Buddha's teaching was wholly concerned with untying the knots in men's minds so that they can be open to reality and free from the greed and ignorance which bind them like chains. I discovered, through meditation, that seeing things in their suchness – the word Buddha uses for the essential nature of all things – seeing them as I did once without any barrier of 'me' to get in the way, was one of the great aims of Buddhism. This was a big relief to me because I didn't want pious talk or a guilty feeling that I should attend some sort of church. I wanted, and found, a straightforward acceptance that man's deepest need is not to live by bread alone but to transcend all his thoughts and feelings and to *know* the meaning of timeless reality, and of God.

In this account phrase after phrase confirms the analysis suggested by split-brain physiology. As a child her intuitive self was aware of 'the Presence' in nature. She suppressed this because 'the everyday world had

*Quoted from a BBC talk, 'A Crowning Clarity', in the series 'The Light of Experience', and published in a book of the same title.

attractions for me too' – and it is the logical, left-brain self that has to be cultivated in order to deal efficiently with the everyday world of experience. But an overdose of everyday experience – what Wordsworth meant when he said, 'The world is too much with us' – left her feeling that she had become 'really futile' – the Ecclesiastes effect. The dominant self had forgotten the existence of its non-dominant partner. A night of deep introspection made her once again aware of the existence of this hidden self. She began seeing the world through the eyes of the 'other self', and experience became intense and direct, no longer strained through what T. E. Lawrence called 'the thought-riddled nature'.

Her 'crowning experience' consisted of what Douglas Harding has called 'having no head'. In his book *On Having No Head* (1972), Harding described how, looking out over the Himalayas, he suddenly lost all sense of identity:

What actually happened was something absurdly simple and unspectacular: I stopped thinking. A peculiar quiet, an odd kind of alert limpness or numbness, came over me. Reason and imagination and all mental chatter died down. For once, words really failed me. Past and future dropped away. I forgot who and what I was, my name, manhood, animalhood, all that could be called mine. It was as if I had been born that instant, brand new, innocent of all memories. There existed only the Now, that present moment and what was clearly given in it. To look was enough. And what I found was khaki trouserlegs terminating downwards in a pair of brown shoes, khaki sleeves terminating sideways in a pair of pink hands, and a khaki shirtfront terminating upwards in – absolutely nothing whatever. Certainly not in a head.

It took me no time at all to notice that this nothing, this hole where a head should have been, was no ordinary vacancy, no mere nothing. On the contrary, it was very much occupied. It was a vast emptiness vastly filled, a nothing that found room for everything – room for grass, trees, shadowy distant hills, and far above them snow-peaks like a row of angular clouds riding the blue sky. I had lost a head and gained a world.

Harding describes the sensation as being 'utterly free of "me", unstained by any observer. . . . Lighter than air, clearer than glass, altogether released from myself, I was nowhere around.'

Yet split-brain physiology suggests that we should not regard this 'me-less' (i.e. 'left-brain-less') state as entirely desirable. After all we possess left brains for a perfectly good reason – to enable us to cope with the complexity of everyday life. We may recall that Anne Bancroft deliberately began to develop her left-brain faculties at the age of sixteen because she found the real world so interesting. The same reasoning suggests that Buddhism may not be the ultimate solution to the world's

51

problems. The fundamental parable of Buddhism tells how Prince Gautama was brought up by his father in total ignorance of pain and suffering; but in three unauthorized excursions from the palace, he saw an old man, a sick man and a dead man. These led him to recognize that human life is basically suffering, and that the answer lies in relinquishing all desire and regarding the world with total indifference. This attitude of wholesale world-rejection will strike most Westerners as another name for pessimism – or the tendency to throw out the baby with the bath water. The left brain is a kind of microscope whose purpose is to examine the world in detail; the right is a kind of telescope whose purpose is to scan wide vistas of meaning. It is true that 'close-upness' deprives us of meaning, but that is not the fault of the microscope but our own stupidity in forgetting that we can correct its limitations with the telescope.

Anne Bancroft's account contains several more important clues – for example her remark that she wished she could know everything in the same way that she knew the rhododendron and the sudden realization, 'Why not? It was only myself that was stopping me. There was no limit to the amount of love that I could give to everything that I saw.' Here again she is making an observation that can be explained in simple psychological terms. Because the left brain is always in a hurry it turns things into symbols, because symbols are simpler to handle than complex realities: you could say it turns real men into matchstick men. And it has to make continual decisions about how much attention to give each of these symbols or ideas – for, as Whitehead observed, movements of thought are like cavalry charges in a battle: you can only make so many of them. When tired or worried the left brain tends to ration its attention to a minimum, and the world begins to look increasingly unreal. A peak experience instantly restores the sense of reality and makes us aware that it was our own fault for failing to give *enough attention* to the world around us. Anne Bancroft had simply rediscovered the central recognition of the philosopher Edmund Husserl: that perception is *intentional*. That is to say that when we look *at* something, we fire our attention at it like a grappling hook. When you walk into a picture gallery you automatically 'fire' more attention at each picture than you would bestow on a passing bus. *We* control the amount of energy we put into perception, so Anne Bancroft was quite correct when she said, 'Why not? It was only myself that was stopping me.' The answer lies in *energizing the perceptions*. Our minds have a 'concentrative faculty', a certain power of intensifying our power of 'focusing', which could be compared to pulling back a spring-loaded piston or the bolt of a rifle. This faculty has the power of suddenly increasing our sense of reality; in fact, it might be labelled – in a phrase borrowed from the French psychologist Pierre Janet – 'the reality function'. The 'reality function' is undoubtedly one of the major keys to the problem of mystical experience.

The 'Bergsonian' approach to the problem has certainly yielded unexpected dividends. Let us see whether it is possible to build on these insights to reach some general understanding of the 'visions' of the mystics.

Bertrand Russell's objections make a convenient starting point. Almost without exception, mystics claim to have achieved some kind of flash of understanding *of the universe*. Now Russell admits that the aim of philosophy is to understand the universe. But he points out that before we can understand *anything*, we have to add one and one together to make two. The 'one-and-ones' that the scientist adds together are *facts*. And Russell objects that the mystics cannot possibly be in possession of enough facts to understand the universe. Nobody is.

To this objection, the mystic replies as follows:

All insights involve a kind of *leap*. When a psychologist puts a banana outside a monkey's cage just out of his reach but leaves a walking stick in the cage, the monkey has to make a *leap* of insight before it sees it can use the stick to reach the banana. When our minds become tired, it is hard for us to make these leaps. On the other hand the mind is apparently a very strange kind of computer. Some mathematical prodigies can work out twenty-four-figure primes within seconds. So is it not conceivable that in certain moments, our minds might make a series of leaps that suddenly reveal the meaning?

William James describes such an experience in an essay called 'A Suggestion about Mysticism':

> In each of the three like cases, the experience broke in abruptly upon a perfectly commonplace situation and lasted perhaps less than two minutes. In one instance, I was engaged in conversation, but I doubt whether my interlocutor noticed my abstraction. What happened each time was that I seemed all at once to be reminded of a past experience; and this reminiscence, ere I could conceive or name it distinctly, developed into something further that belonged with it, this in turn into something further still, and so on, until the process faded out, leaving me amazed at the sudden vision of increasing ranges of distant facts of which I could give no articulate account. The mode of consciousness was perceptual, not conceptual [James means it was right-brain rather than left] – the field expanding so fast that there seemed no time for conception or identification to get in its work. There was a strongly exciting sense that my knowledge of past (or present?) reality was enlarging pulse by pulse, *but so rapidly that my intellectual processes could not keep up the pace.* [My italics.] The *content* was thus lost entirely to introspection – it sank into the limbo into which dreams vanish when we awake. The feeling – I won't call it belief – that I had had a sudden *opening*, had seen through a window, as it were, into distant realities that incomprehensibly belonged with my own life, was so acute that I cannot shake it off today.

We can see that James had simply experienced a less powerful version of

53

Ouspensky's mystical insight. In between two words of the conversation his intuition suddenly zigzagged towards the horizon like a flash of lightning, revealing the basic 'connectedness' of everything and operating at such a speed – and revealing so many connections – that language was left behind, dragging its feet. Like Ouspensky, James *saw* this vast continuum of interconnected 'fact' – 'the mode of consciousness was perceptual, not conceptual.' And if he had had time to investigate the experience he would undoubtedly have found, like Ouspensky, that he could have answered any question, because 'the answer to [any] question included the answer to all possible questions.'

When I was in Majorca in 1969 I asked Robert Graves whether he had ever had a mystical experience, and he told me to read one of his short stories entitled 'The Abominable Mr Gunn'. In it he described how, as a schoolboy, he was sitting on a roller behind the cricket pavilion when he received a sudden 'celestial illumination'.

> It occurred to me that I knew everything. I remember letting my mind range rapidly over all its familiar subjects of knowledge, only to find that this was no foolish fancy. I did know everything. To be plain: though conscious of having come less than a third of the way along the path of formal education, and being weak in mathematics, shaky in Greek grammar, and hazy about English history, I nevertheless held the key of truth in my hand, and could use it to open the lock of any door. Mine was no religious or philosophical theory, but a simple method of looking sideways at disorderly facts so as to make perfect sense of them.

Graves explains that he tried out his insight on 'various obstinate locks: they all clicked and the doors opened smoothly'. The insight was still intact when he woke up next day. But when, after a morning's lessons, he tried to record it in the back of an exercise book, 'my mind went too fast for my pen, and I began to cross out – a fatal mistake – and presently crumpled up the page.' When he later tried to write it down under the bedclothes, 'the magic had evaporated' and the insight vanished. Writing about his experience he says that what struck him at the time was 'a sudden infantile awareness of the power of intuition, the supra-logic that cuts out all routine processes of thought and leaps straight from problem to answer.'

And as a further illustration of this curious ability Graves tells the story of a fellow pupil, F. F. Smilley, who had apparently developed the powers of a calculating prodigy. The master, Mr Gunn, had set them a complicated mathematical problem. Smilley simply wrote down the solution and sat gazing out of the window. Asked how he did it without written calculations, Smilley replied, 'It just came to me – I just looked at the problem and saw what the answer must be.' Mr Gunn accused him of looking up the answer in the back of the book; Smilley replied that the answer got two of

54

the figures wrong anyway. Mr Gunn sent him to the headmaster with a note ordering him to be caned for cheating and gross impertinence.

Graves's description of his own experience is less clear than it might be. When he says he 'knew everything' we are naturally inclined to believe that he is speaking of general knowledge – like knowing dates in history. But this is obviously not so, for he goes on to say that it was a method of 'looking sideways' at disorderly facts to make order out of them. This brings to mind Eileen Garrett's remark that her clairvoyance depends on 'a fundamental shift of one's awareness'. And when Graves goes on to compare his 'celestial illumination' with Smiley's ability to solve mathematical problems at a single glance, it is clear that he is talking about Ouspensky's 'bird's-eye vision', James's glimpse of 'increasing ranges of distant facts'. But James says he could give no articulate account of them, while Graves was sufficiently in control of his insight to apply it to various problems and to try to write it down. It seems obvious that Graves's experience was in many ways similar to James's, but that *what* he saw was something about human nature or the working of the human mind. At a later stage in this book it may be worthwhile to try to define it more precisely. Meanwhile one thing is clear: Graves's illumination concerned the right brain, or the workings of intuition. But his insight seems to contradict our normal assumption that the right brain is simply a natural counterpart of the left, complementing its powers of logical analysis with an ability to perceive patterns. Graves' comment that the insight was of 'a sudden infantile awareness of the power of intuition, the supra-logic that cuts out all routine processes of thought and leaps straight from problem to answer', means that he is claiming that its powers go far beyond mere 'pattern-perception' and come much closer to what we would call 'occult' or paranormal.

2

The Other Self

A few hours before beginning to write this chapter I had an extraordinary dream. I dream a great deal, but most of my dreams are the usual confused muddle and have little or no story-line. In this dream I was in some kind of 'fun house', presumably on a fairground or amusement park. This was some new and very up-to-date attraction. Everyone was swept at a breathtaking pace, on some kind of moving belt, through strange and bewildering tableaux, most of which I have forgotten. But I can clearly remember the most extraordinary of the effects. The belt passed through some powerful magnetic field, and this had the effect of somehow distorting the upper part of my body as if in a fairground mirror, and inducing a most peculiar, light-headed sensation. Now in most of my dreams, I wake up if anything very unusual happens. In this one, I went through the whole strange experience with a vivid sense of reality. At one point the 'field' somehow lifted my hat off my head, and I remember being puzzled and wondering if there was some metal in my hat to account for the phenomenon. And while most of the other people on the belt were swept straight through and out at the other end, I found some method of dodging back through a stairway or tunnel so I could keep on experiencing the effects of this strange 'distorting field', which induced a delightful and rather 'giddy' sensation, unlike anything I have ever known. I woke up feeling as though I had just been through an extraordinary experience.

Before going to bed I had been thinking about the beginning of this present chapter, which was to be about Thomson Jay Hudson and the remarkable powers of the right brain, particularly in dreams. It was as if the 'stranger' in my right brain had said, 'You want an example of my sheer inventiveness? All right, here's one you won't forget . . . .'

So now let us return to the business in hand.

In the 1880s, largely as the result of the researches of the famous Professor Charcot, the subject of hypnosis once again regained a certain academic respectability. In America, one of its leading exponents was the celebrated Professor Carpenter of Boston. At the Salpêtrière Hospital in Paris, Charcot liked to make his hypnotized patients bark like dogs or flap their arms like birds. Professor Carpenter preferred more civilized manifestations: he enjoyed demonstrating that hypnosis can enhance the powers of the human mind. One of his most impressive presentations took place in Washington DC in the presence of 'an audience of highly cultivated ladies and gentlemen', which included a college graduate who is identified only as 'C.'. C. was placed under hypnosis, then asked by Carpenter if he would like to meet Socrates. He replied that he would esteem it a great privilege if Socrates were still alive. Carpenter explained that he had the power to invoke the spirit of Socrates, and pointing to a corner of the room exclaimed, 'There he is.' C. looked at the place indicated, and his face took on an expression of awe and reverence. Carpenter performed the introductions, and C. looked speechless with embarrassment, although he still retained his wits enough to offer Socrates a chair. Carpenter then explained that Socrates was willing to answer any questions, and C. proceeded with some hesitation to open a conversation. Since Carpenter had explained that he was unable to overhear the philosopher's replies, C. acted as intermediary and repeated everything Socrates said. For two hours this amazing 'conversation' continued, and the answers were so brilliant and plausible that some of the audience began to wonder whether there really *was* an invisible spirit in the room.

Later Carpenter offered to introduce C. to the spirits of more modern philosophers, and with most of these he felt a great deal more at ease than with Socrates. What emerged from these conversations was a 'wonderful system of spiritual philosophy ... so clear, so plausible, so perfectly consistent with itself and the known laws of Nature that the company sat spellbound.' With each new philosopher C.'s manner changed, exactly as if he were speaking to a series of real people, and the language and style of the invisible philosophers changed too: it was all so weirdly real that the audience felt as if they were watching a play.

Among the audience was a Detroit newspaper editor named Thomson Jay Hudson, a man at this time in his mid-fifties, and he watched the demonstrations with baffled amazement. Hudson knew that C. was a total sceptic on the question of 'spirits' – as was Hudson himself. Under hypnosis he accepted the existence of the spirits of the great philosophers because he could obviously *see* them. What seemed most surprising was that the 'spiritual philosophy' expressed was not that of C. himself – he frequently expressed his astonishment at some of the statements of the dead philosophers. Yet the whole philosophy was such a coherent system that according to Hudson, it could have been printed in a book verbatim and would have 'formed one of the grandest and most coherent systems of spiritual philosophy ever conceived by the brain of man'.

There happened to be a number of spiritualists present in the audience, and many of them were inclined to the hypothesis that real spirits were present, until Carpenter disillusioned them by summoning up the spirit of a philosophical pig which discoursed learnedly on the subject of the Hindu doctrine of reincarnation.

At about the time Hudson was witnessing these sessions in Washington, a young Viennese doctor named Sigmund Freud was in Paris, studying medicine under the celebrated Charcot. Jean-Martin Charcot was not only one of the greatest medical men of the late nineteenth century; he was also one of its greatest showmen, and – as already noted – he took immense delight in demonstrating the amazing suggestibility of his hypnotized subjects, by, for example, making a woman shriek with horror and pull up her skirts when he threw a glove at her feet and told her it was a snake. Charcot mollified his less flamboyant colleagues – who were still inclined to believe that hypnosis was some kind of fraud – by assuring them that it was really just a form of hysteria. But this explanation left Freud as troubled as ever. He had seen a man's arm blister after it had been touched with a piece of ice which the hypnotist declared was a red-hot poker; he had seen the swollen stomach of a woman suffering from hysterical pregnancy. Such cases made it perfectly obvious that there must be some part of the mind which is far more powerful than the ordinary conscious will. And on his return to Vienna, Freud gradually formulated his doctrine of the unconscious mind and built upon it the theory of psychoanalysis.

Hudson was equally baffled by what he saw, but he pursued a different line of reasoning. He also reached the conclusion that man has 'two minds', one of which has far greater powers than the other. But what precisely *were* they? According to some ancient philosophers, man possesses a soul *and* a spirit; but that was apparently neither here nor there. As far as Hudson could see, man possesses a 'practical' mind which copes with the problems of the outside world, and a kind of 'non-practical' mind which copes with his *inner* problems. Hudson decided to call these two the 'objective' and the 'subjective' minds. The objective mind deals with the real world through the medium of the five senses, and its highest function is that of reason. The subjective mind prefers to use intuition. 'It is the seat of the emotions, and the storehouse of memory. It performs its highest functions when the objective senses are in abeyance. In a word, it is that intelligence which makes itself manifest in a hypnotic subject when he is in a state of somnambulism.'

Hudson was convinced that the subjective mind is somehow independent of the senses. He knew of experiments in which a hypnotized subject, with closed eyes, was able to read a newspaper held by someone on the other side of the room. He knew of hypnotized subjects who could 'travel' to some distant place and describe precisely what was going on. Moreover the subjective mind seems to be capable of drawing upon a power and energy far greater than the subject could exercise by conscious effort. A Danish hypnotist named Carl Hansen used to tell people that they had become as rigid as planks then order them to lie across two chairs – their heads on one and their heels on the other – while members of the audience stood on the stomach or used it as a seat. It seemed clear that the subjective mind is somehow in charge of our energy supply. The objective mind is the person you call 'you'. The subjective mind seems to be a 'separate and distinct entity', a stranger. And under hypnosis the 'you' is put to sleep and the 'stranger' is able to take charge of the brain and body – with remarkable results.

It was in 1893 that Hudson introduced these ideas to the public in a book called *The Law of Psychic Phenomena*. (By 'psychic', of course, he meant psychological.) He had only another ten years to live; but at least he had the satisfaction of achieving sudden fame and seeing his book sell more than a hundred thousand copies.

What excited the American public was the sheer flamboyant sweep of Hudson's theory. He seemed capable of explaining everything from genius to insanity and from hypnosis to the miracles of Jesus. But perhaps the most exciting idea was that the subjective mind has incredible powers – of memory, of invention, of power over the body – and that we *all* possess a subjective mind. Then why are we not all geniuses? Because our objective minds *cramp the powers* of the subjective mind. We *would* be geniuses if we could release these powers. The subjective mind has an apparently limitless memory. Hudson tells stories of people who, under hypnosis, spoke in foreign languages they had never learned; but it turned out, on investigation, that they had overheard the languages in childhood and unconsciously 'absorbed' them. The objective mind *inhibits* the subjective mind, as a schoolboy feels inhibited when the teacher looks over his shoulder. A person who could 'uninhibit' his subjective mind would presumably be capable of learning a foreign language in a week.

There are some people, says Hudson, who are naturally free of inhibition, and whose subjective mind expresses itself as freely and naturally as a child. These are men of genius, and he offers Shakespeare as an example. He also tells a delightful story of the great American orator Henry Clay, who once asked a friend to tug on his coat-tails when he had been speaking for ten minutes in the Senate. The friend duly pulled on his coat-tails; Clay ignored him. The friend tried jabbing him gently with a pin. Still Clay ignored it. The friend jabbed the pin so hard that it went deep into Clay's leg, but Clay was in full flight and did not even notice. Finally, at the end of two hours of magnificent eloquence, he slumped into his seat, overcome by exhaustion, and asked his friend reproachfully why he had not stopped him at the end of ten minutes. Hudson points out that when he made this speech Clay was almost too ill to stand up, and that it is an example of the 'synchronous action of the two minds' and the subjective mind's power over the body.

This is the kind of story that accounted for the book's popularity – with its implication that we might all learn to make better use of the powers of the subjective mind. After all we all know how easy it is to lose our spontaneity when we become self-conscious. (Hudson pointed out that the subjective mind is totally demoralized by scepticism, which is why people with 'psychic powers' find it so hard to demonstrate them before scientists.) The implication is that if we could learn to relax and trust the 'hidden self' we could all make better use of our latent genius.

Why is it that some people, who appear perfectly dull and ordinary, have some special gift that enables them to write or compose or paint brilliantly? According to Hudson it is not a 'special gift' but a kind of accidental state of harmony between the 'two minds' that allows a free flow of communication between them. It could be compared to accidentally tuning your radio set so that you get perfect reception of some particular station. It could happen to anybody, and undoubtedly *would* happen to most people if they could merely learn not to undermine themselves with self-doubt.

Even more interesting from our point of view is Hudson's assertion that mystics and visionaries – he instances William Blake – are men who have a natural access to the subjective mind. Most of us are *tied* to the external world by a kind of nervous vigilance; we are afraid of what would happen if we 'let go'. Blake was able to 'let go' at will, and see strange visions. Another of these odd powers of the subjective mind is 'eidetic vision', the power to recreate a mental image so vividly that it seems to hover in front of the eyes. The scientist Nicola Tesla insisted that he could visualize his inventions so clearly that he could virtually 'build' them in his head and watch them working. Hudson had also known such a person:

> The writer once knew an artist who had the power to enter the subjective condition at will; and in this state he could cause his visions to be projected upon the canvas before him. He declared that his mental pictures thus formed were perfect in detail and colour, and that all that he had to do to fix them was to paint the corresponding colours over the subjective picture. He too thought his fancies real; he believed that spirits projected the pictures upon the canvas.

All this sounds remarkably close to Eileen Garrett's description of how she 'shifts her point of view'. 'What happens to us at these times is that, as we withdraw from the environing world, we relegate the activities of the five senses to the field of the subconscious, and seek to focus *awareness* . . . in the field of the superconscious – the timeless, spaceless field of the as-yet-unknown.' But this makes it clear that we are already passing beyond the simple – and basically scientific – observations of Thomson Jay Hudson on the 'two minds' to something much more controversial and complex: the notion of 'timeless and spaceless fields' that give access to 'paranormal information'. And this, of course, is also the point at which most scientists would dig in their heels. They can accept a Bergsonian notion of 'two minds' – rational and intuitive – but they would insist that the powers of the intuitive mind are the quite ordinary powers that we associate with intuition – sudden flashes of insight, and suchlike. But how can intuition tell us what is happening a thousand miles away or – worse still – what is going to happen tomorrow?

Hudson himself soon passed beyond psychological observations to the field of the paranormal. His studies in hypnosis convinced him that telepathy is a reality. He had undoubtedly heard of the researches of the

Marquis de Puységur, the disciple of Mesmer who in the year 1780 had accidentally discovered hypnotism. Mesmer believed that there is some strange vital force – called 'animal magnetism' – which can be used to cure illness. Under Mesmer's instructions Puységur had 'magnetized' a lime tree in his park and had tied to the tree a young peasant called Victor Race. While the Marquis was making passes over the patient's head with a magnet – to increase the flow of 'magnetic fluid' – Victor Race went into a trance. When ordered to untie himself he did so, with his eyes still closed. And the Marquis soon discovered, to his amazement, that Race could read his mind when the youth was in a trance. Puységur could address a question to him mentally, and Race would answer aloud. If they were in a room with a third person, the Marquis could direct Race's conversation by giving him mental orders and telling him what to say. It would be another century before Frederick Myers invented the word telepathy, but by 1780 science had established that it was a reality.

Hudson was also impressed by a series of experiments conducted in 1819 by a certain Councillor H. M. Wesermann of Dusseldorf. Wesermann made a mental effort to make telepathic contact with a friend whom he had not seen in thirteen years, and chose the middle of the night for his attempt. The next day he went to call on the friend, who told him with amazement that he had dreamt of him the previous night. After this success Wesermann made an old man dream of the funeral of someone they both knew, and a woman dream about some secret conversation involving Wesermann and two other people. When a doctor friend expressed scepticism about all this Wesermann convinced him by making him dream of a street brawl.

Hudson devotes several pages to one of the most famous of all cases of this type – the Verity case. A young student named Beard was engaged to a girl, Miss L. S. Verity. 'On a certain Sunday evening in November 1881, having been reading of the great power which the human will is capable of exercising, I determined, with the whole force of my being, that I would be present in spirit in the front bedroom on the second floor of a house situated at 22 Hogarth Road, Kensington.' He made the effort at one o'clock in the morning. At that moment Miss Verity woke up, and saw her fiancé standing by her bedside. She screamed and woke her eleven-year-old sister, who also saw Beard. At that point Beard vanished.

In the following year Beard was involved in an even more remarkable experiment. In December 1882 he decided to try and 'appear' in the house in Kew to which Miss Verity and her sister had moved. He sat in a fireside chair and tried to fix his mind on the house. Suddenly he became aware that he could not move his limbs – his own theory was that he had fallen into a 'mesmeric sleep'. And when, some time later, he regained his normal state by an effort of will, he recorded that he had been in a 'trance' state from about nine-thirty until ten. At midnight he made another attempt at 'transmission'. The following evening he went to call at the house at Kew and discovered that his fiancée's elder sister was also

61

staying with her – he calls her Mrs L. Mrs L. told him that she had seen him the previous evening at nine-thirty going from one room to another. At midnight she saw him yet again as he walked into the bedroom, walked to her bed and took her long hair in his hand. After this the 'apparition' had taken hold of her hand and looked at the palm, at which Mrs L. remarked, 'You need not look at the lines, for I have never had any trouble.' When Beard had disappeared again Mrs L. woke her sister, who was in the same bed, and told her what had happened.

Mrs L. volunteered this information without any questioning from Beard, and when she had told him her story Beard took from his pocket his own notes, made the previous evening, in which he recorded going into a 'trance' at nine-thirty and making another effort to 'appear' in the bedroom in Kew at midnight. The interesting part of this second experiment is that the 'apparition' was solid enough to hold Mrs L.'s hair and take her hand – presumably under the impression that she was Miss Verity. Beard himself had no recollection of any of this.

Beard also made this interesting comment about his first experiment:

Besides exercising my power of volition very strongly, *I put forth an effort which I cannot find words to describe.* [My italics.] I was conscious of a mysterious influence of some sort permeating my body, and had a distinct impression that I was exercising some force with which I had been hitherto unacquainted, but which I can now at certain times set in motion at will.

This seems to demonstrate two things: that Beard used not only his conscious will, but also some other kind of will – the power of the subjective mind – and that once he had learned the trick he could sometimes repeat it. In fact he repeated it once more in 1884, when he again appeared to Miss Verity and stroked her hair. (It seems to have been a long engagement.)

This case was thoroughly investigated and recorded by the newly-formed Society for Psychical Research (founded 1882), and probably inspired Frederick Myers to embark upon his immense compilation *Phantasms of the Living* (co-authored by Edmund Gurney and Frank Podmore), the first and most impressive study of this strange ability of some people to 'project' their 'astral doubles' (or *doppelgängers*) to distant places.

Hudson thought that the Verity case was an example of telepathy, which to some extent it undoubtedly was; but there was obviously rather more to it than that. (In fact, Hudson preferred to ignore this other aspect – 'astral projection' – for reasons we shall consider later.) But his chief concern now was to try to prove, to his own satisfaction, the hidden powers of the subjective mind. And like Lawrence LeShan almost a century later, Hudson decided that the best way of proving his theory would be through an attempt at healing. Why healing, rather than telepathy, or 'astral projection', or experiments in clairvoyance? Because Hudson's basic theory is that the subjective mind is so powerful because it is *in harmony* with nature and the universe, and that illness is due to loss of contact with this fundamental harmony. So if one subjective mind can reach out to another, it ought to be able to place it once more in contact with the fundamental harmony. In fact Lawrence LeShan follows much the same line of reasoning, writing, 'It is interesting to note that nearly all the great sensitives had a very unusual amount of *joie de vivre* and *élan vital*, and that typically the person who follows the mystical path and disciplines finds joy, serenity and a non-destructive life of peace and fulfilment of purpose.'*

Bearing in mind that Councillor Wesermann had been successful in transmitting telepathic messages to people who were asleep – a state that is, after all, akin to hypnosis – Hudson decided that the best time to attempt his experiment was when the healer was himself on the verge of sleep, that is when his objective mind was totally relaxed. Hudson's first experiment was with an ageing relative who suffered from agonising rheumatism which was so severe that one leg had become two inches shorter than the other and he was hardly able to walk. Hudson began the 'healing' treatment on 15 May 1890, telling two friends about his intention so that he had witnesses. The method was for Hudson to think about the relative, who lived a thousand miles away, just as he was on the point of sleep, and to send out healing suggestions. A few months later one of the two 'witnesses' met the subject of the experiment and was startled to see that he now seemed to be in good health. She asked when the improvement had begun and the man replied, 'In the middle of May.'

It could, of course, have been coincidence. So Hudson persisted with other sick acquaintances. Unfortuantely he offers no further details of the hundred experiments he claims to have carried out; but he reports that with two exceptions, they were all successful. In the case of the two exceptions, Hudson deliberately broke his usual rule and told his 'patients' that he intended to try to cure them. The result, he believed, was that their objective minds inhibited the natural healing powers of the subjective mind – like the schoolteacher peering over the schoolboy's shoulder.

Hudson's list of cures is impressive: neuralgia, dyspepsia, bowel complaints, sick headaches, torpidity of the liver, chronic bronchitis, partial paralysis, pen paralysis (presumably an acute form of writer's cramp), and even strabismus (squint). He admits that the last case was not treated by himself but by the aunt of the ten-year-old girl concerned, who had been cross-eyed from birth. Hudson remarks that he himself would probably have lacked the confidence to attempt such a case, but the aunt completely cured her niece in three months.

A case that occurred sixty years later provides interesting confirmation of Hudson's observations about confidence. In May 1950 a sixteen-year-

*Lawrence LeShan, *The Medium, the Mystic and the Physicist*, p. 100.

old boy was admitted to the Queen Victoria Hospital, East Grinstead, suffering from an exceptionally unpleasant complaint known as fish-skin disease: the whole of his body was covered with black warts, while his hands were covered in a horny skin that was as hard as his fingernails. A skin transplant was a failure. At this point the anaesthetist, Dr Albert A. Mason, decided that he would try hypnosis. He had often cured warts by hypnosis and saw no reason why multiple warts should be any more difficult than single ones. The boy was placed in a trance and told that the warts on his left arm would go away. A few days later the horny skin softened and fell off, revealing normal skin. Dr Mason communicated his success to the surgeon, who looked at him with incredulity and told him to go and look up ichthyosiform erythrodermia – the medical name for fish-skin disease – in the library. He did, and made the upsetting discovery that his patient's skin had no oil-forming glands and that therefore the disease was incurable; the 'hypnotic cure' was literally an impossibility.

Nevertheless, hypnosis had worked. So Mason went on to hypnotize the patient and suggest that his right arm should clear up. The right arm was 95 per cent cleared of warts. On the legs and feet, about 50 per cent of the warts disappeared. More important, the boy's state of mind improved enormously, and he got himself a job as an electrician's assistant. However three years later Mason decided to try and renew the treatment: on this occasion his former patient turned out to be completely un-hypnotizable.

Between 1953 and 1961 Mason tried curing another eight cases of fish-skin disease by hypnosis: all were total failures. He reached the reluctant conclusion that the fault lay in himself: now he *knew* that ichthyosis could not be cured by hypnosis, he was somehow communicating his doubt to the patients. In the case of the sixteen-year-old boy, neither of them had known the disease was incurable when Hudson first attempted hypnosis and the result was a 100 per cent cure of the left arm. By the time he moved on to the right arm, Mason's confidence had been shaken by the discovery that the disease was 'incurable', but the patient still had every reason to believe him. Result: a partial cure. But by the time Mason decided to try again, the patient himself had become worried and nervous, and could no longer be hypnotized. Hudson would say that his objective mind was now inhibiting the healing power of the subjective mind.

By the time of Dr Mason's experiments in hypnosis the existence of the subjective and objective minds had been verified by science – for it must be obvious that Hudson had simply anticipated the findings of Roger Sperry and Michael Gazzaniga on the right and left cerebral hemispheres. It was in 1952 that Sperry had acted as adviser on brain operations to prevent epileptic attacks, the idea being to prevent the 'electrical storm' from passing from one side of the brain to the other by splitting the brain right down the middle. Observing that a patient who accidentally bumped his left side against a table did not seem to know what he had done, Sperry and Gazzaniga performed a series of interesting tests. If a pencil was placed in the left hand of a blindfolded split-brain patient, the patient would have no idea what he was holding; yet asked to *use* the pencil, he did so in a perfectly normal manner. The right brain knew what it was holding. In one of the most interesting experiments, red or green lights were flashed at random into the patient's right brain (i.e. into the left visual field, connected to the right hemisphere). When the patient was asked what colour he had just 'seen', he had to make a guess. And if he got it wrong, his muscles gave a little jerk. The right brain had overheard the wrong guess and was trying to tell him so by 'kicking him under the table', so to speak. It had no other way of communicating.

Perhaps one of the most important points to emerge from these studies was that in a very basic sense, we are *all* split-brain patients. Mozart once said that tunes were always wandering into his head, ready to be written down: what he meant, of course, was that tunes were always wandering into his left brain. And the source of the tunes – as of all 'patterns' – is the right brain. So Mozart himself (remember the 'I' lives in the left brain) had to sit waiting for the 'other self' to send him the music: he was, in effect, a split-brain patient. And if Mozart was a split-brain patient, then the rest of us less talented mortals most certainly are. (Of course if Mozart had actually undergone the split-brain operation his genius would have vanished – or rather would have become confined to his right hemisphere, which would have been unable to pass it on to the 'amanuensis' in the left.)

Hudson understood how genius functions. His insight enabled him, for example, to demolish the argument that Shakespeare was really Francis Bacon. Bacon and Shakespeare were completely opposite types: Shakespeare the typical childlike intuitive right-brainer, Bacon the typical un-childlike, intellectual left-brainer. Bacon's supporters argue that Shakespeare's plays reveal far too much learning for the son of a Stratford butcher. But, Hudson argues, Shakespeare spent much of his time with the most brilliant and learned men of his age and had the natural capacity of the right-brainer to pick up knowledge quickly and easily.

Hudson also understood the problems of the natural right-brainer. His childlike innocence makes it difficult for him to cope with the complexities of practical life. The result is that he is a natural 'Outsider', since he never really feels at home in this 'world'. Mozart, again, is a good example. Dostoevsky devoted a whole novel, *The Idiot*, to a childlike right-brainer, Prince Myshkin; but Myshkin's innocence finally causes chaos and confusion and he ends by going insane. We *need* a strong left brain to cope with the difficult realities of existence. The trouble is that we can easily overdo it and develop such a cautious and defensive left brain that our natural genius never gets a chance to express itself. In fact we can become so defensive that we totally forget the existence of our ally in the right hemisphere and become over-tense and neurotic. Recognizing the existence of the 'ally' is an urgent necessity of mental as well as physical health.

A few years ago I had an interesting experience of the power of the right brain. A film producer had asked me to go to London to re-think and rewrite an extremely bad film-script. I had ten days to do it, and was placed in a suite in one of London's most expensive hotels with permission to eat and drink whatever I liked. (I had champagne and lobster for lunch every day.) But the script had to be finished on time. The knowledge that it *had* to be done made me nervous, and the sheer luxury of the hotel deepened my anxiety; I spent the first day reading through the awful script with a sinking feeling. That night I found it difficult to sleep. Then, as I lay awake, it struck me that I was getting myself into an increasing state of left-brain tension and cutting myself off from any possible inspiration. Hudson had said that it is important to grasp that the subjective mind is a distinct and separate entity, and another interesting researcher, Max Freedom Long (of whom I shall speak later) even used to address his 'other self' as George. So I spoke to my 'other self' in a tone of friendly urgency. 'Look, I've got to complete this damn script in nine days. I *know* you can manage it. So come on – show me what you can do.' With that I fell into a deep and peaceful sleep. When I re-read the script the next morning I immediately began to see ways of improving it, and did a good day's work. Whenever I felt tired or over-tense, I lay on the bed and reminded my right brain that I was relying on its co-operation, and for the next week progress was excellent. It looked as if there was no possibility of finishing it on time, but on the last day I had only a dozen or so pages to do. I began work at 7 a.m. and wrote quickly and easily all day. I typed the last sentences exactly five minutes before the producer's secretary knocked on the door to collect the day's work. And an hour later, as the chauffeured Daimler drove me to my train, I remembered to say a wholehearted thankyou to my right brain.

It is important to realize that since the right brain is in charge of our 'internal' organization (if Hudson is correct), then it is also the quartermaster in charge of our energy supply. It is also, as Hudson points out, immensely suggestible, so that the more we fall into states of depression and pessimism the more we undermine our own strength, for the 'other self' feels that it would be pointless to throw good energy after bad. On the other hand the least suggestion that we are 'winning' is enough to cause a sudden trickle of energy and delight.

These insights led me to formulate what I called the Laurel and Hardy theory of consciousness. The two 'selves' could be compared to Laurel and Hardy in the old movies: Ollie, the dominant, bossy type, and Stan, the vague and childlike character. The real problem is that Stan is so immensely suggestible. When you open your eyes on a wet Monday morning it is Ollie who assesses the situation and mutters, 'Damn, it's

66

Monday and it's raining . . . .' Stan overhears him and – being suggestible – is thrown into a state of alarm. '*Monday*, and it's *raining*.' So he fails to send up any energy. And if you cut yourself while shaving and spill coffee down your shirt-front and trip over the mat in the hall, each mini-disaster causes Ollie to groan, 'It's one of those days . . .', while Stan becomes practically hysterical with gloom.

Consider, on the other hand, what happens when a child wakes up on Christmas morning. Ollie says, 'Marvellous, it's Christmas,' and Stan almost turns a somersault of delight. And of course sends up a spurt of energy, which produces a feeling of well-being. Everything reinforces the sense of delight: the Christmas presents, the lights on the tree, the smell of mince pies . . . . The result is that before the day is half over, the child can experience an almost mystical sense of sheer ecstatic happiness, a feeling that life is self-evidently marvellous – not just now, but all the year round. For in this mood all mountains are seen as molehills, and no problem seems insurmountable.

It can also be seen that this Stan and Ollie mechanism explains a wide range of psychological states and mechanisms, from clinical depression and neurosis to the peak experience and states of mystical affirmation. Neurosis is simply a state of 'negative feedback' in which Ollie's jaundiced viewpoint plunges Stan into hysterical gloom so that he fails to maintain the energy supply, which makes Ollie feel worse than ever. Once a person has fallen into this vicious circle of depression and low energy it is extremely difficult to escape from it because the depression changes the *perceptions*, like a pair of dark glasses; and since we take it for granted that our senses are telling us the truth, we react with weariness and pessimism. On the other hand a person locked into the 'virtuous circle' of peak experience and optimism feels it equally obvious that the world is a fascinating place, full of marvellous variety and complexity. He also has a sense of 'hidden wonders' behind the present façade of reality. It is arguable that this positive vision is, objectively speaking, more accurate than the negative vision, for our common sense tells us that our senses only reveal a fraction of the variety and complexity of the universe.

Expressed in this way, Ollie sounds like the villain – the person who is responsible for Stan's poor performance. But this is not entirely true. There is a third person involved – the entity I have called 'the robot'. We each have a robot in the unconscious mind whose function is to take over all the *repetitive* tasks of life. For example, the robot is now typing these words for me, while Stan and Ollie between them work out precisely *what* I have to say. Your robot breathes for you and keeps your heart beating regularly. He also drives your car and performs numerous other 'automatic' functions. Note that it was Ollie who had to *learn* to drive the car, with a great deal of effort; then, at a certain point, the robot took over, and proceeded to do it far more quickly and efficiently than Ollie. The robot halves our work for us. But he also has one great disadvantage. He tends to 'switch on' like a thermostat whenever we feel tired, and literally take over our lives. If I am very tired, I may not recall driving home from work: the robot has done it for me. The trouble is that he not only 'takes over' the tasks I would rather avoid but is also inclined to interfere in tasks I would prefer to do myself. I discover a piece of music that moves me deeply: the tenth time I hear it the robot is doing the listening for me, and I fail to *experience* it. I discover a new country walk which I thoroughly enjoy: the tenth time I do it all the freshness has gone, because the robot has taken over.

But it is when Stan and Ollie have got themselves into a state of 'negative feedback' that the robot becomes downright dangerous. As we have already seen, Stan is in charge of the energy supply, and when Ollie feels depressed, Stan fails to send him any energy. When that happens the robot's 'thermostat' switches on, and he takes over most of our routine tasks. Experience suddenly loses its freshness; life loses its savour; reality becomes unreal. As a result, of course, Ollie feels lower than ever and Stan sends up less energy than ever. In this state a human being lives on a far lower level than he is intended for, and he *cannot escape* the vicious circle for he can see no reason for effort. The result may be nervous breakdown, or paranoia, or even suicide.

Now all this throws an entirely new light on the problem of mysticism. We can see, for example, that when Anne Bancroft looked out of the window at the blackbird and felt that she had never really *seen* a blackbird before, she was simply seeing the blackbird through her own eyes instead of through the eyes of the robot. It also explains Ouspensky's recognition that we are living in a 'wooden world', full of wooden thoughts, wooden moods, wooden sensations, where everything moves with a melancholy creaking sound. It is the robot that is creaking. When I experience something directly, intuitively, with what Gottfried Benn calls 'primal perception', I experience an immense delight, a feeling that our world, far from being dull and ordinary, is infinitely beautiful. Even a draught of cool water going down a dry throat can bring this almost painful shock of sheer happiness. It is then that I recognize that the real problem of this world is that most of my experience is 'automatic'. The robot thickens our senses, as if we were wearing a suit of armour with metal gloves. I can raise the visor for a moment, but it slips down almost immediately. Moreover this continual sense of woodenness, of unreality, of blunted sensation, makes me feel thoroughly discouraged, so that everything I do is half-hearted. There is a 'vicious circle effect' in which all our perceptions become down-graded. Yet any sudden crisis can rescue us by driving us to make a convulsive effort of will. William Blake wrote:

> Each man is in his Spectre's power
> Until the arrival of that hour,
> When his Humanity awake
> And casts his own Spectre into the Lake.

Anne Bancroft's 'humanity awoke' and cast her spectre into the lake.

Blake's image makes us aware that the spectre – or robot – can become a kind of octopus that strangles our senses *and limits our vision*. In other words our normal perception is diluted and debased by the robot; when we open our eyes in the morning what we see is *not* objective reality but a highly subjectivized reality, coloured by our doubts and miseries. Epictetus said, 'What alarms and disturbs man are not real things, but his opinions and fancies about things.' And since our civilization has been nurturing these opinions and fancies for several thousand years, most of us find ourselves trapped in a totally false 'communal reality'.

Of course it would be unfair to think of the robot only as a kind of spectre. He is simply a computer – a computer thousands of times more complex than anything that has been developed by IBM – and we would find it impossible to live without him. But when we slip into the 'vicious circle' situation he becomes a kind of Old Man of the Sea, sitting on our shoulders and strangling the life out of us.

Graham Greene's autobiography *A Kind of Life* provides an insight into the mechanisms of the vicious circle. He describes how, at public school, the 'interminable repetitions' of his life finally broke him down. It is clear from his account that it was not a particularly unpleasant public school and he had no real reason to be unhappy. But boredom and a naturally gloomy outlook (probably rooted in self-pity) finally drove him to a number of suicide attempts. He drank a bottle of hypo developing fluid under the impression that it was poisonous, drained his blue glass bottle of hay fever drops, ate deadly nightshade picked on the common and went swimming in the school baths after taking twenty aspirin. (He says it produced a sensation like swimming through cotton wool.) After an attempt to run away he was sent to a psychiatrist in London, and thoroughly enjoyed the break from routine. But the psychiatrist's efforts to 'normalize' him only increased his manic depressive tendencies, and he comments, 'For years, after my analysis, I could take no aesthetic interest in any visual thing: staring at a sight that others assured me was beautiful I felt nothing. I was fixed, like a negative in a chemical bath.'

It was at this point that he discovered a revolver left in a corner cupboard by his elder brother. He had read in some Russian book about Russian roulette, and now took the revolver on to Berkhamsted common to try it for himself. He inserted one bullet, then spun the chambers behind his back, put the revolver to his right ear and pulled the trigger. 'There was a minute click, and looking down at the chamber I could see that the charge had moved into the firing position. I was out by one. I remember an extraordinary sense of jubilation, as if carnival lights had been switched on in a dark drab street. My heart knocked in its cage, and life contained an infinite number of possibilities.'

We can see that what had happened is simply that the self-induced 'crisis', followed by relief, had jerked Greene out of a state of self-induced laziness which was based on a feeling of futility and a *decision* that 'nothing was worth doing'. He had been thoroughly trapped in the negative feedback effect until he was half-strangled by the 'spectre'. When he pulled the trigger, the Old Man of the Sea gave a shriek of alarm and leapt off his shoulders. However when Greene continued to play Russian roulette – six times in all – the effect of the 'drug' wore off and he ceased to experience the sense of renewal.

Greene's use of the word 'drug' makes it clear that he had failed to grasp the essence of the experience. He thought of Russian roulette as a way of releasing adrenalin, failing to grasp the insight that the answer lay in *energizing his perceptions*, making a deliberate effort to throw off boredom and laziness. Twenty years later, in *The Power and the Glory*, Greene again made use of the experience. When his 'whiskey priest', another manic depressive, is about to be shot, he suddenly realizes 'that it would have been quite easy to have been a saint'. But the boredom that hangs over the novel like a stifling fog makes it clear that once again Greene has not grasped the import of his own insight.

What is beginning to emerge is perhaps the most important single insight that any human being could experience. Peak experiences and mystical experiences are not glimpses of some ineffable, paradoxical truth, but simply a *widening* of our ordinary field of perception. The mechanism is described precisely by William James when he says that he was reminded of a past experience, 'and this reminiscence, ere I could conceive or name it distinctly, developed into something further that belonged with it, this in turn into something further still, and so on, until the process faded out, leaving me amazed at the sudden vision of *increasing ranges of distant facts* [my italics] of which I could give no articulate account.' That is to say something reminded him of something else, and that of something else, and that of something else, until – like a flash of lightning – he was grasping a *far wider* range of 'facts' than usual. What he 'saw' was not some mystical vision of God or the universe – merely facts. But he saw them all together, in relation to one another. We are reminded of Ramakrishna's parable of the blind men touching the elephant: the one who touches its leg thinks it is like a pillar, the one who touches its ear thinks it is like a winnowing fan, the one who touches its tail thinks it is like a rope, and so on. But anyone who possessed the power of sight, no matter how stupid, would instantly have seen how all these parts combine to make an elephant. It is as if the problem with our normal perception is that it has somehow been crippled or 'damped down' so that it only works at a mere fraction of its proper efficiency. So instead of perceiving the horizons of distant fact that our brains are capable of grasping we grope short-sightedly at the surface of immediate reality and mistake ears for winnowing fans and tails for ropes.

Now although it may not be immediately apparent, all this constitutes a completely new theory of the nature of reality. For as long as philosophy has existed, philosophers have been passing negative judgements on human life. Ecclesiastes thought that all life is vanity and vexation of spirit. Plato compared human life to men chained up in a cave, forced to look at shadows on the wall. Aristotle said that it is better not to have been born, and death is better than life. The Buddha says that all life is misery and bitterness. Lucretius says that life is a treadmill that leads nowhere, a desire that never finds fulfilment. And in 1818 Arthur Schopenhauer published the longest and most comprehensive attempt so far to prove that human life is meaningless and pointless and that – as Sartre later put it – man is a useless passion. According to *The World as Will and Idea*, 'the world is my idea' and has no objective reality; our perceptions only show us illusions. The only underlying reality is a blind, obstinate will that has no real purpose and therefore dooms us all to perpetual disappointment. One of the book's central paragraphs reads as follows:

> We saw that the inner being of unconscious nature is a constant striving without end and without rest. And this appears to us much more distinctly when we consider the nature of brutes and man. Willing and striving is its whole being, which may very well be compared to an unquenchable thirst. But the basis of all willing is need, deficiency, and thus pain. Consequently, the nature of brutes and man is subject to pain originally and through its very being. If, on the other hand, it lacks objects of desire, because it is suddenly deprived of them by a too easy satisfaction, a terrible void and ennui comes over it, i.e. its being and existence itself become an unbearable burden to it. Thus its life swings like a pendulum, backwards and forwards between pain and boredom.*

The complaint is that we all change from moment to moment and have no permanent being or purpose. Even the pleasure of love, according to Petronius, is gross and brief, and brings loathing after it, a sentiment echoed in Dylan Thomas's lines:

At last the soul from its foul mousehole
Slunk pouting out when the limp time came†

The latter is probably as good a summary as any of the philosopher's basic indictment of the world. When a man falls in love he experiences the same perception that he experiences on spring mornings and holidays and in peak experiences: the sense of *reality*, of the real value of the objects of his enthusiasm. When this collapses into a feeling of satiety and fatigue it seems equally obvious that the whole thing was a mistake, that the sex instinct, whose only purpose is procreation, lured us into this situation in order to fulfil its own dubious aims. Or as T. S. Eliot put it:

The World as Will and Idea, Book IV, Haldane and Kemp translation, p. 402.
†Dylan Thomas, Lament.

71

Birth, and copulation, and death.
Birth, and copulation, and death.
That's all the facts when you come to brass tacks:
Birth, and copulation, and death.

Which is 'true' – the original desire, or the later feeling of disillusionment? According to most philosophers, even this question is meaningless. Neither is 'true'. We just happen to feel one thing one day and another thing another: to ask which is true is like asking whether a rainy day is 'truer' than a sunny one. The same answer applies to the question, why do we experience such a clear sense of meaning and purpose when we are in love – or even merely in a state of erotic excitement? Because the 'conjuror' has chosen to delude us for his own purposes. This is why man 'feels sad after coitus' – because he knows he has been duped again.

Now according to the view of perception that we have developed in the last two chapters, all this is simply untrue. The basic problem lies in the dullness of our senses and our brains, which reveal to us an extremely limited range of reality. And it is the 'close-upness' that deprives us of meaning. Or, as I have expressed it elsewhere, man is like a grandfather clock driven by a watchspring. Or like some enormous watermill whose stream has dried up into a narrow, sluggish flow. As William James put it in an essay called 'The Energies of Man':

> Everyone knows that on any given day there are energies slumbering in him which the incitements of that day do not call forth.... Most of us feel as if a sort of cloud weighed upon us, keeping us below our highest notch of clearness in discernment, sureness in reasoning, or firmness in deciding. Compared to what we ought to be, we are only half awake. Our fires are damped, our drafts are checked. We are making use of only a small part of our mental and physical resources.

And he summarizes the problem by saying that our basic problem is an inveterate 'habit of inferiority to our full self'.

If we can once *grasp* this fact – that our senses are so dull that we are little better than sleep-walkers – then we can also begin to see that when we experience a sense of meaning, it is because our senses have opened a little wider than usual, to admit a wider range of reality. In its normal state, the brain is like a piano whose strings are damped so that each note vibrates for only a fraction of a second. In these 'wider' states of mind the strings go on vibrating and cause other strings to vibrate. One thing suddenly 'reminds' us of another, so the mind is suddenly seething with insights and impressions and ideas. Everything becomes 'connected'. We *see* that the world is self-evidently a bigger and more interesting place than we usually take for granted. There is no question of illusion or of being somehow 'intoxicated' with energy. We are simply in a state of wider perception – both outer and inner perception. The brain is operating a little closer to normality instead of in this grossly subnormal state that usually makes life such a burden.

In 'wider' states, we can also see that a man's response to a pretty girl is not some conjuring trick of nature designed to lure him into fathering her children: it is a genuinely deeper perception of her reality. Sexual excitement also has this effect of widening and deepening the *perceptions*: the 'distant ranges of fact' are, in this case, of a sexual nature. If sadness or disappointment or even loathing succeed this excitement, it is simply because the senses have returned to their usual narrow state; we are once again 'subnormal'.

Now clearly, this view of perception contradicts the whole 'negative' trend in philosophy from Ecclesiastes and Plato to Schopenhauer and Sartre. These philosophers insist that we should distrust our senses because their evidence is 'relative'; therefore the statement that the universe (and human existence) is meaningless is just as valid – or as invalid – as the statement that it has an ultimate purpose and direction. But if the insights of the mystics are valid then this 'melancholy relativism' (as Thomas Mann called it) is quite simply a fallacy. The trouble lies in the curious limitations of everyday consciousness – limitations that seem even more puzzling when we realize that they can vanish in a flash and leave us staggered and overwhelmed by a sense of infinite vistas of meaning.

Oddly enough it was Thomas Mann who gave classic expression to this 'melancholy relativism' in an early story called 'Disillusionment'. The author describes a conversation he had with an unknown man in St Mark's Square in Venice. After asking him whether Venice comes up to his expectations the stranger goes on, 'Do you know what disillusionment is? Not a miscarriage in small, unimportant matters, but the great and general disappointment which everything, all of life, has in store?' He goes on to tell how, as a child, he expected life to be infinitely strange and exciting. His first great disappointment came when his family's house caught fire and they were all forced to watch it burn down in their night clothes: he stood there thinking, 'So this is what it is like to be burned out of house and home? Is that all there is to it?' When he fell in love and the girl rejected him, he thought, 'So this is what it is like to suffer agonies of jealousy – is that all?' And it was just as bad when his desires were satisfied: the same feeling of 'Is this all?' Even the first sight of the sea was an anticlimax, for it had horizons, and he had hoped that it would be infinite. It will probably be the same, he concludes, when death arrives: he will confront it with the feeling, 'Is this all?'

Mann's character is obviously suffering from the same sense of boredom that led Graham Greene to play Russian roulette. 'Staring at a sight that others assured me was beautiful, I felt nothing. I was fixed, like a negative in a chemical bath.' This last comment offers us an important clue. Greene had become 'fixed' in a condition of total *passivity*. But

73

passivity is a highly dangerous condition for human beings, because our natural laziness immediately takes advantage of it until it seems to us self-evident that *nothing* is worth doing. This is the condition in which Samuel Beckett's characters sit around in dustbins or lie on their faces in the mud. Yet all this is an absurd misunderstanding. Man has gained power over the world by turning it into symbols – by turning real men into matchstick men, and so on. But he has gained this mastery at the expense of losing touch with external reality and spending far too much of his time in an unreal world of symbols. In effect modern man spends most of his time inside a sound-proof room inside his own head, staring at a computer screen. This enables him to handle reality with far more efficiency than a child or a savage, but it also means that he tends to forget that there is a 'real' reality *out there*. And when he grows tired and bored with the computer, he thinks he has grown tired and bored with life and decides that all effort is futile and that life is an endless disenchantment.

Having landed himself in this 'unreal' situation, Greene had to 'galvanize' himself out of it by playing Russian roulette. His situation could be compared to that of a man who has convinced himself by logic that his limbs are paralysed, but is forced to swim for dear life when he falls into a river. Greene's real problem was that he failed to *grasp* the insight produced by the Russian roulette: that a certain kind of *mental effort* can produce the recognition that 'life contains an infinite number of possibilities'. It is as if the man had scrambled out of the river and immediately fallen victim again to the delusion that he could not move his limbs.

The point is interestingly underlined in a series of case studies made by the psychologist J. Silverman. He reported that schizophrenic patients, after a stay of more than three years in a hospital ward, simply stopped *seeing* things as clearly as they had (or, as Silverman put it, suffered 'changes towards diminished field articulation and diminished scanning'). The same thing was found to be true of convicts who had been in prison for very long periods. Their perceptions became blurry and they tended to notice far less. Their consciousness, says Silverman, had shifted from the 'active mode' to the 'receptive mode' (i.e. passive mode).* In other words boredom had the effect of making their eyes less efficient, so that they actually *saw* the world as a duller and more boring place. Here, we could say, science is providing us with a kind of proof of the mystic's statement that our senses are telling us lies and that they ought to show us a far richer and more fascinating world.

It must be acknowledged that the main problem here is that it is very hard to see what Greene could actually have *done* about his state of 'diminished perception', short of playing Russian roulette. For this is obviously the most important question of all: what can we actually *do*?

*See Arthur J. Deikman, 'Bimodal Consciousness' in *The Nature of Human Consciousness*, ed. Robert Ornstein, p. 72.

The Russian novelist Artsybashev has a novel called *Breaking Point* about a small Russian town where an increasing number of people become convinced that life is futile and meaningless, and the book ends with an epidemic of suicides. How would a psychologist – or a mystic – go about convincing these people that they are actually committing a schoolboy howler about the nature of consciousness?

Silverman's observation of convicts and schizophrenic patients makes it clear that the trouble was that they had stopped *noticing* things, and finally stopped seeing them. They were not paying attention. A Zen parable tells how a common man asked the Zen Master Ikkyu to write down for him some maxims of the highest wisdom. The Master wrote one word: 'Attention.' 'Will you not add something more?' asked the man, whereupon Ikkyu wrote, 'Attention. Attention.' The disgruntled man said he couldn't see much wisdom in this, whereupon the Master wrote, 'Attention. Attention. Attention.' 'What does attention mean?' asked the man, whereupon Ikkyu replied, 'Attention means attention.'

Hermann Hesse stumbled upon the same insight in his small book *Journey to the East*, a kind of allegory about a group of people who wander off in search of 'salvation'. The narrator records, 'I, whose calling was really only that of a violinist and story-teller, was responsible for the provision of music for our group, and I then discovered how a long time devoted to small details exalts us and increases our strength.' Everyone has made a similar discovery at some time: that exhaustion and fatigue can be reversed simply by becoming deeply *interested* in something and giving it the full attention. It is as if the vital energies, which had become scattered and diluted, are somehow *funnelled* into the object of attention. The moment Ollie murmurs, 'How fascinating!' Stan immediately sends up a trickle of strength and vitality. And we only have to experience this trickle of vitality – what J. B. Priestley calls 'delight' or 'magic' – to grasp our true situation and to realize that the sense of being 'cut off from reality' is not a particularly serious condition. We are 'cut off from reality' because we are standing in front of a computer screen in a sound-proof room inside our heads. But it is easy enough to walk out of the door into the fresh air. We merely have to know that the door is there.

This is what happened to Maslow's students, who discovered that as soon as they began thinking and talking about peak experiences, they had peak experiences all the time. They had recognized the simple fact that 'reality' *is* real and should not be confused with the world of symbols. This recognition comes very easily when we are on holiday or travelling in a strange place, for it is then self-evident that reality is real. Sitting outside a pub, drinking cold beer and eating bread and cheese from a wooden table, or walking through some quiet old cathedral close that looks unchanged since the time of Trollope, we can see that the world is ten times as interesting as we thought and that life holds out far more promise than we had realized. Then we experience Anne Bancroft's insight that our normal perception is too lazy and half-hearted and that we make no real effort because we do not believe we shall see any adequate return for our energy. The feeling of 'absurd good news' that comes in such moments is a sudden recognition that there is no good reason why we should return to our former 'debased' perceptions. If we can merely *hang on* to this recognition, we shall have broken out of the vicious circle of Stan and Ollie and the robot. Then it will merely be a question of arousing ourselves to live with far more determination and effort and optimism – an optimism which, in this state of insight, we can see is richly justified.

The most important insight is the recognition that states of 'delight' can be produced by a more or less co-ordinated effort of will. William James noted that it is continual *effort* that can 'carry us over the dam'. My own efforts to induce these states have convinced me of the truth of Ikkyu's observation that the basic necessity is attention. I have succeeded on a number of occasions in producing states of concentrated awareness which lasted for a period of hours, and on each occasion the first necessity was to convince myself (that is to say, my 'other self') that a continuous effort would produce worthwhile results, exactly like the effort devoted to reading a book – or, for that matter, writing one.

On one occasion a few years ago the initial effort was the result of being caught in a snowstorm in a remote farmhouse. I had gone there to give a lecture to a group of extra-mural students on New Year's Eve, and before I arrived at the farm it had begun to snow heavily. I had arranged to stay the night, and when I woke up the next morning I found that my ground-floor bedroom window was blocked by a snowdrift. My car, and a dozen or so others, were stranded in the farmyard, with no possibility of getting them out. So I was forced to stay there another night. The next morning the weather forecast announced more snow, and it was obvious that unless I wanted to spend a week there I had better make a serious effort to get out. Some of the other 'castaways' felt the same, and a team of us set to work with shovels to clear the entrance to the farmyard. Then the car that was nearest to the gate made an effort to get through. But its wheels spun in the snow, and the driver had to admit defeat. My car was next in line, and to my delight it had no problems in gripping the compacted snow. But there was still half a mile of snow-covered road – much of it uphill – between the farm and the main road. In some places the wind had blown the road clear, in others the snow was three feet deep.

We worked away all morning with our shovels – in one place I avoided a loop in the road by driving straight across a field – and by midday I had reached the gateway that led out on to the main road. We all walked back to the farm for lunch, then I picked up my bag and tramped back to the car. The snow on the main road had been flattened by traffic, but the surface was treacherous. In places, where no cars had disturbed the fresh snow, it was impossible to make out where the road ended and the ditch began. In other places the snow had built up at the side of the road into six-foot banks. It was necessary to drive for mile after mile with extreme caution, knowing that the slightest error might land me in the ditch and leave me stranded in the open countryside for another night.

When, several hours later, I finally arrived on a broad main road where traffic had turned the snow into slush, I experienced an enormous sense of relief. Then as I drove on towards home I realized that instead of fading, this 'glow' of relief and delight was remaining constant. The intense and continuous 'attention' of the past few hours, the perpetual sense of crisis, had somehow 'fixed' my consciousness in a higher state of awareness, so that everything I looked at seemed somehow more real. It was not unlike the state I often experienced as a child on Christmas Day – the feeling that the world is *self-evidently* wonderful and exciting, and that no problem is too great for human will and persistence. There was a feeling that if only I could maintain this vision, I would never experience any serious problems for the rest of my life. The state lasted for the remainder of the drive home, and was still easy to recreate the next morning. In fact I only have to spend a minute or so thinking about the experience to feel a renewal of the basic insight – although, of course, without that 'heightened pressure' of consciousness.

In fact a number of experiences of this sort have convinced me that it is absurd to embark on a long train journey or car ride without taking advantage of the free time to make a deliberate effort to raise the pressure of consciousness by constant effort. The initial effort may be difficult, involving winding myself up into a heightened state of determination in which it becomes self-evident that further effort will lead to further results. Earlier this year (1987) I made a more continuous and sustained effort than I had ever attempted before. I was travelling by train from Cornwall to Northampton, a total journey of eight or nine hours, with a change of stations in London. It took me more than an hour to concentrate my attention into a state of awareness where I was suddenly *noticing* more as I stared out of the window. That is to say the effort was being passed on to my subconscious mind, which was helping me to sustain it. In effect I had finally convinced Stan to wake up and start being helpful. Long before I had reached London I had forced myself into a mildly euphoric state in which the main sensation was of a certain feeling of latent strength. In such states I become aware that our normal low-pressure consciousness views the world with a basic feeling of *rejection* – the feeling we might get if we came upon the decaying corpse of a rat in the garden shed. In states of high-pressure consciousness we actually look at things with a kind of friendliness, as if they had something interesting to tell us.

By the time I had crossed London and was on the train to Northampton I was feeling tired, and ready to relax. But it struck me as a pity to waste the rest of the journey, especially since I had never travelled on this particular line before and was therefore unfamiliar with its scenery. So I stared out of the window and continued to make a sustained and determined effort. It came easily, except that I was aware of an underlying fatigue of attention. Every time I felt tired, it was exactly as if a window – or a door – had started to close, cutting off my view of reality. It was an exhilarating sensation to push the window open again and experience an actual thrill of interest as I looked at wagons standing in a siding or a well-kept back garden. That sense of being continually *told* something was very strong.

I arrived at my destination at about half-past four in the afternoon feeling pleasantly fatigued but still full of energy. It was a publisher's conference at which I was due to make an after-dinner speech. But I regretted my effort as I sat at dinner and experienced such a flood of fatigue that I could probably have slept instantaneously simply by closing my eyes. At one point the heat of the room and the smell of food produced a kind of nausea and a desire to go outside for fresh air. Then I remembered the vision of the train journey and the recognition that my *will* had control over my senses. A curious effort of inwardness, very difficult to describe (but quite familiar to anyone who has ever overcome a feeling of sickness by thinking of something else), and I was suddenly wide awake and prepared to stand up and organize my thoughts.

A major insight of that journey was that our minds are simply out of training, like the body of an overweight man who decides to enter for the London Marathon. These, and other experiences like them, have left me in no doubt that it *is* possible to push our minds up to a higher level of perception and to keep them there for a long time. It is, as James points out, merely a matter of habit. A modern city dweller deals habitually with a complexity of experience that would give a backwoodsman a nervous breakdown.

But it seems to me that the most important insight of the Northampton experience was the clear recognition that our senses are normally in a state of 'rejection'. We look at the world rather as an overworked executive looks at a stranger who is probably about to ask him a favour. Yet we only become aware of this in those moments of 'acceptance' when we find ourselves looking at everything with sympathetic interest. This, I realized, was what the German poet Rilke had meant by the phrase '*dennoch preisen*' – to praise *in spite of*. Rilke had been impressed by Baudelaire's poem 'Carrion', describing how the poet and his mistress come upon the horrible rotting carcass of a dog in a public park, because it made poetry out of something normally considered too disgusting to mention. Rilke saw, in a flash of insight, that this is the real business of the poet: to raise himself to a level of mental intensity where everything in the world, even a rotting carcass, becomes fascinating.

3

Down the Rabbit Hole

On 10 January 1912 the historian Arnold Toynbee had a remarkable experience as he sat on one of the twin summits of the citadel of Pharsalus in Greece thinking about a battle that had taken place on those slopes in 197 BC. As he looked out over the sunlit landscape, he suddenly slipped into what he later called a 'time-pocket'. Instead of the sunlit hillside there was a heavy mist, and he knew that in that mist, two armies were groping their way towards one another: the Romans and the army of Philip V of Macedon. Then the mist parted, revealing the right wing of the Macedonian phalanx charging downhill and carrying the Romans before them. In doing so they opened up a dangerous gap between themselves and their left wing – a gap of which a Roman officer instantly took advantage, wheeling his men at the double to attack the exposed wing in the rear. These uncouth young Latin peasants knew nothing of mercy: even as the Greeks threw down their arms and surrendered, they were hacked to the ground. Toynbee's hallucination was so complete that he averted his eyes from the massacre, and as he did so caught sight of a group of fleeing horsemen of whose identity he was ignorant. A moment later, quite suddenly, the whole scene vanished into thin air, and he again found himself looking at the sunny pastoral landscape.

Compare this with an experience described by the great mountaineer Frank L. Smythe in his book *The Mountain Vision* (1941). Crossing the Scottish hills from Morvich to Loch Duich on a bright, sunny day, with a magnificent view of cloud-dappled hills and the distant sea, he entered a grassy defile near Glen Glomach and became instantly aware of an aura of evil in the place. It was as if something terrible had once happened there. On impulse, Smythe decided to stop for lunch and try to fathom this unpleasant feeling. He seems to have possessed some kind of rudimentary psychic faculty – at least enough to know that he should try to empty his mind and sink into a receptive state. Suddenly:

> . . . a score or more of ragged people, men, women and children, were straggling through the defile. They appeared to be very weary, as though they had come a long way. The pitiful procession was in the midst of the defile when all of a sudden from either side concealed men leapt to their feet and, brandishing spears, axes and clubs, rushed down with wild yells on the unfortunates beneath.

79

There was a short fierce struggle, then a horrible massacre. Not one man, woman or child was left alive; the defile was choked with corpses. I got out of the place as quickly as I could. Screams seemed to din in my ears . . . .

Smythe's book was reviewed in *The Scotsman* and a few days later Smythe wrote a letter to the editor in which he mentioned that his researches had revealed that two massacres *had* taken place on the road near Glen Glomach: one in 1715, when General Wade had laid an ambush and slaughtered a number of Highlanders, and one in 1745, after Culloden. Yet he admitted that neither of these two fitted his 'vision', for the weapons were of an earlier period. What Smythe had seen was apparently a 'tape-recording' of a past event somehow 'imprinted' on the scenery by the violence of the emotions involved. (A later researcher, T. C. Lethbridge, called such recordings 'ghouls' and believed that they are somehow imprinted on the electrical field of water and are therefore to be found most often in damp places.)

Yet it seems clear that Toynbee's 'time-slip' was not quite of this nature. He was intimately acquainted with the history of the battle, and this undoubtedly played an important part in his 'vision'. However this seems to suggest that all that happened was that Toynbee experienced an unusually vivid surge of imagination, which is also unacceptable: there is the odd detail of the fleeing horsemen whom he could not identify. Moreover Toynbee goes on to describe several other similar experiences, some of which happened on the same trip to Greece, when he was twenty-three. His account (in the tenth volume of his *Study of History**) makes it clear that he was often in a curious semi-mystical state on this trip and that his state of mind produced a number of near-hallucinations. Two months later, on 19 March, he rounded the shoulder of a mountain in Crete and found himself looking at the ruins of a baroque villa, probably built for one of the last of the Venetian governors about three centuries ago. As he stood looking at this deserted house he 'had an experience which was the counterpart, on the psychic plane, of an aeroplane's sudden deep drop when it falls into an air-pocket'. He was 'carried down a time-pocket' to a day two hundred and fifty years ago when the house was suddenly evacuated and deserted. Now in this case he knew nothing about the house that he suddenly found in front of him. So the experience of falling into a 'time-pocket' must have been in many respects similar to Frank Smythe's experience near Glen Glomach. It was *aided* by his knowledge of history, but was not actually caused by it.

Another similar experience occurred in the ruins of the open-air theatre in Ephesus when suddenly 'the empty theatre peopled itself with a tumultuous throng as the breath came into the dead and they lived and stood upon their feet.' What Toynbee was watching, apparently, was the episode when Saint Paul and his two companions ran into trouble with

*Arnold Toynbee, *A Study of History*, volume 10, pp. 126–144.

the silvermakers' guild of Ephesus, who were afraid that Christianity would undermine their thriving business of making silver images of the goddess Diana. According to the *Acts of the Apostles* the indignant crowd in the theatre shouted and threatened for two hours before the town clerk succeeded in persuading them to go home. Watching this crowd, Toynbee thought he could actually pick out Paul's two companions Gaius and Aristarchus, and an ineffectual Jew called Alexander. And as the shouts of 'Great is Diana' were dying down, the life flickered out of the scene and Toynbee was 'carried up again instantaneously to the current surface of the Time-stream from an abyss nineteen centuries ago'.

A month later, on 23 April 1912, Toynbee had an experience that makes it clear that he believed he was seeing 'visions' and not merely using his 'historical imagination'. He had clambered up to the citadel of Monemvasía in Laconia, and scrambled through a breach in the ramparts. Lying around among the thorn bushes were a number of bronze cannons whose wooden carriages had rotted away, and once again Toynbee fell into a 'time-pocket', going back to the evening of the day in 1715 when the fortress, previously held by the Venetians, had fallen to the Turks. But when Toynbee later checked on this vivid impression he was puzzled to learn that the fortress had *not* been taken by storm, either in 1715 or in 1821, when the Turks surrendered to the rebel Greeks: on both occasions the surrender had been negotiated peacefully. So Toynbee had to conclude that what he had 'seen' was the victors breaching the walls and dislodging the cannons to put the fort permanently out of action so that it could not constitute a threat in the future. His puzzlement leaves no doubt that he felt he had actually seen it, not merely imagined it.

The best-known of Toynbee's 'time-slips' happened in May 1912 as he was musing on the summit of the citadel of Mistrà, above the plain of Sparta. Mistrà had been a ruin since it had been overrun in the Greek war of independence in the 1820s. Gazing down at the ruins and nibbling a bar of chocolate Toynbee was suddenly carried back to that day when the invaders had poured into Mistrà and massacred most of the inhabitants; from that day onward it had remained a ruin. Again, time stood still and the past became a reality. Toynbee was overwhelmed by a 'horrifying sense of the sin manifest in the conduct of human affairs' – a vision that was to lead him to write the monumental *A Study of History*.

What was the precise nature of Toynbee's 'visions'? A sceptic would dismiss them as 'mere imagination', but Toynbee's own account makes it clear that he believed them to be more than that. Details like the unknown horsemen riding away at Pharsalus, the glimpse of Paul's companions in the theatre at Ephesus, the impression of violence in the fortress of Monemvasía, all suggest that it was closer to a kind of dream: in fact Toynbee refers to himself as 'the dreamer' in speaking about Pharsalus. He admits that these visions lasted only a fraction of a second yet says that the sense of reality was so poignant that he seemed to have slipped back into the past; he compares himself to a palaeontologist who can reconstruct a whole dinosaur from a fragment of bone. Yet this is not a 'time-slip' in the sense of Frank Smythe's experience, for Smythe knew nothing about the massacre in the valley. Toynbee's experience was based on his intimate knowledge of history. In some odd way, he had caused history to 'come alive', not in the sense of a daydream but as something far more vivid and real.

I have suggested elsewhere* that what we are dealing with here is a latent human faculty whose existence we only dimly recognize. It is a curious ability to grasp intuitively the *reality* of some other time or place. In Dr Johnson's novel *Rasselas* the hero contemplates the beautiful scenery of the Happy Valley where he was born and wonders why he cannot be happy like the cows. He reflects sadly, 'I can discover within me no power of perception that is not glutted with its proper pleasure, yet I do not feel myself delighted. Man surely has some latent sense for which this place affords no gratification, or he has some desires distinct from sense which must be gratified before he can be happy.'

His problem is easy to understand. The Happy Valley is pleasant enough. But he is *stuck* there, in the present moment, unable to escape, like a fly on a sweet but sticky fly paper. And when man experiences only *one reality* at a time, he is bored. A child experiences happiness when he is sitting beside a warm fire on a winter's night with the rain beating on the windows, or when he is lying on a beach on a summer day with the great cold expanse of the sea stretching in front of him. For he is in effect in two places at once: in the warm room, and out there in the freezing rain; or on the sunny beach, and out there on the cold and fathomless sea. This is why children love to hear ghost stories when they feel comfortable and secure: it is a way of being in two places at once. Dr Johnson's Prince Rasselas is not only stuck in the present moment, but in a state of mind that might be called 'mono-consciousness'. The child listening to a ghost story is in 'duo-consciousness'.

But there are times when duo-consciousness becomes so intense that it ceases to be an exercise in imagination and takes on a compelling quality of reality. This is the 'latent sense' that Johnson talks about. It seems to be an unknown or unrecognized faculty, and as such I have suggested calling it Faculty X.

It is interesting to note the similarity of this faculty – as illustrated by Toynbee – to Eileen Garrett's 'super-sensory perceptions'. When she held a fragment of the shirt that belonged to the vanishing doctor she immediately knew that he was in La Jolla: she was in two places at once. Elsewhere, she talks about the power to 'see through barriers', and gives an example that obviously qualifies as Faculty X:

A road may wind among hills for any distance. One sees the hills, and as the road reaches away, perspective operates and its further

The Occult, p. 58.

dimensions diminish. . . . Nevertheless, at the same time, one sees the entire road completely, regardless of the intervening hills, and its further reaches are as meticulously discernible as the areas that lie close to the spot from which one is seeing. Each rut and stone is individually seen and can be described with precision. The leaves of trees and the blades of grass are countable throughout the landscape.*

This also brings to mind the experience of the motorcyclist Derek Gibson (pp. 22–3) in which as well as being able to look *into* the trees and grass, he was also aware of every blade of grass and every tree 'as if each had been placed before me one at a time'. And there are other interesting parallels. Gibson's experience began as the sound of his motorcycle seemed to fade to a murmur; this suggests some kind of involuntary withdrawal inside himself, which in turn suggests Eileen Garrett's description of how she achieves her 'superconscious' states by withdrawing from the outside world. As Toynbee sat on the summit of Mistrà or overlooking Pharsalus, he was also in a state of contemplation – that is, deliberate withdrawal from the outside world. Most of us can achieve this state fairly easily: we merely have to think intently of some past event. But Toynbee, Gibson and Eileen Garrett then went a stage *further* – falling into Toynbee's 'time-pocket'. In effect they had learned to withdraw deeper into that inner world, as if they had found a trap-door in the floor with a flight of steps leading down to yet another level – or, like Alice in Wonderland, had stumbled down a rabbit-hole.

All this is rather puzzling, for it seems to contradict our commonsense view of imagination, which is simply another name for fantasy. In ordinary language, imagination means forming an *image* of something that is not actually present, and such an image is bound to be a poor copy of the original. What Toynbee did at Pharsalus or Ephesus is obviously quite different. This was no mere fantasy based on his historical knowledge, but something much more hallucinatory, as if he was actually watching – or rather taking part in – the original event. Ordinary fantasy is passive, like a spectator sitting in a cinema; Toynbee's imagination had taken on an active quality, much more like a film director marshalling the actors in a crowd scene. The fundamental distinction here seems to be between passive and active imagination.

Active imagination involves a sense of participation, as we can see from another example cited in *A Study of History*. Toynbee describes how, as a student, he was reading an account in Livy of the war between Rome and her Italian allies. Mutilus, a Roman who was fighting on the side of the Italians, had succeeded in making his way home to his wife's house in disguise: when his wife refused to let him in, scolding him for having a price on his head, Mutilus plunged his sword into his breast and spattered

*Eileen Garrett, *Adventures in the Supernormal* (1949), p. 172, cited in LeShan, *Towards a General Theory of the Paranormal*, p. 34.

her door with his blood. Toynbee says that as he read this account he was 'transported, in a flash, across the gulf of Space and Time . . . to find himself in a back yard on a dark night witnessing a personal tragedy that was more bitter than the defeat of any public cause'. This flash of 'active imagination', which took place in the year before his trip to Greece, was clearly due to sudden intense personal sympathy with Mutilus, but it presages the experiences of the 'time-pockets' of the following year.

It seems that the mind itself is suddenly raised to a higher level of power – as if the watch-spring in the grandfather clock has suddenly become far more powerful. But this access of power seems to happen by accident, as in the case of William James's sudden glimpse of 'ranges of distant facts'. It as if some natural faculty has been accidentally galvanized. This becomes clearer in Toynbee's account of another 'illumination' that sounds altogether more like the mystical illuminations described in an earlier chapter:

On each of the six occasions just recorded, the writer has been rapt into a momentary communication with the actors in a particular historic event through the effect upon his imagination of a sudden arresting view of the scene in which this long-past action had taken place. But there was another occasion on which he had been vouchsafed a larger and a stranger experience. In London in the southern section of the Buckingham Palace Road, walking southward along the pavement skirting the west wall of Victoria Station, the writer, once, one afternoon not long after the end of the First World War – he had failed to record the exact date – had found himself in communion, not just with this or that episode in History, but with all that had been, and was, and was to come. In that instant he was directly aware of the passage of History flowing through him in a mighty current, and of his own life welling like a wave in the flow of this vast tide. The experience lasted long enough for him to take visual note of the Edwardian red brick surface and white stone facings of the station wall gliding past him on his left, and to wonder – half amazed and half amused – why this incongruously prosaic scene should have been the physical setting of a mental illumination. An instant later, the communion had ceased, and the dreamer was back again in the everyday cockney world . . . .'

It is very plain that Toynbee's mind was raised momentarily to a higher level of power, so that for a moment it *hovered* over the whole of human history like some mythical bird, as the mind of a mathematical prodigy must hover over the whole number field. James found that one thing reminded him of another, and that reminded him of something else, and that of something else – all so fast that his rational intellect had no time to catch up. In Toynbee's case the 'connecting process' seems to have been instantaneous.

It is also clear that these experiences of Faculty X can be explained in simple and logical terms – for example, of brain physiology. Toynbee's experiences may have been due to some sudden surge of vitality which caused the brain to 'glow' as a surge in the electric current causes a light bulb to glow more brightly. Such illuminations are certainly accompanied by a switch from left-brain consciousness to right-brain consciousness. The left brain is always in a hurry, concentrating on the next thing that has to be done, so it has no time to linger over impressions or intuitions. Right-brain consciousness begins with a feeling of relaxation and relief. Instead of rushing forward, consciousness spreads gently 'sideways', taking in the present moment, looking *at* things instead of through them. The result is the sense of increased reality that Anne Bancroft experienced as she looked at the blackbird.

In the same way, right-brain memory seems to be quite different in kind from left-brain memory. Left-brain memory brings back the salient features of what we want to remember; right-brain memory brings back the very *smell* of reality. Proust devoted a whole vast novel to the distinction between the two: *A la recherche du temps perdu*, whose title could be more accurately translated *The Search for the Past* than (as it is in English) *Remembrance of Things Past*. He says gloomily, 'And so it is with our own past. It is a labour in vain to try to recapture it: all the efforts of our intellect must prove futile. The past is hidden somewhere outside the realm, beyond the reach of intellect. . . .' Yet his hero *does* recapture it by accident, coming home cold and tired and tasting a little cake called a madeleine which he dips in herb tea:

> No sooner had the warm liquid mixed with the crumbs touched my palate than a shudder ran through me and I stopped, intent upon the extraordinary thing that was happening to me. An exquisite pleasure had invaded my senses, something isolated, detached, with no suggestion of its origin. And at once the vicissitudes of life had become indifferent to me, its disasters innocuous, its brevity illusory – this new sensation having had on me the effect which love has of filling me with a precious essence; or rather, this essence was not in me, it *was* me. I had now ceased to feel mediocre, accidental, mortal . . . .

Several more tastes of the madeleine dipped in tea finally reveal to him that the 'exquisite pleasure' was due to memories of childhood in a little town called Combray, when his Aunt Léonie used to give him a taste of her own madeleine dipped in lime blossom tea.

But why *should* Proust's autobiographical hero experience this almost mystical sensation of sheer happiness merely because he recalls his childhood? Proust shows himself fairly adept at analyzing the reason. In the second volume he describes how, on a train journey to the seaside town of Balbec, at a small country station, he sees a young girl selling milk and coffee. 'Flushed with the glow of morning, her face was rosier than the sky. I felt on seeing her that desire to live which is reborn in us whenever we become conscious anew of beauty and of happiness.' Proust has undoubtedly placed his finger on the very essence of the human problem. We keep on *forgetting* how delicious life can be, and allow ourselves to slip into a state of mind in which it scarcely seems worth the effort. Proust says, 'And we deliver on life a pessimistic judgement which we suppose to be accurate, for we believed that we were taking happiness and beauty into account, whereas in fact we left them out and replaced them by syntheses in which there was not a single atom of either.' We may believe we have preserved the essence of some past pleasure in the memory: in fact it is really little more than a poor carbon copy – a piece of paste jewellery in place of the original diamond.

Proust's hero experiences the same illumination in the final volume, *Time Regained*, when, feeling rather depressed and discouraged, he is on his way to a reception. In the courtyard he steps back to avoid a car and almost loses his balance on an uneven paving stone. Yet once again, 'all my discouragement vanished, and in its place was that same happiness which had been given to me at various epochs of my life . . . .' And once again he is able to remember why he feels so happy: the uneven flags have suddenly recalled the uneven paving stones in the Baptistery of St Mark's in Venice. Twice more in the next quarter of an hour he experiences similar flashes of 'magic', once when a servant accidentally knocks a spoon against a plate, reminding him of a railwayman testing wheels with a hammer on the Balbec line, and once more when he wipes his mouth with a napkin, releasing a flash of memory of performing the same action on holiday in Balbec. Brooding once again on this problem Proust reaches the conclusion that the reason for that odd feeling of 'immortality' is that such experiences occurred 'outside time'. This explanation arouses understandable misgivings, since the 'flashes' *did* occur in time – if only in a split second.

In fact Proust has stumbled on the real explanation in an earlier sentence, when he says that he 'experienced them at the present moment and at the same time in the context of a distant moment, *so that the past was made to encroach upon the present . . .*' (my italics). This also answers the question about why these *memories* of Balbec and Venice cause such intense pleasure when the original experiences were often rather boring. The explanation, we can see, is not that the 'flashes' were timeless, but that they caused a state of *duo-consciousness*. *This* is what produces the flood of delight, the sensation of 'ceasing to feel mediocre, accidental, mortal'. It is the recognition that consciousness is not restricted to the boring, down-to-earth present in which we are all stuck for most of our lives. It can achieve a strange double-focus that can suddenly arouse in us 'the desire to live which is reborn whenever we become conscious anew of beauty and of happiness' – Graham Greene's sudden recognition that life contains an infinite number of possibilities.

Once again we confront that most baffling of all problems: how is it possible that human beings can *cease* to want to live? Whenever we experience intense happiness – or danger – we suddenly feel that it would be perfectly easy to go on living forever. It is the feeling Dostoevsky expresses in *Crime and Punishment* when Raskolnikov reflects that if he had to stand on a narrow ledge forever, in eternal darkness and tempest, he would still prefer to do that rather than die at once. The same recognition came to Hans Keller, former head of the BBC music department, when he was in Germany in the late 1930s. Keller was aware that fellow Jews were vanishing into concentration camps, and described in a broadcast how it had suddenly struck him that *if only* he could escape from Germany he would never be unhappy again for the rest of his life. Then how is it possible for us to lose that vision? The answer lies in Bergson's recognition that the intellect was not made for grasping the living quality of experience; it keeps on reducing the world to symbols and measurements. And we *forget* just how marvellous life can be.

Apart from Proust, the modern writer who was most continually concerned with this paradox was – oddly enough – G. K. Chesterton, although the light-hearted style in which he expresses it has tended to obscure the importance of what he is saying:

The Gallows in my garden, people say,
Is new and neat and adequately tall.
I tie the noose on in a knowing way
As one that knots his necktie for a ball;
But just as all the neighbours – on the wall –
Are drawing a long breath to shout 'Hurray!'
The strangest whim has seized me . . . . After all
I think I will not hang myself today.

Tomorrow is the time I get my pay –
My uncle's sword is hanging in the hall –
I see a little cloud all pink and grey –
Perhaps the Rector's mother will *not* call –
I fancy that I heard from Mrs Gall
That mushrooms can be cooked another way –
I never read the works of Juvenal –
I think I will not hang myself today.

It was Chesterton who coined the phrase 'absurd good news' to express these flashes of 'immortality'. And in *The Man Who Was Thursday* he demonstrates his insight into Faculty X when he makes the hero ask, 'When you say, "thank you" for the salt, do you mean what you say? No. When you say, "the world is round", do you mean what you say? No. It is true, but you don't mean it.' A moment before Proust's hero tastes the madeleine dipped in tea he could have said, 'I was a child in Combray,' but he would not have meant it. As he tastes the madeleine he can say, 'I was a child in Combray', and *mean* it. Yet in a sense he has only grasped the obvious: the reality of the past. But he 'knows' the past is real anyway. Proust's experience only underlines the fact that our normal consciousness is a consciousness of unreality. Our left-brain perception separates us from reality as if we were enclosed by a wall of sound-proof glass. In fact it is easy to fall into a pessimistic view of the left brain as our jailer. Eliot writes:

We think of the key, each in his prison
Thinking of the key, each confirms a prison

Yet, as already pointed out, it would be a serious mistake to think of 'Ollie' as the villain. On the contrary, it is left-brain perception that makes life interesting and exciting. This emerges with almost painful clarity in a passage of a letter written in 1887 by Mrs Sullivan, the teacher of a blind deaf-mute child called Helen Keller. Mrs Sullivan tells her friend:

In a previous letter I think I wrote you that 'mug' and 'milk' had given Helen more trouble than all the rest. She confused the nouns with the verb 'drink'. She didn't know the word for 'drink', but went through the pantomime of drinking whenever she spelled 'mug' or 'milk'. This morning, while she was washing, she wanted to know the name for 'water'. When she wants to know the name of anything, she points to it and pats my hand. I spelled 'w-a-t-e-r' and thought no more about it until after breakfast. Then it occurred to me that with the help of this new word I might succeed in straightening out the 'mug/milk' difficulty. We went out to the pump-house and I made Helen hold her mug under the spout while I pumped. As the cold water gushed forth, filling the mug, I spelled 'w-a-t-e-r' in Helen's free hand. The word coming so close upon the sensation of cold water rushing over her hand seemed to startle her. She dropped the mug and stood as one transfixed. A new light came into her face. She spelled 'water' several times. Then she dropped on the ground and asked for its name and pointed to the pump and the trellis, and suddenly turning round she asked for my name. I spelled 'Teacher'. Just then the nurse brought Helen's little sister into the pump-house, and Helen spelled 'baby' and pointed to the nurse. All the way back to the house she was highly excited, and learned the name of every object she touched, so that in a few hours she had added thirty new words to her vocabulary . . . .
PS . . . Helen got up this morning like a radiant fairy. She has flitted from object to object, asking the name of everything and kissing me for very gladness. Last night when I got into bed, she

stole into my arms of her own accord and kissed me for the first time, and I thought my heart would burst, so full was it of joy.*

It is almost impossible for us to imagine the world of a blind deaf-mute. But as we read these lines, we can suddenly grasp the overwhelming happiness of the child who realizes that *everything has a name*. Before that she was in a state of confusion about 'mug' and 'milk' – she thinks that words are interchangeable. And now, suddenly, this seven-year-old child has been handed the key to the understanding of all life, and her excitement is so immense that she learns thirty new words in a few hours. And from then on, she wants to know the name of everything she touches; she drops the signs and pantomimes and prefers to spell out her desires in words. In a few hours she has become the *master* of her environment. She has ceased to feel mediocre, accidental, helpless, mortal . . . . And all this because she has learned the proper function of the left brain: *mastery* of life.

This recognition is of central importance, for it is too easy to fall into the error of regarding the left brain merely as a jailer who prevents us from having peak experiences. The left brain is, on the contrary, the key to our evolutionary destiny. 'Vision' is important, but control is even more important. The point is powerfully underlined by the novelist Joyce Collin-Smith in her autobiography *Call No Man Master*. In the 1960s she became a follower of the Maharishi Mahesh Yogi, who was convinced that the world could be transformed by transcendental meditation. The Maharishi 'initiated' her one day by teaching her to repeat her personal mantra, then left her to meditate. She described how she immediately slipped into a state of blissful serenity that lasted for most of an afternoon and evening. After this she found it easy to achieve states of 'inwardness' in which hours passed like minutes. According to the Maharishi, the mind will turn naturally towards the source of its own being if it is shown an easy technique. This is the 'kingdom of God within', and the source of all existence. 'Great happiness, energy, creativity, love, can be tapped by this simple means,' he said, 'for the mind easily transcends this world and enters the field of the Being. So the initiate finds all tensions, world-weariness and all negative emotions falling away from him. He goes deep within and emerges renewed and refreshed.'

This sounds unexceptionable. But it soon became clear that 'plunging within' had some disadvantages. 'A desire to withdraw from life, and to be committed to no one and to nothing, seemed to be growing in them' [the initiates]. Some initiates could not be prevented from remaining in meditation almost permanently. A few began to have alarming experiences – a kind of cataleptic trance in which they were unable to move or open the eyes. (As we shall see in a later chapter, such a state often precedes an 'out-of-the-body experience'. Finally Joyce Collin-Smith

*Helen Keller, *The Story of My Life*.

began to experience doubts about the Maharishi himself, as success changed the childlike guru into a kind of super-tycoon, and after a period of disillusionment she left the movement. Then, quite suddenly, she was oppressed by a sense of boredom and futility:

> Then slowly everything began to turn, not just depressing and heavy, but completely sinister. I found I couldn't hold my mind steady at all. I perceived what the intellect had always known but experience had not as yet appreciated: that everything in life is in a perpetual state of flux; that there is no stability anywhere; that the only constant is continual unrelenting change.
> Looking at my hands, I saw them dissolving from the competent ring-clad hands of a middle-aged woman to the slim, smooth young hands of a girl, the little fists of a small child, the tiny curled buds of the baby in the womb. And at the same time they were old and gnarled with the knuckles of an aged crone, and finally the skeleton hands crossed in the grave.

Soon this experience began to happen with everything she looked at: a cup would become a heap of china clay and a few broken shards, a table would be simultaneously a pile of unplaned timber and broken fragments of worm-eaten firewood; nothing would 'hold still'. After a night in which she saw the world as a kind of Dante's Inferno, full of helpless misery, she decided to kill herself. She took a rope and sat underneath an oak tree, trying to decide how to go about it. As she did so she noticed that the rope was 'holding steady'.

> In my recent state the rope would have been dissolving into strands, into hemp, into flax growing in a field, flowering and seeding, being gathered, soaked and plaited, and at the same time fraying and disintegrating . . . .
> Now I saw that my deep concentration on the moment, on the rope as it was at that time – not what it had been or what it would become – had caused it to hold steady in its present moment of time. . . . The tree had also remained steady, neither dying nor becoming a sapling or a seed. It was like the television technique of stopping characters and situations in mid-action, leaving everything poised and immobile . . . .
> The secret of recovering 'normality', then, must lie somehow in holding attention steady in the present moment; not allowing any slippage in the mind . . . . The intense concentration and narrowing down of my mind as I contemplated my own intention with the rope had apparently triggered off a mechanism that, in the normal state, enables one to function in the world. It was evidently an automatic function, operated in some way by attention, or perhaps by *intention*, but normally completely unobserved.

This led Joyce Collin-Smith to realize that 'directed attention . . . must somehow be the key to getting back my sanity'. And she soon re-acquired the trick of focusing upon the present moment. 'For months I had been looking at life as through an unfocused microscope, seeing far too much, far more than I could use profitably in any way at all.' As soon as she grasped that, she again became 'normal'.

Her symptoms had been very like those of a bad psychedelic trip. Transcendental meditation had taught her the knack of escaping the limitations of the left brain and of relaxing 'into the right', with all its wider connections with other areas of being. Her terrifying experience taught her that the purpose of evolution is not to escape the limitations of the left brain, but to put them to good use.

Since we have got hold of this problem by the coat tails it would be a pity to let it go without a determined attempt to get to the bottom of it.

We can see that Toynbee's flashes of Faculty X were a *controlled* version of Joyce Collin-Smith's unnerving 'glimpses'. Toynbee was also catching a glimpse of reality – so that he was able to say something and *mean* it. Because he was actually in the citadel of Mistrà looking down on the plain of Sparta, he could say, 'A century ago, invaders came over that wall *there*,' and almost *see* them doing it. Whether that was all that happened is a matter we shall discuss in a moment. But the 'flash of reality' was certainly the starting point of the experience.

Why, in that case, can we not summon the experience at will? We can see, to begin with, that Toynbee summoned the experience by *telling* himself that it was true. And because he was in Mistrà, and because the place held for him such fascinating associations, he was somehow able to 'convince' his senses that it had happened five minutes ago.

It seems clear that when the senses are 'convinced', they are perfectly willing to reveal another dimension of reality. And this in turn raises the natural question, why do our senses not normally show us 'reality'? Part of the answer is plain enough. The left brain is always in a hurry. Its job is to 'cope' with everyday life and its endless complications. It has very little time to 'stand and stare'. When I am driving in heavy traffic I cannot afford to notice the make of every car that comes towards me, or even its colour; all that concerns me is its speed and what it intends to do next. So, for perfectly sound reasons, the left brain reduces the real world to a set of symbols. The problem is to persuade the brain to go behind these symbols – to galvanize it into a sense of reality, as Graham Greene's Russian roulette galvanized his devitalized senses. William James said that what we need is 'the moral equivalent of war', meaning some imaginative experience that would galvanize us like the trumpet for battle.

But if we examine this problem more closely we can see that it is not entirely a matter of symbols. The real problem is the way we interpret these symbols. The trouble is that faced with a rather dull-looking world (which is dull because we have turned it into symbols), we allow

91

ourselves to groan with despair and turn away in disgust. When this happens we experience what Sartre calls 'nausea', and Camus 'the absurd'. In Sartre's novel *Nausea* the hero, Roquentin, describes how it first happened to him. When he was in Cambodia, an acquaintance tried to persuade him to accompany him on an archaeological mission. He happened to be staring at a Cambodian statue at the time. Then, suddenly, he seemed to wake up 'from a six-year slumber':

> The statue seemed to me unpleasant and stupid and I felt terribly, deeply bored. I couldn't understand why I was in Indo-China. What was I doing there? Why was I talking to these people? Why was I dressed so oddly? My passion was dead. For years it had rolled over and submerged me; now I felt empty. But that wasn't the worst: before me, posed with a sort of indolence, was a voluminous, insipid idea. I did not see clearly what it was, but it sickened me so much that I couldn't look at it. All that was confused with the perfume of Mercier's beard.

And Sartre's hero abruptly refuses to go on the mission.

We can see that what has happened is simply that Roquentin has been overwhelmed by the 'Oh No!' feeling, and that *he has been taken in by it*. He has fallen into the elementary error of telling himself that this is 'the truth' and that his previous feeling that life is quite interesting was a delusion. He has been overtaken by the 'Ecclesiastes effect'. And he makes the enormous mistake of believing that it is a *revelation* of meaninglessness, instead of recognizing that he has simply *allowed* himself to 'let go', like an exhausted man clinging to a window ledge.

Camus falls into the same error. He writes in *The Myth of Sisyphus* about the problem of boredom. 'Rising, streetcar, four hours in the office or the factory, meal, streetcar, four hours of work, meal, sleep, and Monday, Tuesday, Wednesday, Thursday, Friday and Saturday according to the same rhythm.... But one day the "why" arises, and everything begins in that weariness tinged with amazement.' That is to say the feeling of 'absurdity' begins with a sense of futility, with the question, 'Why on earth am I wasting my life like this?' He goes on:

> Men, too, secrete the inhuman. At certain moments of lucidity, the mechanical aspect of their gestures, their meaningless pantomime, make silly everything that surrounds them. A man is talking on the telephone behind a glass partition, but you see his incomprehensible dumb-show; you wonder why he is alive. This discomfort in the face of man's own inhumanity, this incalculable tumble before the image of what we are, this 'nausea', as a writer of today calls it, is also the absurd. Likewise the stranger who at certain seconds comes to meet us in a mirror, the familiar and yet alarming brother we encounter in our own photographs, is also the absurd.

These examples reveal the flaw in Camus's argument. If you turn down the sound of the television at a moment of high drama the faces of the characters look absurd, with their mouths opening and closing like fishes. But this is because you have deliberately robbed them of a dimension of reality – a dimension necessary to grasp fully what is going on. Similarly, if you walked into a play halfway through it would mean less to you than to someone who had watched it from the beginning. But you would not argue that your lack of understanding is somehow 'truer' than the view of the other person. The same argument applies to the man gesticulating in the telephone booth. You have been denied certain essential clues that would enable you to complete the picture, but it is obvious nonsense to allege that your incomprehension somehow proves his 'inhumanity'.

Now it should be clear that Sartre's 'nausea' and Camus's 'absurdity' are not very different from our normal perception of the world. For as Ouspensky points out, the essence of normal perception is that everything is *separate*; the world is 'cut into little pieces'. Nausea is just this separateness carried to an extreme: *all* 'connectedness' has vanished. In short, *ordinary consciousness is a form of nausea*. The left brain has deprived us of a whole dimension of meaning. If by 'normal' we mean something that tells us the truth, then Faculty X is far more normal than our everyday awareness and the reality seen by the mystics is the most normal of all.

We can also see why the flashes of duo-consciousness are accompanied by the sense of 'absurd good news', the 'all is well' feeling. Our analysis has shown that narrow, left-brain consciousness is *not* 'normal' consciousness but a rather specialized and abnormal form developed as a tool for controlling the world. (Language is its first and most important means towards that end, as we saw in the example of Helen Keller.) The form of consciousness Proust experienced in his 'flashes' was normal – even if, paradoxically, human beings only experience it in flashes. We were *intended* to have this richer and more complex form of consciousness, and – as Wordsworth pointed out – most children actually do possess it. Our consciousness of the world was intended to have a richness and warmth that would make everything appear to be 'apparelled in celestial light'. This is the kind of consciousness that most adults experience only during holidays, when the actual sight of new and interesting places awakens in them a sense of the complexity and variety of the external world. But the original sense of 'glory and freshness' is lost as they are forced to cope with an increasingly complex environment and the 'shades of the prison house begin to close'.

This seems to suggest an answer to one of the most puzzling questions about the brain: why does it possess two apparently identical halves which appear to duplicate one another's functions? So far no physiologist has succeeded in offering a convincing answer to this problem, the most plausible suggestion being that one half is intended as a 'spare' in case the other half is damaged. The experiences of Toynbee and Proust suggest another answer: the brain has two halves so we can be in two places at the same time. Which brings us, of course, back to our former question – and the question to which Proust devoted the twelve volumes of *A la recherche du temps perdu*: is there some *method* by which we could summon 'duo-consciousness' at will?

The foregoing analysis offers one important clue. The real problem is what *prevents* us from achieving such states at will? One basic obstacle is that we accept 'everyday' consciousness as 'normal', and it is this acceptance that keeps us trapped in our mechanical expectations. Consider again the case of Toynbee on Mistrà. As he looks at the scenery he *tells* himself that this place was destroyed by invaders in the Greek war of independence; he is actively *imposing* his knowledge of history upon the evidence of his senses. And his brain responds with some kind of 'surge' that transforms history into reality. An ordinary tourist, looking down on Mistrà, would lack two of Toynbee's advantages: his knowledge of Greek history and the sudden imaginative conviction that caused the 'surge'. In short the attitude of the tourist is relatively passive; Toynbee is using his imagination actively.

But the problem is not merely one of passivity. We can see, in the example of Sartre's Roquentin, that there is an actively negative element, which sets in motion the 'vicious circle effect'. This can be seen even more clearly in the well-known episode of the chestnut tree in *Nausea*. Roquentin begins the diary entry by admitting that he feels crushed, but at least he now knows what he wanted to know. 'The Nausea has not left me and I don't believe it will . . . but I no longer have to bear it, it is no longer an illness or a passing fit: it is I.'

He had, he explains, just been sitting in the park:

> The roots of the chestnut tree were sunk in the ground just under my bench. I couldn't remember it was a root any more. The words had vanished and with them the significance of things, their methods of use, and the feeble points of reference which men have traced on their surface. I was sitting, stooping forward, head bowed, alone in front of this black, knotty mass, entirely beastly, which frightened me . . . . And then all of a sudden, there it was, clear as day: existence had suddenly unveiled itself. It had lost the harmless look of an abstract category: it was the very paste of things, this root was kneaded into existence. Or rather the root, the park gates, the bench, the sparse grass, all that had vanished: the diversity of things, their individuality, were only an appearance, a veneer. This veneer had melted, leaving soft, monstrous masses, all in disorder – naked, in a frightful, obscene nakedness.

What has happened is similar to his experience in Indo-China. Boredom, a sense of futility, causes a collapse of his will power, a sudden feeling of 'What am I doing here?' It is a little like stage-fright – a sudden desire not to go on. But this experience then goes a stage further than stage-fright. We do not need to know that Sartre's own experiences of nausea were due to a bad mescalin trip to understand what happens next. The writhing, snake-like appearance of the roots produces a mixture of revulsion and terror. He *knows* it is a tree and perfectly harmless, but the collapse of his will power, of his will to live, makes him feel totally vulnerable. It is basically the same mechanism of revulsion and *mistrust* that makes Dylan Thomas regard a girl's sexual organs as a 'foul mousehole'.

We are all subject to a more or less permanent degree of mistrust. If you reach out to open a door and the doorknob is wet and sticky, you snatch your hand away in disgust. If you pick up a fallen apple from under a tree and find a slug on the underside, you drop it in disgust. We are always vaguely prepared for things to be not as they seem: that is part of our self-preservation mechanism. But if we allow it to go too far, it develops into the state known as paranoia. The Victorian scientist Sir Francis Galton wanted to find out how easy it was to slip into a state of paranoia, and deliberately induced a persecuted state of mind by telling himself that everyone he passed in the street was a spy. He was alarmed to discover how easy it was to make himself feel persecuted: when he passed a cab-stand he even had a feeling that all the horses were staring at him. Professor Peter McKellar was intrigued by this experiment and tried persuading friends in a restaurant that the waiter had something against them and was determined not to serve them; in *Mindsplit* he records that it was surprisingly easy to induce a state of mild paranoia. And when Aldous Huxley took mescalin he also realized how frighteningly easy it would be to 'embark upon the downward, the infernal road. . . . If you started the wrong way, everything that happened would be a proof of the conspiracy against you. It would all be self-validating. You couldn't draw a breath without knowing it was part of the plot.'

All this is explained, of course, by the Stan and Ollie mechanism. Ollie tells himself that everybody is against him, but he doesn't really believe it. But Stan believes it, and before long Ollie is horrified to realize that he has become the victim of Stan's negative responses. And this is what has happened to Sartre's Roquentin. He knows the root is not a snake or a writhing octopus, yet the sense of paranoia is so strong that the root seems to exude alien menace.

The important thing to note is that Roquentin's intellect tells him that he is looking at the root of an ordinary tree, but his negative emotions convince him that it is nasty and frightening. His paranoia assures him that he ought not to take the root for granted; his attitude should be one of mistrust. But we can also see that the real problem is that Sartre's intellect then ratifies the whole transaction. Instead of telling himself, 'Nonsense, this is just a chestnut root,' he proceeds to convince himself that the world is really a far nastier and more frightening place than most of us realize. He tells himself that when we look at things, we do not *really* believe they exist; we treat them as if they were stage scenery. And now he suddenly realizes that things exist in their own right, and that their sheer reality seems to mock our attempt to keep them in their 'proper place'. *This* is the real root of Sartre's problem: he has allowed his emotions to convince his intellect that human existence is short, brutal and futile, and that – as he says in *Being and Nothingness* – 'it is meaningless that we live and meaningless that we die.'

And here, at last, we have come to grips with the very heart of the problem: the tendency of intellect to confirm our negative judgements on life. A child can feel just as depressed and miserable as an adult, yet a child seldom commits suicide. Why? Because he merely *feels* depressed. The adult *thinks* depressed, and – if he happens to be a Sartre or Samuel Beckett – tells himself that life is meaningless and futile anyway.

In an amusing story called 'The Unknown' Maupassant provides an illustration of the workings of this 'negative mechanism'. A young man-about-town describes his acute embarrassment at being overtaken by sexual impotence. He has frequently passed a dazzlingly attractive girl in the street and wondered how to make her acquaintance – once even trying to follow her home. One day he summons up his courage to speak to her and, to his surprise, finds that she has no objection to coming to his apartment. (This already begins to worry him – it is a little too easy.) A few caresses, and she begins to take off her clothes – asking him, as she does so, not to look at her. He glances at her naked back – and sees that she has a curious black stain between the shoulder blades. Absurd ideas flash through his mind – of fatal enchantresses in the *Arabian Nights* who lure men into their clutches. And when it comes to the time to 'sing his song of love', he finds he has no voice. The girl looks at him with mild contempt, says, 'It seems a pity to have put me to so much trouble', and walks out on him.

Maupassant's story only underlines a mechanism with which we are all familiar. The machine I am using to type these words has an erase key, a highly convenient modern development. If I strike the wrong key or write 'hte' instead of 'the', I merely press the erase key, and the mistake vanishes. Our brains already have an erase key, so that we can correct our conversation as we go along. It will even cancel something I am *about* to say or do: if I am about to make a tactless remark, I can catch myself just in time and say something else. If I am feeling very nervous or embarrassed, my finger hovers permanently over this erase key, to the great detriment of my spontaneity. The sight of the black birthmark causes Maupassant's hero to press the erase key and destroy his own sexual desire. And Sartre's hero is in such a permanent state of nausea that he keeps his finger on the erase key most of the time.

Let us look a little more closely at the way this mechanism works, for it is obviously the key to the question, what prevents us from experiencing 'duo-consciousness' at will?

What actually *happens* when Maupassant's hero suddenly loses his potency or Roquentin feels that a chestnut root has become frightening and menacing? The answer is obvious: the intellect has been overruled by a negative emotion. This is the basic mechanism of nausea and mistrust. Or to put it another way, his intellectual values have been overruled by his emotional values. (A value, of course, is simply a feeling that something is good or bad.)

We have, in fact, three distinct sets of values: physical, emotional and intellectual. And of these three, the intellectual values are by far the most reliable. My physical values have a nasty habit of changing from one hour to the next, so that I can feel marvellous at nine in the morning and utterly miserable by ten, merely because I feel hungry, or tired, or have a headache. There is an excellent example of the awful power of our physical values in C. S. Lewis's *Screwtape Letters*, when the demon Screwtape explains to his nephew Wormwood one of his most effective techniques for preventing human beings from thinking clearly:

I once had a patient, a sound atheist, who used to read in the British Museum. One day, as he sat reading, I saw a train of thought in his mind beginning to go the wrong way. The Enemy [i.e. Jesus], of course, was at his elbow in a moment. Before I knew where I was I saw my twenty years' work beginning to totter. If I had lost my head and begun to attempt a rational argument I should have been undone. But I was not such a fool. I struck instantly at the part of the man which I had best under my control and suggested that it was just about time he had some lunch. The Enemy presumably made the counter-suggestion . . . that this was more important than lunch . . . . When I said, 'Quite, in fact much *too* important to tackle at the end of the morning,' the patient brightened up considerably; and by the time I had added, 'Much better come back after lunch and go into it with a fresh mind', he was already halfway to the door.

The first major obstacle to our powers of insight is the body itself, with its continually changing moods.

The second set of obstacles was clearly recognized by Anne Bancroft. 'I saw that I had become really futile, so much a slave to my emotions, so involved with my own feelings . . . that my life had narrowed down to the compulsive behaviour of a zombie.' This sounds like a contradiction in terms – surely feelings should make you feel more alive, not less? Yet we all know precisely what she means. When we are truly happy, there is a blissful sense of being free of our emotions. Emotions are like heavy mist, while real happiness is like being surrounded by clean, pure air.

But my intellect stands above these physical and emotional values. For example, when I am feeling angry or jealous or upset, another part of me looks down on it all with cool detachment and tells me not to be such a fool. On the whole my intellect tells me the truth – or at least does its

97

best. My physical and emotional values tend to distort my perception of reality and often assure me that life is horrible or futile or meaningless. My rational self tells me that I am lucky to be alive.

The central problem of human existence is that our lives are dominated by these 'trivial' values of the body and the emotions, so that we are in a permanent state of confusion – like someone who is blindfolded at the beginning of a game of blind man's buff, then whirled round a dozen times until he is dizzy. There are times when our 'trivial' values and our rational values fight a duel to the death. William James tells the story of a man who suddenly fell out of love. For two years he had been violently enamoured of a girl who was a coquette. His reason told him that she was simply not the right person for him but his emotions – and no doubt his physical desires – were so involved that he remained a slave. Then one day, on his way to work, he felt as if 'some outside power lay hold of me', and he rushed home and burned all her letters and photographs, feeling 'as if a load of disease had suddenly been removed from me' – as, in a sense, it had. It is significant that he felt as though some 'outside power' had laid hold of him, when it was merely his common sense that had revolted. He had come to so identify himself with his 'trivial' values that he could not recognize that it was his own mind that had intervened to release him from his slavery. All that had happened was that his mind had resumed its *rightful place* as the ruler and controller of his emotions.

Sartre once remarked that he had never felt so free as during the war when he was in the French Resistance and in constant danger of arrest. The reason is obvious. With the threat of danger hanging over him he could not *afford* to allow trivial emotions to dominate his judgement. The same is true of Graham Greene when he placed the gun to his head and pulled the trigger. In the surge of alarm, all his negative emotions were scattered to the four winds and a more mature 'self' took charge.

Maslow's story of the young mother makes the same point. As she watched her husband and children eating breakfast, she was preoccupied with immediate problems – getting her husband off to work and the children off to school – and therefore with 'trivial' values. Then, in a flash, her mind rose above such trivialities, and she *grasped her situation objectively*, as if she were coolly assessing someone else's life. The result was a perception, 'My God, aren't I lucky!', and a surge of joy. Here we can see that *the peak experience is simply the experience of grasping the world clearly and rationally*. The real trouble with physical and emotional values is that they are so *short-sighted*. And when we feel tired or depressed or bored – or simply passive and indifferent – it is because we are allowing our 'trivial' values to dominate our intellectual values. In effect we are holding our values *upside-down*.

This is a recognition of vital importance. When a clear state of rationality is suddenly overcast by heavy clouds of emotion and *we allow ourselves to be taken in by them*, it is exactly as if our feet have turned into gas-filled balloons and we are suddenly floating upside-down. And when we come to recognize this state we realize with horror that most human beings spend their lives 'upside-down'. It applies even to philosophers, which is why the history of philosophy is so full of pessimism and confusion.

We might turn this insight into a parable in the manner of Confucius, and say that when the intellect is the emperor and emotion is the grand vizier, the kingdom is harmonious and happy. But when emotion usurps the throne and forces intellect to become its servant, the kingdom falls into chaos and misery.

The chief problem of being 'upside-down' is that the 'trivial' values are so short-sighted and tend to plunge us into a state in which the difficulties of life seem just not worth the effort. 'Trivial' values induce the 'Ecclesiastes effect'. When I am driven by a powerful sense of purpose, my intellect tells me that it *is* worth making tremendous efforts and I summon my vital energies accordingly – or rather, Stan summons them for me. When emotional values are allowed to dominate, my vitality sinks – for it is Ollie who suddenly feels that life is just not worth the effort and whose pessimism infects Stan.

It is important to emphasize that we are not now talking about some relatively rare state of anger or jealousy or self pity. The 'upside-down' state happens to us a hundred times a day, so that we literally forget whether we are on our head or our heels. Most of us recognize the problem and do our best to fight against it. But we all know people who have allowed themselves to become completely dominated by envy or self-pity or a sense of defeat, and who seem bent on ruining their own lives and the lives of everyone they come into contact with. Permanent 'upside-downers' are the most dangerous people in the world.

Yet our proneness to 'upside-down' states is an inevitable consequence of human evolution. Human beings can cope with more complexity than any other animal. To cope with this complexity we have developed a 'microscopic' vision, rather like a watchmaker's eyeglass. But the eyeglass condemns us to 'close-upness', and close-upness (another name for nausea) deprives us of meaning. Nausea is a kind of 'collapsed consciousness', a consciousness *minus* a dimension of meaning. And once we recognize that, we have to face the depressing insight that 'normal' human consciousness *is* a form of nausea. And human beings who are stuck in this narrow, 'collapsed' consciousness are particularly prone to 'upside-down' states – for 'close-upness' also makes us easily discouraged.

Now we have grasped the true nature of our everyday consciousness, we can see that far from being 'normal', it is actually subnormal. It lacks a whole dimension of meaning, like the television with the sound turned down. On the other hand we can also see that Toynbee's glimpses of Faculty X at Mistrà or Pharsalus were 'everyday consciousness' *plus* a dimension of meaning. In other words Toynbee was experiencing a brief flash of genuinely normal consciousness.

This recognition is the all-important first step in answering the question, how can human beings set about achieving Faculty X at will? We must recognize *precisely* what is wrong with our subnormal everyday consciousness. We must also recognize that our tendency to 'upside-downness' constitutes a major obstacle to learning to achieve genuinely normal consciousness. 'Upside-downness' blinds us to reality. A philosopher who tries to understand the 'meaning of life' without grasping this insight is in the position of a matador who tries to give a good performance even though his hat keeps slipping over his eyes.

The first step towards achieving normal consciousness is to grasp the precise mechanisms of 'upside-downness'. When Maupassant's hero glimpsed the black birthmark between the girl's shoulders he instantly turned upside-down, and the result was impotence. Five minutes before he had been quite certain that he wanted the girl: now he suddenly felt it was a mistake. But at least this was only a temporary reversal. The character in Thomas Mann's 'Disillusionment' is in a permanent state of 'upside-downness', for he has *decided* that life is one long disappointment. He has ratified the 'upside-down' state with his intellect. It is rather as if the emperor decided that he had never had any right to the throne after all, and that the grand vizier and his descendants should be emperors in perpetuity. (This is why writers like Sartre, Graham Greene and Samuel Beckett are so dangerous – they have ratified 'upside-downness' with the intellect, and their negative vision is passed on to adolescent students with all the authority of a modern classic.)

Another example of the 'upside-down' mechanism is to be found in Arthur Koestler's autobiography *Arrow in the Blue*. He had spent an afternoon playing poker and lost far more than he could afford. At a party that evening he got drunk, then discovered that his car radiator had frozen and the engine block had burst. A girl he did not like offered him the hospitality of her flat. When he woke up the next morning with a hangover, lying beside a girl he found unattractive, and remembered that he had no money and no car, he experienced a wave of violent indignation with life in general that led to the decision to join the Communist Party. There was no logic in the decision: simply the desire we all feel, when goaded beyond endurance, to go and do something spectacular. It took another seven years of bitter experience to make him realize that he had walked into an intellectual cul-de-sac, and to undo the consequences of a single day's 'upside-downness'.

The way in which this subsequent reversal took place is equally instructive. In 1937 Koestler was a foreign correspondent in Spain; he was recognized as a member of the Communist Party and thrown into a fascist prison. Executions took place every day, and Koestler had no doubt that his turn would come soon. The crisis caused what he described as 'a loosening up of psychic strata close to rock bottom'. He passed the time scratching mathematical problems on the wall of his cell with a broken bed-spring, and one day tried hard to remember Euclid's proof that there is no greatest prime number – in other words that the number of primes (numbers that cannot be divided exactly) is infinite. As he scratched the proof on the wall he experienced a sense of enchantment, and recognized the reason:

> . . . the scribbled symbols on the wall represented one of the rare cases where a meaningful and comprehensible statement about the infinite is arrived at by precise and finite means . . . . The significance of this swept over me like a wave. The wave had originated in an articulate verbal insight; but this had evaporated at once, leaving in its wake only a wordless essence, a fragrance of eternity, a quiver of the arrow in the blue. I must have stood there for some minutes, entranced, with a wordless awareness that 'this is perfect – perfect'; until I noticed some slight mental discomfort nagging at the back of my mind – some trivial circumstance that marred the perfection of the moment. Then I remembered the nature of this annoyance: I was, of course, in prison and might be shot. But this was immediately answered by a feeling whose verbal translation would be, 'So what? is that all? Have you nothing more serious to worry about?' – an answer so spontaneous, fresh and amused as if the intruding annoyance had been the loss of a collar-stud. Then I was floating on my back in a river of peace, under bridges of silence. It came from nowhere and flowed nowhere. Then there was no river and no I. The I had ceased to exist.

The experience was a turning point in Koestler's life, the beginning of his rejection of Marxism.

It is interesting that the essence of the experience is a purely rational and logical insight. He is in prison, waiting to be shot – an experience that would turn anyone into an 'upside-downer'. But the crisis arouses deep reserves of vital energy. And when the mathematical insight brings a sudden recognition of the sheer power of reason, the result – as in the case of Maslow's young mother – is an almost blissful sense of objectivity, of the power of the human mind to grasp the world clearly and rationally.

Another example from Koestler's autobiography makes the point even more effectively. Koestler tells how he was sitting on a park bench in Vienna with a pile of books beside him; he was reading a pamphlet about atrocities against Jewish pioneers in Palestine and was overcome with a feeling of impotent rage. Then he picked up a book on Einstein and read the comment that relativity had led the imagination 'across the peaks of glaciers never explored before by any human being'. The phrase brought an image of Einstein's relativity formula hovering in a kind of haze over snow-covered peaks, and the feeling of rage dissolved into a 'sense of infinite tranquillity and peace'.

Einstein himself had said something very similar. He declared that his supreme aim was the 'perception of this world by thought, leaving out everything that is subjective'. He also wrote that 'one of the strongest motives that lead men to art and science is to escape from everyday life, with its painful crudity and hopeless dreariness, *from the fetters of one's own ever-shifting desires* [my italics]. A finely tempered nature longs to escape from personal life into the world of objective perception and thought; this desire may be compared with the townsman's irresistible longing to escape from his noisy, cramped surroundings into the silence of high mountains . . . .' Here we can see precisely the same feeling that swept Koestler away as he worked out Euclid's proof on the wall of his prison cell: a longing to escape from the stifling world of personal emotions and anxieties and into a world of objective contemplation.

What is so interesting about Toynbee's experiences is that he apparently achieved this objectivity without any effort. What was the secret? His account of his experience at Mistrà suggests the answer. He had sat 'musing and gazing . . . through most of a long summer's day', so was in a state of contemplative calm, the same calm that Wordsworth declared to be the essential condition for poetry. And although he was meditating on 'the cruel riddle of Mankind's crimes and follies' he was not, like Koestler, in a state of seething indignation. It was this freedom from negative emotion, this calm intellectual contemplation, that provided the basic condition for the leap of imagination that placed him above human history. Nietzsche had had a similar experience above Lake Silvaplana in Switzerland, when he was seized with the inspiration for *Thus Spake Zarathustra*. He wrote in his journal: 'Six thousand feet above men and time . . . .' Both Toynbee and Nietzsche had fulfilled the basic condition: they were 'the right way up'.

4

The Information Universe

One day in 1968 Mr P. J. Chase of Wallington, Surrey was waiting for a bus, and since the next bus was not due for some time he strolled a short distance along the road. Soon he found himself standing in front of two pleasant thatched cottages with attractive gardens; these had a profusion of flowers, and Mr Chase particularly noticed some hollyhocks. A date above the door of one of the cottages indicated that it had been built in 1837.

The next day Mr Chase mentioned the cottages to someone at work – his place of work was not far from the bus-stop. The other man thought about it and shook his head. There were no such cottages on the site, he insisted – only two brick houses. The following evening Mr Chase walked back to the site, and discovered that his workmate was correct; there were only two brick houses. But an old resident of the area verified that there *had* been two cottages on the site; they had been demolished some years earlier.

Mr Chase recounted this story to the historian Joan Forman, and she has published it in a book called *The Mask of Time*. The sensible reaction to such an anecdote is that it is pure invention – the kind of thing that happens in ghost stories, but not in real life. Yet the evidence of 'time-slips' is too strong for that. Undoubtedly the most famous 'time-slip' concerned two principals of an Oxford college, Charlotte Moberly and Eleanor Jourdain, who on 10 August 1901 visited the Trianon park at Versailles and were surprised to see many people in eighteenth-century costume. Both felt oddly depressed and experienced a 'dreamlike' sensation. It was when they compared notes that they decided that something rather strange had happened. Three years later they returned and found everything changed: the place had been 'modernized' – yet the changes they noted had not taken place in the past three years. Careful study of books on the period convinced them that they had somehow revisited the age of Marie Antoinette – and had probably actually seen her in person. The story of their strange experience, *An Adventure*, caused a sensation. Nevertheless, when Dame Joan Evans became the literary executor of the two ladies she decided to allow the book to go out of print on the grounds that what they had seen was almost certainly a fancy-dress party organized by a fashionable lady called Mme de Greffuhle, a friend of the novelist Proust. In fact later investigation showed that the fancy-dress party had taken place seven years before the Trianon visit, and that Mme de Greffuhle left Versailles for the country during the month of August. So the most famous 'time-slip' of all remains unexplained.

I myself collected a similar experience at first hand from Mrs Jane O'Neill, a Cambridge schoolteacher.* When she and a friend visited Fotheringhay church – where Mary Queen of Scots was executed – in the autumn of 1973 she was greatly impressed by a picture of a crucifixion behind the altar. Later, when it happened to come up in discussion, her friend denied seeing the picture. Jane O'Neill rang the Fotheringhay postmistress, who arranged the flowers in the church every Sunday, and was told that no such picture existed. When the two women revisited the church a year later Jane O'Neill found its interior quite different. Some historical research revealed that the church *she* had seen in 1973 was the one that had been pulled down in 1553.

Jane O'Neill's 'time-slip' had been only one of a series of similar experiences that followed a severe shock earlier that autumn: she had been the first at the scene of a bad motorway accident near Heathrow and had helped to pull injured passengers from the wreck. On her way home later that night she had begun to 'see' injured passengers in front of her – a phenomenon known as 'eidetic imagery'. On holiday in Norfolk soon afterwards she continued to 'see' things – but this time, apparently, they were visions from the past, and in each case she felt exhausted afterwards. So her 'vision' in Fotheringhay church was almost certainly a piece of eidetic imagery which she mistook for present-day reality. What is strange is that her vision corresponded so closely to the church as it had been before its demolition.

Now in the case of Jane O'Neill we can at least form some rough idea of what happened. A bad shock has the effect of 'loosening the psychic strata' and shaking us out of habit patterns. It makes us more vulnerable, yet in a sense more alive – more sensitive to the reality that surrounds us, instead of taking it for granted. In this state of 'wide-openness' one becomes like a highly sensitive camera that can take photographs in a semi-darkness that would defeat an ordinary camera. So Jane O'Neill's experience in the church is not dissimilar to Toynbee's experience above Pharsalus – with this single difference: she mistook her 'vision' for reality. And the same explanation seems to fit Mr Chase's two thatched cottages and the experience of the two ladies at Versailles.

But if we are to accept this explanation, then we must make one absolutely basic assumption: that 'information' about the past is somehow 'stored' exactly like a tape-recording, and that our minds have some natural method of 'retrieving' this information. For the most part it seems to happen accidentally when the mind is 'wide-open' and in a state of relaxation. Then there is the experience that Toynbee describes as falling into a 'time-pocket' and that Eileen Garrett calls 'a fundamental

*The story is told in detail in *Mysteries*, pp. 361–3.

shift in one's awareness'. The mind suddenly relaxes *below* its usual threshold of relaxation and falls 'down the rabbit-hole'. What it then seems to encounter is some more solid and permanent level of reality than our changing world. There is a feeling of timelessness, as if what is 'glimpsed' is happening *now*. In one of his last books J. B. Priestley speaks of his own experiences of such 'glimpses':

> ... on these occasions I have been recalling a person or a scene as clearly and as sharply as I could, and then there has been, so to speak, a little click, a slight change of focus, and for a brief moment I have felt as if the person or scene were not being remembered but were really there *still existing*, that nobody, nothing, had gone. I can't make this happen; either it happens or it doesn't. . . .*

This is obviously Toynbee's experience of the reality of history, Faculty X, and again there is the 'little click, a slight change of focus', a kind of shift of awareness as if diving down inside oneself. And this is followed by the sense of being in touch with some more permanent reality. Sometimes, what is 'glimpsed' is logical and rational, like the battle of Pharsalus or the inside of Fotheringhay church. Sometimes it makes no sense at all.

The biologist Ivan Sanderson records such an experience in the final chapter of *More Things*, a book concerned mainly with zoological oddities: the chapter is called 'An Hallucination?' After stating that he has never been interested in 'the occult', he tells how he and his wife were living in Haiti, engaged on a biological survey. One day, on a drive to Lake Azuey, they made the mistake of taking a short cut that landed them up to their axles in mud and had to spend most of the night walking back. Sanderson and his wife were walking together, their assistant Frederick G. Allsop walking ahead, when:

> ... suddenly, on looking up from the dusty ground I perceived absolutely clearly in the now brilliant moonlight, *and casting shadows appropriate to their positions*, three-storied houses of various shapes and sizes lining both sides of the road. These houses hung out over the road, which suddenly appeared to be muddy with patches of large cobblestones. The houses were of (I would say) about the Elizabethan period of England, but for some reason, I *knew* they were in Paris! They had pent roofs, with some dormer windows, gables, timbered porticos and small windows with tiny leaded panes. Here and there, there were dull reddish lights burning behind them, as if from candles. There were iron-frame lanterns hanging from timbers jutting from some houses and they were all swaying together as if in a wind, but there was not the faintest movement of air about us . . . .

*J. B. Priestley, *Over the Long High Wall*, p. 60.

I was marvelling at this, and looking about me, when my wife came to a dead stop and gave a gasp. I ran smack into her. Then she went speechless for a time while I begged to know what was wrong. Finally she took my hand and, pointing, described to me *exactly what I was seeing*. At which point *I* became speechless.

Finally pulling myself together, I blurted out something like, 'What do you think's happened?' but my wife's reply startled me even more. I remember it only too well; she said, 'How did we get to *Paris* five hundred years ago?'

We stood marvelling at what we apparently *both* now saw, picking out individual items and pointing, questioning each other as to details, and so forth. Curiously, we found ourselves swaying back and forth and began to feel very weak, so I called out to Fred, whose white shirt was fast disappearing ahead.

I don't quite remember what happened then but we tried to run towards him and, feeling dizzy, sat down on what we were *convinced* was a tall, rough curbstone. Fred came running back asking what was wrong but at first we did not know what to say. He was the 'keeper' of the cigarettes, of which we had about half a dozen left, and he sat down beside us and gave us each one. By the time the flame from his lighter had cleared from my eyes, so had fifteenth-century Paris, and there was nothing before me but the endless and damned thorn bushes and cactus and bare earth. My wife also 'came back' after looking into the flame. Fred had seen nothing. . . .

A young native later commented to Sanderson, 'You saw things, didn't you? You don't believe it, but you could *always* see things if you wanted to.' Presumably he meant that Sanderson was 'psychic'. This could certainly help to explain the vision of ancient houses. Their situation may also have played its part: they were tired, plodding along a road in bright moonlight, feeling a little nervous, so their senses were 'wide-open'. Sanderson's wife may have seen the ancient houses by 'tuning in' to her husband – husbands and wives are often telepathic. But all that still leaves the mystery of what fifteenth-century houses were doing in twentieth-century Haiti. It is true that Haiti was occupied by the French, but this was two centuries later. Is it possible that there *were* once old 'Elizabethan' houses on that bare country road? That, on the whole, seems the likeliest explanation. Yet it seems unlikely that they could have vanished without leaving any trace. And if this explanation has to be abandoned, then the vision of fifteenth-century Paris in twentieth-century Haiti remains incomprehensible.

In *The Mask of Time* Joan Forman makes a creditable attempt to explain 'time-slips' in scientific terms. Her suggestion is that events are 'recorded by a material medium (stone seems to be a common recorder) . . . at a time when energy patterns were being created in the neighbourhood'. The culprit, she thinks, could be 'Schumann waves', ultra-violet energy of very short wavelength, which are present between earth and the ionosphere and which operate on the same frequency as our 'brainwaves'.

A similar explanation of haunted houses had been advanced towards the turn of the century by Sir Oliver Lodge, who suggested that powerful tragic emotions, like those associated with murders or suicides, might be 'recorded' in the walls of houses where such events have occurred. Half a century later a retired Cambridge don named T. C. Lethbridge came independently to the same conclusion. Lethbridge had often experienced 'unpleasant sensations' in certain spots, as if something 'nasty' had happened there and left traces behind. Lethbridge called these sensations 'ghouls', and believed that they were basically 'recordings'. In one case he and his wife Mina were visiting Ladram beach to collect seaweed and both experienced an 'unpleasant feeling' near a stream that ran down the cliff: when Mina went to make a sketch at the clifftop she had the feeling that someone was urging her to jump. Lethbridge later discovered that a man *had* committed suicide from that spot and assumed that Mina was somehow 'picking up' a 'recording' of his emotions just before he jumped. On another occasion Lethbridge and his mother had been walking in the great wood near Wokingham when both had experienced acute depression; they discovered later that they had been walking close to the corpse of a man who had committed suicide.

Lethbridge observed that the site of such an occurrence is usually damp and concluded that the 'recording medium' may simply be the electrical field of water. He suggested that ghosts are nothing more than 'tape-recordings' which for some reason become suddenly visible to human beings.

This explanation seems to be favoured by Joan Forman. One of her correspondents had visited the Long Gallery at Hampton Court and experienced an 'agony of distress' at the door leading to the antechamber of the royal pew, and then again in the pew itself. Catherine Howard, the wife of Henry VIII, had been arrested at Hampton Court in 1541 and charged with misconduct: she had escaped from the guards and rushed screaming along the gallery to try to see the king, who was in his pew in the chapel; but the door was closed. Joan Forman, who had herself experienced a feeling of 'utter misery and extreme physical coldness' in the gallery, suggests that the two 'recordings' are, respectively, those of Catherine Howard and those of Henry VIII, who heard her screams. But Catherine was executed in the following year, and Henry VIII lived on for another six years. So it seems unlikely that their 'ghosts' haunt the spot. According to Joan Forman, a sudden tragic intensity of emotion is all that remains of the event: a permanent 'tape-recording' that can be 'picked up' by those who are sensitive enough.

The first person to stumble on this notion of 'recordings' was an American professor, Joseph Rodes Buchanan, who has already been introduced in the opening chapter. When Buchanan first began experimenting with his students, handing them various chemicals wrapped up in

107

brown paper packages and asking them to try and 'sense' what was inside them, he believed that our bodies are surrounded with a 'nerve aura' which has exactly the same kind of sensitivity as our tongues. So his students were really identifying the chemicals as they might have identified the taste of salt or sugar in their mouths. And when some of his 'sensitives' were able to hold sealed letters and describe the people who wrote them, Buchanan simply extended his theory and concluded that the personality of the writer had somehow 'imprinted' itself on the letter. His sensitives were in effect psychic bloodhounds who were able to distinguish between one 'smell' and another. However this pleasingly simple and logical theory soon ran into difficulties. The sensitives were able to produce equally precise descriptions if he handed them a photograph sealed in an envelope (photography was a recent discovery in the 1840s). At first that seemed reasonable enough – after all, most photographs have been in contact with their subjects and must have picked up something of their 'smells'. Then Buchanan discovered that it worked just as well with newspaper photographs. And that was absurd. The 'nerve aura' theory had to be abandoned – or at least modified. Buchanan had to fall back on the notion of 'clairvoyance', and this undoubtedly helped to destroy his reputation with his scientific colleagues. By the 1860s few people still took him seriously.

But by this time his disciple William Denton, a professor of geology at Boston, was producing even more remarkable results with geological specimens wrapped in thick paper. His chief sensitives were his wife, his sister-in-law Mrs Cridge and, later on, his son Sherman. Denton's book *The Soul of Things* remains one of the most fascinatingly readable books in the whole field of paranormal research. He arrived at the conviction that every object in the world carries its own history hidden inside it and that most people can develop the ability to 'read' this history simply by holding it in their hands. A fragment of volcanic rock produced visions of an exploding volcano with a river of lava pouring into the ocean. Mrs Cridge even 'saw' ships on the ocean. In fact the lava was from the eruption in 1840 of the volcano of Kilauea on Hawaii, when the United States fleet had been visiting the island. A meteorite brought visions of empty space, with the stars looking abnormally large and bright. A fragment of dinosaur bone summoned a vision of aquatic dinosaurs on a prehistoric beach. And when Denton tried the same fragment on Mrs Cridge a month later (without telling her what was in the parcel) she also saw water and bird-like creatures with membranous wings – probably pterodactyls. A piece of a mastodon's tooth produced an image of a monstrous creature with heavy legs, an unwieldy head and a very large body. A pebble from a glacier produced a feeling of being buried for a long time in a depth of ice. A pebble from Niagara brought an impression of the sound of a torrent and a deep hole full of something like steam (she thought it might be a hot spring). A piece of hornstone from the Mount of Olives brought an image so accurate that Denton's wife deduced she was looking at Jerusalem.

Denton's theory was astonishing enough, yet in another sense quite logical. For every object *does* carry its history imprinted in it. To begin with light falling on the surface of a stone must destroy some of its outermost molecules, producing a kind of blurred photograph. (E. T. Bell's science-fiction novel *Before the Dawn* was based on the idea of a machine that could 'unscramble' these pictures and so read the history of ancient rocks.) If strong human emotions can be 'imprinted' on scenery, then presumably so can other kinds of energy. Denton was merely suggesting that the human mind possesses its own powers of 'decoding' these ancient recordings.

However when Thomson Jay Hudson came to write *The Law of Psychic Phenomena* in the early 1890s he dismissed Denton's claim that we all possess a natural 'telescope into the past'. He felt that Denton's results could all be explained by the extraordinary powers of the subjective mind. As an example he cited the case of a piece of Roman mosaic pavement which Denton knew to be from the villa of the orator Cicero. Denton's wife decribed a Roman villa, a squad of Roman soldiers and a fleshy man in a toga with a commanding presence. In order to guard against any cheating – even unconscious cheating – Denton went through an elaborate double-blind procedure before he handed over the Roman fragment. He first of all wrapped it in brown paper then mixed it up with many other specimens in identical wrapping, so that he himself had no idea which was which. This was in case he gave his wife some unconscious hint or even transmitted information to her telepathically. (The word telepathy was invented by Frederick Myers in the early 1880s but the idea of 'thought transference' was familiar long before that.)

That sounded convincing enough, but Hudson was unimpressed. He pointed out that the memory of the subjective mind seems to be practically limitless. So it would know precisely what each parcel contained even if Denton mixed them with his eyes closed. Denton's own historical know-ledge would provide the 'pictures' from the past, and his wife would have no difficulty picking them up from him by means of telepathy . . . . So that disposed of Denton's belief that every event is 'recorded' on its sur-roundings.

As it turned out Hudson could not have chosen a worse example. Denton had himself been puzzled by the fact that his wife had not seen Cicero: the man she had seen was fleshy, but Cicero had been tall and thin. It was when Denton came to republish the book fifteen years later, in 1888, that he revealed a discovery he had made in the meantime. Cicero's villa had previously been owned by the dictator Sulla, and Sulla corresponded very accurately to Mrs Denton's image of a broad, fleshy man with an aloof, majestic air, yet whose face also revealed 'a good deal of geniality'. Hudson might still object, of course, that Denton already knew that Sulla had owned the villa before Cicero and had simply forgotten. But if we accept Denton's word that he learned about it for the first time after the 1873 edition of *The Soul of Things*, then Hudson's objections collapse and the 'recording' theory remains unshaken.

Since the 1880s psychometry – as Buchanan christened the 'recording' theory – has been generally ignored by science. Even 'psychical researchers' seem to find it embarrassing and prefer not to mention it. Yet it is probably the best authenticated of all 'psychic faculties' and there are hundreds of impressive examples in the history of psychical research. In 1921 a sceptical French novelist named Pascal Forthuny discovered – to his amazement and embarrassment – that he was an excellent psychometrist. He was present at the Metapsychic Institute in Paris when Dr Gustav Geley, a leading French investigator, was about to test a clairvoyant. Someone asked for a letter to be passed across the room to the clairvoyant: Forthuny grabbed it on the way, clapped it against his forehead, and began a mocking improvization: 'I see a crime . . . a murder . . . .' When he was finished he was told that the letter was from the French 'Bluebeard' murderer Landru. Forthuny was equally accurate with two more objects, a fan and an officer's cane, describing their history in striking detail. He was later subjected to a series of scientific tests by Geley's assistant, Dr Eugene Osty, whose book on the subject leaves no doubt of the genuineness of Forthuny's remarkable powers.

Forthuny seems to demonstrate that objects can 'record' the emotional history of their owners – illnesses, personal tragedies and so on. But what of Denton's belief that *everything* records its own life history, including rocks and meteorites? It sounds scientifically indefensible, yet another series of tests a few years earlier suggest that Denton may have been correct after all.

Just before the First World War Dr Gustav Pagenstecher, a German doctor who had settled in Mexico City, was treating an insomniac patient named Maria Reyes de Zierold. Drugs were useless but hypnosis seemed to work. And one day, under hypnosis, she told him that her daughter was listening outside the door. He opened the door and found this was true. Of course the explanation might have been simply that Maria's senses were exceptionally acute under hypnosis. But Pagenstecher also observed that baffling phenomenon first observed in the nineteenth century by Alfred Russel Wallace, 'community of sensation'. Maria could see, hear and taste through Pagenstecher's senses. She could see him and describe what he was doing even when he was behind her or in the next room. He also discovered that she had remarkable powers of psychometry: a meteorite produced a detailed description of falling through space; a seashell led her to describe an underwater scene. One of her most convincing demonstrations concerned a sea bean picked up on the beach by Dr Walter Franklin Prince, who was sent to investigate by the American Society for Psychical Research. Maria described a tropical forest with a river nearby. Prince was convinced she was wrong, but Pagenstecher said he would prefer to believe Maria. When they took the sea bean to an expert, they learned that it was actually a nut from a tree that grew in tropical forests and that it had been carried down to the beach by a river . . . .

Maria de Zierold offers us an interesting glimpse of her procedure. As

110

she held the object she 'identified' with it, exactly as she had earlier identified with Pagenstecher: if it was moistened with alcohol, she tasted the alcohol; if a lighted match was held underneath it, she felt the burning sensation. And once she had 'entered into' the object she became aware of its life history.

This has some exciting implications. Bergson had said that we have two ways of knowing an object: by analysis, which means grasping it from *outside*, and by intuition, which means going *inside* it. The latter sounds nonsensical, since we cannot really 'enter into' an object. Yet if Maria's evidence is to be accepted, this is not true. When she 'shared' Pagenstecher's consciousness she felt that she was connected to him by a kind of 'luminous cord' with some 'electric' quality. When she 'entered into' an object it became connected to her by the same kind of cord. If Maria de Zierold's descriptions are to be taken seriously, it would seem that Bergson was correct and we *can* 'enter into' objects.

But how about 'reading' the life history of the object? Again this sounds absurd, since an object is not alive. A possible explanation could lie in the suggestion of Bergson's contemporary philosopher Alfred North Whitehead. He argued that *everything* in the universe is, in some sense, alive and capable of 'feeling'. The universe should be regarded as a single living organism. (Whitehead's philosophy is known as the philosophy of organism.) Both Whitehead and Bergson insisted that the underlying reality of the universe is *an underlying web of connections*. But in order to survive human beings have to focus upon one thing at a time, so we have learned to 'screen out' the connections. Moreover our survival depends upon our sense of individuality – feeling ourselves to be quite separate from the rest of the universe – and so, once again, man has learned to 'screen out' the sense of one-ness with Nature and to become intensely aware of himself in isolation. Both mysticism and paranormal research strongly support the view of Bergson and Whitehead that this isolation is an illusion.

All this is certainly supported by what we know about the right and left halves of the brain. Left-brain perception is essentially narrow and concentrated, like a fast-flowing stream. Right-brain perception is broad and relaxed, like a wide, slow river. Left-brain perception could also be compared to the headlights of a car, which cut into the darkness and enable you to drive at ninety miles an hour; however, travelling at this speed you are aware of nothing but the objects illuminated by the headlights. If you want to become aware of the scenery around you then you had better switch off the headlights, open the window, and slow down to a walking pace: then, as your eyes adjust to the darkness, you will become aware of the hedges and the trees. Bergson achieved this state as he strolled around the countryside of the Auvergne, and all we have learned of mediums and mystics suggests that they make use of the same technique, 'slowing down' until their eyes have adjusted to the darkness.

But if relaxation can lead to 'psychic awareness', then why are we not all psychic? The answer has already emerged in the last chapter. As Toynbee sat on the summit of Pharsalus or Mistrà he was in a state of total relaxation. Then he went a stage *further* and fell into the 'time-pocket' or down Alice's 'rabbit hole'. When this happens it is as if – to return to the previous analogy – the car driver has decided to stop and switch off his engine. And now, in the silence, he can hear the sound of the wind in the trees, the water running in the ditch, the cry of night birds. The poet Rilke once experienced such a state as he leaned in the fork of a tree in the garden of the Castle Duino. He later described the experience (in the third person):

> . . . in this position immediately felt himself so agreeably supported and so amply reposed, that he remained as he was, without reading, completely received into nature, in an almost unconscious contemplation. Little by little his attention awoke to a feeling he had never known: it was as though almost imperceptible vibrations were passing into him from the interior of the tree . . . . It seemed to him that he had never been filled with more gentle motions, his body was somehow being treated like a soul, and put in a state to receive a degree of influence which, given the normal apparentness of one's physical conditions, really could not have been felt at all . . . . Nevertheless, concerned as he always was to account to himself for precisely the most delicate impressions, he insistently asked himself what was happening to him then, and almost at once found an expression that satisfied him, saying to himself that he had got to the other side of Nature.

Rilke goes on to describe his state of strange detachment and explains that 'all objects yielded themselves to him more distantly and, at the same time, somehow more truly'. He had somehow left behind the 'close-upness' that deprives us of meaning. And when, on another occasion, he experienced a sense of deep peace as he sat reading in a billiard room in the early morning, he described a sensation of 'inner space', 'a space as undisturbed as the interior of a rose'.

What seems to happen in these moments of 'inner silence' is that time slows down. Most of the mystics record this curious experience – the sense that time has come to a stop, or that hours of experience have been packed into a split second. What actually happens, presumably, is that our inner metabolism slows down to accommodate some important insight and the result is 'extended time'. In his suggestive little book *Stalking the Wild Pendulum* Itzhak Bentov suggested that this power to 'bring time to a stop' is well within the abilities of the average person, and outlines an experiment to test this. The only piece of apparatus required is a clock or watch with a second hand. The first step is to sit at a table with the watch lying face upward and to sink into a state of relaxation. The next step is to close the eyes and to withdraw from the

external world, sinking into a kind of daydream of any favourite activity –
for example lying on a beach. But it is important to try to imagine this
activity as clearly as possible – try to feel the warmth of the sun and hear
the sound of waves. Then open the eyes and allow the gaze to fall
casually on the watch, 'as if you are a disinterested observer of this whole
affair. If you have followed the instructions properly, you may see the
second hand stick in a few places, slow down and hover for a while. If
you are very successful, you'll be able to stop the second hand for quite a
while.'

I myself have recently observed this phenomenon occurring spontaneously. Not long ago I had a new battery put into my wrist-watch, and
for a few days afterwards it developed the irritating habit of stopping
until I had removed the back and re-adjusted the battery. On several
occasions I glanced at the watch and thought, 'Oh damn, it's stopped
again' – then realized that the second hand was in fact moving. The
second hand on my watch moves in little jerks, a second at a time, so I
had obviously glanced at it in the fraction of a second when the hand was
stationary. Yet even so it appeared to remain stationary far longer than
usual. My sense of time had somehow slowed down.

In the same way the blur of railway sleepers seen from the window of
a moving train often seems momentarily to pause. This phenomenon was
first pointed out to me by the American writer Jesse Lasky when we were
travelling together, and at first I failed to understand what he was talking
about. Since then I have frequently observed it. The sleepers are rushing
past so fast that they are nothing more than a blur. Then, suddenly,
one of them becomes as clearly visible as if the train had come to a halt.
The explanation must be that our inner time has slowed down for a
moment.

Two things should be noted about Bentov's description of how to
make time 'stop'. First, that the withdrawal into an inner world sounds
like Eileen Garrett's description of how she induces states of clairvoyance. Second, that his insistence on precise visualization sounds like the
procedure described by Priestley: ' . . . on these occasions I have been
recalling a person or a scene as clearly and as sharply as I could, and then
there has been, so to speak, a little click, a slight change of focus, and for
a brief moment I have felt as if the person or scene were not being
remembered but were really there *still existing* . . . .' The effort of precise
visualization seems to cause the experience of 'falling down the rabbit
hole'. This, presumably, is the mechanism of Arnold Toynbee's 'time-
pocket' experiences.

All this is obviously of immense importance. If Bentov and Priestley
are correct, then we have greater control over our inner world than we
realize. The effort of 'withdrawal' into an inner world causes a slowing
down of 'psychological time' and a suddenly intensified sense of reality.
And this of course is logical enough. The sense of unreality is caused by
being in a hurry; the more we rush, the less real the external world

113

becomes. So it follows that a deliberate effort of relaxation – Priestley's 'little click' may be the actual switch from left-brain to right-brain consciousness – should have the effect of intensifying the sense of reality and producing something like the 'time-slip' experience.

It should by now be clear that most of the experiences we have so far discussed in this book – experiences of mediums and mystics, experiences involving 'time-slips' and clairvoyance and psychometry – all point towards the same basic conclusion: that we are living in an *information universe*. Mediums and psychics are always obtaining pieces of information that they have 'no business knowing'. This leaves no possible doubt that the information is somehow 'there for the asking', as if stored on microfilm in a library, but that most of us do not know how to ask. Denton believed that this information includes every event that has ever occurred in the history of the universe, and that everyone can gain access to it if he goes about it in the right way.

The simplest and most straightforward way to gain entry to this library of information, apparently, is to 'fall down the rabbit hole'. But there are other ways. Sometimes the information has been so strongly 'recorded' that under certain circumstances we can pick it up without our normal senses. That is what seems to have happened to Mr Chase, who saw the two thatched cottages so clearly that he had no doubt that they were real. The same explanation seems to apply to the vision of fifteenth-century Paris seen by Ivan Sanderson and his wife (which as we know may well have been a vision of a group of old houses that had once stood on the spot). In his book *The Undiscovered Country* Stephen Jenkins describes how, on a track near Mounts Bay in Cornwall, he had a sudden vision of a host of armed men among the bushes. As he tried to run towards them a sensation like a curtain of heated air wavered in front of them, and they vanished. And in *The Mask of Time* Joan Forman describes how, in the courtyard at Haddon Hall in Derbyshire, she saw a group of four children playing near the entrance to the Hall, shrieking in helpless merriment, almost hysterical with mirth. She was particularly struck by a nine-year-old girl wearing a lace cap and a dress of grey-green silk. As soon as Joan Forman stepped forward the vision (which she compared to a dream) was gone. But inside the hall she saw the portrait of the nine-year-old girl – identified as Lady Grace Manners. It seems likely that the sheer force of their merriment somehow 'recorded' the scene, exactly as if someone had taken a photograph.

One of the most remarkable examples of this kind of 'recording' occurred at Edgehill in Northamptonshire, where one of the great battles of the Civil War was fought. After the battle people in the area were disturbed by sounds of cannon and shouting and the clash of arms. In 1642 a pamphlet was published about it: *A great Wonder in Heaven, shewing the late Apparitions and Prodigious Noyse of War and Battels, seene on Edge-Hill, neere Keinton, in Northamptonshire*. It described how, on four successive Saturday and Sunday nights, visitors to the battlefield had witnessed sights and sounds of battle; these included a Justice of the Peace and a number of army officers, who recognized old comrades among the combatants. King Charles I was so intrigued that he sent a commission led by Colonel Lewis Krike to investigate: they witnessed the phenomena and testified before the king, swearing statements about what they had seen. The sounds continued at intervals for three centuries, so that a twentieth-century clergyman, the Rev. John Dering, was able to collect accounts from many living witnesses who had heard the battle sounds.

Lethbridge's theory about the magnetic field of water is obviously inadequate to explain these phenomena: to begin with a hill would presumably be less damp than the low-lying country surrounding it. But another incident described by Stephen Jenkins seems to offer a clue. In April 1973, near Acrise in Kent, Jenkins paused to take a map-reading and found, to his surprise, that he was unable to do so. His sense of direction seemed to be affected and he experienced a curious light-headedness. He walked on a few yards and the problem immediately vanished. When he went back to the previous spot, it returned again. A year later, on Yes Tor in Dartmoor, he had a very similar experience. Standing by a stone he called the Wedge, he set out to walk to the nearby Merlin Stone. His companion called him back – he was walking off in the wrong direction, south-east instead of south. He took his bearings and tried again; this time he went west. Even when the mist cleared he was still unable to orient himself. The experience puzzled him, and in the following year he took a group of three pupils to the site near Acrise and asked them to take a map-bearing – without mentioning his own previous experience. They all experienced the same disorientation, and were unable to do it.

Jenkins concluded that the solution to the riddle lay in the fact that the spot was a crossing point of two ley lines – lines of earth magnetism. The earth is, of course, a weak magnet, and there is evidence that birds and animals use these magnetic forces for homing. (The homing pigeon, for example, has a piece of tissue between its eyes which contains the mineral magnetite: if a bar magnet is strapped to the pigeon's back, it is unable to find its way home.) There are certain areas on the earth's surface known as magnetic vortices, and birds who fly into these lose their sense of direction and fly around helplessly. So Stephen Jenkins could be correct in believing that at the nodal point of two ley lines, his own inner compass became affected by a kind of magnetic vortex.

That human beings possess an inner compass was proved conclusively by Dr Robin Baker, a zoologist at Manchester University, in the late 1970s. Baker would blindfold his subjects, then take them from their homes and drive them through narrow, twisting lanes. At a secret destination they were asked to get out of the car and point in the direction of their homes. Most of them did so with surprising accuracy. After that some of the subjects had a bar magnet strapped to their heads while

115

others were fitted with a brass bar that obviously had no magnetic properties (the idea being that the subject should not know which he had). They were then taken for another circuitous drive and once again asked to point towards their homes. Those with the brass bar were still remarkably accurate, but the ones with the bar magnet were completely disoriented.

Many years after his experience of the 'phantom army' Stephen Jenkins returned to the place at Mounts Bay where he had seen it. And as he walked through it there was once again a momentary hallucination of armed men. As before he realized that he was standing on a nodal point of ley lines. When he moved a step forward the 'army' vanished.

Jenkins' theory – which has since been accepted by many 'ley hunters' – is that nodal points form some kind of magnetic vortex which can somehow 'record' events – particularly strong emotions like those associated with a battle. Orthodox science has remained suspicious of the idea of ley lines, and some sceptics have even gone to considerable trouble to prove that they cannot exist. Part of the reason for this suspicion lies in the fact that an interest in ley lines usually runs in tandem with another highly suspect activity: dowsing. The dowser, or diviner, holds in his hand a forked twig (two plastic strips tied together at one end will do equally well), grasping the end of both forks in either hand. As he walks over underground water the dowsing rod twists in his hands. Dowsing is almost universally accepted by country people who have seen it in action; the sceptics are usually scientists or official bodies (such as the United States Geological Survey) who have convinced themselves in advance that such phenomena are superstitions. But in the 1960s a series of impeccably designed experiments by Dr Zaboj V. Harvalik, a professional physicist and adviser to the US Army, finally placed dowsing on an unshakeable scientific basis.

Intrigued by dowsers in his native Czechoslovakia, Harvalik continued his researches when he became a physics teacher at the University of Missouri. One of the first things he noticed was that his dowsing rod would always react to an electric wire on the ground: this suggested that dowsing was basically electrical. Next he drove two lengths of water-pipe vertically into the ground, separated by a distance of sixty feet, and connected their exposed ends to a powerful battery. When he switched on the current his dowsing rod responded immediately. He then began to practise on friends and discovered that *all* of them could dowse provided the current was high enough – above 20 milliamps. The remaining 20 per cent proved to be even better dowsers who could detect a current as low as 2 milliamps – some even responded to a half milliamp. And most people improved steadily with practice. He also found that dowsing ability was improved if the dowser drank a few tumblers of water before he began, and made the fascinating discovery that people who seemed to possess no dowsing ability would suddenly begin to dowse after half a tumbler of whisky: the alcohol relaxed them and thus enabled them to 'tune in'.

Harvalik's conclusion was that the human body is itself a magnetic

116

detector – for primitive man it must have been a matter of life and death to locate underground springs, and Australian aborigines can still 'sense' water even without the aid of a dowsing rod – and that some part of the body picks up the change in magnetic gradient and passes the information on to the brain, which in turn causes the muscles to convulse, twisting the rod. Professor Yves Rocard of the Sorbonne had already performed experiments in 1962 which showed that weak changes in the earth's magnetic field produced changes in the dowser's muscles. Now Harvalik performed similar experiments with a German master dowser, Wilhelm de Boer – which satisfied him that the 'organ' that detects water is the group of glands known as the adrenals, just above the kidneys. (These are the glands that flood us with adrenalin when we experience a shock.) But a strip of aluminium foil wound around the head just above the ears also blocked all dowsing signals; so did a single square of aluminium foil pasted in the centre of the forehead.

De Boer was able to detect incredibly small signals – a mere thousandth of a milliamp. And working with de Boer confirmed something Harvalik had always suspected – that dowsers can *select* the signals they want to 'tune' into. De Boer could even detect various radio stations which broadcast on different frequencies. Harvalik would tell him which frequency to look for, and de Boer would turn round slowly until he was facing the direction of the radio station. Then Harvalik would check his accuracy by turning a portable radio in that direction.

The fact that dowsers can *select* what they want to 'pick up' was certainly one of the most important observations of all. If a dowser is looking for underground minerals, he can make his dowsing rod ignore water. He can even detect different articles placed under a carpet – coins, matches and so on – merely by deciding what he is looking for. This sounds amazing enough, yet it is no more remarkable than our ability to listen to a conversation in a crowded bar. In this respect the dowser's inbuilt electromagnetic detector is immensely superior to the best magnetometers built in laboratories, for they pick up every signal from underground water and power lines to human brainwaves. The dowser can decide which signal he wants to detect.

The invention of a magnetometer sensitive enough to detect brainwaves – between .5 and 50 Hz – suggested to Harvalik that a good dowser ought to be able to detect brain rhythms. He would stand with his back to a screen in his garden with earplugs in his ears, and ask people to walk towards him from the other side of the screen. His dowsing rod revealed their presence when they were ten feet away. When he asked them to think 'exciting' thoughts – for example, about sex – he could detect them at twenty feet. Harvalik's experiment offers a possible explanation of how telepathy functions. It certainly seems to explain why so many of us feel uncomfortable when someone stares at the back of our heads, and why women can often detect the gaze of a sexually interested male even when he is walking behind them.

117

Perhaps the most impressive thing to emerge from Harvalik's investigations was the remarkable accuracy of which a dowser is capable. Harvalik could not only fix the direction of a reservoir from many miles but could even state how many feet of water were in it. Christopher Bird* tells how Harvalik was able to point out the direction of a reservoir in Sydney, Australia and accurately estimate its distance as 12.6 miles. The water-board engineer asked him if he could tell him how deep it was: Harvalik said sixty-eight feet. The engineer checked his booklet and told Harvalik that he was fairly close: the actual depth was seventy-five feet. But when they visited the reservoir the following day Harvalik was found to be correct: the water level had dropped by seven feet.

Clearly our ability to 'read' the information that surrounds us is far greater than we normally assume (although it would certainly not have surprised Thomson Jay Hudson). T. C. Lethbridge had made the same discovery when he moved to Devon in 1957 and began a series of experiments with a pendulum (which many dowsers prefer to the usual forked twig). Most pendulum dowsers use a fairly heavy weight on a short piece of string (so that it is not unduly affected by wind). Lethbridge decided it might be more interesting to use a long piece of string – wound round a pencil, so that its length could be varied – and to see whether different substances would cause it to react at different lengths. He began by placing a silver dish on the floor and suspending his pendulum above it. When the length of the string reached twenty-two inches, the pendulum stopped swinging back and forth and went into a circular motion. Lethbridge assumed this to mean that the 'rate' for silver was twenty-two inches – and went on to detect a tiny piece of buried silver in the courtyard of his house. It was not even necessary to stand above the silver. He could stand with the pendulum in his hand and the other arm outstretched in front of him, slowly moving in an arc. When the pendulum started to swing in a circle he noted the direction of the pointing finger, then went and stood somewhere else and repeated the procedure. Where the resulting two lines crossed he dug down, and usually found what he was looking for. He noted that each substance seemed to register at a precise rate: carbon at twelve inches, tin at twenty-eight, copper at thirty and a half, grass at sixteen, apples at eighteen, elm at twenty-three. It even responded to abstractions such as sex, anger, evolution, male and female. (These had to be clearly visualized.) He and his wife Mina tried picking up stones and throwing them against a wall, then testing the stones with a pendulum: it was able to detect which stones had been thrown by each of them by its male or female response.

Lethbridge was convinced that he had discovered a fundamental secret of nature – that everything has its own 'rate'. Harvalik would undoubtedly treat this assertion with scepticism. He discovered that dowsers can

*Christopher Bird, *The Divining Hand*, p. 273. I am indebted to this book for the above account of Harvalik.

118

decide in advance how they want the pendulum to respond: they can 'programme' it to swing back and forth for 'No' and in a circle for 'Yes', or vice versa: they can 'programme' the forked twig to twist up or down as preferred. So Lethbridge's 'rates' may have been arbitrary, 'programmed' by his unconscious mind. Yet this is obviously a minor point. What matters is that the pendulum can detect an astonishing range of information that would normally be undetectable by our senses. And if Harvalik is correct, it does this through the body's response to incredibly small magnetic gradients.

Yet even Harvalik had to admit that his 'magnetic theory' had its limitations. His researches soon brought him into contact with dowsers who claimed to be able to detect water just as well by dangling their pendulum over a map: he not only found their claims to be true, but discovered that he could do it himself. A map dowser can dowse not only for water but also for oil and coal and other substances – most large mineral combines have one on their payroll. The psychic Uri Geller has become a multi-millionaire by dowsing for oil and mineral companies, and the fact that he is paid by results demonstrates clearly that his results are real. Moreover a good dowser can use his pendulum to obtain other kinds of information. In 1960 a Swiss dowser named Edgar Devaux was asked to help trace a missing housewife. He held his pendulum over a photograph of the woman and announced that she was dead – his pendulum had swung from north-east to south-west. Then, using a map of Basel, he traced a line along the river and made a cross. 'She is there.' Divers went down at the spot indicated and one of them touched the body: as he disturbed it, it floated away. Devaux walked along the towpath, tracing its progress as it floated down the river, but had to abandon the chase when houses made it impossible to continue. A few days later, however, the corpse was found at the barrage where the water was sieved before turning the turbines of a power station.*

But although map dowsing defies all attempts to explain it in terms of magnetic fields, it is no more startling than Eileen Garrett's ability to detect a missing man from a fragment of his shirt. The major difference is that Eileen Garrett somehow acquired 'direct access' to information by using her ability to 'withdraw' into a clairvoyant state, while Devaux gained his information by handling a photograph (and a slipper provided by the woman's sister) and then 'questioning' his pendulum. Both cases suggest that we are living in an 'information universe'; the difference lies in the manner of gaining access to the information.

Let us pause to survey this bewildering profusion of data.

The notion that we are living in an 'information universe' – a universe in which everything that has ever happened is 'on record' – is certainly a strange one, but it cannot be dismissed as unscientific. We now know that whole pages of information can be condensed on to a microdot and that a

*For a fuller account of this story see *Mysteries*, pp. 151–2.

long message can be compressed and transmitted in one supersonic 'beep'. Moreover we know that the whole rich sound of an orchestra can somehow be captured by a wavy line on a plastic disc. And this in itself seems an absurdity. We know that Edison first recorded sound by speaking into a trumpet with a needle attached to its narrow end and allowing the needle to make a mark on a revolving drum covered with tinfoil. Then he put the needle back to the beginning of the scratch and turned the crank: his own voice came out of the trumpet reciting 'Mary had a little lamb'. That sounds straightforward enough, for a voice is a fairly simple sound. But how can the same 'scratch' record *all* the instruments of the orchestra? – surely you would need a different scratch for each one?

But at least this analogy makes us aware that there is nothing illogical about the notion of events being 'recorded' on matter. If tinfoil can record Edison's voice with the aid of a few vibrations, then the walls of a house may well be able to record some tragedy that has taken place there by means of emotional 'vibrations'. And if Joan Forman is correct in believing that these vibrations are of the same frequency as our brainwaves, then each of us has a 'gramophone' to play back the 'time-recordings'.

Harvalik's experiments place all this on a commonsense foundation. They demonstrate that the human body is, among other things, a complicated electronic device for measuring energy. Of course we already know that our ears detect sound waves and our eyes detect light waves. But Harvalik demonstrated that our bodies can also detect radio waves far below the red end of the spectrum, and radioactivity, which is far above the violet end. It is true that Caspar Hauser was able to *see* heat waves, and that Yuliya Vorobyeva can apparently see X-rays. Even master dowser Wilhelm de Boer cannot actually see radio waves and gamma rays. But his divining rod can detect them, which is the next best thing.

Equally important is Harvalik's demonstration that the dowser can 'programme' himself to select the signals he is interested in – so that de Boer could trace the Washington radio station on 570 kc then turn his attention to some other radio or TV station broadcasting on a different wavelength. Of course de Boer could only pinpoint the direction of the broadcast. But since we know that dowsers can improve with practice there is obviously no reason why he should not eventually be able to listen in to the programmes. The same applies to Harvalik's discovery that he could detect the brainwaves of people who walked towards him across a lawn. With a great deal more practice, there seems to be no logical reason why he should not be able to detect what they are thinking about.

I have myself taken part in a demonstration that involved a kind of

120

telepathy. In 1972 I was researching the dowsing abilities of the 'psychic' Robert Leftwich. In one experiment I held the dowsing rod while Leftwich stood with his back towards me; I was then ordered to walk forward down my drive. The aim was to detect an underground water-main: I knew its position but Leftwich didn't. As I walked over the pipe, my dowsing rod twisted in my hands and Leftwich shouted, 'Stop, you're on it.' He had somehow picked up the signal from my brain. Harvalik's experiments place these observations on a scientific basis. We now know that nothing particularly 'occult' was taking place – merely the detection of magnetic gradients by the piece of electronic apparatus known as the human body. Then could this not also apply to Buchanan's psychometry'?

While I was engaged on the writing of the present chapter, my wife took two guests to look at the old gaol in Bodmin, which is open to the public. My wife is an excellent dowser; the other two were novices. There were two places in the gaol where even the novices obtained a powerful response from the rods: the condemned cell and the execution shed. All three sensed an unpleasant atmosphere in these places while they were dowsing. It is possible of course that the rods may have been responding to underground water, and that the unpleasant atmosphere was pure imagination. But if we can accept the psychometric hypothesis then there is obviously an alternative explanation: the walls of the condemned cell and the execution shed have 'recorded' a great deal of human anguish over the centuries. The narrow range of our everyday left-brain consciousness prevents us from becoming aware of these 'recordings'. But the right brain – Hudson's subjective mind – is a 'record-player' that can 'play back' these 'recordings', and even though it is not capable of communicating its knowledge to the objective mind it can register the information through the medium of the dowsing rod, causing the muscles to convulse.

A single step further, and the same argument provides a logical explanation for telepathy. In *The Psychic Detectives* I have cited a case concerning the remarkable 'telepath' Dr Maximilien Langsner. In July 1929 four people were shot to death by an unknown killer at a farm in Edmonton, Alberta. The police were called by a farmer's son, Vernon Booher, whose mother and brother had been among the victims (the other two being hired hands). Langsner, who happened to be in the area at the time, attended the inquest and later told the chief of police that the killer was Vernon Booher and that he had hidden the murder weapon in a clump of prairie grass behind the house. Langsner then accompanied the police to the house and wandered around at the back – the police chief commented that Langsner reminded him of a dowser with a hazel twig. A rifle recovered from a clump of grass proved to be the murder weapon. Vernon Booher was then placed in protective custody as a major witness, while Langsner sat outside his cell. After a while Langsner got up and left. He was then able to tell the police exactly why Vernon had

121

committed the murders. Vernon had come to hate his mother and, after a quarrel, had shot her in the head with his rifle. He then had to kill his brother, who was in the next room, and two farm hands who had heard the shots and knew he was in the house. Confronted with this story, Vernon Booher confessed that he had killed his mother after a quarrel about a girl: he wanted to marry the daughter of a farm-worker and his mother, a highly dominant woman, had enraged him by telling him precisely what she thought of the girl. Booher was hanged in 1929.

We can see that after murdering his mother in a fit of rage, Booher would be in a highly-charged emotional state. If violent emotions can 'record' themselves on the walls of an execution shed then it seems logical to suppose that they can also be detected by a good dowser, or 'psychic', like Maximilien Langsner. In fact they should be far more powerful and distinct, since he is picking them up directly and not at second hand through a 'recording'.

If we also take into account the dowser's ability to 'select' the set of impressions he is interested in – so that de Boer could distinguish between various radio stations – then it is possible to see how a 'sensitive' might actually pick up one particular scene rather than another. William Denton had already observed that his wife and his sister-in-law might 'see' quite different scenes from the history of the object they were holding. And we can also see that if the observer happened to be in a relaxed frame of mind, then he might 'accidentally' pick up some 'recording' and be quite unaware that he was catching a glimpse of the past. When Joan Forman 'saw' the children playing in front of Haddon Hall she was aware that she was seeing 'a mental picture, as one does in dreams'. But although the two English ladies at Versailles experienced a 'dreamlike sensation' they were unaware that they were seeing a mental picture. When Mr Chase saw the two pretty nineteenth-century cottages he was tired – having finished a day's work – and also relaxed, since he was waiting for a bus on a fine evening. If he had actually tried to walk into one of the gardens he would probably have received a shock as the cottages vanished and were replaced by two houses. If Jane O'Neill had tried to touch the painting of the crucifixion it would probably have disappeared and she would have found herself standing in the modern church at Fotheringhay instead of the church as it was four centuries ago.

Now this, admittedly, is a little difficult to swallow. Surely we can all tell the difference between a reality 'out there' and a thought inside our own heads? But the matter may not be that simple. For more than two-and-a-half centuries philosophers have been suggesting that perhaps our senses play a part in *creating* the world 'out there'. The argument – as presented by thinkers like Locke, Berkeley, Hume and Kant – runs something like this. Consider a piece of chocolate. You would say that it is sweet, brown, sticky and has a 'chocolatey' smell. But if you hold your nose as you eat it, it suddenly has no smell and very little taste – so these things depend on your senses. The brownness depends on your sense of sight; to a colour-blind man it might look grey. The stickiness depends on the temperature of your fingers; if they were as cold as icicles, the chocolate wouldn't be sticky. All this led Bishop Berkeley to suggest that there may not be a 'real' world out there: perhaps our senses are *creating* the whole thing. Kant went a step further and suggested that perhaps our senses also create space and time and logic.

Berkeley's contemporaries thought it was all rather a joke and Dr Johnson thought he had refuted him by kicking a stone. Yet we now know that these philosophers were not all that far from the truth. Science tells us that the 'truth' about the chocolate is a swarm of electrons organized into atoms and molecules by sub-atomic forces. Strictly speaking it has no smell or taste or colour. These things are 'added' by our senses – or our brains. As we have already noted, our eyes distinguish between light wavelengths of 16 and 32-millionths of an inch by 'colour coding' one of them as red and the other as violet. As Whitehead once commented, the poets ought to sing their praises to the human brain, not to Nature.

In recent years two scientists have advanced a revolutionary theory which is really an updated version of the philosophy of Berkeley and Kant. Their names are Karl Pribram and David Bohm, and the theory has become known as 'the hologramatic universe'. To understand it we have to know what a hologram is. A hologram is a kind of three-dimensional photograph which hangs in space and looks exactly like a solid object. Such a photograph cannot be taken by ordinary light: it requires a laser beam – light in which all the waves have been made to 'march in step' like a squad of soldiers. If two laser beams cross one another, they form an interference pattern – just as, if you throw two stones into a pond, two sets of circular ripples will interact with one another. Now imagine that the two laser beams interact on a glass photographic plate and that one of the two beams has just 'bounced off' a human face. The interference pattern on the photographic plate does not look in the least like a human face – rather like a pattern of ripples. But if you shine a laser beam through it the face will suddenly appear suspended in space, looking quite solid and three dimensional. The light has 'interpreted' the interference pattern into a face. What is odder still is that if you break off a small corner of the photographic plate and shine a beam of laser light through it, the complete face will still appear in space, although looking rather blurrier than when the whole plate is used. In other words every part of the interference pattern contains the whole face.

Pribram, whose speciality is the brain and its functions, was suddenly struck by an awe-inspiring idea: suppose the world around us is actually a hologram and the reality 'behind' it is simply a kind of interference pattern? Kant said that the world is made up of the 'phenomena' – the things we see and hear – and the 'noumena', *the reality that lies behind them*. Pribram was suggesting that the noumena is an interference pattern.

123

At this point Pribram learned that a British physicist had proposed an almost identical idea. David Bohm had been trying to explain some of the paradoxes of quantum theory, particularly the strange fact that two particles, flying apart at the speed of light, can apparently affect one another. That should be totally impossible – unless their 'apartness' is somehow an illusion. So Bohm proposed a theory which he outlined in his book *Wholeness and the Implicate Order*, to explain this paradox. Expressed very simply, Bohm says that the underlying reality of the universe – the noumena – is rather like one of those small pellets which, when dropped into water, unfolds, and you are suddenly looking at a flower. The only fault with this analogy is that in Bohm's theory, the pellet continues to exist even when the flower has unfolded in the water. And since Bohm backed up his theory with scientific argument, his 'implicate order' theory could be regarded as a scientific justification of Pribram's flash of absurd inspiration. (Readers who find all this difficult to follow may be reassured by Pribram's admission that he does not understand his own theory.)

In one obvious sense, Bohm and Pribram are clearly correct. My eyes and brain 'interpret' energy with a wavelength of 16 millionths of an inch so that it appears as the colour red. And when I put on a gramophone record my brain reconstructs all those sound waves generated by wavy lines and turns them into a Beethoven symphony. (A young child finds this far more difficult to do: classical music sounds like a chaotic jumble of notes.) Our brains are interpreters of reality, exactly as if they were translating Japanese into English.

Now let us assume, for a moment, that what my wife 'picked up' in Bodmin gaol was a 'tape-recording' of the anguish of men who knew they were soon going to be hanged. We do not know the mechanism of this recording but it cannot be all that much more complicated than a compact disc. My wife's objective mind is not sensitive enough to 'pick up' this 'recording', but her subjective mind has the power to 'play it back' and communicates something of its distress to her muscles, which cause a response in the dowsing rod. Some of this flood of information communicates itself to her objective mind, producing the 'unpleasant atmosphere'.

Now our brains can certainly distinguish between their own thoughts – or imaginings – and the world 'out there'. But the powerful impressions my wife experienced in the gaol were *not* her own thoughts or imaginings. They were as real, in their way, as the light that registers on her eyes and the sounds that make her eardrums vibrate. If she were sensitive enough to *see* these energy frequencies, is it not possible that she might have mistaken them for reality, just as a hologram can be mistaken for the real thing?

All this sounds most satisfyingly logical. We might even feel justified in claiming that we have placed 'the paranormal' on truly scientific foundations. With the aid of the 'tape-recording' theory we can explain

124

all kinds of baffling phenomena, from ghosts and 'visions' to telepathy, psychometry and clairvoyance. Yet there is still one problem that defies all attempts at logical explanation: glimpses of the future. Consider the following story:

In 1935 Wing Commander Victor Goddard – who later became Air Marshal Sir Victor Goddard – decided to visit a disused First World War airfield at Drem, near Edinburgh. It proved to be in a state of dilapidation, with disintegrating hangars and cracked tarmac. Cattle grazed on the old airfield. Later that day Goddard took off in his Hawker Hart biplane from Turnhouse, Edinburgh, to head for home. But he soon encountered thick cloud and heavy rain, and as he tried to descend below the cloud ceiling the plane spun for a few moments out of control. He managed to straighten out close to the ground – so close that he almost hit a woman who was running with a pram. Ahead of him was the Firth of Forth, and Goddard decided to head for Drem airfield to get his bearings.

It was still raining heavily as he crossed the airfield boundary. Then an odd thing happened: he suddenly found himself in bright sunlight. And Drem airfield was no longer an overgrown field, but a neat, orderly place, with four yellow planes parked in front of open hangar doors and mechanics in blue overalls walking around. Both these things surprised Goddard, for in those days all RAF planes were painted with aluminium and mechanics wore khaki overalls. Moreover the mechanics did not even glance up as the plane roared a few feet overhead: Goddard had the feeling that they did not see him. He also had the feeling of 'something ethereal about the sunlight'.

When he landed he told his immediate superior about his 'hallucination', and was advised to lay off the whisky. So Goddard said nothing about his 'vision' in his official report. It was not until four years later, when war broke out, that he received an even greater shock. Next time he saw Drem it had been transformed into the airfield of his vision. The 'trainers' were now painted yellow and the mechanics wore blue overalls. A monoplane he had failed to recognize four years earlier he now identified as a Miles Magister.

Recordings from the past are a reality, as every film and gramophone record demonstrates. But a recording from the future sounds preposterous. Even if we assume it was a hallucination, and not a 'time-slip' into the future, it remains just as impossible.

David Bohm would not agree: he has stated, 'The implicate order is there all at once, having nothing to do with time.' Neither would Eileen Garrett: she said about her experiences of precognition, 'The experience remains as "real" as any other and suggests that there must be a timeless and spaceless communion between our intuitive selves and the eternal laws of nature' – a comment that becomes twice as significant if we substitute 'right brain' for 'intuitive selves'. She has also said that 'on clairvoyant levels there exists a simultaneity of time'. All of which, of course, leaves us just as bewildered as ever. Yet one of her statements about clairvoyance seems to throw a little light on this baffling process. 'In clairvoyant vision I do not look *out* at objects . . . as in ordinary seeing, but I seem to draw the perceived object towards me, so that the essence of its life and the essence of mine become, for the moment, one and the same thing.' Now this sounds very like Maria de Zierold's comment that she seemed to *become* the objects she psychometrized, which in turn reminds us that Bergson said that we can know objects by somehow 'getting inside them'. And that in turn reminds us that Bergson also said that we can only *know* time 'intuitively'. As soon as we think about it we shatter it into unreal fragments. Is it possible that in trying to explain Goddard's experience in 'logical' terms, we are already erecting an insuperable barrier between ourselves and the reality? But Eileen Garrett has not yet finished her remarks on clairvoyance. She goes on, 'Thus, to my sense, clairvoyance occurs in states of consciousness whose relations exist as a fact in nature, *on levels of being that transcend the present perceptive capacities of our sensory faculties*' [my italics]. Stated in simple terms, this means that clairvoyance is a glimpse of a reality that exists on another level of being. We are back to Kant's 'noumena' and David Bohm's 'implicate order'. Eileen Garrett even goes on to use an analogy that sounds like an 'interference pattern'.

In the clairvoyant experience, one follows a process. Light moves in weaving ribbons and strands, and in and out of these, fragmentary curving lines emerge and fade, moving in various directions. The perception consists of a swiftly moving array of these broken, shifting lines, and in the beginning one gathers meaning out of the flow as the lines create patterns of significance which the acutely attentive clairvoyant perception senses.*

This certainly sounds as if Eileen Garrett is glimpsing the underlying 'interference pattern' of reality. And if we merely recall that every fragment of the 'interference pattern' contains a complete image of the whole, then we can suddenly catch an intuitive glimpse of how Eileen Garrett could 'know' that a missing doctor was in La Jolla, California.

One more fact emerges very clearly. Whatever happened to Goddard, his was not a passive vision of the future. It involved the sudden activation of *an unknown power of his own mind*. And this is something that cannot be overstressed. In this chapter we have tried to understand 'time-slips', psychometric visions and dowsing in terms of an 'information universe', of 'recordings' that can be 'picked up' by some dormant human faculty. All this seems to emphasize the notion that we are merely passive observers. But the theme that has emerged from the first page of this book is that man possesses '*hidden powers*'. He is not a passive

*All these quotations are from Eileen Garrett *Adventures in the Supernormal, A Personal Memoir* (1949), chapters XV and XVI.

creature. The 'passive fallacy' is one of the greatest mistakes human beings can make; it condemns us to miss the whole meaning of life. Buckminster Fuller once remarked, 'I seem to be a verb,' and this recognition is the first step in understanding the paranormal. Eileen Garrett underlines the same point when she writes:

> I have referred to an inner condition of 'alertness' which is *the* essential factor in many of these activities. It is a realization of superior vital living. I enter into a world of intensely vibrant radiation; I am extra competent, I participate fully and intimately in events that move at an increased rate of movement, and though the events that I observe are objective to me, I do more than observe them – I *live* them.

The conclusion is obvious. Clairvoyance has something to do with being *more alive*.

5

Intrusions?

In his autobiographical book *Rain Upon Godshill* J. B. Priestley describes a disturbing dream:

> One night last year I dreamed myself into some foreign city and though I had no name and did not know what I looked like, I *felt* I was a younger and smaller man, really somebody else, a student or something of that kind; and I crept into a room where there were a number of tiny models of some military or naval invention; and I had just taken one of these from the table when two uniformed officers rushed in, and as I was running out of the opposite doorway one of them fired several times at me, wounding me severely, and as I staggered out into the street I could feel my life ebbing away. I was actually wounded during the war but not in this fashion, and have never in waking existence felt my life fast ebbing away, and I do not believe I could invent that vast throbbing gush of weakness. No doubt most of the dream was my own invention, though I am not given to melodrama of this kind, but I will swear that that swaying progress from the office into the street and the blind weakness that washed over me there were somebody's last moments and that my consciousness had relived them.

It hardly matters whether the dream really involved the last moments of a man who had been killed: what is interesting here is Priestley's feeling that it was *all totally real* and not the usual disconnected fantasy we experience in dreams. Everyone has experienced something of the sort: a dream that seems so real and alien that it seems to be an intrusion into our minds from *elsewhere*.

I personally find that most of these 'intrusions' happen when I am hovering on the point of sleep, or as I am waking up in the morning. Strange images float through my mind, voices make extraordinary but meaningless statements, people I have never seen before introduce themselves and vanish. Such voices and visions are known technically as 'hypnagogic phenomena'* (or hypnopompic if they occur on waking), and they often leave behind a powerful sense of their independent reality.

The American psychiatrist Wilson Van Dusen came to believe that the

*The traditional spelling is hypnogogic.

128

hypnagogic states can be a vital key to self knowledge. He observed that 'even very average people who explore this region can run into strange people and strange symbolic conversations that look like visitations from another world.' He taught himself to fall into these semi-waking trances and was often startled and amused by the comments he heard. On one occasion a voice commented, 'I didn't want anything to happen to my sphere so I read Chekhov. Your sphere will have a repair letter on it.' This is typical of those authoritative yet apparently meaningless statements made by hypnagogic voices. Yet the hypnagogic stranger could also give sensible answers. On another occasion Van Dusen asked him (or it) whether he should change his job and circumstances. He received an image of a river that had worn a deep gorge over the centuries, and the words, 'Wear down like a river.' He took this as a clear indication that he should stay where he was – that moving from place to place would only reduce his long-term effectiveness. On yet another occasion, about to 'wake' himself out of the hypnagogic state, he heard a voice ask, 'Don't you like my sister?' He asked, 'Who is your sister?', and received the reply, 'Heaven. Talk to me now.' He asked, 'Tell me of your nature,' and was told, 'Handsome breath.' This seemed meaningless, but on reflection Van Dusen saw that 'handsome breath' could mean noble spirit, and that the notion of noble spirit, whose sister is heaven, made good sense – perhaps profound sense. His feeling that the hypnagogic states were capable of revealing something of importance was increased when, awakening from the trance, he saw the gigantic image of a mandala, intricately carved of wood, with a four-fold design representing the four-fold nature of the real self. The centre of the design was 'an empty hole through which the fearsome force of the universe whistled'. Jung believed that the mandala is one of the great 'archetypal' images of the psyche.

As a psychiatrist working in a state mental hospital (Mendocino), Van Dusen came to believe that hypnagogic hallucinations could help him to understand the delusions of the insane. And here again he experienced that baffling sense of the ambiguity of this unknown region – the feeling that it may after all possess its own independent reality. One of his patients was a woman who had murdered 'a rather useless husband'. She had a hallucination of the Virgin Mary which told her to drive to southern California and stand trial for murder. By way of authentification, the Virgin revealed that there would be an earthquake at Mendocino on the day she left and another at her destination when she arrived. On the evening she left Van Dusen was talking to the chaplain when an earth tremor made the brick building sway. He later read in the newspaper that there had been an earthquake in the south at the time the woman was due to arrive.

Van Dusen was also greatly intrigued by the hallucination of a schizophrenic gas-pipe fitter. He saw, quite clearly, a spritely little woman describing herself as 'An Emanation of the Feminine Aspect of

129

the Divine', and, through him, Van Dusen could carry on conversations with the lady. One of her more charming habits was to hand over her panties when Van Dusen or the fitter said something she approved of. But if this seemed to be a proof of her dreamlike insubstantiality, her intellectual acuteness suggested otherwise. The fitter was far from bright but the lady's knowledge of religion and myth seemed to be considerable. The fitter described a Buddhist wheel mandala made of intricately woven human bodies that rolled through the office. Van Dusen spent an evening studying Greek myths, paying special attention to their more obscure parts, and asked her about them the next day. He records, 'She not only understood the myth, she saw into its human implications better than I did.' Van Dusen asked her to write Greek letters, and the lady obliged. Van Dusen couldn't see them of course, but the fitter – whose sparse education had not included Greek – was able to copy the letters, which were the real thing. When Van Dusen engaged her in a discussion on religion he became aware that her understanding was greater than his own and that she seemed to have a considerable knowledge of history. After his conversation the gas-pipe fitter turned round as he was leaving the room and asked for just one clue to what they had been talking about.

Experiences like this seem to confirm the uneasy feeling that what goes on inside our heads may not be as personal as we think. Another American psychologist, Dr Jean Houston, has recorded a similar experience. One of her subjects lay on a settee wearing an eye-mask, and recorded what he 'saw' as a result of a dose of LSD. He said that he was on the Athens water-front having a conversation with Socrates. 'What does he have to say?' asked Dr Houston. 'I don't know. He's talking in Greek and I don't understand Greek.' 'I do,' said Dr Houston, who had studied it for six years, 'Repeat the words.' Whereupon the patient proceeded to repeat classical Greek.

Thomson Jay Hudson would have no difficulty in explaining this: in fact he does so in the fourth chapter of *The Law of Psychic Phenomena*, citing a peculiar case described by the poet Coleridge in his *Biographia Literaria*. An illiterate servant girl who was suffering from 'nervous fever' began to speak quite clearly in Greek, Latin and Hebrew. Whole sentences were noted down, and they made sense. Some of the Hebrew came from the Bible; other things seemed to be from Rabbinical texts. A young doctor became so fascinated by the mystery that he set out to uncover the girl's past life. At her birthplace he traced an uncle who was able to tell him that she had been taken in by an old Protestant pastor. He then tracked down the pastor's niece, who had also been his housekeeper, and learned that the old man was in the habit of walking up and down a corridor outside the kitchen reading aloud in Greek, Latin and Hebrew. The girl's 'subjective mind' had 'recorded' what she had heard, although she had no conscious memory of these languages, and the words had come back to her in her delirium.

In the case of Jean Houston's patient this explanation sounds reasonable enough – perhaps he had spent some time in childhood in the house of a pastor who read aloud Plato's dialogues in Greek. But where Van Dusen's Emanation of the Feminine Aspect of the Divine is concerned, the explanation seems dubious. Perhaps the gas-pipe fitter *had* learned the Greek alphabet unconsciously. Perhaps he had also 'absorbed' volumes on religious myth and symbolism without realizing it. But since he was perfectly conscious while Van Dusen was 'conversing' with the erudite lady it is hard to understand why he was unaware that all this knowledge originated in his own mind . . . .

The most thorough research so far conducted into hypnagogic states was carried out at Brunel University by Dr Andreas Mavromatis. He managed to teach himself – and his students – to relax deeply, then to drift in the state between sleeping and waking without relaxing into sleep. This seems to be the most difficult part of the technique but can be achieved by practice. I myself achieved it by accident after reading Mavromatis's book *Hypnagogia*. Towards dawn I half woke up, still drifting in a pleasantly sleepy condition, and found myself looking at a mountain landscape inside my head. I was aware of being awake and of lying in bed, but also of looking at the mountains and the white-coloured landscape, exactly as if watching something on a television screen. Soon after that I drifted off to sleep again. The most interesting part of the experience was the sense of looking *at* the scenery, being able to focus it and shift my attention, exactly as when awake.

Mavromatis's most interesting experience occurred when he was half dozing in a circle of students, one of whom was 'psychometrizing' some object which he held in his hand – trying to describe its history. As the student began to describe his impressions Mavromatis also began to 'see' various scenes. Soon after this he became aware that he was seeing the scenes that were being described by the student. Mavromatis then began to alter his hypnagogic vision – a faculty he had acquired by practice – and discovered that the student began to describe these altered visions.

As far as Mavromatis was concerned this established beyond all doubt that hypnagogic states encourage telepathy. He verified this conclusion at evening classes with students by asking them to 'pick up' various scenes he envisaged. Although the results were mixed, some were too accurate to be dismissed as mere chance. All this finally led him to the amazing conclusion (which he hides away modestly in the last sentence of an appendix) that 'some seemingly "irrelevant" hypnagogic images might . . . be meaningful phenomena belonging to another mind.'

Now this is an immensely exciting conclusion, for it suggests that deliberately-induced hypnagogia might be the open sesame to the whole field of the paranormal. The real problem with psychical research is that it is almost impossible to 'do' it in the laboratory. In the late 1930s Professor J. B. Rhine made an important breakthrough when a gambler told him that he could will the dice to make him win. Rhine tested him and found that his score was far above average, and that many other

131

people could achieve the same high scores by concentrating on the dice and willing double sixes to appear. But once Rhine had proved that dice can be influenced by the mind it was difficult to think of where to go next. Like Uri Geller's demonstrations of his ability to bend keys by stroking them, Rhine's experiment was interesting but induced the response, 'So what?' If, as Mavromatis believes, the hypnagogic experience is a kind of gateway into the world of paranormal powers, it could well be the breakthrough that psychical research has been hoping for since the 1880s.

In fact Mavromatis's suggestion has already been anticipated many times in this book – for example by Thomson Jay Hudson, who believed that the best time for 'healing' experiments was when falling asleep or when first waking up in the morning. Hudson recognized that the real problem is that the 'objective mind', with its inborn scepticism, seems to block the powers of the 'subjective mind'. And the findings of split-brain research bring us an even clearer insight into the problem. One of its most significant discoveries is that the left brain (the 'you') works much *faster* than its non-dominant partner. The left is always in a hurry; the right takes its time. And in civilized society the problem is compounded by the sheer pace of the rat race.

Yet it is perfectly obvious that when we are in a hurry experience turns into a kind of 'non-experience'. If I swallow my food too fast, it is difficult to taste it. If I watch television or read a book in a state of impatience, I fail to take half of it in. Yet in the course of the past five thousand years man has come to accept this over-stressed consciousness as the real thing. And the result of the non-stop stress is Proust's feeling of being 'mediocre, accidental, mortal'. Why *should* a cake dipped in tea bring a feeling of ecstatic happiness? After all it only had the effect of reviving Proust's childhood, and he already knew he was once a child in Combray. The real significance of the experience is that the taste of the madeleine *slowed him down* and made him suddenly aware of the sheer delight of living at a much slower pace. And Hermann Hesse's Steppenwolf, describing a similar experience, uses the significant phrase, 'Suddenly I could breathe again . . . .' The most important thing that modern man could possibly learn is how to genuinely *relax*. It has the effect of opening up a whole new mode of consciousness, a consciousness that 'spreads out sideways' instead of rushing forward at a breakneck speed. And it is *this* mode of consciousness that offers access to paranormal experience.

In the early 1920s the wife of the American novelist Upton Sinclair began to go through a 'middle-age crisis' in the course of which she started to develop telepathic powers. In fact she had been telepathic in childhood, when she would feel instinctively that her mother wanted her and be on her way home before the negro servant could set out to find her. Upton Sinclair found it a little uncomfortable that his wife should know exactly what he was doing when he was away from her. In a book called *Mental Radio* he described a series of experiments in the transmission of drawings which demonstrate beyond all doubt that his wife could read other people's minds. In the eighteenth chapter of that book May Sinclair described how she achieved the state in which she became telepathic. First, she said, she needed to be in a state of concentration – not concentration *on* anything in particular, but simply in a high state of mental alertness. And at the same time she had to go into a state of complete relaxation. The relaxation would bring her into a state of *hovering on the verge of sleep*. And once she had achieved this state she was ready to begin telepathy.

Obviously May Sinclair and Mavromatis are talking about precisely the same thing. And the same conclusion can be drawn: that when we can relax into this broad, unhurried type of consciousness, we can begin to exercise our 'hidden powers'.

The distinguished psychical investigator Guy Playfair had the same experience. When in Rio de Janeiro in the early 1970s he accidentally stumbled on the trick of sinking into hypnagogic states. The nights were so hot that it was extremely hard to get to sleep, and he often lingered in a 'borderline' state. In these states he experienced visions, 'as though a colour slide had been projected on an invisible screen in the darkness in front of my closed eyes'. The 'slide shows' became an almost nightly event and, like other 'hypnagogic dreamers', he was fascinated by the apparent reality of the scenes that floated in front of his eyes. He later found that a good method of inducing such states was to 'think blue', until his whole field of vision was a sheet of blueness. (May Sinclair also began by inducing a 'blank state of consciousness'.) Playfair later learned that experimenters in the paranormal were using this same method to induce telepathy. They would slice billiard balls in half and place the halves over the eyes of the subject so that he could see nothing but a field of blank whiteness. (A pair of goggles with white paper on the lenses is equally effective.)

Playfair began to take part in experiments with a Cambridge researcher, Dr Carl Sargent. One day, as he was returning to London, he and Sargent agreed to try a telepathic experiment around midnight that night. He lay in bed and induced a 'blank' state, then waited. Quite suddenly he 'saw' a picture. It was a man standing on a pedestal with a halo of light around him – Playfair thought it might be a statue of Mao Tse Tung. The next day he checked with Sargent to ask what kind of picture Sargent had been trying to 'send'. It was a picture by William Blake called 'Glad Day' in which a man with outstretched arms stands on a pinnacle of rock, with a halo of light behind him. Playfair's hypnagogic vision was unmistakably a 'hit'.

On a later occasion Playfair decided to try telepathy with a whole audience. He began by filling the room with white noise by turning a radio on to an unused wavelength and picking up the typical hissing noise, and telling his audience to relax – even to fall asleep if they wanted to. Then he selected one of four postcards at random – it was of Chatsworth House – sat behind a screen, and tried to 'broadcast' the picture of his audience. He did this by staring intently at the picture and mentally repeating the words, 'castle, bridge, river, trees'. Finally he turned off the radio and asked the audience what they had 'picked up'. Among the first replies were 'trees, river, bridge'. Then he passed the four cards round the audience and asked them to take a vote on which of them he had tried to 'send'. Chatsworth House received by far the largest vote – 35 per cent. The next largest vote was for a Flemish painting of a castle with trees (25 per cent.) The remaining two pictures received a mere 10 and 12 per cent respectively. It seemed again a fairly conclusive demonstration that telepathy is natural to us when we are relaxed.*

In his book *The Paranormal* the psychologist Stan Gooch cites an even more remarkable example. It concerned a chemist named Marcel Vogel, who also happened to be a psychic. In 1974 Gooch was present at a lecture given by Vogel, and when Vogel told his audience that he intended to project an image into their minds Gooch's reaction was, 'No, don't attempt that.' He felt that Vogel was putting his head on the block. They were asked to close their eyes, and Vogel announced that he was beginning the transmission of an image. At this point Gooch 'saw' in his mind's eye 'a triangle on which seemed to be superimposed a rather less clear circle'. Vogel then said he was giving the image colour: Gooch's mental image became blue, then red. Vogel now told them to open their eyes and asked how many had seen an image. When the first person to raise his hand said that he had seen a triangle, Gooch almost fell off his chair. Vogel then told them that he had projected the image of a triangle enclosed in a circle, and that he had first coloured it yellow, then red. (Blue is the 'complementary' colour of yellow: if you stare fixedly at a bright-yellow object, then look at a blank wall, a blue after-image will appear.) Gooch comments, 'I spent the rest of that lecture in what I can only describe as a state of joy. At the close the audience clapped enthusiastically. But why did they only clap? We should have stamped and shouted and broken the chairs in honour of this world-beater.'

Vogel, like Playfair, had demonstrated that the projection of a telepathic image is *not* a hit-or-miss affair, and the experiments of Mavromatis with hypnagogia point unmistakably to the same conclusion.

A case cited by Brian Inglis in his book *The Power of Dreams* seems to suggest that hypnagogia is even conducive to precognition. In a letter to the Koestler Foundation, his correspondent describes how she woke up one morning,

> . . . to find I was not in my own bed, in my flat, but in the bed of a male colleague. Although I had never been in his flat before, I knew immediately where I was; but I did not have any of the feeling of surprise, horror or exhilaration that might be associated

*Described in Guy Playfair's book *If This Be Magic* p. 117.

134

with such an event. I should perhaps emphasize that I grasped the situation through tactile rather than visual evidence, as I hadn't yet opened my eyes.

When she opened her eyes she realized that she was in her own bed.

She had paid very little attention to the colleague in question, for she was in love with someone else and she knew the colleague had a girlfriend. Yet that evening, at some official university function, he invited her to slip out to a pub and they ended in a 'necking situation' which would probably have ended in his bed. Recalling her 'dream' of that morning, she refused to let it go any further. Thinking it over later, it struck her that in those days of inadequate contraception – it was 1956 – she might well have found herself pregnant, faced with a shotgun wedding or single parenthood, and that her hypnagogic illusion had been, in fact, a warning not to yield to a pleasant impulse.

How precognition can possibly work – in hypnagogia or any other state – is a subject that must be considered in the next chapter. For the moment it is enough to observe that this case reinforces the notion of a link between hypnagogia and the paranormal.

Another distinguished student of occultism, Rudolf Steiner, stated that the best time to communicate with the dead is before falling asleep or just after waking up. Steiner's personal experience left him in no doubt that communication with the dead is possible. Brought up in a tiny village in Austria among mountains and woods, Steiner always had a capacity for sinking into deep states of contemplation. He claimed that the peace of nature made him aware 'not only of trees and mountains . . . but also of the Beings who lived behind them, the spirits of nature that can be observed in such a region'. In his autobiography he tells how, as a small boy, he was sitting in a station waiting-room when a strange woman came in. Steiner noticed that she bore a strong resemblance to other members of his family. The woman said to the boy, 'Try and help me as much as you can', then walked into the stove and vanished. Not long after Steiner learned that a female relative had died at exactly the same time he had seen the 'ghost'.

As a result of such experiences, Steiner formulated his basic doctrine:

I said to myself: the objects and events seen by means of the senses exist in space. This space is outside man; but within him exists a kind of soul-space, which is the setting for spiritual beings and events. It was impossible for me to regard thoughts as mere pictures we form of things. To me they were revelations of a spiritual world seen on the stage of the soul . . . . I felt that knowledge of the spiritual world must actually exist within the soul as an objective reality, just like geometry.

This is a baffling doctrine, for it seems to contradict our everyday

135

experience. If I sink into a state of revery, I do not see 'revelations of the spiritual world' and I certainly do not see ghosts. yet throughout his life Steiner insisted that the world inside us *is* the spirit world. But by now we should at least be able to catch a glimpse of what he meant. 'Entering the inner world' was not merely falling into a state of revery: it was *falling down the rabbit hole*.

Like Arnold Toynbee, Steiner had an ability to make imaginative contact with the past. In my book on Steiner I summarized it as follows:

> On the same trip [to Weimar] he visited Martin Luther's room in the Wartburg, as well as spending time in Berlin and Munich. There can be no doubt that this first journey into the greater world was of immense importance for Steiner. His natural capacity for floating off into mental worlds meant that every historical site and art gallery was a vital imaginative experience. Most of us find historical sites a fairly superficial experience; the guide assures us that such and such an event took place there, and we take his word for it; but we are more aware of the other tourists and the souvenir shops and the ice-cream vans. All his life, Steiner had the ability to enter into the spirit of a place, to conjure up scenes that had taken place in the past. So in front of Goethe's statue in Weimar he felt that 'a life-giving air was being wafted over everything', while his visit to the Wartburg impressed him so much that he felt it was one of the most memorable days of his life.*

Another mystic, William Blake, held precisely this same view of the inner world. He wrote in his *Descriptive Catalogue:* 'This world of Imagination is the world of Eternity; *it is the divine bosom into which we shall all go after the death of the vegetated body* [my italics]. This world of Imagination is infinite and eternal .... There exist in that eternal world the permanent realities of everything that we see reflected in this vegetable glass of nature.' This last sentence sounds very like the conclusion reached in the last chapter: that we are living in an 'information universe' where everything is somehow 'on record', and it reminds us that Steiner also believed that the history of the universe is available to inspection by mystics. Steiner borrowed a term from Madame Blavatsky's Theosophy and called this 'library' the Akashic Records. Many Theosophists claimed to be able to 'read' the Akashic Records. The scholar G. R. S. Mead wrote a book called *Did Jesus Live 100 BC?*, based on a Jewish document called the *Toldoth Jeschu* about a certain Rabbi Jeschu who lived about 100 BC, suggesting that Jesus and Jeschu were the same person. In the introduction he admitted that one of his reasons for entertaining this hypothesis was that many friends with 'clairvoyant faculties' were unanimous in declaring that the historical Jesus lived a century before the traditional date. 'They, one and all, claim

*Rudolf Steiner, The Man and his Vision (1985), chapter 3, p. 84.

that, if they turn their attention to the matter, they can see the events of those far-off days passing before their mind's eye, or rather, that for the time being they seem to be in the midst of them, even as we ordinarily observe events in actual life.' These friends are identified, in a little book called *Occult Investigations* by C. Jinarajadasa, as Annie Besant and C. W. Leadbeater of the Theosophical Society. Another member of the Theosophical Society, W. Scott-Elliott, wrote a history of Atlantis and Lemuria based upon his own investigations of the Akashic Records. Steiner himself produced a kind of history of the universe, called *Cosmic Memory*, in which he includes accounts of Atlantis and Lemuria.

The normally sceptical reader will find it hard to swallow these accounts of 'earth history' by Steiner, Scott-Elliott and 'Bishop' Leadbeater. Yet this is in itself no reason for rejecting the idea of 'cosmic memory'. William Denton devoted the third volume of *The Soul of Things* to 'astronomical examinations' which consist largely of the 'visions' of his son Sherman of the planets Mars, Venus and Jupiter. After the first two volumes, with their impressive evidence about ancient Greece and Rome, it is a keen disappointment. Venus has giant trees like toadstools which are full of sweet jelly. Mars has men with four fingers and blonde hair, while Jupiter is peopled by blue-eyed blondes who can float in the air. It is clear that Sherman's unconscious mind had been pulling his leg. Yet the evidence based upon psychometric examination of objects in the first two volumes remains very impressive indeed. The lesson to be learned is that in these 'borderland' areas of the mind, 'clairvoyant' perceptions can easily blend into dreams which possess all the amazing reality of hypnagogic imagery.

Steiner's explanation of 'cosmic memory' is that:

> . . . in the spiritual sense, what is 'past' has not really vanished, but is still there. In physical life men have this conception in regard to space only. If you stand in front of a tree, then go away and look back . . . the tree has not disappeared. In the spiritual world the same is true in regard to *time*. If you experience something at one moment, it has passed away the next as far as physical consciousness is concerned; spiritually conceived, it has not passed away. You can look back at it just as you can look back at the tree.

A comment like this ceases to be baffling if we recall Toynbee's experiences in Greece in 1912: he was somehow able to look back on past events as if they were actually happening in the present moment. In everyday life, our physical senses hurry us along so that experiences quickly fade and disappear. Yet we know that they are all stored in memory, and that some chance occurrence – like Proust's cake dipped in tea – can revive them in all their reality. Steiner is declaring that if we can learn to retreat deep inside ourselves – 'down the rabbit hole' – we can contact not only our own past memories but those of the race. He also declares that it is through this ability to enter his own 'inner world' that he is able to converse with the dead. In a lecture called 'The Dead Are With Us' he explains:

> Besides waking life and sleeping life there is a third state, even more important for intercourse with the spiritual world . . . . I mean the state connected with the act of waking and the act of going to sleep, which lasts only for a few brief seconds . . . . At the moment of going to sleep the spiritual world approaches us with power, but we immediately fall asleep, losing consciousness of what has passed through the soul.

If we wish to ask a question of the dead, we should 'carry it in the soul' until the moment of sleep, and then put the question. It must be imbued with deep feeling and with will, so it is committed to the subconscious mind. Then the answer will come from inside us. In his autobiography Steiner describes two occasions on which he became 'intimately acquainted' with the souls of the dead. On the first occasion he had been introduced into the family of a fellow student but had not met the father, who was an invalid and a recluse. Yet when the father died Steiner knew so much about his life and personality that he was asked to deliver the funeral oration. Eight years later, in Weimar, Steiner took lodgings in the house of a widow named Anna Eunicke, whose husband had recently died: once again, Steiner claimed that he was able to get to know the dead man intimately.

Unfortunately there is no corroborative evidence of Steiner's claims. But this is not so in the case of another mystic, Emanuel Swedenborg, who also claimed to be able to enter the 'spirit world' at will, and whose *Spiritual Diary* makes it clear that he used hypnagogic states to gain access to that world. In 1761 the widow of the Dutch ambassador told Swedenborg that a silversmith was dunning her for payment for a tea service which she was convinced her late husband had already paid for. A few days later Swedenborg told her that he had spoken to her husband in the spirit world and that he had a message from him: the receipt for the tea service would be found in a secret drawer in his bureau together with some secret correspondence. Both the receipt and the correspondence were found where Swedenborg said they would be. On another occasion Swedenborg was asked by the Queen of Sweden to give her regards to her dead brother. When he next saw her he told her that her brother apologized for not answering her last letter, and would now do so through Swedenborg. As Swedenborg delivered the message the Queen turned pale and said, 'No one but God knows this secret.'

We may of course prefer to dismiss the notion that Swedenborg derived his information from the dead: what *is* clear is that he was able to obtain information 'paranormally', and that he made use of hypnagogic states to enter this 'inner world'.* His own words echo those of Steiner: 'Nay, there is another kind of vision which comes in a state between sleep and wakefulness. The man then supposes that he is fully awake, as it were, inasmuch as all his senses are active . . . .' Swedenborg called this state 'passive potency', underlining Eileen Garrett's point that the mind needs to be in a strange state that is at once passive and active.

There seems, then, to be a remarkable unanimity of opinion that entering 'psi states' involves a withdrawal from the external world and a relaxation into an 'inner world' that goes far deeper than ordinary relaxation. What continues to be difficult to grasp is this notion that entering our 'inner' world can somehow give us access to a *wider* reality – after all, the world 'out there' *is* 'out there' and not inside us. But then if Mavromatis is correct when he suggests that 'hypnagogic images may be meaningful phenomena belonging to another mind' – that is, they seem 'alien' because they *are* alien – then the 'inside' of our own minds may be our point of contact with a wider reality. Mrs Upton Sinclair made the same suggestion when she wrote that 'if clairvoyance is real, then we may have access to all knowledge. We may really be fountains, or outlets of one vast mind.' If telepathy is real, 'then my mind is not my own . . . . I and the universe of men are *one*.' Upton Sinclair expanded these comments:

> What telepathy means to my wife is this: it seems to indicate a common substratum of mind, underlying our individual minds, and which we can learn to tap. Figure the conscious mind as a tree, and the subconscious mind as the roots of that tree: then what of the earth in which the tree grows, and from which it derives its sustenance? What currents run through that earth, affecting all the trees of the forest? If one trees falls, the earth is shaken, and may not the other trees feel the impulse?
>
> In other words we are apparently getting hints of a cosmic consciousness, or cosmic unconsciousness; some kind of mind-stuff which is common to us all, and which we can bring into our individual consciousness. Why is it not sensible to think that there may be a universal mind-stuff, just as there is a universal body-stuff, of which we are made, and to which we return?

Comments like this immediately induce the modern reader to think of Carl Jung and the 'collective unconscious'. But Sinclair was writing *Mental Radio* in the late 1920s, when Jung's name was scarcely known outside Switzerland. In fact Jung had already developed his own peculiar technique for falling 'down the rabbit hole', although at that time it was known only to a few of his patients and colleagues. It was only revealed to the general public in 1960, with the publication of his autobiography, *Memories, Dreams, Reflections*. In it Jung tells how, after the break with

*See Wilson Van Dusen, *The Presence of Other Worlds* and *The Natural Depth in Man*.

Freud in 1913 – which shook him to his foundations – he began to experience severe states of self-doubt and depression. On a train journey in October 1913 – when no one had any reason to expect war – he experienced a hallucination that all Europe was submerged by a flood and covered with floating rubble and drowned bodies; finally the water turned into blood. Since the 'vision' lasted an hour, he suspected he was close to insanity. 'I was living in a constant state of tension; often I felt as if gigantic blocks of stone were tumbling down on me.' As the hallucinations persisted Jung tried to hold his tensions in check with yoga exercises, but he often found himself whispering aloud: the forces of the unconscious were trying to break loose. The idea of surrendering to these forces aroused resistance and fear. Then one day he decided to take the risk:

I was sitting at my desk once more, thinking over my fears. Then I let myself drop. Suddenly it was as though the ground literally gave way beneath my feet, and I plunged down into dark depths. I could not fend off a feeling of panic. But then, abruptly, at not too great a depth, I landed on my feet in a soft, sticky mass. I felt great relief, although I was apparently in complete darkness. After a while my eyes grew accustomed to the gloom, which was rather like a deep twilight. Before me was the entrance to a cave, in which stood a dwarf with a leathery skin, as if he were mummified. I squeezed past him through the narrow entrance and waded knee deep through icy water to the other end of the cave where, on a projecting rock, I saw a glowing red crystal. I grasped the stone, lifted it, and discovered a hollow underneath. At first I could make out nothing, but then I saw there was running water. In it a corpse floated by, a youth with blond hair and a wound in the head. He was followed by a gigantic black scarab and then by a red, newborn sun, rising up out of the depths of the water. Dazzled by the light, I wanted to replace the stone upon the opening, but then a fluid welled out. It was blood. It seemed to me that the blood continued to spurt for an unendurably long time. At last it ceased, and the vision came to an end.

Jung came to believe that the youth was Siegfried, and that he symbolized the Kaiser's Germany, determined to have her own way. But he also symbolized Jung himself, trying to impose his will upon the forces of the unconscious. Siegfried had to be killed and the unconscious allowed to well up like blood.

From then on Jung discovered the secret of 'falling down the rabbit hole'. The method involved imagining a steep descent. 'The first time I reached, as it were, a depth of about a thousand feet; the next time I found myself at the edge of a cosmic abyss. It was like a voyage to the moon, or a descent into empty space.' He found himself in a crater and felt he was in the land of the dead. Then he saw two figures: a white bearded old man and a young girl. They identified themselves as Elijah and Salome and Jung had a long conversation with Elijah 'which, however, I did not understand'.

This inevitably recalls Wilson Van Dusen's conversation with the Emanation of the Eternal Feminine, and the gas-pipe fitter's request to be given just one clue as to what they had been talking about. It also recalls Van Dusen's remark about hypnagogic states: 'Even very average people who explore this region can run into strange people and strange symbolic conversations that look like visitations from another world.' Clearly Jung had stumbled upon his own method of entering this 'third state of consciousness'. In fact Jung encountered a figure called Philemon, another old man, who seemed to him to have an independent existence:

> Philemon and other figures of my fantasies brought home to me the crucial insight that there are things in the psyche which I do not produce, but which produce themselves and have their own life. Philemon represented a force which was not myself. In my fantasies I held conversations with him, and he said things which I had not consciously thought. For I observed clearly that it was he who spoke, not I. He said I treated thoughts as if I generated them myself, but in his view thoughts were like animals in a forest, or people in a room, or birds in the air . . . . It was he who taught me psychic objectivity, the reality of the psyche.

Jung is here making a point of crucial importance. He remarks that after his visions of Europe covered with blood an inner voice told him, 'Look at it well: it is wholly real and will be so. You cannot doubt it.' And in August 1914 it became real. May Sinclair makes the same point. Sometimes her telepathic 'visions' were like fantasies, but on other occasions they had an odd quality of 'truth' that left no doubt. 'I think a study of them shows that a true vision comes into the subconsciousness, not directly from the drawing [which she is trying to guess], but from another mind which has some means of knowing, and sending to consciousness *via* the subconsciousness . . . .' The true visions brought a hunch, and if she asked, 'Is this right or not?', 'this question seemed to receive an answer, "Yes", as if some intelligent entity was directly informing me.'

Now this is in fact a vitally important step in the argument of this book. We began by considering 'visions' like those of Eileen Garrett and trying to explain them in terms of some mysterious human faculty, the power of falling 'down the rabbit hole'. There followed the suggestion that everything that has ever happened is somehow 'on record', and that the human mind can extract information from the record by means of the 'subjective mind'. But in the case of the missing doctor it is hard to see how such a faculty could operate, since the fragment of shirt handed to

141

Eileen Garrett had been worn by the doctor on the day *before* he left home. One possible explanation, of course, is that the doctor had already decided to vanish to La Jolla before he left home and that the decison had somehow been 'imprinted' on his shirt. In this particular case, such an explanation is plausible. But it would be possible to cite dozens of other cases in which this is not so. In 1956 a pretty typist named Joy Aken disappeared after leaving her office in Durban, South Africa. Her family approached a psychic named Nelson Palmer and asked if he could help. Palmer told them to bring some items of the girl's underwear to his home. As he rested his hands on the clothing, Palmer told Joy's mother that the girl was dead and that her body lay in a culvert. He then guided a group of searchers to a culvert sixty miles away where the girl's body – with gunshot wounds in the head – was discovered. A man named Clarence Van Buuren was later hanged for her murder.*

It is clearly impossible that this girl's clothing could have somehow 'recorded' information about her murder since she was not wearing it at the time. But May Sinclair provides a possible explanation when she states that, 'it was as if some intelligent entity was directly informing me'. The intelligent entity could, of course, be Hudson's 'subjective mind'. But that still leaves us with the problem of how the 'subjective mind' of a psychometrist could obtain information from a garment that had no connection with a crime.

We have already encountered this same problem in the field of dowsing. Harvalik's magnetic gradients provide a perfectly satisfactory explanation for the dowser's ability to find underground water or minerals, but they totally fail to explain how a map dowser can detect the same things by dangling his pendulum over a map. (It need not even be a printed map; I have described in *Mysteries* how the Welsh dowser Bill Lewis accurately traced the course of a stream on a map I had sketched with a pencil, even indicating the point where a pipe ran off at a right angle to carry water to our cottage.) Most books on dowsing prefer to avoid the subject, to escape embarrassment. Yet most dowsers seem to feel that this odd ability is as 'normal' as their power to locate water with a divining rod. One of the most famous of French dowsers, the Abbé Mermet, 'explained' map dowsing by commenting that thought waves can travel round the world with the speed of light, and that therefore it is just as easy to dowse for something on the other side of the globe as in your own back garden; but he did not bother to explain how 'thought' can locate – for example – a sunken wreck in the middle of the Pacific Ocean. Here again the intelligent entity hypothesis seems to offer a more straightforward explanation.

Jung's attempt to resolve the mystery has something in common with David Bohm's 'implicate order' theory – the notion that the 'underlying reality' of the world contains information about the whole universe – as well as with Rudolf Steiner's Akashic Records. According to Jung, the

*The story is told more fully in my book *The Psychic Detectives*.

'collective unconscious' of the human race also contains knowledge of everything that has ever happened. He goes on to use this theory to explain a curious 'psychic' experience. One of his patients had relapsed into a state of depression:

At about two o'clock – I must have just fallen asleep – I awoke with a start, and had the feeling that someone had come into the room; I even had the impression that the door had been hastily opened. I instantly turned on the light, but there was nothing. Someone might have mistaken the door, I thought, and I looked into the corridor. But it was still as death. 'Odd,' I thought, 'someone did come into the room!' Then I tried to recall exactly what had happened, and it occurred to me that I had been awakened by a feeling of dull pain, as though something had struck my forehead and then the back of my skull. The following day I received a telegram saying that my patient had committed suicide. He had shot himself. Later I learned that the bullet had come to rest in the back wall of the skull.*

The straightforward explanation of this experience would seem to be telepathy – perhaps the patient was thinking about Jung as he prepared to blow his brains out. Jung preferred something more complicated:

The experience was a genuine synchronistic phenomenon such as is quite often observed in connection with an archetypal situation – in this case, death. By means of a relativization of time and space in the unconscious it could well be that I had perceived something which in reality was taking place elsewhere. The collective unconscious is common to all: it is the foundation of what the ancients called 'the sympathy of all things'. In this case the unconscious had knowledge of my patient's condition. All that evening, in fact, I had felt curiously restive and nervous, very much in contrast to my usual mood.

To understand this passage we have to recall that Jung believed that Philemon, Elijah and Salome were 'intelligent entities' who had their own independent existence outside his own mind. He believed, in effect, that he had walked out of his own personal 'unconscious' and had met them in the common ground of the collective unconscious. So if we brush aside the screen of abstractions about 'the relativization of time and space in the unconscious', he is really suggesting that his knowledge of his patient's suicide came from 'intelligent entities' – exactly as May Sinclair does.

As Jung learned the techniques of plunging 'down the rabbit hole', he began to enter into a curious relationship with these intelligent entities. Another entity called Ka – more demonic than Philemon – made his

*Carl Jung, *Memories, Dreams, Reflections* p. 136.

143

appearance, and Jung began writing accounts of his encounters in a notebook he called his Black Book. One day as he was writing he asked himself the question, 'What am I really doing?', and a female voice inside his head answered clearly, 'It is art.' It was the voice of a female patient who had been in love with Jung. When, later, he asked the same question, the same voice replied clearly, 'It is art.' Whereupon Jung invited 'her' to explain exactly what she meant: as a result she came through with a long statement. Jung then decided that this 'inner woman' was an essential part of his own soul and christened it 'the anima' – the female component in men. And he came to suspect that her assertion 'This is art' was an attempt to persuade him to see himself as a great misunderstood artist and so to bring about his destruction. (Unfortunately he failed to explain precisely why his anima should wish to destroy him.)

In 1916 the 'entities' seemed to escape from his unconscious (or the collective unconscious) into the real world. The air seemed to be full of ghosts. His eldest daughter saw a white figure passing through the room while the blanket was twice snatched from the bed of his youngest daughter. Later the following afternoon the doorbell began ringing frantically, but when they answered it there was no one there.

> Then I knew that something had to happen. The whole house was filled as if there were a crowd present, crammed full of spirits. They were packed deep right to the door, and the air was so thick it was scarcely possible to breathe. As for myself, I was all a-quiver with the question, 'For God's sake, what in the world is this?' Then they cried out in chorus, 'We have come back from Jerusalem where we found not what we sought.'

Jung snatched up his pen and began to write: in three evenings he had written a curious work entitled *Seven Sermons to the Dead*, written in the rather pompous, inflated style which Jung says is typical of the 'archetypes'.

Does this mean that Jung felt he had been dealing with real 'spirits'? Apparently yes. He says, 'The intellect, of course, would like . . . to write the whole thing off as a violation of the rules. But what a dreary world it would be if the rules were not broken sometimes!'

It must be emphasized that at the time Jung kept these experiences very much to himself. He had his career to think of. Nothing would have delighted Freud more than for Jung to openly declare himself a believer in 'the occult' so that he could say, 'I told you these weird ideas would drive him mad . . . .' The result was that Jung played his cards very close to his chest. In 1920 he rented a cottage near London and was disturbed by knocking noises, unpleasant smells and sounds as if a large animal was rushing around the bedroom – typical 'poltergeist phenomena'. One night, as the walls echoed to a storm of blows, Jung opened his eyes to find himself looking at half a head – of an old woman – on his pillow. He left hastily and the cottage was pulled down. Yet as late as 1948 he wrote a postscript to an article on 'spirits' in which he claimed they were 'projections of the unconscious' stating that he could not make up his mind whether spirits really existed 'because I am not in a position to adduce experiences that would prove it one way or the other.' This sounds – to put it mildly – slightly disingenuous. And it was not until two years later that he finally dared to relate his experience in the haunted cottage in the introduction to a book called *Ghosts: Reality or Delusion?*

Jung also preferred to keep silent about another 'occult' interest, the Chinese book of oracles known as the *I Ching*. This ancient text contains sixty-four 'oracles', and is consulted by a chance procedure involving coins or yarrow stalks. The simplest method is to throw down three pennies. A preponderance of heads gives a straight line; a preponderance of tails a broken line. When placed on top of one another, these lines form a hexagram which indicates which of the sixty-four oracles contains the answer to the question. (The question must be clearly formulated in the mind before consulting the oracle.)

Obviously there is no possible scientific justification for the procedure; yet Jung was studying – and consulting – the *I Ching* from 1920 onward. He did not admit to it until 1950 when, after an accident that brought him to the verge of death, he obviously felt that it was time to speak frankly. Then he justified his interest in the *I Ching* by discussing what he called 'synchronicities' – those baffling, apparently meaningful coincidences that give us the feeling that fate is trying to tell us something. Jung gives an example from his own experience: after making a note about a mythical creature that was half man and half fish, he had fish for lunch, someone mentioned the custom of making an 'April fish' (April fool) of someone, a patient showed him a picture of a fish, he saw an embroidery of fishes and sea monsters, and, finally, a patient told him about a dream of a fish that night. On the day he wrote all this down, he found a large fish on the wall by the lake.

Writing an introduction to Richard Wilhelm's translation of the *I Ching* Jung was confronted with the problem of how to justify such 'occult' notions in scientific terms. He compromised by describing synchronicity as 'an acausal connecting principle' – a completely meaningless term meaning a cause that is not a cause. But it sounded more or less scientific, and Jung later tried to justify it by publishing his essay on synchronicity in a book that also contained an essay by the physicist Wolfgang Pauli, arguing that the astronomer Kepler had invented the idea of 'archetypes'.

Pauli, oddly enough, was himself an amusing example of what Jung meant by synchronicity. He seemed to have some odd power of making things go wrong. One day in Göttingen a complex piece of apparatus suddenly collapsed without apparent cause, and Professor J. Franck remarked jokingly, 'Pauli must be around somewhere.' He wrote to ask

Pauli where he was at the time and discovered that Pauli was actually on the railway platform in Göttingen, changing trains.

Having convinced himself – and many other respectable psychologists – that synchronicity was a scientifically justifiable idea, Jung continued to use it to explain anything that he felt might sound suspiciously 'occult'. We have seen, for example, how he explained his telepathic experience of his patient's suicide by describing it as 'a genuine synchronistic phenomenon such as is quite often observed in connection with an archetypal situation' – an explanation which obviously has no relation to what actually happened but which sounds comfortingly scientific.

In fact most of the examples Jung mentions in his lecture 'On Synchronicity' are not about synchronicity at all. He mentions a student friend who had a dream of a Spanish city: when he went to Spain on holiday he recognized the scene of his dream, even to a carriage with two cream coloured horses. This is obviously precognition. Jung then mentions some of Rhine's experiments in card guessing – but this, again, is not synchronicity but ESP. It is only then that he comes to a case that fits his own definition of synchronicity as a meaningful coincidence. He was having considerable difficulty with a young female patient 'who always knew better about everything' and whose rationalism seemed impregnable. One day, as she was telling Jung about a vivid dream of a golden scarab, there was a tapping on the window: Jung opened it and a gold-green scarab – a rose-chafer – flew into the room. Jung caught it and handed it to the patient. 'Here is your scarab.' This 'punctured the desired hole in her rationalism' and broke the ice of her resistance.

A far more impressive example is noted in Jung's short book on synchronicity. In 1914 a mother took a photograph of her son in the Black Forest and left it to be developed in a shop in Strasbourg, but the outbreak of war made it impossible to collect it. In 1916 she bought a film in Frankfurt and took a photograph of her baby daughter. When the film was developed it proved to be a double exposure, with the photograph of her son underneath that of her daughter – somehow, her original film had got back into circulation among new films. Jung took the story from a book called *Chance* by Wilhelm von Scholz, who suggests that these coincidences are arranged 'as if they were the dream of a greater and more comprehensive consciousness which is unknowable'. Another psychiatrist, Herbert Silberer, encapsulated his own feeling in the title of a book, *Chance: the Kobold-tricks of the Unconscious* (a kobold being a mischievous hobgoblin).

Odd coincidences certainly produce in us the 'creepy' feeling that fate is nudging us in the ribs, attempting to make us realize that life is more meaningful than we thought. In the opening sentence of 'the Mystery of Marie Roget' Poe writes, 'There are few persons, even among the calmest thinkers, who have not occasionally been startled into a vague yet thrilling half-credence in the supernatural, by *coincidences* of so seemingly marvellous a character, that, as mere coincidences, the intellect has been unable to receive them.' This sentence was itself one of a series of synchronicities that occurred when I began to write an article on the subject of synchronicity. The decision to write the article, in an encyclopaedia of unsolved mysteries, arose when I was about to write an article on whether Joan of Arc was really burnt at the stake. While looking for something on a library sheet I noticed a series of bound volumes of the *International History Magazine* and decided that it might be worth spending some time looking through them for unsolved mysteries. I opened the first volume at random and found myself looking at an article on Joan of Arc which raised the question of whether she survived her execution. Soon after this I noticed a newspaper cutting that my wife had left outside my study – she told me she had cut it out because it contained an interesting reference to Ernest Hemingway. In fact it proved to be an article about strange coincidences concerning lost manuscripts. These 'coincidences' made me decide to add an article on synchronicity to the encyclopaedia. But first I had to write an article on the case of the disappearance of the New York 'cigar girl' Mary Rogers, on which Poe based his Marie Roget story. Its opening sentence, quoted above, confirmed the decision to write the synchronicity article.

It is obviously important to distinguish between ordinary coincidence and synchronicity, which might be defined as a coincidence so outrageous that it cannot be shrugged off as coincidence. Here are two personal examples which I would dismiss as coincidence. In 1967 my wife and I were flying to Phoenix, Arizona when I commented suddenly, 'The famous meteor crater ought to be around here somewhere.' My wife looked out of the window and said, 'There it is.' In fact we were flying over it. In 1974 we were flying to Beirut across the Mediterranean and I said, 'We ought to be flying somewhere near Santorini at some point.' We looked out of the window and discovered we were flying over it at that moment.

Here is an example – which occurred in the past twenty-four hours – which seems to me to stretch the definition of the word 'coincidence' without breaking it. During the morning, tidying a pile of books and magazines in a corner of the bedroom, I found a copy of the *Journal of the Society for Psychical Research* containing a review of a book – which I have recently read – debunking the whole field of the paranormal. In the course of the piece the reviewer mentions the researcher S. G. Soal, who is attacked in the book, and mentions that there is no positive evidence that he cheated. Later, in my morning post, I found a review of my book *Afterlife* by D. Scott Rogo in which he reproached me for citing that well-known fraud, S. G. Soal. I wrote a letter to Mr Rogo citing the *SPR Journal* review. An hour later, searching for a book in my untidy study, I came across a volume lying open under a pile of books: it was about parapsychology in South Africa and was open at an article by Basil Shackleton – the 'psychic' with whom Soal worked – in which he gave reasons for not believing Soal to have been a cheat.

This seems to me a borderline case of synchronicity. But the following example has the truly outrageous touch.

In the course of writing my article on synchronicity in the *Encyclopedia of Unsolved Mysteries* I described an example recounted by the computer expert Jacques Vallee. Vallee had become interested in a Californian sect called the Order of Melchizedek – named after the Biblical prophet – and was doing all he could to find information about the original Melchizedek. There proved to be very little. One day Vallee took a taxi to the Los Angeles Airport and asked the driver – a woman – if he could have a receipt. She handed him a receipt signed 'M. Melchizedec'. Struck by the coincidence, Vallee wondered how many other Melchizedecs were in the Los Angeles telephone directory. The answer was, only one – his taxi driver. Vallee said he felt as if he had stuck a note on some universal notice-board, 'Wanted, Melchizedecs', and fate had asked, 'Is this one any good?' 'No, for heaven's sake! That's a taxi driver . . . .'

When I had finished telling this story I broke off my article to take my dogs for their afternoon walk. About to leave my study, I noticed a book lying on my untidy camp-bed; it was one I had no recollection of seeing before, although I had obviously purchased it for I had had it bound by Remploy. It was *You Are Sentenced to Life* by Dr W. D. Chesney, and was about the evidence for life after death. I tossed the book on to my armchair and glanced through it when I returned from my walk. At the top of the page there was a heading, ORDER OF MELCHIZEDEC, followed by a letter from one Grace Hooper Pettipher, an Instructress in the same Order of Melchizedec that Vallee had been researching. I have just about thirty thousand books in this house, and I doubt whether any other contains a reference to the Order of Melchizedec. But I had to stumble on this one after writing about Vallee's remarkable coincidence. It was as if fate was saying, 'All right, if you *really* want me to show you what I can do, how about this?'

In the early 1970s Arthur Koestler became intrigued by synchronicity and wrote an article in the *Sunday Times* appealing for examples, the most striking of which were published in a book *The Challenge of Chance*. A doctor pointed out, for example, how often he would come upon some rare ailment during surgery and then encounter several more cases during the day. A typewriter specialist mentioned that after he received some unusual model for repair other models of the same make would turn up immediately afterwards.

Koestler pointed out that synchronicity sometimes looks like extra-sensory perception. He tells of how Dame Rebecca West was in the London Library researching the Nuremberg war trials when she found, to her annoyance, that the trials are published in no proper order. After an hour of fruitless search she approached a librarian and said, 'I can't find it . . .', reaching out casually as she did so and taking down a volume at random. It opened at the trial she had been searching for. Hudson would say that her subjective mind already knew where the trial was to

148

be found – perhaps by some form of 'dowsing' – and had guided her to it. But in another case involving Rebecca West this would have been impossible. She recounts how she was in the London Library waiting for a copy of Gounod's memoirs to arrive. An American approached her and asked her whether it was true that she possessed some lithographs by the artist Delpeche. They were still talking about Delpeche when the assistant brought her the book. She opened it casually and found herself looking at a passage in which Gounod mentions Delpeche's kindness to his mother . . . .

Jung himself believed in the subjective mind explanation. He explains that 'the archetype has the tendency to gather suitable forms of expression round itself', and goes on to say, 'The factor which favours the occurrence of parapsychological events is the presence of an active archetype, i.e. a situation in which the deeper instinctual layers of the psyche are called into action.'* Archetypes are symbolic figures, like the Mother, the Temptress, the Wise Old Man – Salome and Elijah being examples of the last two. Since Jung believed that the archetypes have an existence apart from the individual mind, we seem to be back to something very like the intelligent entity theory.

But if the archetypes are responsible for synchronicities, they seem to select some singularly trivial examples. Jung cites one of the most famous in his book, a case originally recounted by Camille Flammarion in his book *The Unknown*. The poet Emil Deschamps described how as a child he had been presented with a piece of plum pudding by a certain M. Fortgibu, who had become acquainted with this rare dish on a trip to England. Years later Deschamps saw a plum pudding in the window of a Paris restaurant and went in to ask if he could buy one. He was told that, unfortunately, the pudding had been ordered by someone else: the someone turned out to be M. Fortgibu, who offered to share it. We can see that Deschamps would regard the coincidence as an astonishing one. But there was yet more to come. Years later he attended a party at which plum pudding was to be served and – inevitably – he told his story about M. Fortgibu. At that moment the door opened and M. Fortgibu – now an old man – walked in. He had been invited to another apartment in the same building and had mistaken the door.

Camille Flammarion tells another equally impressive story of a coincidence concerning himself. One day when he was writing a book, a gust of wind carried some pages out of the window. Since it was raining he decided that they were not worth recovering. A few days later the chapter arrived from his printer. It seemed that the porter of the printing office had walked past, seen the pages on the ground, and assumed he had dropped them: so he sorted them out and delivered them to the printer. The subject of the chapter? The wind . . . .

What emerges very clearly from Jung's book is that in spite of all his talk about the archetypes and acausal connecting principles his real

*Carl Jung, *Collected Works*, vol. 18, pp. 509–11.

feeling about synchronicities is a certain excitement, as if they were 'messages from God' – or at least from some benevolent intelligence. It is true that the Fortgibu case sounds more like an example of the 'kobold-tricks of the unconscious' – or what Charles Fort called 'the cosmic joker', yet that is beside the point. The important thing is that synchronicities produce a sense of the underlying meaningfulness of the universe, the feeling that in spite of all appearances, we are not accidents of nature who have been stranded in a universe of chance. According to Sartre, the underlying truth about human existence is 'contingency', the feeling that 'existence is not necessary', and that we are ultimately victims of chance. We all experience that feeling when life is going badly – sometimes even the feeling that fate is actively malevolent. Synchronicities *feel* like a nudge in the ribs from some benevolent entity, telling us not to take our problems too seriously. Most scientific parapsychologists would dismiss that idea with scorn – and then experience precisely the same feeling next time they encounter an interesting synchronicity.

I summarized my own feeling about synchronicities as follows:

It is my own experience that coincidences like this seem to happen when I am in 'good form' – when I am feeling alert, cheerful and optimistic, and not when I am feeling tired, bored or gloomy. This leads me to formulate my own hypothesis on synchronicity as follows. As a writer, I am at my best when I feel alert and purposeful: at these times I feel a sense of 'hidden meanings' lurking behind the apparently impassive face of everyday reality. But this is not true only for writers: it applies to all human beings. We are *all* at our best when the imagination is awake, and we can sense the presence of that 'other self', the intuitive part of us. When we are tired or discouraged we feel 'stranded' in left-brain consciousness . . . . We can be jarred out of this state by sudden crisis, or by any pleasant stimulus, but more often than not these fail to present themselves. It must be irritating for 'the other self' to find its partner so dull and sluggish, allowing valuable time and opportunity to leak away by default. A 'sychronicity' can snap us into a sudden state of alertness and awareness. And if the 'other self' can, by the use of its peculiar powers, bring about a synchronicity, then there is still time to prevent us from wasting yet another day of our brief lives.

All this is implicit in Jung's book on synchronicity, although he preferred to leave it unsaid. And its implications are clearly momentous. Even if we only suppose that the 'other self' can 'steer' us towards synchronicities – as it seems to have steered Rebecca West to the right book on the Nuremberg war trials – then it looks as if it *knows* far more than we know consciously. But Jung's lifelong use of the *I Ching* suggests that he thought there was more to it than that. If the coins fall in a certain order in response to a mental question, then the implication is that the 'other self' can cause them to fall in that order and can actually influence physical events.

The implications of Rebecca West's Delpeche experience are even odder. When the American introduced himself to her the librarian had *already* gone to collect Gounod's memoirs, with its reference to Delpeche, thus setting the coincidence in motion. One explanation – apart from straightforward coincidence – would be that her subjective mind directed her attention to the Delpeche reference *as a result* of her conversation with the American. The only alternative would seem to be that her subjective mind was able to foresee the future . . . .

As incredible as it sounds, both explanations for synchronicity have been tried and tested in the laboratory. Admittedly this was not part of the intention, yet it amounted to the same thing. A physicist, Dr Helmut Schmidt, was trying to devise foolproof tests for extra-sensory perception in his laboratory at Durham, North Carolina. A piece of radioactive substance – whose rate of decay was completely unpredictable – was wired up to four lamps, causing one at a time to light up in random order. Three 'psychic' subjects were asked to guess which lamp would light up next. Since there were four lamps, their chances of a correct guess were 25 per cent, and since they were allowed a vast number of guesses – 63,000 – the chance result should have been *precisely* 25 per cent. In fact it was 27 per cent – which amounted to seven hundred more correct guesses than there should have been.

Next Schmidt asked his subjects to try to *influence* the way in which a row of lamps would light up – either clockwise or anticlockwise. Over a large number of tries a 'chance' score should have been precisely 50 per cent clockwise and 50 per cent anticlockwise. In fact their efforts scored between 52 per cent and 53 per cent – again, a significant variation.

Now comes the unbelievable part of the experiment. Schmidt decided to *pre-record* some random numbers and try out the pre-recorded tapes on his subjects. Obviously it should have been totally impossible to influence the direction in which the lamps lit up, for it was 'predestined'. Incredibly, the 'psychics' were *still* able to influence the lamps.

There can be only two explanations. One is that the minds of the subjects were somehow able to alter the way the lamps lit up, thereby proving 'mind over matter', the basis of any theory about how synchronicity works. The other sounds even more extraordinary: it is that the tapes themselves were influenced – at the time they were being recorded – by the *future* efforts of the subjects. This sounds preposterous until we recall a series of experiments, conducted in 1939 by S. G. Soal, in which a housewife named Gloria Stewart was asked to read someone's mind and draw a series of pictures which were selected at random. Her score was poor until Soal realized that she was frequently drawing the *next* picture, which had not yet been selected. Her 'ESP' was operating on the future. So Schmidt's suggestion that the tapes were being

151

influenced by the future efforts of his subjects may be less absurd than it sounds. This whole subject must be examined more fully in the next chapter.

Jung always took good care never to suggest that synchronicity might be *caused* by 'mind over matter' – that is, that events might be somehow influenced by the human mind. Yet that is clearly the real implication of the idea of synchronicity. At the very least, he regarded it as some kind of unrecognized 'correspondence' between the mind and the physical world.

Jung derived this notion of a 'correspondence' from alchemy, which he had started to study at about the same date as the *I Ching*. The fundamental tenet of alchemy is the saying attributed to its legendary founder, Hermes Trismegistos, 'As above, so below', which is generally taken to mean that the pattern of the greater universe (macroscosm) is repeated in the smaller universe of the human soul (microcosm). But these speculations about synchronicity suggest another interpretation.

It is obvious that external events influence our states of mind (or soul). But as we have seen in this book, the fundamental tenet of 'occultism' is that the human mind possesses hidden powers that can influence the external world, possibly by a process of 'induction' not unlike that of an induction coil. Most of us are acquainted with the latter in the form of simple transformers: for example, if I wish to use an American electric razor in England I have to buy a small transformer which will 'step down' the English current of 240 volts to the standard American level of 120 volts. A transformer consists of two coils of wire, one wrapped around the other. If a current is passed through one coil, its electric field induces a current in the other. And if the second coil has twice as many turns as the first, then the induced current will be twice as strong.

'As above, so below' may be taken to mean that, under the right circumstances, the human mind can induce its own 'vibrations' in the material world, causing things to 'happen'. One result may be psychokinesis (PK), as when Schmidt's subjects influenced the electric lights. Another could be synchronicity.

In the previous chapter we encountered the suggestion that certain places can 'record' the emotional vibrations of events that have taken place there, and that the force involved may be connected with earth magnetism. In the case of some tragic event – like the arrest of Catherine Howard at Hampton Court – the negative 'vibrations' may be so strong that they can be 'picked up' by later visitors to the scene. It has been suggested – by T. C. Lethbridge among others – that ancient stone circles like Stonehenge may have been a kind of 'transformer' set up at some place of powerful earth magnetism so that their vibrations could interact closely with those of the priests who conducted their fertility rituals there. This may also explain why Christian churches are so often built on the sites of pagan temples: the earth, so to speak, provides a ready-made 'transformer' which can 'step up' the vibrations of the worshippers.

With their power of 'amplifying' emotional currents, such sites obviously have a powerful potential for both good and evil.

If human beings can induce 'positive' vibrations in the external world, it should also be clear that they can induce 'negative' vibrations. If that is so, then 'As above, so below' becomes a warning that a sense of pessimism or discouragement, the gloomy certainty that we are destined for bad luck, can cause 'negative induction', so that the bad luck becomes a self-fulfilling prophecy.

So it seems that the ultimate implication of Jung's theory – although it is one that he himself took care never to state – is that it should be possible for us to influence events by our mental attitudes: that people whose attitude is negative 'attract' bad luck, while those whose attitude is positive attract 'serendipity'. This in turn suggests that if we could learn to induce moods of optimism we could somehow *make* things go right. And although such an attitude may be scientifically indefensible, most of us have a gut-feeling that it contains more than a grain of truth.

6

Memories of the Future

During the Second World War Wilbur Wright – later a best-selling novelist – was a fighter pilot in the RAF. In March 1945 his closest friend, Doug Worley, came to him early one morning and handed him a wrapped bundle of his possessions. 'See my family get this stuff – I won't be back from the next trip.' He had foreseen his death in a dream, and Wright noted that he seemed neither worried nor frightened. Wright told him he was talking nonsense: the Squadron Commander repeated that view and suggested that Doug Worley should stand down for the day. Worley declined: he said that if it didn't happen in flight it might happen under the wheels of a truck. Later that day eight Tempests went in to strafe the German airfield at Schwerin. Wilbur Wright, diving next to Doug Worley, saw his friend's petrol tank explode into flame and watched as Worley deliberately flew his blazing aircraft straight into the doors of a hangar.

Wilbur Wright was haunted by Doug Worley's death – not so much by the tragedy of it, occurring a few weeks before the end of the war, as by the question it implied. Was Doug Worley *destined* to die that day, as he obviously believed? If so, then is everything that happens also predestined? Is belief in free will an illusion?

Wright had no doubt that this was a genuine case of precognition – he had known other pilots who had accurately foreseen their own death. Years later, in Germany, he met an anti-aircraft gunner named Schwab who had been among those who were defending the Schwerin airfield that day. He told Wright that the Germans had been expecting the attack – they had all been awakened at four that morning and told to remain on the alert. (Wright thought that a double agent had betrayed them.) So Doug Worley's dream *could* just have been some form of telepathy. But in that case how did he know that he would die and that Wilbur Wright would survive to hand over his possessions to his family?

After the war Wilbur Wright began to have his own experiences of telepathy. In 1946, 1948 and 1954 he dreamed the winners of three major horse-races. The dream always took the same form. He was at a race-course – although in fact he had never visited such a place – and some companion was standing beside him. In each dream he asked the companion, 'What won the big race?' and was told the name of the horse. In 1946, for example, it was Airborne. Wright would comment, 'There's

154

no such horse running,' and his companion would reply, 'Well it won anyway.'

After that first dream Wilbur Wright learned that a horse called Airborne *was* running in the St Leger, but the odds were sixty-six to one and no one expected it to win. He mentioned the dream to a few friends on the base, but none of them took him seriously. Not being remotely interested in horse-racing, Wright did not bother to place a bet himself. But when Airborne won there were some dejected faces among his friends. Two years later, when the dream-companion told him that a horse called Arctic Prince would win the Derby, they hastened to place their bets: once again Wilbur Wright did not bother. His friends won a great deal of money – so much that the local booky came to see Wright to ask him where he got the tip.

The next dream occurred in 1954 when Wilbur and his wife were staying with a Mrs Cheesewright in Newark. The same procedure was repeated, but with a minor difference. When he found himself standing on the race-course beside his companion, Wright suddenly realized he was dreaming. He turned to his anonymous friend and said, 'Oh no! Not you again!' Then followed the usual procedure: 'What won the big race?' 'Radar.' 'There's no such horse running.' 'Well it won anyway.' Then Wright woke up. He could remember quite clearly the look of annoyance on the man's face, as if saying that he was 'on duty', just doing his job, and that he wasn't there to be insulted.

It turned out that there was no such horse as Radar, but there was a Nahar running in the Cambridgeshire that day. Mrs Cheesewright was a racing enthusiast and she immediately rang her booky. Wilbur, as usual, did not bother. But Nahar won, and Mrs Cheesewright was obviously well satisfied with her winnings.

This was the last time the dream tipster made an appearance: possibly he was offended by Wright's 'Not *you* again,' with its implied comment that he couldn't imagine why the tipster was wasting his time. And Wilbur Wright has often wondered why the tipster bothered in the first place – announcing winners to someone who wouldn't even take the trouble to place a shilling each way.

Dream winners are by no means a rarity. The present Earl Attlee has described how he had a vivid dream of being at a dog-meeting and suddenly knowing that he held in his hand the winner and second of the Grand National. The ticket contained two numbers. Like Wilbur Wright, Attlee was not a racing enthusiast, and he attached no importance to the dream. On Grand National day he was sitting in the office when he heard someone call out to ask if anyone else wanted to place a bet. He mentioned the two numbers and was told that the names were required. Someone fetched a paper and they looked up the horses who were running under the two numbers. Attlee placed a modest bet on each, and – as his dream had foretold – they came in first and second. In fact he had dreamed the numbers of the winners before the numbers had been allocated.*

*In *I Saw a Ghost*, edited by Ben Noakes (1986).

In 1946 an Oxford student named John Godley, who later became Lord Kilbracken, woke up with the names of two horses running in his head: Bindle and Juladdin. A check on the newspapers revealed that both horses were running – in different races – that day, and Godley made over £100. A few weeks later he dreamed of a winner called Tubermor. The only horse with a similar name was Tuberose, running at Aintree: once again Godley won a respectable sum. Not long after he dreamed that he was ringing his bookmaker to ask for the winner of the last race: he was told it was Monumentor. He discovered that a horse called Mentores was running that afternoon at Worcester, and backed it: again it won. More winners followed in 1947: then he began to dream losers, and stopped backing them. But ten years later he dreamed that the Grand National had been won by a horse called What Man? In fact Mr What won, and Godley was better off by £450. He became the *Daily Mirror*'s racing correspondent on the strength of his fame as a 'psychic punter'.*

Perhaps the most significant case of its kind was that of Peter Fairley, science correspondent for Independent Television. In a radio talk called 'Halfway to the Moon' Fairley described how, in 1965, a virus afflicted him with temporary blindness. One day, in a depressed state, he recollected his experiences of watching the space launches at Cape Kennedy and suddenly thought – with a desperate sincerity – 'If *only* I could help other blind people to understand what it's like.' At that moment the telephone rang. It was someone ringing on behalf of the blind asking him if he would give a talk about space probes.

After this curious synchronicity, extraordinary coincidences began to happen all the time. One day, driving into London through a place called Blakeny, he heard a request on the car radio for a Mrs Blakeny; a few minutes later he heard a reference to another – totally unconnected – Blakeny. At the office he heard the name again; this time it was the name of a horse running in the Derby. He backed it and it won. From then on, he explained, he could pick winners by merely looking down at a list of horses: the winner would 'leap off the page' at him. Asked if he had won a great deal of money in this way, he admitted apologetically, 'Yes.' But as soon as he began to think about it and wonder how it worked, the faculty vanished.

In this case it seems that Fairley somehow activated the faculty by a feeling of sheer desperation and by wishing from the bottom of his heart that he could help the blind. But the first time he was able to pick a winner it was not through a premonition or a dream, but through synchronicities. This is highly significant because it suggests that whatever 'agency' can cause premonitions can also cause synchronicities; in fact in this case, a synchronicity was *intended* to be a form of precognition. The Blakeny experience cannot be dismissed as coincidence because it was followed by full-blown precognitions of winners. In the same programme Fairley described a number of odd synchronicities – too

*The story is told at length in *Mysteries*, pp. 147–9.

long to recount here – which seem to confirm that in his case at any rate, synchronicity became a method by which some 'entity' – or unknown part of his own mind – tried to communicate with him.

Wilbur Wright had two more experiences of dream-precognition. In 1972 he had a clear dream of an airliner crashing on a crowded airfield: the odd thing was that the plane was painted bright red. A few months later he saw the crash on television: it was the Russian Concordski airliner which crashed at the Paris Air Show. Yet although Wright recognized the airliner and the scene, he was puzzled that the airliner was not bright red but the usual silver colour. Then it came to him: the redness was symbolic; the unknown 'dream producer' in his unconscious mind was trying to tell him that the plane was Russian.

Here again the implication is clear. The 'dream producer' was trying to tell him that the airliner was Russian, just as his racing companion had been trying to tell him the names of winners. Again it looks as if we are dealing with May Sinclair's 'intelligent entity', not merely with some accidental precognitive faculty.

Wilbur Wright's other precognitive experience was curiously trivial. He dreamed of standing in jungle underbrush staring down at a large diamond-patterned snake that was flowing past a gap in the bushes: the dream was so vivid that he told his wife about it. That evening, watching a David Attenborough nature programme on television, he saw the diamond-patterned snake flowing across the screen. He and his wife looked at one another and said, 'Snap'.

Both these dreams bring to mind the series of precognitive dreams described by J. W. Dunne in his famous book *An Experiment with Time*, whose publication in 1927 made him an international celebrity. Dunne was an aeronautics engineer who, ever since childhood, had been possessed by the conviction that he would bring an important message to mankind. He proved to be correct. Dunne's book was the first to direct wide attention to 'precognitive dreams'. In his twenties he dreamed that his watch had stopped at half-past four and that a crowd was shouting, 'Look, look!' He woke up and discovered that his watch *had* stopped at half-past four. The next morning he realized that the watch was still showing the right time, so he had awakened at the moment it stopped. The experience convinced him that it was worth paying close attention to his dreams, and he soon noticed that all kinds of minor events – newspaper headlines and suchlike – were clearly foreshadowed in them.

Dunne caused a sensation by suggesting that everybody has precognitive dreams, but that most of us fail to notice them simply because we forget them the moment we open our eyes. He made a habit of keeping a pencil and paper by his bedside and noting down his dreams the moment he awoke. Most of the precognitions were quite trivial: for example, he was reading a book describing a type of combination lock when he recollected that he had dreamed about it the previous night. A more 'important' dream concerned the great volcanic eruption on Martinique in 1902: Dunne dreamed that four thousand people had been killed. When he saw a newspaper headline about the eruption shortly afterwards it stated that forty thousand people had been killed, but Dunne misread it as four thousand and did not discover his mistake for fifteen years. This indicates clearly that his dream of the eruption was, in fact, a precognition of his own experience of reading an account of it in a newspaper, not of the event itself. (In fact the final figure for the dead was between thirty and thirty-five thousand.)

In 1969 Tom Lethbridge (whom we have already met in connection with dowsing) decided to try Dunne's 'experiment with time', and began recording this dreams. His interest in the subject had been awakened five years earlier when a young cameraman named Graham Tidman accompanied a television team to Lethbridge's Devon home. Something in Tidman's manner made Lethbridge ask him if he had been there before. Tidman had – in his dreams. In the garden he was able to say, 'There used to be buildings against the wall.' There had – but many years before. Tidman had dreamed of the place as it had been before his birth. From plans more than half a century old, Lethbridge was able to confirm Tidman's accuracy.

Lethbridge's own experiments soon convinced him that Dunne was correct, and that precognitive dreams are far commoner than we think. (J. B. Priestley reached the same conclusion when he made a public appeal for precognitive dreams and received thousands of replies.) Again they were mostly very minor 'glimpses': the face of an unknown man seen a few hours later; items seen in newspapers the following day. Some of his correspondents had had dreams of catastrophes that had subsequently happened: a hotel fire; the collapse of a block of flats in a gas explosion. But once again it seemed clear that the dreams were of subsequent newspaper or television reports, not of the actual events.

Lethbridge reached the conclusion that there are other 'levels of reality' beyond our material level, and that they exist on higher 'vibrational rates'. Immediately beyond the material level, he suggested, there is a 'timeless zone', in which the future is as real as the present or the past. It is, he thought, possible that the 'spirit' (or 'astral body') passes through this timeless zone immediately after sleep or immediately before waking, and that this explains precognitive dreams.

Dunne's theory is altogether more ambitious. He began by pointing out that when we say time goes quickly or slowly we must be *measuring* it against some other standard, and that this standard must be some other kind of time – he called it Time 2. And presumably there must be another kind of time by which we measure Time 2, and so on ad infinitum. And there are also probably an infinite number of 'me's' who correspond to each level of time.

In fact we tumble into this kind of speculation the moment we admit that time is something more complicated than a simple one-way flow. If *any* kind of precognition is possible then we must be capable of a kind of

158

'time travel'. And time travel also implies that there are an infinite number of 'me's'. For example, if I could travel forward into tomorrow I could presumably encounter 'me' as I shall be in twenty-four hours' time. And I could keep on doing that indefinitely, meeting dozens – or billions – of 'me's'. It was this kind of reasoning that led Dunne to conclude that our human time is in some sense an illusion. In a book called *The New Immortality* he compares human life to a long strip of film that contains everything that happens to us between birth and death. The 'real you' stands opposite that film, able to direct its attention to any part of the film. But along that strip of film there travels an entity he calls 'Observer 1', whose attention is usually taken up entirely with moment-to-moment impressions. If nothing much is happening, however, and he can relax, Observer 1 sometimes catches glimpses of other parts of the film. These are glimpses of the past and precognitions.

Dunne has a particularly poetic section which seems to be the crux of the book, and which was given as a television lecture in 1936. A pianist was told to play the whole keyboard, from bottom to top. That, says Dunne, is what everyday life is like – just 'one damn thing after another'. In sleep the 'pianist' can jump back and forth, hitting keys at random – and creating a horrible cacophony. But after death the 'Observer' can choose what keys he likes and strike them so as to make them into a pleasant little tune or even a piano sonata. (At this point the pianist was instructed to play Mendelssohn's Spring Song and Beethoven's Funeral March.) It is a charming illustration, but still leaves us rather baffled as to Dunne's basic beliefs about time. One point, however, emerges fairly clearly. Human beings, he says, mistake a 'hybrid' form of time for real time. The result is that we feel that life is a disappointing business, which opens with high hopes and sounding trumpets, moves on to frustration after frustration, and ends in a disillusioned crawl into the grave. If we can once grasp 'real time' and the 'real me', we shall realize that everything that is in existence remains in existence. 'A rose which has bloomed once blooms for ever.'

In the last analysis what Dunne seems to be saying is that there is a 'real you' which exists up above time – roughly what the philosopher Husserl meant by the 'transcendental ego'. It occupies a kind of permanent four-dimensional universe and possesses a kind of freedom that is unknown to the physical self.

Now this view certainly seems to echo some of the mystical insights we examined in the second chapter. The *Bhagavad Gita*, for example, says, 'There never was a time when I did not exist, nor you, nor any of these kings. Nor is there any future in which we shall cease to be . . . . That which is non-existent can never come into being, and that which is can never cease to be.' It seems encouraging that Dunne believed he had arrived at these insights through purely scientific reasoning, even though no one I have ever met has succeeded in following his reasoning. But it still seems to leave us with the problem that worried Wilbur Wright. If my life is already 'on film', so to speak, then presumably everything that happens to me is predestined and my feeling of having free will is an illusion?

This was an aspect of Dunne's theory that worried a successful young novelist named John Boynton Priestley who had achieved overnight fame with *The Good Companions* in 1929. When he began writing plays in the early 1930s he made an attempt to dramatize Dunne's theory in a tense little play called *Dangerous Corner*, in which he splits time in two and tries to show what might have happened as well as what did happen. This, and a second 'time play' called *Time and the Conways*, seemed to echo the fatalistic view that our lives are preordained. But by 1937 Priestley had discovered another theory of time in the work of P. D. Ouspensky, whose 'experimental mysticism' was considered in an earlier chapter (p. 40). Ouspensky argued that time, like space, has three dimensions: duration, speed and direction. So time is, so to speak, a cube rather than a straight line. We only see the straight line, because we are stuck in time, so to us it seems inevitable that one event follows another like the notes on a piano keyboard. But if time is a 'cube' and not a line, then its forward flow can go up or down or sideways within a three-dimensional space. And this obviously means that the next point on the line is not rigidly predetermined, for it might be up or down or sideways. Life is full of non-actualized potentialities, says Ouspensky in the 'Eternal Recurrence' chapter of his *New Model of the Universe*, and when it comes to an end it starts all over again, so we go on living the same life forever. (He used this idea in a remarkable novel called *The Strange Life of Ivan Osokin*.) But it does not have to be exactly the same: only dull and lazy people live the same life over and over again. More determined people strive to actualize their potentialities, and although the events are predetermined, they can choose to pour more energy and determination into them. So their lives are changed infinitesimally each time.

In his chapter 'Experimental Mysticism' Ouspensky offers some clues about how these ideas were developed. He speaks of the curious feeling of a 'lengthening of time', so that seconds seem to turn into years or decades. He emphasizes that the normal feeling of time remained as a background to this 'accelerated time', so that he was – so to speak – living in two 'times' at once. Our ordinary time merely has 'duration', but the second time has 'speed'. And since time has a flow from past to future, it would also seem to possess a third dimension – 'direction'.

These experiments also seem to have convinced Ouspensky that the future is, in some sense, predetermined. On one occasion he asked himself whether communication with the dead was a possibility and immediately 'saw' someone with whom he urgently wanted to communicate. But what he 'saw' was not the person but his whole life, in a kind of four-dimensional continuum. At that moment Ouspensky realized that it was pointless to feel guilt about his own failure to be more helpful to this particular person because the events of his life were as unchangeable as the features of his face. 'Nobody could have changed anything in them, just as nobody could have changed the colour of his hair or eyes, or the shape of his nose . . . .' In other words, what happened to the man was his 'destiny'.

It was also during these experiments that Ouspensky had a clear premonition that he would not be going to Moscow that Easter, as he fully intended to. He was able to foresee a sequence of events that would make his visit impossible. And in due course this sequence occurred exactly as he had foreseen it in his mystical state. Ouspensky, therefore, had no doubt that precognition is a reality.

Priestley borrowed Ouspensky's idea for his third 'time play', *I Have Been Here Before*, in which a thoroughly unsatisfactory character who has committed suicide out of self-pity produces a determined effort the 'second time round', and makes an altogether better job of his life.

In his book *On Time*, Dr Michael Shallis, an Oxford don, recounts two personal anecdotes which seem to offer support for Ouspensky's theory. Dr Shallis remembers how, when he was twelve, he came in through the back door of his house and called to his mother, who was upstairs, to say that he was back: as he did so he was overwhelmed by the feeling that this had happened before, and that his mother would call down that they were going to have salad for dinner – which she did. Now this case could be labelled 'doubtful', for it is my own experience that such feelings may be the reactivation of some half-forgotten memory, or perhaps some malfunction in the computer known as the brain, which tells us that an experience is 'familiar' when it is actually not. (His mother's information about the salad could have been coincidence – or perhaps they always had salad on that day of the week.) But Dr Shallis's second case seems altogether odder.

Shallis was giving a tutorial on radioactivity when he was again swamped with the *déja-vu* feeling. He felt that the next thing that 'had' to happen was that he should suggest that he needed a certain book from his office, and then go to fetch it. He decided that he would break the pattern by resisting the urge to go and get the book. Yet even as he made this resolution he heard his voice saying, 'I think I had better show you some examples of this. I will just pop down to my office and get a book.' This certainly seems, on the face of it, an example of the 'predetermination' Ouspensky speaks about.

In fact J. B. Priestley came to accept the Ouspensky theory as altogether more realistic than Dunne's 'serial time'. But he still had some basic reservations. In his book *Man and Time* (1964) he illustrates these with a case borrowed from Dr Louisa Rhine. A mother described a dream in which she was camping with some friends on the shores of a creek. She took her baby down to the creek, intending to wash some clothes. Then she remembered that she had forgotten the soap and went back to the tent, leaving the baby throwing stones into the water. When she came back the baby was lying face down in the creek: she pulled him out and found he was dead.

161

That summer she went camping with some friends, and they chose a spot on the banks of a creek. She decided to do some washing and took her baby down to the water: then she recalled she had forgotten the soap and started back for it. As she did so the baby started to throw stones into the water and her dream flashed into her mind. She realized that everything was exactly as it had been in the dream, even to the baby's clothes. So she picked up the baby and took him back to the tent with her . . . .

Here, clearly, is a case where the 'precognition' enabled her to avert a catastrophe, and it seems to demonstrate clearly that the future is not rigidly determined. And this view could be supported by many other cases, two of which can be found in a classic study of precognition, *The Future is Now* by Arthur W. Osborn. An eldest son was visiting his family who were on holiday in a cottage in Hobart, Tasmania. Before he left to drive back to Kingston his mother warned him that she had had a premonition that he would have an accident on the way home, and to drive carefully. Halfway home the young man remembered his mother's warning and slowed down to twenty-five miles an hour. A few seconds later the car skidded on a patch of ice – the only one on the entire journey – and landed in the ditch after hitting the embankment. The car was badly damaged, but he was unhurt: if he had still been travelling at twice that speed he would have been killed or seriously injured.

In the second incident, a friend of Osborn's – a music master at a public school – was standing behind a pupil who was playing the piano when the music paper seemed to vanish and he saw a portion of the road he would be driving up that afternoon. As he watched a car came round a bend on the wrong side of the road, driving very fast. Then the scene faded and the music paper was restored to normal. That afternoon, approaching the bend, he suddenly recollected his 'vision'. Without even thinking he pulled over to the other side of the road. As he did so a car came round the bend on the wrong side, driving very fast, just as he had 'seen' it.

These cases are puzzling, for they seem to suggest that far from being predetermined, the future can be altered. And since the premonition was the direct cause of the alteration, it looks as if the warning was deliberately given so that the future *could* be altered – which begins to sound very much like May Sinclair's 'intelligent entity'. This seems to suggest two alternative theories: (1) that the future is *not* predetermined, but that it is nevertheless possible for us to catch glimpses of what it holds. This sounds so self-contradictory that it suggests the alternative theory (2) that the future *is*, to some extent, predetermined, but that it can be changed by deliberate effort on the part of human beings.

There is, however, a third possibility, which can best be illustrated by a famous story. This also concerns Air Marshal Goddard, who caught his strange glimpse of Drem airfield in the future. In 1946 Sir Victor Goddard was attending a party given in his honour in Shanghai. He was talking to some friends when he overheard someone behind him announcing that he – Goddard – was dead. He turned round and found himself looking into the face of a British naval commander, Captain Gerald Gladstone. Gladstone immediately recognized him, and looked appalled. 'I'm terribly sorry! I do apologize!' 'But what made you think I was dead?' 'I dreamt it.'

Gladstone went on to describe his dream. He had seen the crash of a transport passenger plane, perhaps a Dakota, on a rocky coast: it had been driven down by a terrible snowstorm. In addition to its RAF crew the plane also carried three civilians, two men and a women: they had emerged from the plane, but Air Marshal Goddard had not. Gladstone had awakened with a strong conviction that Goddard was dead, and throughout that day he expected to hear the news.

Goddard was not too worried: he *was* due to fly to Tokyo in a Dakota, but there would be no civilians on board. He and Gladstone spent a pleasant half hour or so discussing Dunne's theory of time. But during dinner there were alarming developments. A *Daily Telegraph* journalist asked if he could beg a lift to Japan. Then the Consul General told Goddard that he had received orders to return to Tokyo immediately and asked if he could travel too; he also asked if they could find room for a female secretary. With deep misgivings, Goddard agreed. And when the plane took off from Shanghai, he personally had no doubt whatever that he was about to die.

The Dakota was caught in heavy cloud over mountains – another detail Captain Gladstone had 'seen' – then ran into a fierce snowstorm. Finally the pilot was forced to crash-land on the rocky coastline of an island off the shore of Japan. But Gladstone proved to be mistaken about Goddard's death: everyone on board survived.

We can see that in this case, Gladstone's premonition made no practical difference to Goddard: there was nothing he could *do*, short of refusing to go to Tokyo. So, unlike the 'dreamers' in the earlier anecdotes, he was unable to take evasive action. Yet Gladstone's premonition of his death was unfulfilled. The logical conclusion seems to be that the future is to some extent predetermined, but not rigidly so. Perhaps the very fact that Goddard knew – or thought he knew – about the crash somehow altered the course of events so that the fatal accident did not take place.

This is, of course, a conclusion that human beings find extremely disturbing. The very thought of predetermination is enough to arouse the suspicion, which we feel in our worst moments, that life is no more than a dream. Yet this is, in a sense, absurd. We accept *spatial* 'predetermination' every day without feeling worried by it. On the contrary I would feel very uneasy if I didn't know whether the next bus would take me to Picadilly or Pontefract. Moreover I recognize that spatial predetermination makes no difference to my free will: I can *choose* whether to go north, south, east or west.

163

But are we not talking about something totally different? Time is quite different from space, in the sense that something that has not yet happened is *not* predetermined – something quite different may happen. But a moment's thought shows us that this is also untrue. Astronomers can predict the movements of stars for centuries ahead, and if they had sufficient knowledge could do so for millions of years. As I now look out of the window I can see the wind blowing washing on the line and also swaying the syringa bush. To me, the next movement of the bush or the clothes seems purely a matter of chance: in fact they are just as predetermined as the movements of the stars – as the weatherman could tell you. What *is* true is that living beings introduce an element of genuine chance into the picture: my wife may decide to water the garden instead of hanging out the washing. But the bushes, although alive, can introduce very little chance into the picture. Moreover even free will can be described in terms of statistics. The sociologist Durkheim was surprised to discover that it is possible to predict the suicide rate with considerable precision. This seems to imply that with sufficiently detailed knowledge, we could predict exactly who will kill himself next year. This is not quite true, of course, for human beings possess some degree of free will: yet it serves to remind us that in a basic sense, time is just as 'predetermined' as space.

To some readers this may seem to be an extremely gloomy picture. But if we grasp its true meaning we shall see that the contrary is true. In *The Man Who Was Thursday*, the anarchist poet Gregory talks about the delights of chaos:

> Why do all the clerks and navvies in the railway trains look so sad and tired . . . ? It is because they know that whatever place they have taken a ticket for that place they will reach. It is because after they have passed Sloane Square they know that the next station must be Victoria, and nothing but Victoria. Oh, their wild rapture! Oh, their eyes like stars and their souls again in Eden, if the next station were unaccountably Baker Street!

But Gregory's opponent rejects this.

> The rare, strange thing is to hit the mark; the gross, obvious thing is to miss it. We feel it epical when man with one wild arrow strikes a distant bird. Is it not also epical when man with one wild engine strikes a distant station? Chaos is dull; because in chaos the train might indeed go anywhere, to Baker Street or Baghdad. But man is a magician, and his whole magic is this, that he does say Victoria, and lo! it is Victoria.

This is obviously true: the fact that there are laws of nature – and railway timetables – means that we can become masters of the chaos that surrounds us. When we are tired and discouraged, laws may seem an obstacle; when

164

we are feeling excited and optimistic, we see that what matters is not the law but our freedom to take advantage of it.

Now where 'predetermination' is concerned, the real problem is that there are no timetables to tell me what will be happening next week so that I can avoid being in a place where there will be an earthquake or a hurricane. Yet even this is not a rigid law for, as we have seen, people are always foreseeing the future with an accuracy that leaves no doubt that in addition to powers of dowsing, telepathy, psychometry and clairvoyance, human beings also possess remarkable powers of precognition.

In April 1912 a man named J. Connon Middleton dreamed for two nights running of a ship floating keel upwards, with passengers swimming frantically around. He was deeply concerned, since in ten days' time he was due to sail to New York on the *Titanic* for a business conference. But he felt unable to cancel his trip on account of a mere dream, and was greatly relieved when the conference was cancelled a week before he was due to sail. A marine engineer named Colin Macdonald also had strong premonitions of disaster about the *Titanic* and declined three increasingly tempting offers to sign on as its second engineer. The engineer who took the job was drowned when the *Titanic* went down on 14 April 1912.

The newspaper editor W. T. Stead was less sensible. He was interested in 'the occult', and had been warned by two fortune-tellers that he would meet his death on a ship sailing to America. He even wrote a story about an ocean liner that sank because it did not have enough boats, and concluded with the words, 'This is exactly what might take place, and what will take place, if liners are sent to sea short of boats.' But Stead was one of those who drowned because the *Titanic* did not have enough lifeboats.

But the most remarkable example of apparent precognition of the sinking of the *Titanic* occurred fourteen years earlier. In 1898 an American writer named Morgan Robertson wrote a novel called *The Wreck of the Titan* about a giant 'unsinkable' liner that struck an iceberg and sank – just as the *Titanic* did. His *Titan* was 70,000 tons; the *Titanic* was 66,000. Both were triple-screw vessels capable of 25 knots. The *Titan* had 24 lifeboats; the *Titanic* had 20. Both ships were on their maiden voyages from Southampton to New York. Morgan Robertson was a peculiar writer in that his creative activities were semi-automatic. He felt himself to be the tool of some other writer who 'took over' when he felt inclined: at other times he was incapable of writing a line. During these 'dry periods' he could only wait until his invisible companion chose to manifest himself. It seems a logical conclusion that *The Wreck of the Titan* was a genuine piece of precognition rather than a 'coincidence'.

Jung would prefer, of course, to call it a synchronicity, and in the practical sense it obviously makes no difference which we choose to call it. For it is surely obvious by this time that we are speaking about the same thing. We could say that when Rebecca West reached out and found the Nuremberg trial she wanted she was exercising a kind of clairvoyance with respect to space; when she opened Gounod's memoirs and saw a reference to Delpeche – about whom she had been speaking *before* she ordered the book – she was exercising a kind of clairvoyance with respect to time. And if this is correct then we could regard synchronicity, far from being a proof of predetermination, as a proof of human free will. It is as if our 'other self' (or 'unknown guest' as Maeterlinck preferred to call it) had a railway timetable of future events and so could engineer 'significant coincidences'.

Some recent discoveries about identical twins seem to reinforce this argument. They were made in the late 1970s by an English social worker named John Stroud. In 1979 he was approached by a thiry-nine-year-old woman from Dover, Barbara Herbert, who was searching for her twin sister. Their mother, a Finnish student in London, had abandoned them at the beginning of the Second World War and they had been separately adopted. Barbara discovered her true identity when she applied for a copy of her birth certificate to join a pension scheme. She wrote to a Finnish newspaper, and eventually learned that her mother had committed suicide in 1943. With John Stroud's help she traced the midwife who had delivered her and even took the registrar general to court in an attempt to learn who had adopted her sister. Eventually she learned that her twin was called Daphne Goodship and that she lived in Wakefield, Yorkshire. Daphne agreed to come to King's Cross station to meet her twin. When they finally met, both were wearing a beige dress and a brown velvet jacket. And this proved to be only the first of an astonishing series of coincidences. Both were local government workers, as were their husbands; both had met their husbands at a dance at the age of sixteen and married in their early twenties in the autumn – elaborate weddings with choirs; both had suffered miscarriages with their first baby, then had two boys followed by a girl; both had fallen downstairs at the age of fifteen and both had weak ankles as a consequence; both had been girl guides; both had taken lessons in ballroom dancing; both had lived in Silchester; both read a particular woman's magazine and had the same favourite authors . . . . Altogether John Stroud listed thirty coincidences. Some could be explained by the fact that they *were* identical twins – fear of heights, physical mannerisms, dislike of the sight of blood, food preferences. But accidents like falling downstairs or miscarriages could hardly be explained in terms of their genes.

By a coincidence that seems typical in such matters, the subject of identical twins had become a subject of national attention in America at the same time, when identical male twins appeared on the Johnny Carson chat show and told their incredible stories. When Jim Lewis, of Lima, Ohio, was nine years old he learned that he had an identical twin who had been adopted at birth. Thirty years later – at exactly the same age as Barbara Herbert – he decided to see if he could find him. Unlike British courts, American courts are inclined to be helpful in such cases, and Jim

166

Lewis soon learned that his twin was called Jim Springer and lived in Dayton, Ohio. And as soon as they met they discovered a string of the same kind of preposterous coincidences that had amazed Barbara and Daphne. Both had married a girl called Linda, then divorced and married a girl called Betty; both had called their sons James Allan, although Jim Lewis spelt Alan with only one l; both had owned dogs named Toy; both had worked part time as deputy sheriffs; both had worked for the McDonald's hamburger chain; both had been filling-station attendants; both spent their holidays at the same seaside resort in Florida and used the same beach – a mere 300 yards long; both drove to their holidays in a Chevrolet; both had a tree in the garden with a white bench around it; both had basement workshops in which they built frames and furniture; both had had vasectomies; both drank the same beer and chain-smoked the same cigarettes; both had put on ten pounds at the same point in their teens, and lost it again; both enjoyed stock-car racing and disliked baseball.

Their case was written up in *Science*, the journal of the American Association for the Advancement of Science. And a psychologist named Tim Bouchard, who had been studying twins at the University of Minnesota, was so interested that he raised a grant to study identical twins who had been separated at birth. John Stroud soon heard about his researches, and some of his identical twins were quickly on their way to America. (Typically, John Stroud and Tim Bouchard soon acquired the same number of identical twins to study – sixteen pairs.) Professor Bouchard quickly realized that the coincidences in the lives of the 'Jim twins' were, so to speak, no coincidence. Where twins were concerned, coincidences were the rule rather than the exception. Terry Connolly and Margaret Richardson had married on the same day of the same year within an hour of each other; both had four children who were conceived and born at roughly the same time; both had intended to name their first daughters Ruth but had changed their minds. Two other twins, Dorothy Lowe and Bridget Hamilton, had kept a diary for one year, and had filled in exactly the same days. Male twins Oscar Stohr and Jack Yufe had been taken off in opposite directions by their parents, and while Jack had been brought up an orthodox Jew in America, Oscar had gone to Germany and become a member of the Hitler Youth. When they met at the airport in 1979 both were wearing square wire-rimmed glasses, blue shirts with epaulettes and identical moustaches; both flushed the lavatory before and after using it, stored rubber bands on their wrists and had identical speech rhythms, although one spoke English and the other German. In England, John Stroud brought together Eric Boocock and Tommy Marriott, who were both wearing square wire-rimmed glasses and goatee beards and who both worked as charge hands in Yorkshire factories. He also noted that coincidences continued to pursue Barbara Herbert and Daphne Goodship who, although they were living at opposite ends of the country, often bought the same book at the same time and changed the colour of their hair at the same time without consulting one another.

What can we make of such preposterous coincidences? Obviously there is nothing surprising in discovering that identical twins have the same health problems, the same tastes in clothes and the same speech rhythms. After all, identical (or monozygotic – MZ for short) twins are formed by the splitting of the same ovum and therefore have identical genes. So we have no trouble accepting that Jeanette Hamilton and Irene Read discovered that they both suffered from claustrophobia and dislike of water, both sat with their backs to the sea on beaches, both got a pain in the same spot in their right legs in wet weather, and were both compulsive calculators. But coincidences involving the same jobs, the same dates and the same towns are obviously impossible to explain genetically. Even the assumption that MZ twins remain in telepathic contact fails to explain how they could fall downstairs at the same time or both have miscarriages. All this sounds more like Charles Fort's 'cosmic joker'.

But if we can accept the logical consequences of precognition it becomes altogether less difficult to understand. As we have seen, precognition at first seems to suggest that our lives are rigidly predetermined, like a film. But some precognitions enable their subjects to *change* the future, like the music teacher who avoided a head-on collision or the young man who slowed down just before a patch of ice. (In that case, we may presume that Wilbur Wright's friend Doug Worley made a fatal mistake in not accepting the squadron leader's suggestion that he stand down for the day.) So the future cannot be *that* rigidly predetermined.

But once we begin to think about this matter, we can see that life *is* far more predetermined than we realize. Human beings undoubtedly possess free will – for, as William James pointed out, we can decide to *think* one thing rather than another. But even so we habitually overestimate the amount of free will we normally exercise. If we carefully observe ourselves, we realize how many of our actions are merely responses to the things that go on around us. The Russian philosopher Gurdjieff insisted that human beings are 'machines' whose ordinary state of consciousness is a form of sleep. His disciple Ouspensky was suddenly struck by the truth of this when, at the beginning of the First World War, he saw military lorries loaded up with crutches – crutches for limbs that were not yet blown off.

In short, the world of matter is rigidly predetermined; every earthquake, every avalanche, every hurricane, is already scheduled in some 'railway timetable' of the future. Of course, some natural disasters are 'man made', but if we examine these with an open mind we shall have to admit that human free will plays very little part in them: for the most part, we are merely reacting to circumstances. And once we recognize that human free will operates on an extremely small scale, inside our own heads, we also recognize that our lives are far more 'predetermined' than we care to admit. The curious enigma of the identical twins underlines that point. The 'Jim twins' must have felt that it was entirely a matter off personal choice that they had married girls called Linda, then girls called Betty, that they called their sons James Allan and James Alan and their dogs Toy. Barbara Herbert and Daphne Goodship must have felt the same about falling in love at sixteen, getting married, planning a family and so on. But the whole matter of extraordinary coincidences in the case of MZ twins suggests that the things that happen to them are as 'inevitable' as their genetically inherited health problems.

Schopenhauer would certainly accept such an admission as evidence that human life is a shadow-play of illusion. But he would be missing the point: what matters is not the extent to which our lives are predetermined, but the extent to which we can exercise freedom of choice. As I walk down a crowded city street my freedom is limited in a thousand ways. I have to avoid bumping into people, avoid traffic as I cross the street, avoid twisting my ankle on uneven pavements, avoid banging my head on scaffolding . . . . If I also happen to be tired and hungry then I may well feel that I am a 'plaything of the gods', a creature of circumstance. But for the most part I cope with all these limitations perfectly well and go about my business with an unshaken conviction that I possess freedom of choice. And for the most part, I am correct. Freedom depends upon how much I choose to 'put into' life.

This becomes perfectly obvious if we consider 'positive' precognitions – precognition of some desirable event. The wife of Arthur W. Osborn, the author of *The Future is Now*, tells of her first glimpse of her future husband:

> I had written a paper on Robert Browning, but as I was recovering from an illness I arranged for someone else to read it. The paper was read in a moderately large hall to an audience of about 300 persons. I sat at the back of the hall.
>
> After the lecture questions were requested, and several people asked them. But there was one man sitting near the front who asked a rather critical question and tended to challenge my authority for a certain statement I had made. I could only see the man's back, but I felt a sense of personal significance as between him and myself, though he was a complete stranger to me. It was of a joyous nature in spite of the extreme embarrassment his question was causing me. I have always regarded the experience as one of recognition. I just *knew* him. It would not have mattered who or what he was – the relationship was there. I learned later that this man had only that day arrived from England on his first visit to Australia.

We might object that this was not a case of true precognition. Although she could not see her future husband's face, Mrs Osborn may well have found his voice attractive and recognized instinctively that he was 'her type'. But the same objection cannot be raised against an example cited by J. B. Priestley:

Dr A. had begun to receive official reports from Mrs B., who was in charge of one branch of a large department. These were not personal letters signed by Mrs B., but the usual duplicated official documents. Dr A. did not know Mrs B., had never seen her, knew nothing about her except that she had this particular job. Nevertheless, he felt a growing excitement as he received more and more of these communications from Mrs B. This was so obvious that his secretary made some comment on it.

A year later he had met Mrs B. and fallen in love with her. They are now most happily married. He believes – and so do I after hearing his story – that he felt this strange excitement because the future relationship communicated it to him; we might say that one part of his mind, not accessible to consciousness except as a queer feeling, already knew that Mrs B. was to be tremendously important to him.

Priestley cites this case in *Man and Time*. In a later book he admitted that he himself was Dr A. Mrs B. was his future wife Jacquetta Hawkes, who was Archaeological Adviser for the Festival of Britain, in which Priestley was also involved (even to the extent of writing a novel about it). If Priestley is being entirely accurate, he had no reason whatever to feel excitement at receiving duplicated letters from Jacquetta Hawkes, and it sounds like a genuine case of 'positive precognition'. And it is very clear that any sense of 'predestination' that Priestley experienced was a feeling of pleasurable anticipation rather than of trapped inevitability.

The same applies to another case cited by Priestley, of a man who experienced an odd feeling of anticipation whenever he passed a certain cottage on the bus; he had no idea of who lived there but felt that there was somehow a connection between himself and the cottage. Later he met and married the woman who lived there, and it was she who rescued him from periodic nervous breakdowns.

Priestley calls these cases of FIP – the Future Influencing the Present, and at first it is not clear what he means by this, or why he bothers to distinguish it from ordinary precognition. But his meaning becomes very clear when he mentions a case of a man who suffered periodic attacks of nausea and vomiting. During these attacks he would lie in a darkened room with a blinding headache. Towards the end of each attack he experienced a succession of brilliant colours – reds, blues, greens and purples. Then they would all seem to fly apart, and he would vomit. After this he would recover. Years later, in the Second World War, the man was in Malaya, and as Japanese fighters machine gunned their convoy he made a dive for a small ravine. A bomb exploded and the world burst into jagged splinters of red, blue, green and purple: then he was violently sick. The attacks of nausea and vomiting ceased from that moment on.

Priestley is convinced that 'the explosion, so to speak, went in two different Time directions', the future and the past. And its effect was so powerful that it influenced the man's past self.

Now all this sounds very convincing – and quite incomprehensible. In our universe, light cannot go backwards into the past. Besides, if the future can influence the past in this way, then we find ourselves facing all the paradoxes we considered earlier – of a 'multiple universe' in which there are millions of 'parallel times'. For if the event has *already* taken place while it is still several years in the future, then it must have taken place in a parallel universe . . . .

The sensible alternative here is surely the one we have already considered: that the explosion was, so to speak, listed in the timetable for the future, but that, like a train, it may not run on time. And in that case, precognition is simply another form of the faculty we call extra-sensory perception or clairvoyance – the faculty that warned tiger-hunter Jim Corbett that a man-eater was lying in wait for him. It may even be the same as the faculty that enables calculating prodigies to decide that some vast twenty-digit number is a prime when even a computer could not do it in the same time; the same faculty that enabled Robert Graves's schoolfriend to 'see' the answer to a difficult mathematical problem at a single glance. If this is true then we have to make the assumption that the future is a great deal more 'fixed' than we would like to believe. But at least it provides us with a sensible and logical explanation of precognition.

A further case from Priestley's archives reinforces the argument. A woman correspondent told him how, during Matins in St Martins-in-the-Fields, she began to cry uncontrollably, but with no idea of what was upsetting her. Two days later, as she travelled home by train, it happened again. And as she got off the train and was met by her husband and son she suddenly knew that her sense of foreboding was related to her son. Three weeks later he became ill, and died within a few months.

The same mother tells how, during her son's illness, he suddenly remarked, 'A dog is going to bark a long way off.' A few seconds later she heard the faint bark of a dog. Then he said, 'Something is going to be dropped in the kitchen and the middle door is going to slam.' Within seconds both things had happened. When she told the doctor about it he said that he had known of this happening before, and that her son's brain was working 'just ahead of time'.

Now in the case of this woman's two 'precognitions' of her son's death, it is significant that she was sitting quietly – on the first occasion in a church, on the second in a train. Her subconscious 'computer' had a chance to scan the future and became aware of the tragedy in store for her. It was not that the tragedy had already taken place in some parallel universe or some other time dimension. And the case of the barking dog and the slamming door reinforces this interpretation. As 'precognitions' they are pointless: it can make no possible difference to know that a dog will bark in a moment or that the door will slam. On the other hand we can also see that there is a more 'scientific' explanation. When the dog barked in the distance – say, a couple of miles away – its sound waves

171

took about ten seconds to reach the bedroom. (Sound travels at about twelve miles a minute.) So the dog had already barked when the boy made the prediction. Now this cannot be true of the door slamming below – the sound would have reached him almost instantaneously. Yet we can easily conceive that the same 'superconscious computer' that enabled him to 'hear' the dog before its sound reached his bedroom also anticipated the slamming of the door.

The 'super-computer' theory has its drawbacks, yet it is the only realistic alternative to the 'serial universe' theory. This theory, as we have seen, is the notion that, in some sense, all future events have already taken place. And since they have obviously not taken place in *our* universe, we have to assume the existence of 'parallel universes' or parallel times. Dunne landed himself in this intellectual cul de sac, with an infinite number of times – Time 1, Time 2 and so on – and an infinite number of selves. J. B. Priestley pointed out sensibly that we do not need an infinite number of selves to explain our experience of time: three is enough. First there is the 'me' who merely observes the world – who gazes blankly out of a window. If I become suddenly interested in something that is going on, a second 'me' comes into existence, the self-aware 'me'. And since I can also observe that change from 'me-gazing-blankly' to 'me-gazing-intently', there must be a third 'me', a kind of eternal observer who looks on the world with cool detachment.

We have already encountered a very similar notion at the end of chapter 4, when discussing the 'three value systems': physical, emotional and intellectual. And we can immediately see that these three 'systems' correspond closely to Priestley's three selves. The 'me-gazing-blankly' is the 'me' that confronts the world when I awaken from a deep sleep or when I am so tired that I am incapable of thought: the 'physical me'. The 'me' that proceeds to take an active interest in the world around me is the 'me' that experiences desires, the emotional self. (For example, the stimulus that arouses a cat into a state of attention may be a movement that indicates a mouse or a bird: in the case of a man, it may be the sight of a pretty girl.) The 'me' that observes the world with detachment is the intellectual self. (It may be worth mentioning, in passing, that Rudolf Steiner made a similar three-fold distinction. The consciousness of plants is purely physical, and would be regarded by human beings as a form of sleep. Animal consciousness involves desires and hopes and fears – in short, emotions. Only man, according to Steiner, possesses *self-awareness*, the ability to look on his body and emotions with detachment.)

So in rejecting Dunne's 'infinite selves' theory in favour of Priestley's more sensible 'three selves', we have also rejected the view that future events have already taken place – that our lives are some kind of movie that has already been made. Instead we recognize that the future is fairly rigidly predetermined but not absolutely so, and that human beings have a certain limited power to alter it. But since most human beings

172

habitually follow the path of least resistance, most lives are, to all intents and purposes, predetermined.

What then follows is a simple extension of the 'information universe' theory of chapter 5. Psychometry *seems* to indicate that everything that has ever happened is somehow 'on record' and is accessible to some remarkable faculty possessed by human beings: the 'hidden power'. We can see that this in itself seems to suggest some kind of super-computer. A piece of film only has to record one set of events. A meteorite or a stone from Cicero's villa would be like a billion photographs superimposed on one another, yet the 'super-computer' of a psychic seems to be able to disentangle them. Our theory of precognition merely demands that the same super-computer should be able to make a highly sophisticated set of predictions. The main thing a computer needs to make predictions is sufficient information about the present state of affairs. Psychometry appears to indicate that the super-computer of the 'hidden self' has – potentially – the whole past of the universe at its disposal.

Its problem is then how to convey its 'predictions' to the 'everyday self'. And here the main problem is obvious: we are simply too preoccupied with our immediate concerns. Everyday life demands a fairly constant state of alertness, and this prevents us from paying attention to the still small voice of the other self. Which explains why so many 'intrusions' seem to occur when people are in a state of relaxation, or hypnagogia, or even dreaming.

Wilbur Wright, whom we met at the beginning of this chapter, was understandably obsessed by this problem of dream precognition and in the early 1980s decided to undertake the kind of exhaustive study of parapsychology and modern physics that might provide him with the answer. The results of his study challenge comparison with Dunne and Ouspensky and establish him as one of the major time-theorists of the twentieth century.* He writes:

> I was obliged to recognize that events yet to happen, of which we gain knowledge by paranormal means, must, *per se*, have existence in some domain outside our three-dimensional universe.
>
> What sort of universe, I wondered, could accommodate a Time mechanism in which events existed permanently in potential, but were activated only when matter in motion integral with the advancing Present Moment coincided with their spatial location? And given such Fixed Time Events, how was it possible for a facet of our human subconscious to view them?

Wright underlines his point by citing the case of Robert Morris snr, an American agent for a Liverpool shipping firm, whose son, Robert Morris jnr, was one of the framers of the American Constitution. The story of his

*I am deeply indebted to Wilbur Wright for allowing me to quote from his so-far unpublished work *Immortality and the I Ching*.

father's peculiar death is told in the biography of Morris jnr. On the night before the arrival of a ship in the harbour of Oxford, Maryland, Morris snr dreamed that he received a mortal wound from a salvo fired in his honour. But when he told Captain Mathews of the *Liverpool* that he had decided not to come on board, the captain accused him of superstition. Morris replied that his family was reputed to have the gift of precognition. So the captain assured him that no salute would be fired. However, when Morris was enjoying the party on board, the captain told him that the crew felt upset at not firing the customary salute. Morris replied, 'Very well, but do not fire until I or someone else gives the signal.' In due course Mathews accompanied Morris in the boat that was to row him ashore. A fly settled on his nose, and he brushed it off. The gunner, thinking this was the signal he was waiting for, fired the salute. The wadding from one of the guns struck Morris's elbow, breaking the bone: a few days later, he died of the infection.*

The story seems to add support to the case of Doug Worley who, you will recall, was convinced that he was due to die whatever he did. Yet as Wilbur Wright points out, such a view involves us in contradictions. Morris did his best to avoid his death: were these attempts also part of his fate? Was his precognitive dream also predetermined?

Wilbur Wright's solution is that there must be 'a series of versions of each individual event, differing only in detail while preserving the main ambient flow of the events.... All future human events, we can postulate, exist as possibilities ...' unlike the future of the heavenly bodies, which is routinely predictable. And since any future possibility will either be advantageous or inimical to us, we could say that our problem is to decide which to choose. The *I Ching*, Wright points out, could be regarded as a binary computer whose purpose is to decide which of two possibilities we should choose: in other words a kind of do-it-yourself 'timetable of the future'. He then goes on to suggest, like Ouspensky, that time has three dimensions, of which we are aware of only one: duration. These three dimensions constitute what he calls the 'Fixed Time Field'. He believes that a 'migratory' aspect of our minds can catch glimpses of this 'Fixed Time Field' in the same way that an astronaut can look down on both sides of the earth at once.

In fact most writers on time, from Dunne onward, have tried to solve the mystery by evoking the notion of other 'dimensions', with which they usually associate the name of Einstein, with his four-dimensional 'space-time continuum'. Wilbur Wright points out that if we could see the sun from this four-dimensional point of view it would look like a golden cylinder stretching through space, rather like those photographs of a horse in motion which show a whole series of overlapping horses.

There is a great deal to be said for this theory of other dimensions. At the very least it helps us to break some of our bad old habits of thinking. There is an astonishing experiment in modern physics that helps to

*See Herbert B. Greenhouse, *Premonitions: A Leap into the Future*.

underline the point. Human beings are accustomed to the fact that if they turn round through 360° (through a full circle) they find themselves facing in the direction they started from. Not so an electron. By passing it through a certain kind of magnetic field its 'axis of spin' can be tipped through 360°, which ought to restore it to its original position. But it doesn't. The electron has to be turned through yet *another* full circle before it behaves as it did before. We cannot distinguish the difference between the two circles: the electron can. Which seems to suggest that in the sub-atomic world, a 'full circle' is not 360°, but 720°. In our world we have somehow lost half the degrees we ought to have. Or to put it another way, there may be another dimension in the sub-atomic world.

And while we are speaking of physics, this may be the place to mention another paradox: the fact that electrons behave like practical jokers with a warped sense of humour. And this could offer an important key to the whole field of the paranormal. If I shine a beam of light through a pinhole it will form a circle on a screen (or photographic plate). If two pinholes are opened up side by side the result – as you might expect – is two overlapping circles of light. But on the overlapping portions there are a number of dark lines. These are due to the 'interference' of the two beams – the same effect you would get if two fast streams of traffic shot out on to the same roundabout. Now suppose the beam is dimmed so that only one photon at a time can pass through either of the holes. When the image finally builds up on the photographic plate you would expect the interference bands to disappear. Instead they are there as usual. But how can one photon at a time interfere with itself? And how does a photon flying through one hole 'know' that the other hole is open? Could it possess telepathy, as Einstein jokingly suggested . . . ? Perhaps the photon splits and goes through both holes? But a photon detector reveals this is not so; only one photon at a time goes through one hole at a time. Yet, oddly enough, as soon as we begin to 'watch' the photons, they cease to 'interfere' and the dark bands vanish. The likeliest explanation is that the photon is behaving like a wave when it is unobserved, and so goes through both holes and interferes. The moment we try to watch it, it turns into a hard ball. Of course we know that this is because our photon detector affects the photon itself: you cannot literally 'see' something as small as a photon but have to detect its presence by making it collide with something else and cause a flash. The odd thing is that this apparently makes it curl up into a ball like a hedgehog. Wilbur Wright even suggested that the photon behaves as if it is alive. The physicist Neils Bohr did not go that far: he merely said that we should regard photons and electrons as 'waves of probability'.

It may seem that the particle's odd behaviour is simply due to the clumsiness of our experimental methods, which could be compared to trying to pick your teeth with a broom handle. But according to Bohr this is not so: the 'uncertainty' is inherent in the very nature of these sub-atomic levels. And it is certainly true that electrons seem to behave in a wildly unpredictable manner. At one point physicists thought that they might be able to pin the electron down a little more precisely by measuring the direction of its spin – for, like the earth, electrons seem to spin on an axis. The experimenter had to begin by setting up a 'reference direction' to measure it by – just as, if you were about to set up a signpost at a crossroads, you would need to know the direction of at least one of the places it pointed to. He chose an electric field. And he discovered that the spin seemed to point exactly along the line of the field. No matter how many times the direction was changed, the electron changed too.

Electrons show the same unpredictability if they are fired at a barrier – an electric field or an array of atoms. Sometimes electrons with more than enough force to break through the barrier bounce off it; sometimes electrons without enough force go straight through it. They seem to behave according to how they feel at the moment. It begins to look as if Nature is indulging in a leg-pull. It seems to be saying, 'I decline to pander to your conceited view that reason can explain everything. When you look at the night sky you are confronted by the mystery of where space ends. And when you look inside the atom you are confronted by another insoluble mystery, to which I flatly refuse to yield the answer.'

Einstein grew very irritable about this casual behaviour of the electron – particularly about what Heisenberg called 'the uncertainty principle', which means simply that you cannot measure both the speed and the position of an electron. 'God does not play dice,' said Einstein indignantly. And he and two colleagues called Rosen and Podolsky thought up an experiment conclusively to disprove the uncertainty principle. Let us, they said, shoot two electrons at one another so they fly apart at the speed of light in opposite directions. What is to stop us from measuring the speed of one and the position of the other? And since they are behaving as mirror-images of one another, we should then be able to establish both the speed and position of the same electron.

We have already mentioned – on p. 174 – the astonishing experiments that revealed that Einstein was wrong. They were performed at Berkeley in 1974 by Stuart Freedom and John Clauser, and in the early 1980s, with much more precision, by Alain Aspect at the University of Paris. They showed, in effect, that the particles *were* 'telepathic', and that no matter how far they flew apart, an alteration in the direction of one would cause a similar alteration in the direction of the other, thus confirming a theorem known as Bell's Inequality.

The result of all this is that in experiments involving quanta of energy, the scientist can never actually pin down the particle he is interested in. He knows where it is when it leaves his electron gun and where it is when it hits a screen at the other end of the apparatus, but in between there is only a haze of probability that *cannot*, by the very nature of things, be resolved into something more definite. Niels Bohr compared it to a huge, smoky dragon whose tail is in the mouth of the apparatus and

176

whose head is at the other end of the laboratory, but whose body is merely a kind of shimmering cloud.

Some modern physicists have even gone so far as to say that we help to *create* the particle by observing it. And one of them, John Wheeler, has gone even further and suggested that perhaps we play some role in creating the universe itself. (He calls it 'the participatory anthropic principle', and we shall consider it in the last chapter of this book.) Oddly enough it was this same John Wheeler who caused a stir at a meeting of the American Association for the Advancement of Science in 1979 by demanding that the paranormal researchers – whom he called 'pseudos' – should be 'driven out of the workshop of science'. Yet it can be seen that his suggestion about the mind helping to 'create' the universe is in accord with the Jungian notion of synchronicity – that is, the idea that our minds somehow *interact* with the universe to cause apparently preposterous coincidences and other anomalies.

We can underline the point by an illustration used by Dr Danah Zohar in her book on precognition, *Through the Time Barrier*. To explain Bell's inequality theorem, she asks us to imagine identical twins who have not met since birth, one living in London and the other in New York. If Einstein were told that each of them had been injured playing football at the age of sixteen and smashed his car at twenty-five, he might suspect that there was some unknown connection between them. Bell has suggested, in effect, pushing one twin downstairs in London to see whether the New York twin would also fall downstairs. In fact Aspect's particle experiments show that there *is* such a connection between identical-twin electrons. And we have already seen that there is evidence for some equally odd connection between identical-twin humans. So the odd coincidences that seem to befall identical twins may not be, after all, a violation of the laws of common sense, but simply the expression of some basic law of nature.

This digression on physics is, for the time being at least, at an end, and we can ask, 'How far does it help us to *understand* paranormal events?' In the sense of providing some exact and logical explanation, hardly at all. Yet it begins to show us a glimmering of light in the darkness. Consider, for example, the following curious case of 'time-retrocognition'.

In the summer of 1954 a couple who prefer to be known as Mr and Mrs Allan set out for a day in the country. Both had been overworking recently, and they badly needed a break. They woke up feeling oddly depressed, although neither mentioned this to the other. They took a bus in Dorking, but went past their stop and alighted at Wotton Hatch, near the village of Wotton, birthplace of diarist John Evelyn. Instead of walking back they decided to go and look at the Evelyn family church. And when they finally came out of the churchyard they turned right and found themselves facing an overgrown path with high bushes on either side. It led uphill to a clearing with a wooden seat. There they had a view over the valley, and they decided to sit down and eat their sandwiches.

They could hear the sound of a dog barking, and someone chopping wood. But Mrs Allan felt oddly uneasy.

Suddenly a silence descended and the birdsong ceased. Mrs Allan was overcome by a sense of foreboding and went icy cold. At that moment she became aware that three men had entered the clearing behind her: although she had her back to them she could 'see' them quite clearly. All three wore what looked like clerical garb. The man in the middle had a round, friendly face, but the other two seemed to 'radiate hatred and hostility'. When Mrs Allan tried to turn round she found she was paralysed and unable to move. Then the experience passed. She asked her husband if it had gone cold, and he touched her arm and said she felt like a corpse. They got up and left hastily. Neither is clear about what happened next except that at some point, they fell asleep on the grass. Then they found themselves in Dorking, both in a state of confusion and unable to remember clearly how they got there. They took the train home for Battersea.

Two years later Mrs Allan decided to return. She went into the church without looking around outside. When she emerged she turned right, expecting to find the path uphill. Then she was surprised to discover that there was no 'uphill': the countryside was quite flat. She went home and told her husband, who thought she was being 'silly'. The following Sunday he made the same journey – only to find that his wife had been telling the truth. There was no overgrown path, no clearing, no wooden seat. A local woodman told him there was no wooden seat on the whole estate.

It was at this point that the couple decided to report their experience to the Society of Psychical Research. They told their story to its Honorary Secretary, Sir George Joy, and to a senior Council member, G. W. Lambert. But the Society was in process of changing its premises and their account seems to have been mislaid. In 1973 they again told their story, this time to a solicitor, Mary Rose Barrington, who was also a member of the SPR and who delivered a paper on it to the Society in 1974. By this time she and a member of the SPR Council had spent some time investigating the area around the church and verified that there was no hill and no bench. But in John Evelyn's diary for 15 March 1696 they discovered an entry in which Evelyn mentions his approval of the sermon that morning and then speaks of the recent execution of 'three wretches', one of them a priest, who had been involved in a plot to assassinate King William. But that, of course, still fails to explain how Mrs Allan could have seen the three men on a hill that did not exist.*

The 'information universe' theory, according to which everything that has ever happened is 'on record', suggests that the Allans experienced a 'time-slip' of much the same nature as those experienced by Jane O'Neill and the two English ladies at Versailles. But the 'information universe'

*I am indebted to the account of the case given by Andrew MacKenzie in *The Seen and the Unseen* (1987), chapter 30.

theory also involves the assumption that these 'recordings' are like images on film – merely a 'picture' of the past. Mr and Mrs Allan undoubtedly climbed a real hill and sat on a real bench before Mrs Allan experienced her unpleasant vision of the three men. But – and this will remind readers of the two ladies at Versailles – they actually spoke to some of the people they saw and received replies, and crossed a small bridge which later proved not to exist. We may also note that Jane O'Neill took it for granted that the church she had entered was real. It seems that 'time-slip' cases often involve a sense of tactile reality. And this is completely unexplainable in terms of a 'tape-recording' theory of 'time-slips'.

But in the subatomic world there is no difference between the sense of sight and the sense of touch: both involve a collision of basic particles with our nerve-ends. And throughout this book we have observed that 'psychics' and clairvoyants seem to have a more direct method of grasping reality than through the nerve ends. If the study of quantum physics serves no other purpose, it reminds us that we should not accept materialistic common sense as a touchstone of reality. Wheeler's belief that we play a part in creating reality suggests that there are other possible realities that our minds might 'tune in to'. But even if one rejects Wheeler's theory as too extreme (as I do), quantum physics still offers a vitally important insight. We cannot know exactly what goes on at the subatomic level because our observation interferes with what we are observing. This is not, of course, true of everyday life: a rock is too big to be affected by the light that bounces off it. The result is that we take it for granted that we are mere observers of the world around us. Moreover the development of left-brain awareness, with its detached, sanitized quality, encourages a sense of helplessness and passivity. We come to take it for granted that the world takes no account of us.

Synchronicities suggest that this is simply untrue. They suggest that even in the perfectly ordinary world that surrounds us, there is some sense in which we *interact* with reality and affect it in the same way that the 'observer' affects subatomic events. The level at which this happens is obviously not the level of the everyday self. But it *is*, presumably, the level that is able to 'read' the information encoded in the reality around us. And this in turn reminds us that it is not entirely true to say that a rock is too big to be affected by the light that bounces off it. If psychometry is not a delusion, a rock can record information exactly like a photographic plate. And there is a level of the human mind that can decode it.

All this begins to afford us a glimpse into what happened to the Allans, as well as to Jane O'Neill, the two ladies at Versailles and Ivan Sanderson and his wife in Haiti. The fact that the Allans were run down, overworked and depressed – and therefore in a passive rather than an active state of mind – may explain why their minds failed to 'tune in' to the everyday reality of 1954, and in some erratic way selected the reality of another time and place.

179

All this suggests that Wilbur Wright could be close to the truth with his view of the 'Fixed Time Field', in which human beings move forward like a man in a railway carriage, regarding the passing scenery as the 'present reality'. Or perhaps a better image might be one of those artificial streams in an amusement park, in which passengers climb into a boat – held temporarily at rest by an attendant – and are then swept off by the flow of the water, through ghostly tunnels and strange landscapes, where skeletons descend from the sky and crocodiles rise at the side of the boat. Once in the boat, the passenger has no way of escaping the forward-flow; yet the attendants can walk along the banks in either direction. If this view contains some element of the truth, then time is not some kind of illusion, as most time-theorists suggest. The stream and the boat and the landscapes are perfectly real; but the passenger in the boat has been subjected to a kind of *limitation* that does not apply to the attendants – and which will not apply to himself when he gets out of the boat at the other end.

If we consider the total picture that seems to emerge from the evidence for 'time-slips' and precognitions, it certainly seems clear that there is some sense in which the past continues to exist with its own kind of solid reality. (Otherwise the Allans could not have sat on a non-existent seat, and the two English ladies at Versailles could not have crossed a non-existent bridge.) There also seems to be some sense in which the future already exists as *some* kind of reality – Air Marshal Goddard was quite convinced that he was flying over a real airfield. And there is certainly overwhelming evidence that human beings possess a faculty that can grasp these other realities. In that case, it could be argued that the past, present and future form a total 'field', which ought – under the right circumstances – to be accessible to all of us, just as a total view of London is accessible to anyone who flies over London in an aeroplane.

But the 'Fixed Time Field' view should also be treated with some caution. It implies that we live in a kind of four-dimensional (or perhaps six-dimensional) museum in which everything is fixed and static. But the very essence of human existence is our feeling that the past has happened and cannot be 'unhappened', and that the future has not yet happened, and therefore cannot be precisely known. Time is not 'unreal'. The alternative view, suggested in this chapter, is that the past is accessible to a certain level of the human mind because we are living in an information universe in which everything is 'on record'. The future is also accessible because we are living in a largely predetermined universe in which human beings can (but not necessarily do) introduce an element of freedom. But the future – like the quantum universe – is a world of possibilities. The very essence of this theory is the recognition that human beings possess the freedom to choose between these possibilities.

Then how can human beings exercise their freedom? The basic answer seems to be: in the extent to which they accept or reject their experience. When I catch a train, I know in advance where it will take me, and even what time it will arrive. But *I* decide whether to sit blankly gazing out of the window, or whether to try to force my mind into a state of wider perception. Our basic human problem lies in our failure to *grasp* our freedom. And this is the real irony of the human situation. The freedom is *there*. It is merely the dullness of our physical senses, and the dreary narrowness of our minds that prevents us from grasping it. And, more important, grasping what can be done with it.

7

Minds Without Bodies?

The story of the Allans yields another important clue to the mystery of paranormal experience. When the three 'ghosts' appeared behind Mrs Allan she felt paralysed, unable to turn her head. This sensation of paralysis appears again and again in accounts of paranormal experience. The student S. H. Beard experienced the same sensation when he tried to 'appear' to his fiancée Miss Verity, as decribed in chapter 3: 'I must have fallen into a mesmeric trance, for although I was conscious, I could not move my limbs.' It is as if the mind and the body have drifted slightly out of alignment.

Another case is cited by Dame Edith Lyttelton – one-time president of the Society for Psychical Research – in her book *Our Superconscious Mind*. In June 1889 Mrs F. C. McAlpine went to meet her sister off the train in Castleblaney and, when she failed to arrive, decided to go for a walk by the lake.

> Being at length tired, I sat down to rest upon a rock at the edge of the water. My attention was quite taken up with the extreme beauty of the scene before me. There was not a sound of movement, except the soft ripple of the water on the sand at my feet. Presently I felt a cold chill creep through me, and a curious stiffness in my limbs, as if I could not move, though wishing to do so. I felt frightened, yet chained to the spot, as if impelled to stare at the water straight in front of me. Gradually a black cloud seemed to rise, and in the midst of it I saw a tall man, in a suit of tweed, jump into the water and sink.
>
> In a moment the darkness was gone, and I again became sensible of the heat and the sunshine, but I was awed and felt eerie . . . . On my sister's arrival I told her of the occurrence: she was surprised but inclined to laugh at it. When we got home I told my brother: he treated the subject in much the same manner. However, about a week afterwards a Mr Espie, a bank clerk (unknown to me), committed suicide by drowning at that very spot. He left a letter for his wife, indicating that for some time he had contemplated his death . . . .

It seems clear that Mrs McAlpine's state of total relaxation created the right circumstances for her experience. We can assume either that her 'subjective mind' received a precognition of the suicide – after all,

182

probably the most arresting event in the immediate future of the lake – or that she simply entered into telepathic contact with the bank clerk who was brooding on his suicide at that spot. The problem was then for the 'subjective mind' to convey the information to everyday awareness. If Mrs McAlpine had been asleep or in a semi-doze, a dream or hypnagogic image would have served the purpose. But at least she was in a state of complete relaxation. A slight 'nudge' was enough to send her 'down the rabbit hole', where the information could be conveyed in the form of a visual impression. But the 'rabbit hole' state is close to trance, so it involves a feeling of paralysis.

The literature of the paranormal offers many more examples in which feelings of paralysis are associated with 'clairvoyant' states. The psychic Robert Cracknell has described an experience that he had in the RAF, when he was guard commander. He was supposed to stay awake all night but decided to take a nap in one of the cells:

> I was lying on the bunk fully dressed, drifting into sleep, and it was as though I suddenly woke up. I could quite distinctly hear the voice of the orderly officer in the main guardroom asking where the guard commander was . . . . I tried to get up and found, to my horror, that I was completely paralysed.
>
> I knew in a strange way that I was not asleep. This was not a dream. And yet I could not move a muscle, and for what seemed to be at least three minutes I tried to call for help. The words formed in my mind but I was incapable of making myself heard. At this point I was conscious of panic. I constantly struggled to get up from the prone position, but could not do so, and from somewhere at the back of my mind came the impression that I should relax. The panic, however, was far too strong, and I went on wrestling with my state of paralysis. I heard someone walk down the corridor and a voice said, 'Quick, Corp, wake up.'
>
> I managed to master my paralysis and stood by the side of the bunk completely bemused, drenched in sweat and unable to grasp what was going on. Then I heard the voice of the orderly officer calling out, 'Where's the guard commander?'*

In fact the orderly officer had only just arrived at that moment, and Cracknell was there to receive him. The dream – or rather the hypnagogic experience, for he points out that it happened as he was drifting into sleep – had been a precognition. For Cracknell it was the first of many such experiences. It was only later that he learned – from a book called *Projection of the Astral Body* by Sylvan Muldoon and Hereward Carrington – that such states of 'paralysis' often precede so-called 'out-of-the-body experiences'.

Muldoon is probably the most famous of the 'astral projectors' – at

*Robert Cracknell, *Clues to the Unknown*.

least until recent years, when that position was challenged by another American, Robert Monroe. Muldoon had his first out-of-the-body experience (usually abbreviated to OBE) at the age of twelve, when he and his mother were visiting the Mississippi Valley Spiritualist Association at Clinton, Iowa. He woke up in the middle of the night in a state of bewilderment and when he tried to move, found that he was paralysed. He had a sense of floating up into the air, then looked down and, to his amazement, saw his own body lying on the bed. He seemed to be joined to his body by a kind of cable that extended between their heads – the kind of 'cable', we may recall, that seemed to join the psychometrist Maria de Zierold to Dr Pagenstecher (see p. 110). Assuming he was dead, he tried to awaken the other sleepers, without success. 'I clutched at them, called to them, tried to shake them, but my hands passed through them as though they were but vapours. I started to cry . . . .' Then, as he wandered around the place, he felt an increasing resistance on the 'cable'. It pulled him back towards his physical body, and once again he felt paralysed, unable to move. As he re-entered his body all his muscles jerked and he experienced intense pain, 'as if I had been split open from head to foot'. Then he was awake and conscious again.

Many thousands of examples of out-of-the-body experiences have been reported in the literature of the paranormal: one eminent researcher, Robert Crookall, devoted nine volumes to such cases. Another, the South African investigator J. C. Poynton, collected 122 cases as a result of a single questionnaire published in a newspaper. A similar appeal by the English researcher Celia Green brought 326 cases. One survey even produced the incredible statistic that one in ten persons have had an out-of-the-body experience.

A few investigators, notably Dr Susan Blackmore, have expressed doubts as to whether these experiences are any more than dreams. One of my correspondents, Mr D. R. Mitchell, has sent me a paper in which he argues that out-of-the-body experiences can be explained in terms of a mechanism in the brain called the Reticular Activation System, which acts as a valve between the senses and the brain and which closes the channel between the brain and the muscles (producing, obviously, a sense of paralysis). He also suggests that as soon as we begin to fall asleep, a mechanism called the Silt Removal System is activated to get rid of surplus calcium ions in the synapses of the nerves. The neurons 'fire', and this causes memories to appear in the nervous system. (This could also explain hypnagogic images, as well as dreams.) But if something jarred the sleeper partially awake he would find himself in a kind of sensory limbo, unable to move – because the Reticular Activation System's 'valve' was still half closed – and aware of the input of memories being 'dumped' by the Silt Removal System. This, Mr Mitchell believes, explains the out-of-the-body experience, which is merely a waking dream.

It is a convincing explanation, but would be rejected by most people with any experience of 'astral projection'. Obviously, the question of proof is all-important. Muldoon's fellow author, Hereward Carrington, was an eminent member of the American Society for Psychical Research and made something of a speciality of exposing fraudulent mediums, but he was finally convinced by Muldoon's ability to obtain correct information about distant events by 'travelling' there in his astral body. In fact Carrington himself once conducted a series of experiments in which he tried to 'project' himself into the room of a young lady when he was on the point of sleep. He had no idea of whether he had succeeded. But the young lady told him not only had he 'appeared' to her, but she had been seized by an impulse to practise 'automatic writing' and had written a poem. The 'poem' turned out to be the opening lines of a song called 'When Sparrows Build' which she did not know, but which was a favourite of Carrington's.

In the 1960s the psychologist Charles Tart studied a borderline schizophrenic girl whom he called Miss Z., who told him that she had been leaving her body ever since childhood. To test whether these experiences were dreams Tart told her to try an experiment: she was to write the numbers one to ten on several slips of paper, scramble them up, then choose one at random when her light was out and place it on the bedside table. If she had an out-of-the-body experience in the night she had to try to read the number (she claimed to be able to see in the dark during her OBEs). She tried this several times and found she always got the number right. So Tart decided to test her himself. The girl was wired up to machines in his laboratory and asked to try and read a five-digit number which Tart had placed on a high shelf in the room next door. Miss Z. reported correctly that the number was 25132.

In 1972 a book called *Journeys Out of the Body* by the American businessman Robert Monroe aroused widespread interest. Monroe had begun to experience what he called 'vibrations' on the point of sleep when he was experimenting with data learning during sleep. When this happened he became powerless to move. Then one day when the 'vibrations' came he happened to be lying with his hand over the side of the bed. He tried scratching the rug and found that his fingers went through it, then through the floor to the ceiling of the room below. A few weeks later he found himself floating in the air looking down at his own body on the bed. From then on, he was able to leave his body more or less at will. He soon confirmed, to his own satisfaction, that this was not some kind of dream: he observed what friends were doing during his 'trips' and later confirmed that he had been correct. He even pinched a woman friend, who jumped and later showed him a bruise at the same spot. (People in OBE states seem to have some slight ability to influence the physical world.)

Charles Tart investigated Monroe in his laboratory and found that, like Miss Z., he could report accurately on things that were happening elsewhere. Other psychologists were understandably sceptical. Glen O.

Gabbard and Stuart W. Tremlow produced a classic study of 'out-of-the-body experiences' based on 339 case studies. They noted that as a child, Monroe had had a fascination with flying, and speak of his 'Daedalus fantasies' (Daedalus being the Greek mythological character who invented wings, with which his son Icarus flew too close to the sun and crashed.) They say that 'the fascination with out-of-body "travel" seen in Monroe is likely an adult derivative of this Daedalus fantasy.' But when Tremlow studied Monroe in his own laboratory in 1977 he and a colleague were baffled to see a 'heat-wave-like distortion beginning at Monroe's waist, so that it was difficult to get a clearly focused picture of his upper body, although his lower body was in clear focus'. This was a few moments before Monroe began to move again at the end of his trance-like sleep. They also observed a slowing down in his brainwaves when he was in his trance-state. It looks, on the whole, as if Monroe had the last word in this argument.

The title of Gabbard and Tremlow's book, *With the Eyes of the Mind*, is taken from Goethe's autobiography *Poetry and Truth*, Part 3, Book Eleven, which describes a curious episode in which Goethe was confronted by his own double. He had just taken leave of Frederika, a girl he had been tempted to marry, and was in a state of gloom:

I now rode along the footpath towards Drusenheim, and here one of the most singular premonitions took possession of me. I saw, not with the eyes of the body, but with the eyes of the mind, my own figure coming towards me, on horseback and on the same road, attired in a dress which I had never worn: – it was the grey of a pike, with something of gold in it. As soon as I shook myself out of this dream, the figure disappeared. It is strange, however, that eight years later, I found myself on the very road, to pay one more visit to Frederika, in the dress of which I had dreamed, and which I was wearing not from choice but by accident . . . .

It looks as if Goethe's 'superconscious mind' was attempting to relieve his depression by showing him a picture of himself returning to see Frederika in eight years' time – and in fact it did have that effect: 'the strange illusion calmed me in those moments of parting.'

The German for 'double' is *doppelgänger*, but the above case is obviously an example of premonition rather than of the 'projection' of a double. On another occasion, however, Goethe saw a genuine *doppelgänger*. It was of his friend Friedrich, who was apparently strolling along the street in front of Goethe after a heavy shower. The odd thing was that Friedrich was wearing Goethe's dressing-gown. Goethe arrived home to find Friedrich – in the same dressing gown – standing in front of the fire. He had been caught in the rain and had borrowed Goethe's dressing-gown while his own coat dried out.

Now here – as in many other cases – the *doppelgänger* is obviously a 'thought projection', some kind of telepathic image transmitted accidentally or deliberately (but usually accidentally) by someone who happens to be thinking of another person or another place. Another poet, W. B. Yeats, describes in his autobiography how, 'one afternoon . . . I was thinking very intently of a certain fellow student from whom I had a message . . . . In a couple of days I got a letter from a place some hundreds of miles away where the student was. On the afternoon when I had been thinking so intently I had suddenly appeared there amid a crowd of people in a hotel and seeming as solid as if in the flesh . . . .' The student had asked him to come again when he was alone, and Yeats apparently reappeared in the middle of the night and gave him a message. Yeats adds, 'I myself had no knowledge of either apparition.'

When the Society for Psychical Research was first formed in 1882 one of its leading members, Frederick Myers, realized that there were so many cases of this type that they deserved to be collected and classified. *Phantasms of the Living*, a massive 1,300 page work by Myers and his friends Edmund Gurney and Frank Podmore, is the first attempt at a cool, scientific evaluation of *doppelgängers*, and the sheer quantity of its material can leave no possible doubt of the reality of the phenomenon. The immense variety of the 'apparitions' is bewildering, but one thing soon becomes apparent: the great majority are related to serious crises – illness or sudden death. This one is typical:

> In 1877 I was living in Dublin, and was very anxious about my father, who was dangerously ill with congested lungs, in Wales. Awaking suddenly one night I distinctly saw him sitting on a chair near me, with his face covered by his hands. When I jumped out of bed he vanished. So startled was I that, next day, I crossed to Wales and found that he had been delirious for two days. When I entered the room he at once said he had gone the day before to tell me where he had left a topcoat [in Dublin] . . . [Case 499].

In another case (634) a child suddenly told her adoptive parents that there was a young woman looking at her and talking to her. Her description made it clear that she was seeing her real mother (whom she could not remember). The alarmed parents took her to a neighbour's house, hoping the 'hallucination' would vanish, but it came with them and stayed for most of the afternoon before suddenly vanishing as if 'in a flash of fire'. The adoptive parents heard later that the child's mother had died in a fire at the same time she had appeared to her daughter.

Wilbur Wright has made the interesting suggestion that all human beings possess these powers of 'projection' but that most of us never have the occasion – or the desire – to use them. They can however be released by the stimulus of sudden danger or the prospect of death – hence the enormous number of 'crisis apparitions' in the literature of the paranormal. It also seems very clear that some of these peculiar powers can be released if the desire is strong enough. One clergyman relates (Case 641) how a young lady fell violently in love with him, and how he soon began to have the odd feeling that she was with him when he was alone. Then the girl began to tell him where he had been and what he had been doing. At first he thought that someone had told her, but she began to describe the circumstances and surroundings with such accuracy that it was obvious she had really been there. She then admitted that she only had to think about him intently to begin to see him. When it first happened she thought it was her imagination – until the clergyman later admitted the total accuracy of her 'visions'. As soon as he realized that the girl had the power to 'project' herself into his life he took care to avoid her. But the psychic link remained. Ten years later, walking on the cliffs at Ramsgate with his wife, he suddenly felt so oppressed that he had to sit down. Suddenly the girl was standing in front of him, introducing her husband and asking to be introduced to his wife. Once again he terminated the acquaintance as soon as he decently could.

On a visit to Milwaukee in the autumn of 1987 I collected the following remarkable case from James Pease, the director of the Bauer Contemporary Ballet Company. In 1972 his wife Susie Bauer went to New York to continue her dance studies. Pease relates:

My brother Mitchell moved into the Milwaukee apartment with me to share expenses. Susie and I were quite miserable.

One night about a week after she had left Milwaukee she went into her bedroom with a bottle of wine, put a record on the stereo and sat down on the floor leaning against her bed. She was unhappy, and felt trapped by the decision she had made: and, in an attempt to tune out her thoughts, she immersed herself in the music.

Meanwhile Mitchell and I had finished our, ahem, gourmet dinner in front of the television. Mitch was sitting on the couch; I was in an easy chair with my back to the archway leading to the dining room.

Suddenly I caught a glimpse out of the corner of my eye of what I thought to be Susie standing at the edge of the archway over my left shoulder, as if she was entering the room. It took a few micro-seconds to recall that Susie was in New York and couldn't be entering the living room. My double-take at this apparition was violent enough to cause Mitch to turn his head from the TV and ask what was going on. I replied something like, 'I could have sworn that I just saw Susie starting to come into the room,' shrugged it off and we continued to watch the tube.

A minute or two later the phone rang. It was Susie calling from New York and she seemed quite upset. Her exact words were, 'I was just there,' and I responded, 'I know.' She went on to tell me how we had arranged the furniture – with perfect accuracy – where we were sitting, where the beer cans were, what dinnerware we had used, and where the dirty dishes were located, and that Mitch had used an end table as a TV table. She described Mitch as sitting back into the sofa with his feet up on the end table (all true) and that I had just reached for my beer when she became frightened because she thought I had seen her. I had to think about that for a moment and then realized that it was true.

Susie described the experience as going into a trance and feeling herself lifted out of herself, hovering above her body as if from the ceiling. Looking down on herself, she thought how ridiculous it was to feel so miserable about a circumstance of her own making, that if she didn't want to be there she should do something about it. Suddenly she found herself walking past the bedroom of our apartment in Milwaukee, across the entrance room . . . and as she entered the dining room, turned and approached the archway to the living room, she became conscious of the 'fact' that she couldn't be there. When she thought I had noticed her, she became frightened at what would happen, and opened her eyes sitting on the floor of her bedroom in New York . . . .'

Pease adds that after the experience Susie 'felt completely uncomfortable, as if she was in a body she didn't know', and that it took about a day to get over this feeling of 'wrong-bodiness'.

Susie Bauer's experience seems to suggest that most of us could, if we wanted to, experience 'bilocation' at will. The following strange case from *Phantasms of the Living* (number 642) makes the same point and also suggests that the ability might be put to sinister use. It concerns a nineteen-year-old girl who began having dreams about a man with a mole on the left side of his mouth, who caused her a feeling of repugnance. The dreams always began with a sensation of some 'influence' coming over her, accompanied by a feeling of 'Here it is again'. The dreams were not unpleasant in themselves, she said, but were always dreadful to her because 'a kind of struggle between two natures within me seemed to drag my powers of mind and body two ways.' (This modest Victorian young lady is obviously saying that the man was arousing her sexual feelings.) She would wake up shivering, with her teeth chattering.

Two years later, at a dance in a private house in Liverpool, the girl began experiencing the 'influence' again – feeling 'cold and stony' while her head began to burn. She stood up, 'knowing what I was going to see', and found herself looking into the face of the man of her dreams. He was already acquainted with her companion, so he was introduced to her and went with them to the refreshment room. He asked her where they had met and she insisted that she had never seen him before. He seemed annoyed and puzzled. Later that evening the girl asked her sister if she recalled her description of the man she had seen in her dreams and asked her if she thought there was anyone like him at the party. The sister had no difficulty in identifying the man.

189

From then on this man began to pursue the girl: she found that he seemed to be at every party she went to. He began to talk about dreams, then asked her if she had ever travelled to various places. In fact she had dreamed that she had been in these places with the man and had even described them at the time in a dream notebook she kept. She was often tempted to admit that she had dreamt about him, but felt instinctively that if she did so, 'I should be as completely his slave and tool as I had been in dreams.' So she continued to deny everything and eventually wrote to ask her parents to recall her.

The key to this strange story seems to be an admission that the man had made. He had seen her before the dreams began, at a Birmingham music festival, and on that occasion she had fainted. At the time she had thought that this was due to 'the heat and the excitement of the music'. Later, thinking it over, she realized that the swoon had been preceded by the same feeling of the 'influence' creeping over her. The inference seems to be that the man immediately recognized her as the kind of person over whom he could exercise a certain power and had somehow succeeded in establishing some kind of telepathic contact in her dreams, in which he sexually 'enslaved' her. (Gurdjieff is credited with the same power: in *God is My Adventure* Rom Landau has described how, sitting at the next table to an attractive female novelist, Gurdjieff began to inhale and exhale in a peculiar way. Suddenly the novelist went pale, declaring later, 'I suddenly felt as if I had been struck right through my sexual centre – it was beastly.') It is also worth noting that the girl was, to some extent, 'psychic'. Elsewhere in the book *Phantasms of the Living* she describes how she dreamed accurately of the death of her brother in a cavalry charge during the Indian Mutiny. Her aunt pointed out that her brother was in the infantry, but in due course news of his death in a cavalry charge was confirmed.

Early investigators, like Myers and the French astronomer Camille Flammarion (whom we have already met in connection with the manuscript pages that blew out of his window), felt that it was enough to collect vast numbers of such cases – where possible supported by signed statements from witnesses – to convince any intelligent reader of the reality of these 'strange powers'. Flammarion's 1,000 page *Death and Its Mystery* is another amazing treasure house of paranormal incidents. What neither Myers nor Flammarion recognized was that no sceptic is going to read through so many pages and so grasp their sheer consistency. What is basically necessary is some kind of a theory to connect the cases, and it is this that is lacking in their books.

Are we, then, in any better position? The answer, on the whole, is yes. The Victorians had accumulated an impressive body of material – about clairvoyance, about hypnosis, about psychometry and crisis apparitions – but most of it was anecdotal and was simply ignored by Victorian scientists and philosophers. Flammarion, for example, tells a well-authenticated story about an operation performed upon a certain

Madame Plantin, who was under hypnosis, by a Dr Cloquet, while Madame Plantin's daughter, also under hypnosis, looked on. The hypnotized woman was able to describe her mother's internal organs in specific detail ('The right lung has shrunk.... The liver is white and discoloured') and added the information that she would die early the following day. Mme Plantin died as predicted and an autopsy revealed the accuracy of her daughter's descriptions of her organs. Flammarion adds with understandable bitterness, 'Nevertheless, I have seen grave "scholars" burst out laughing while listening to these "cock-and-bull stories."' Nowadays parapsychologists can point to laboratory evidence to support their claims about telepathy, psychometry and clairvoyance, and the sceptics are reduced to picking holes in the evidence instead of bursting into shouts of laughter.

Does this mean that laboratory evidence is better than anecdotal evidence? Obviously not. It is extremely difficult to persuade paranormal events to manifest themselves in the laboratory, although a few exceptionally gifted psychics have succeeded. The sheer richness of the anecdotal evidence assembled by Flammarion and Myers convinces through its inner consistency. So many people, from dukes to dustmen, have seen dying relatives at the moment of death that only the most dogmatic rationalist could dismiss it all as pure invention. By comparison, laboratory evidence seems unexciting and rather flimsy. Its real importance is that it forms such powerful support for the anecdotal evidence, which points quite clearly towards certain basic conclusions, the most important of which is that all human beings possess certain paranormal powers which can be developed by effort and practice. Our powers are normally limited by the fact that we seem to be tied down to the physical body and its habits. Paranormal powers seem to indicate that this assumption is untrue. Our tendency to identify ourselves with our bodies is largely a matter of laziness and habit. And the habit can be broken.

Where 'out-of-the-body experience' is concerned, the theory was tested by an eminent psychical researcher, Professor Arthur Ellison. He was inspired by *The Projection of the Astral Body* to attempt to carry out Muldoon's instructions:

The principle was to loosen the grip of the physical body on the astral body by . . . imagining oneself, in the astral body, consciously rotating about an axis from head to feet, observing first the ceiling, then the wall, then the floor and other wall . . . .

For one hour of every night for a month I tried these methods on retiring to bed. At last I had success. The first sign was that in accordance with the book, I found myself in a cataleptic state – unable to move a muscle . . . . I used my will – or was it my imagination? – to make myself float upwards, and the experience was quite fascinating. I felt as though I were embedded in the mud at the bottom of a river, and the water was slowly seeping into the mud and reducing its viscosity, so that eventually I was borne upwards by the water. Slowly I floated upwards, still cataleptic, like an airship released from its moorings. I reached the ceiling and floated through it into the darkness of the roof space. Then I passed through the roof tiles, and the sky, clouds and Moon became visible. I increased my 'willing' (or 'imagining'), and my velocity of ascent up into the sky increased. I have the memory of the wind whistling through my hair clearly to this day.

Ellison goes on to emphasize, 'From the moment of getting into bed to this point up in the sky I had no break of consciousness.' So although he is willing to concede that the whole thing could have been a dream, there was certainly no moment at which he fell asleep.

The second – and last – time he tried it he determined that he would try to float beyond what Muldoon calls 'cord activity range' – far enough to break loose of the 'cord' that seems to attach most 'astral projectors' to their physical bodies.

This time it took only three or four nights to repeat the projection. However, on this occasion I stopped the vertical movement at ceiling height and changed direction. Still cataleptic, I floated horizontally, feet first, towards the first floor window of the room. Floating smoothly through the top of the window frame, I was aiming to describe a smooth parabola down onto the lawn where, I hoped, I should be outside 'cord activity range' and the real work of acquiring evidence could begin. It did not happen like that. As I cleared the window and started the descent to the lawn I had one of the most intriguing experiences to date. I felt two hands take my head, one hand over each ear, move me (still cataleptic) back into the bedroom and down into the body. I heard no sound and saw nothing.

By this time, Ellison admits, he was so tired during the day from lack of sleep that he ceased the experiments. But his curiosity remained, and he decided to continue the investigations in the laboratory. The basic aim of the experiment was the same as Charles Tart's experiment with Miss Z.: to get the 'astral projector' to read a number during the 'out-of-the-body' state. However there was one obvious flaw in Tart's experiments: since Tart himself knew the number, Miss Z. might have picked it up from him by telepathy. Ellison decided that this flaw could be eliminated in his experiment if he made sure that he himself did not know the number. So he constructed an electronic box that generated random numbers. When he pushed a button a three-digit random number would appear at the other side of the box, hidden from both Ellison and the 'astral projector'. The 'astral projector' would be asked to read this number and repeat it:

192

Ellison would then enter the number on a dial and the box itself would tell him whether it corresponded to the number on the back of the box. It seemed foolproof.

On the trial run it looked as if Ellison had taken a wise precaution. His subject was a girl who claimed to be able to achieve 'astral projection'. To save time Ellison looked at the numbers while the girl tried to tell him what they were (presumably she 'projected', took a look at the numbers, and returned to her body). It was an amazing success: on a number of occasions the girl got the number completely right. Then Ellison tried the 'blind' procedure and immediately the girl began to experience difficulties, saying the numbers were too small to read. This seemed to show that she had been reading his mind.

The next subject was a famous American clairvoyant who said he did not need to 'project' his astral body – the numbers would appear in his mind. He scored an amazing eight out of twenty. But when Ellison tried it the next day the box recorded that he also had scored eight out of twenty, and he realized that the electronic nought on the box was turning into a figure eight due to some malfunction of the micro-circuit: when Ellison cleaned it his score dropped to its usual zero.

The next subject was a famous British psychic. This time Ellison and his assistant did test runs before the experiment: they scored nought, as usual. Then the psychic tried, and scored eight. Ellison and his assistant tried again, and also scored eight. Again they cleaned the component, and he and his assistant achieved their usual zero score. The psychic tried again, and scored eight. Ellison cleaned the component and tried again: he scored zero. It looked as if the 'cosmic joker' was having a joke at Ellison's expense – either that or, as he himself suspected, the psychic might have been somehow acting upon the circuit by psychokinesis (mind over matter) to get a high score.

A similar attempt by the American researcher Dr Karlis Osis produced a more positive result. He constructed an ingenious box in which the circuitry superimposed various images to give an apparently normal picture. But the subject had to stand in a particular position in front of the box in order to see the picture. A psychic named Alex Tanous was asked to 'project' himself and look into the box from the correct position. Tanous was able to see the picture correctly, indicating that some part of him had left his body and was looking through the glass window into the box.

It can be seen at once that these experiments, while interesting, are not half as convincing as Ellison's own experience of 'astral projection'. To be truly convinced we need to be able to experience some sense of 'the human equation' – or better still, to have direct experience. When Ernest Hemingway was blown up by a shell in the First World War he experienced a sensation that he described as follows, ' ... my soul or something coming right out of my body, like you'd pull a silk handkerchief out of a pocket by one corner. It flew around and then came

193

back and went in again and I wasn't dead any more.' But while this may have convinced Hemingway that he had died briefly, it is open to the obvious objection that it may just have been a 'feeling' caused by physical crisis.

There are nevertheless cases in which there seems to be a certain amount of hard evidence that physical consciousness can survive the 'death' of the body. One of the most striking occurred at the Hartebeespoort Snake and Animal Park near Pretoria in South Africa. Its owner, Jack Seale, was a releasing a twelve-foot black mamba into its cage when an over-officious research assistant asked if he had checked it for parasites. Seale's attention was distracted for a moment and the snake turned and sank its fangs into his ankle. Seale knew that his chances of survival were minimal: no one has ever been known to survive the bite of a full-grown black mamba. When he saw venom squirting out of his ankle he knew the mamba must have injected a massive dose.

Seale had about 10 ccs of serum on the premises, but he required at least four times that amount. So after injecting himself with all he had, he was driven to Pretoria General Hospital.

Luck was with him. The surgeon on duty was a friend to whom he had often expounded his favourite theory about snakebite treatment. Mamba venom is a neurotoxin that paralyses the central nervous system. Jack Seale had always believed that if the snakebite victim was connected to a heart-lung machine he stood a good chance of remaining alive. This notion was based on an observation he had made a few years before. A Pretoria researcher, Gert Willemse, was trying to determine exactly how much venom it would take to kill a rabbit when Jack Seale arrived. Willemse decided to take a tea break after injecting the rabbit with a massive dose of venom. He left it connected to a heart-lung machine, and when they returned an hour later they were amazed to see that the rabbit was still alive.

As the surgeon forced his mouth open and inserted an air tube down his throat, Jack Seale thought, 'Thank God, thank God . . . .' Then he died. (It was later discovered that the snake had injected enough venom to kill fifty men.) A few hours later he returned to consciousness to hear a harsh rasping sound and a 'peep, peep, peep' noise: it gradually dawned on him that he was listening to his own breathing and heartbeat. When he tried to move he discovered he was completely paralysed. The monitors showed that his brain was dead; they failed to record the fact that consciousness had returned.

For the next eight days Jack Seale remained completely paralysed, yet able to hear everything that went on. When two young nurses inserted a catheter he heard one of them remark that he had the smallest dick she'd ever seen: she was much embarrassed when he reminded her of this later. A doctor shone a torch into his eye and expressed the opinion that he had been brain-damaged: Seale heard that too. Later he heard them tell his wife that even if he recovered he would be brain-damaged for life. And

194

on the third day he heard a doctor say, 'That poor woman is going to be stuck with a vegetable for the rest of her life. The best thing we can do is to pull the plug . . . .' After further discussion they decided to leave him on the machine because the case was clinically interesting.

On the eighth day he succeeded in moving a finger. A doctor told the nurse it was an involuntary nerve spasm. Seale moved the finger again. The doctor said, 'Mr Seale, if you can hear me, move your finger twice.' Seale concentrated all his will power and moved the finger twice. There was immediate pandemonium as the room filled up with doctors, nurses and interns. Nine hours later his eyelids fluttered. According to Jack Seale's account, normal consciousness then returned 'layer by layer'. And eight days later he was allowed to leave the hospital. One of the first things he did was to catch the snake that had bitten him and milk it of its venom. For months he found it impossible to sleep without the light on, since waking up in darkness immediately brought back the sense of living death – as in Poe's 'The Premature Burial'. His comment on the ordeal was, 'I know what it feels like to die. It's not such a terrifying thing . . . .'

Medically speaking the case only proves that consciousness can remain intact when the body is technically dead. Yet for those who insist that life is inseparably connected with the body there remains the puzzle of how Jack Seale remained conscious when monitors indicated brain-death. It takes very little to deprive us of consciousness – a whiff of anaesthetic, a blow on the head, a rush of blood from the brain if we stand up too quickly. Yet Jack Seale's consciousness survived total bodily death. Consciousness seems to be rather less fragile than we generally assume.

The major problem is plain enough. When we close our eyes and fall asleep, we simply disappear: the next sign of consciousness we experience is when we begin to dream. So there seems to be no realistic evidence whatsoever of a part of us that 'migrates' during sleep. It is certainly quite logical to believe that death is merely a permanent 'disappearance'. To some extent this objection was countered by one of the first and most remarkable of the 'dream researchers', Frederik Van Eeden, who began studying his own dream experiences in the late 1890s. After a while he began to experience 'lucid dreams' – that is dreams in which he was aware he was dreaming.

In January 1898 . . . I dreamt that I was lying in the garden before the windows of my study, and saw the eyes of my dog through the glass pane. I was lying on my chest and observing the dog very keenly. At the same time, however, I knew with perfect certainty that I was dreaming and lying on my back in my bed. And then I resolved to wake up slowly and carefully and observe how my sensation of lying on my chest would change into the sensation of lying on my back. And so I did, slowly and deliberately, and the transition – which I have since undergone many times – is most wonderful. It is like the feeling of slipping from one body into

195

another, and there is distinctly a *double* recollection of the two bodies. I remembered what I felt in my dream, lying on my chest; but returning into the day-life, I remembered also that my physical body had been quietly lying on its back all the while. This observation of a double memory I have had many times since. It is so indubitable that it leads almost unavoidably to the conception of *a dream body*.

(This could also explain Susie Bauer's experience of 'wrong-bodiness' when she returned to her physical body.)

We are so accustomed to identifying the ego with consciousness that it is very hard to grasp the notion of a double consciousness – that is a part of us with its own consciousness that can migrate elsewhere. Yet this is a concept we encounter repeatedly in accounts of 'out-of-the-body experiences'. One of the most eminent scientific men to describe such an experience was Sir Auckland (later Lord) Geddes, professor of anatomy at Dublin University. In a paper presented before the Royal Medical Society in 1937 Geddes describes how he had been suffering from food poisoning and how, seated in his chair, he became paralysed. At this point he realized that 'my consciousness was separating from another consciousness which was also me'. One consciousness was attached to his body, which remained seated in the chair, while the other was attached to his ego. (Note that he says 'attached to', not identical with, his ego.) This second consciousness seemed to be outside his body. In this state, he says, he could see the whole house and garden and then things in London and Scotland. He felt that he was 'free in a time dimension of space, wherein "now" was in some way equivalent to "here" in the ordinary three-dimensional space of everyday life', an observation that seems to bear out the notion that some part of human consciousness can rise 'above' time. Geddes was discovered soon after his heart had stopped beating and given a camphor injection that restored him – reluctantly – to everyday consciousness.

Oddly enough that reluctance seems to be a recurrent feature of such 'near death' experiences. In 1871 a professor of geology from Zurich, Albert Heim, fell seventy feet from a snow-covered ledge and experienced a slowing-down of time accompanied by a delightful feeling of peace and serenity:

Mental activity became enormous, rising to a hundredfold velocity .... I saw my whole past life take place in many images, as though on a stage at some distance from me. . . . Everything was transfigured as though by a heavenly light, without anxiety and without pain. . . . Elevated and harmonious thoughts dominated and united individual images, and like magnificent music a divine calm swept through my soul. . . .

196

All this took place in a three-second fall.

In her autobiography *The Passionate Years* the American socialite Caresse Crosby describes a similar experience when, as a child, she came close to drowning. Her two brothers held on to her ankles as she fell into the foaming river.

When my head had plunged beneath the water's surface, I took one long frightened gulp and I never got another breath of air, my lungs expelled once and refilled with tide water. The blood rushed from my toes to my nose and suddenly my head seemed to expand and explode, but softly as though it were a cotton ball fluffing out and out and out. Into my ears poured strange sea lullabies and little by little, there beneath a flood a dazzling prismatic effulgence cleared my vision – not only did I see and hear harmony, but I understood everything. And slowly, as a bubble rises to the surface, I rose to the surface, rose up through the wooden platform, rose to where I could dominate the whole scene spread out beneath me. I watched my father at work on his boat, my brothers deathly frightened hanging on to my spindly heels and I, my hair like seaweed pulled flat against the submerged bottom of the float. Thus, while I drowned I saw my father turn and act, I saw my frightened brother run homeward, I saw the efforts to bring me back to life, *and I tried not to come back*.

It was the most perfect state of easeful joy that I ever experienced, then or since. There was no sadness or sickness from which I wished to escape, I was only seven, a carefree child, yet that moment in my life has never been equalled for pure happiness. Could I have glimpsed, while drowned (for I was drowned), the freedom of eternal life? One thing I know, that Nirvana does exist between here and the hereafter – a space of delight, for I have been there.

Albert Heim's own experience of 'ecstasy' on the point of death led him to begin collecting similar experiences from other mountaineers who had been involved in climbing accidents: he discovered that 95 per cent of them had had experiences similar to his own.

Lyall Watson became so intrigued by such experiences that he devoted a book to them, *The Romeo Error* (the error in question being Romeo's assumption that Juliet is dead when she is alive). He also recorded many experiences that indicated that people on the point of death often experience 'ecstasy'. Watson had himself had an 'out-of-the-body experience' when his minibus overturned on a safari in Kenya and came to rest on the edge of a gully.

I found myself standing outside the small bus, looking at the head and shoulders of a young boy in the party who had been pushed halfway through the canvas roof on the last roll and would be crushed if the vehicle moved any further – as it seemed bound to do. Then, without pause, I recovered consciousness in the front seat of the bus, rubbed the red dust out of my eyes, climbed through the window, and went round to help the boy free himself before the battered vehicle settled itself into its final resting position. My memory of the details 'seen' while still unconscious is still vivid and there is no doubt in my own mind that my vantage point at that moment was detached from my body . . . .

In this case we observe that Watson experienced no sense of floating free of his body and looking down from above. He simply found himself standing beside the bus, as if his mind had been shaken free of its normal limitations. This raises the interesting question of whether the notion of an 'astral body' is really necessary. It may be simply that in these states of 'detachment', the mind continues to see itself in its usual guise, as a human being. Camille Flammarion, the most encyclopaedic of French 'occultists', had no doubt that clairvoyant faculties are not some extra 'sense' but simply the normal ability of the mind to escape the limitations of the body. Writing about Friederike Hauffe, the 'Seeress of Prevorst' who could read a book placed open on her stomach, or about the young girl described by Lombroso who could read with her ear, he writes, 'The result of this research is *the affirmation that the human being can see without eyes, with the spirit.*' And by way of supporting this assertion he goes on to offer almost sixty pages of impressive examples, beginning with a document by the Archbishop of Bordeaux describing a young priest of somnambulist tendencies who used to get up in the middle of the night and write his sermon – with his eyes closed – then re-read it and make corrections. Thomson Jay Hudson would immediately object that this is merely an example of the power of the subjective mind: that in his 'sleep-walking' state the priest could visualize the page on which he was writing and remember it so accurately that he could even go back and make corrections. There is no need for 'vision without eyes'.

But other cases cited by Flammarion cannot be explained in the same way. Alexis Didier was one of the most famous hypnotic subjects of the nineteenth century, and his feats occupy many pages of Eric J. Dingwall's *Abnormal Hypnotic Phenomena*. He became a somnambule by accident. One day at the theatre, he volunteered to go on stage to be hypnotized and made such an impression that his employer decided to give up commerce and become his manager. By far his most spectacular feat was playing cards while blindfolded. This sounds, of course, like an ordinary stage magician's trick – a conclusion also reached by the famous stage magician Robert Houdin (after whom Houdini named himself). But a session with Didier left Houdin shattered and convinced. The latter had brought a pack of marked cards with him to guard against trickery, but it proved to be quite unnecessary. Houdin shuffled, and as he laid the first card down on the table Didier identified it as a king. As the game proceeded he proved to be correct. Although Houdin played with his own hand under the table, Didier would advise him which card to play next. This, of course, sounds like telepathy. But Didier played his own cards *without turning them over*, and they always proved to be in perfect agreement with the ones Houdin had just played.

Didier also demonstrated psychometric abilities under hypnosis. Alexandre Dumas handed him a ring: Didier described its history and that of the man who had given it to Dumas, then went on to describe Tunis, where the ring had originated, although Didier only knew it by name.

Another of Didier's feats was to project himself mentally to places mentioned by those who were testing him, an ability known as 'travelling clairvoyance'. Again this sounds like a matter of ordinary telepathy, but Didier often proved otherwise by describing things of which his companion was unaware. A certain Captain Daniell asked Didier to 'travel' to his father's house. After Didier had correctly described ornaments, furniture and other details, Daniell told him he had been wrong about only one thing, the colour of the curtains. But when he checked later Daniell found that Didier was correct.

On another occasion a highly sceptical magistrate named Séguier went to see Didier and asked him where he – Séguier – had been at two o'clock that day. 'In your study,' said Didier. 'It is cluttered with papers – twists of tobacco – drawings – and little machines. There is a pretty little bell on your desk.' Séguier denied the last observation emphatically. But when he got home he found the bell, which his wife had placed there that afternoon. This seems to demonstrate that Didier made use of telepathy *and* 'travelling clairvoyance'. The telepathy told him where Séguier had been at two o'clock that afternoon but it was 'travelling clairvoyance' that showed him the bell that had been placed on the desk since Séguier left home.

'Travelling clairvoyance' was demonstrated most clearly in a case of theft. In 1849 a clerk named Dubois vanished from his place of work, the Mont-de-Piété, with two hundred thousand francs; a lawyer friend of the manager decided to go and consult Didier. Without prompting, Didier told his visitor the sum stolen and the name of the thief: Dubois. He added that Dubois was at present in Brussels, in the Hôtel des Princes. The lawyer hurried there, only to find that the clerk had left a few hours earlier. Didier now stated that he saw the clerk in a casino at Spa and that he would have no money left by the time he was arrested. The lawyer rushed off to Spa (in Belgium), and again missed the clerk by hours. Back in Paris, Didier told him that the clerk had been to Aix-la-Chapelle but was now back in Spa gambling away the remaining money. This time the clerk was arrested but – as Didier had foretold – he was penniless.

This account makes it clear that Didier possessed the same powers that enabled Eileen Garrett to locate the whereabouts of the missing doctor. But these powers were the result of hypnosis, not of some inborn 'psychic faculty'. What Flammarion's chapter demonstrates is that the powers that can be released by hypnosis are far greater than modern medical science would admit. (The same point is demonstrated repeatedly in Dingwall's *Abnormal Hypnotic Phenomena*.) In the twentieth century we have come to take it for granted that the powers displayed by hypnotized subjects are merely the result of 'suggestion'. At the time of writing Dr Graham Wagstaff, a Liverpool professor, has just announced that all the effects of hypnosis can be explained away in terms of role-playing (i.e. play-acting), a return to the kind of total scepticism that prevailed at the beginning of the nineteenth century. But unless Robert Houdin and many eminent Victorian scientists were downright liars, such a view is grotesquely inadequate to explain the observed facts.

Flammarion had no doubt that both telepathy and will power play some part in hypnosis – or can do. 'The action of the will at a distance is not subject to doubt, as those who have studied this subject know very well.' Mesmer, the discoverer of a form of hypnosis, demonstrated this to the scholar Seifert, who viewed mesmerism as 'all humbug'. When Seifert demanded proof Mesmer offered to demonstrate his powers through a brick wall. The subject – one of Mesmer's patients – was placed on one side of the wall and Mesmer on the other, while Seifert stood where he could watch them both. When Mesmer made some angular movements from right to left the subject complained that he felt 'as if everything within me were swinging from right to left'. When Mesmer began to make oval motions with his fingers the man complained, 'Now everything is turning about in a circle.' All this happened in 1775, some years before Mesmer's pupil Puységur discovered hypnosis, so Mesmer's subject was fully conscious. But a century later two eminent psychologists, Pierre Janet and Julian Ochorowicz, collaborated on a series of experiments that proved beyond all doubt that people could also be hypnotized from a distance and would then respond to telepathic commands. Janet was puzzled by the results of a doctor in Le Havre, J. H. A. Gibert, who was able to hypnotize a peasant woman by 'peripheral muscular stimulation' – pressure on her hand. But Gibert found that it only worked if he concentrated: if he tried to do it without proper attention the woman did not respond. This clearly indicated that Gibert's 'thought pressure' played some part in the hypnosis. So Gibert tried hypnotizing the woman by thought alone – and it worked. Janet began working with the same peasant woman and found that he could induce a hypnotic trance from the other side of Le Havre merely by thinking about her, and could call her to him.

Ochorowicz, a hard-headed medical man, began to move beyond his materialistic assumptions when he discovered that his hypnotized subjects obtained unusually high scores in card guessing games. Ochorowicz and Janet began to collaborate with Dr Gibert, using his peasant woman, Mme B., as a subject. They established that even when Mme B. was half a mile away from the hypnotist (either Janet or Gibert) she could be put into a trance and then given mental orders which she would obey. Moreover if the hypnotist pinched himself Mme B. would react as if she were being pinched in the same place. It was the old 'community of sensation' that had been observed by Alfred Russel Wallace and William Barrett (and which would later be observed by Dr Pagenstecher). But Mme B. (later known as Léonie) also demonstrated powers of 'travelling clairvoyance'. Asked to visit the famous paranormal researcher Charles Richet in Paris, she declared that his laboratory was on fire – and proved to be correct. The result of all these researches, published in Ochoro-wicz's *Mental Suggestion* (1887) caused a sensation, and many medical men hastened to confirm these results. A Dr Dufay of Blois conducted experiments with a subject called Maria in which she displayed remark-able psychometric powers. In the *Revue Philosophique* Dufay described how Maria had been hypnotized then handed a package containing a small portion of a necktie belonging to a man who had used it to commit suicide in gaol. She was able not only to describe the man's crime – murdering someone with a hatchet – to the examining magistrate, but was also able to tell them where to find the murder weapon. She went on to demonstrate that simply by handling objects belonging to various prisoners, she could tell what crime they had been gaoled for.

The result of all these experiments points to the same unmistakable conclusion: that suggestion can be transmitted direct from one mind to another and that the will can play an active part in hypnosis. Flammarion might have strengthened his case by citing a criminal trial of 1865 in which a club-footed beggar named Timotheus Castellan was sentenced to twelve years in prison for the rape of a twenty-six-year-old peasant girl named Josephine. Castellan had begged a night's lodging from her father, a poor peasant, claiming to be a healer. The next morning the girl's father and brother went to the fields leaving her alone with Castellan. A neighbour who called claimed that she saw Castellan making signs in the air behind the girl's back. Over the midday meal Castellan made a sign with his fingers, as if dropping something on the girl's plate, and she felt her senses leaving her. He carried her into the next room and raped her; she said she was conscious but unable to move. Later Castellan departed, taking her with him. At one farm where he stayed the night he demonstrated his power over her by making her crawl around on all fours like an animal and burst into peals of laughter. He was eventually arrested.

The well-known Heidelberg case of 1934 has many of the same features. A woman was arrested for attempting to kill her husband. The police psychiatrist, Dr Ludwig Mayer, eventually discovered that she had made six attempts on her husband's life on the orders of a criminal named Franz Walter. Walter had met the woman on a train and told her he was a healer. As she accompanied him for a cup of coffee he touched her hand, and she suddenly felt as if all her will power had deserted her. She accompanied him to a room in Heidelberg where he placed her in a trance

201

by touching her forehead and raped her. He subsequently made her earn money for him by prostitution, then ordered her to murder her husband. Walter was sentenced to ten years in prison.*

These cases throw an interesting light on the experience of the girl cited in *Phantasms of the Living* who became a man's sexual slave in her dreams (see p. 189). The obvious hypothesis about the women who became victims of Castellan and Walter is that they were prone to hysteria and allowed themselves to be 'paralysed' by suggestion. But in the case cited in *Phantasms of the Living* this is obviously impossible, since the girl did not even see the man of her dreams until months later. In this case, the likeliest explanation is that the man immediately recognized her as the kind of person whom he could bend to his will by means of telepathic suggestion and deliberately set out on a course of long-distance dream-seduction. And if that possibility can be admitted then it seems likely that Castellan and Franz Walter used a similar method. This view is supported by the observations of a modern researcher, Dr Ferenc Andras Völgyesi, whose *Hypnosis of Man and Animals* has become a classic. Völgyesi came to accept that will power plays a part in the hypnosis of animals and birds by snakes and often witnessed 'battles of will'. His book contains photographs of these mental struggles taking place between a giant toad and a cobra and between a rattlesnake and a bird of prey.

The implications of these ideas may seem more revolutionary than they actually are. After all if we can accept the evidence for telepathy – and the evidence in its favour is now overwhelming – then we have already accepted the idea that one mind can influence another. The only surprising thing that emerges from Flammarion, Ochorowicz and the rest is that it seems far easier than we might assume. In *Over the Long High Wall* J. B. Priestley tells how, at a boring literary dinner in New York, he decided to try an experiment in telepathic suggestion: to make one of the poets wink at him. He chose a sombre looking woman, 'obviously no winker', and concentrated on her: suddenly she turned to him and winked. Later she came over to apologize. 'It was just a sudden silly impulse.'

The same 'knack' was apparently possessed by Elsie, Lady Abercrombie, who is described in Joyce Collin-Smith's autobiography *Call No Man Master*.

At an early age she had discovered it to be possible to influence other people's words and actions. Once, in India, banished by her mother from a formal gathering, she had returned to her schoolroom and set herself in pure mischief to influence events downstairs. They would all start talking compulsively of something silly, something irrelevant, and be unable to stop, she determined.

*Both cases are described more fully in *Mysteries*, pp. 486–8.

Her mother, knowing her gift, came sternly half an hour later and shook her: 'Stop it at once, you naughty girl! They're all talking and talking about. . . .'

'Camels?' said Elsie with an innocent look. And so it proved to be.

Pressed for further information about Lady Abercrombie, Joyce Collin-Smith sent me the following anecdotes:

. . . I do know she had no clear idea how she did it . . . . Once at a meeting in a studio behind a house belonging to Michael Macowen, head of LAMDA, Elsie muttered to me, 'Cold. Better end it.' She was quite elderly then, and felt the cold a lot. A moment later Michael said, 'It seems to have got cold in here. We'll stop early and go in for coffee.' It might have been a coincidence but for the wicked twinkle and chuckle which made me sure she had manipulated it somehow.

Another curious episode was when I took her a large potted hydrangea, which I thought lovely. I put it near her chair. An hour later I was astonished to notice it had drooped completely as though absolutely dead, though it had stood the long journey in my car without harm. When I mentioned it, she glanced at it and said balefully, 'I hate hydrangeas.' As I apologized for bringing her an unacceptable gift she stared at it for a long time, then went on talking. Ten or fifteen minutes later I was absolutely astonished to find it had perked up, and was almost visibly lifting its petals, as though exorted to live after all, rather than hurt my feelings.

One of my correspondents, John Jacobs, has suggested that the 'knack' involved is a quality he calls 'in-betweenness'. This is a state that combines relaxation with a certain degree of deliberate purpose. He describes how as a child he was astonished to see his younger brother opening a good-quality padlock with a paper-clip. 'I asked him how he did it and he replied, "It's easy", and did it again for me. After I finally expressed my great amazement, it was curious that he could no longer open the padlock. My postulation is that he did not realize that people weren't supposed to be able to do such things. After I expressed my amazement I succeeded in indoctrinating him into the world-view that such things are impossible.'

Jacobs described another incident that took place when his brother was five.

We were cleaning the corn crib and . . . there were quite a few mice and rats liberated in the process. I was standing by my brother when a rat ran by about five or ten feet away. My brother had been pretending he was an Indian and had become totally involved in the

203

imaginary play-acting. When he saw the rat he hurled his paper-weight knife at it and – amazingly – it went through the animal and killed it. Under normal circumstances, that knife would have bounced off a balloon, let alone killed an animal. I believe that, in his child innocence, my brother caused another reality to manifest – the reality of himself as a mighty Indian hunter.

This story immediately brings to mind Dr Albert Mason's 'miracle' cure of the boy with fish-skin disease by hypnosis (p. 64). Mason had no idea that fish-skin disease was incurable and the result was that he cured it: as soon as he knew it was incurable he began to fail. And all this in turn suggests that 'magical' powers may be no more than the powers we can naturally exercise when in a relaxed and confident state. Everyone who has been actively involved in sport has noticed the same phenomenon: there are certain states when 'everything goes right' and when the most unlikely kick will score a goal. I have occasionally noticed the same thing when playing darts: I am normally an indifferent player but on a few rare occasions I have begun to play with an accuracy that astounded me. On such occasions I have noticed that I have reached a high degree of inner tension *combined with* deep relaxation: the result is John Jacobs' 'in-betweenness'.

Since the use of such powers involves relaxation it would seem to follow that the first step towards learning to use them would be to learn to relax – so, for example, they ought to be enhanced by transcendental meditation. Joyce Collin-Smith tells a number of stories about the Maharishi that suggest that this is so. When he was holding court in an Oxford hotel an aristocratic old lady on the same floor complained to the management about the noise, and the Maharishi was asked if he would mind moving to another floor. Joyce Collin-Smith was deputed to deliver the message. The Maharishi replied that he had no intention of moving, then added casually, 'Don't worry – she won't bother us again.' And to Joyce Collin-Smith's amazement, she didn't. The Maharishi, it seems, could exercise the same peculiar power as Lady Abercrombie. Joyce Collin-Smith's account of her 'initiation', and the deep relaxation she experienced immediately thereafter, suggest that the Maharishi may have used the same power to positive effect on his followers.

What seems clear is that these powers somehow involve the positive use of the imagination. This was an observation I made a few years ago when trying out an experiment in psychokinesis recommended to me by the dowser Robert Leftwich. The apparatus required is extremely simple: a needle, a cork, and a two-inch square of paper. The paper is first folded diagonally from corner to corner twice, thus making an X, then in half again, vertically and horizontally – so the resulting pattern looks rather like a Union Jack. This can then be pinched into a paper dart with four 'fins'. The needle is stuck in the cork and the paper dart placed umbrella-wise on top of it, so the end product looks like a tiny

204

roundabout. After tying a handkerchief round his face (to prevent him breathing on it), Leftwich placed his hands around his 'roundabout' and concentrated for a moment: the roundabout began to revolve – first clockwise, then counter-clockwise. But when I tried it, the utmost efforts of concentration failed to make it move. I tried keeping it at the side of my typewriter and trying to "will" it to move whenever I felt relaxed. And one day, as I stared at it and imagined it moving, it began to move. It was no fluke; I found that I could make it stop, then revolve the other way. The trick, obviously, was to use the imagination as well as will power.

In *Mysteries* I have described a similar experiment, suggested by the theatre historian John Melling. I was made to stand in the middle of the room with my eyes closed. Four people stood around me with their hands raised to the level of my shoulders but not touching me and tried to 'will' me to sway in a pre-selected direction. After a few minutes I began to feel dizzy, then found myself swaying forward – the direction they had chosen – as if an invisible force was pushing me. The 'trick' worked with everyone in the group. Yet when I tried demonstrating the same thing in front of television cameras at eleven o'clock in the morning it failed utterly. At that hour and in that setting we were not in the correct mood of 'in-betweenness'.

If these powers are so easy to demonstrate, why do we not bother to develop them? The answer seems to be because they are irrelevant. The snake needs its power to 'hypnotize' a rabbit. But of what earthly use would it be to be able to make strangers wink at you? Myer's story of the man who tried to seduce a girl by means of 'dream telepathy' seems to underline the point: the man went to an enormous amount of trouble, all to no effect. But in fact these objections are really an illustration of our human tendency to laziness and inertia. If such powers exist they are of immense importance and deserve to be investigated and understood: their implications could be as momentous as those of splitting the atom.

The bewildering variety of evidence presented in this chapter all seems to point in the same direction: a human being is not merely a physical body that happens to be 'alive'. A more representative picture is that a human being is a presiding entity – let us call it a mind or spirit – whose basic function is the *control* of the physical body and the emotions. This in turn seems to amount to an assertion that the mind is somehow independent of the body and might therefore be expected to survive physical death. But at this point a basic objection arises. When I fall asleep I 'disappear' and have no more memories until I begin to recover consciousness. In other words, when the body falls asleep *I* fall asleep. This seems to suggest that 'I' am my body.

What seems equally puzzling is that in the majority of cases of 'phantasms of the living', the 'projector' has no idea of whether he has succeeded or not. S. H. Beard had no idea of whether he had 'appeared' to Miss Verity and her sister yet his 'apparition' stroked the sister's hair and took her hand. Yeats 'appeared' to his student friend, and later reappeared in the middle of the night and gave him a message, while his body was sleeping, oblivious, in bed. Hereward Carrington succeeded in 'appearing' to his woman friend yet had to ask her if the experiment had been successful.

Equally strange is an anecdote in Robert Monroe's *Journeys Out of the Body* in which he described 'projecting' himself into the study of the paranormal investigator Andrija Puharich, with whom he was in correspondence. He spoke to Puharich and says that he replied and apologized for neglecting their project. Later Monroe discovered that his memories of Puharich's study were accurate, yet Puharich had no memory of speaking to him. This implies either that the 'visit' was basically a dream or that Monroe's 'astral body' was able to communicate directly with Puharich's 'astral body' without Puharich's physical self being aware of it.

Other cases seem to suggest that human consciousness may be somehow 'divided'. D. Scott Rogo has cited the case of a woman who was lying in bed, fully awake, when she saw a 'roll of mist' near the ceiling.

> I could feel its presence and its motion as though I, Helen, *was* the mist, and the knowledge came with the words, 'Oh, I am up on the ceiling.' I was not asleep. I was not dreaming. I could see it there, though not with my bodily eyes.... There was no fear, no questioning – simply a quiet acceptance of the fact that I was outside my body, hovering over it. There was a sensation of pushing against the ceiling, lightly, and of being stopped by it, as a toy balloon which has got away would be stopped ... it ended when I was aware of being back in my body.*

It seems that the centre of this woman's consciousness remained in her body, although she was also aware that 'the mist' was herself. We should also note that she saw herself with 'the eyes of the mind' – as Goethe did – another shred of evidence to support Flammarion's view that it is the mind that perceives 'paranormally', not the physical senses.

In that case we would presume that Yeats's friend saw him with 'the eyes of the mind', and that when he spoke to Yeats his mind was communicating directly with a *subconscious* level of Yeats's mind – or as Hudson would say, with Yeats's subjective rather than his objective mind.

A glimmer of daylight begins to appear. In an earlier chapter we tentatively identified Hudson's 'two minds' with the two hemispheres of split-brain physiology. (It should be emphasized that the identification

---

*Quoted in *The Unfathomed Mind: A Handbook of Unusual Mental Phenomena* compiled by William D. Corliss, p. 571.

itself is not important: what matters is the established fact that we have two 'selves', not whether they are really located in the left and right cerebral hemispheres.) We also concluded that in a certain sense, all human beings are 'split-brain patients' whose rational ego is out of touch with the intuitive non-ego. On this level at least it is an established fact that human beings experience 'divided consciousness'. Rational consciousness is narrow and, as we realize in states of deep relaxation, only a fragment of our possible total consciousness. Pierre Janet observed that the consciousness of hysterical patients became increasingly narrow until in some cases they actually experienced 'tunnel vision'. He also discovered that he could sit beside one of these hysterical patients and converse with both aspects of the patient's mind. If he said in a low voice, 'Raise your left hand,' the patient would obey. If he then said, in his normal voice, 'Why have you got your left hand in the air?' the patient would look up in amazement. This phenomenon is no more mysterious than the fact that we can bruise ourselves when we are in a hurry and not even notice we have done it until later. 'Divided consciousness' is a matter of everyday experience. And if we consider that the rational ego is the product of millions of years of evolution, we can begin to understand why it has lost contact with the instinctive self and why our 'normal' human consciousness is little better than tunnel vision.

Goethe's vision of his own *doppelgänger* riding to meet him was an example of divided consciousness: his 'other self' apparently sent the image to comfort him in his misery. Helen's vision of herself floating near the ceiling as a roll of mist is another example. One of the most amusing examples can be found in the autobiography of a remarkable English 'psychic', Rosalind Heywood. She describes how one sleepless night she lay beside her husband and decided to wake him up to make love to her:

Before I could carry out this egoistic idea I did something very odd – I split in two. One Me in its pink nightie continued to toss self-centredly against the embroidered pillows, but another, clad in a long, very white, hooded garment, was now standing, calm, immobile and impersonally outward-looking, at the foot of the bed. This White Me seemed just as actual as Pink Me *and I was equally conscious in both places at the same time* [my italics]. I vividly remember myself as White Me looking down and observing the carved end of the bed in front of me and also thinking what a silly fool Pink Me looked, tossing in that petulant way against the pillows. 'You're behaving disgracefully,' said White Me to Pink Me with cold contempt. 'Don't be so selfish, you know he's dog-tired.'

Pink Me was a totally self-regarding little animal, entirely composed of 'appetites', and she cared not at all whether her unfortunate husband was tired or not. 'I shall do what I like,' she retorted furiously, 'and you can't stop me, you pious white prig!'

She was particularly furious because she knew very well that White Me was the stronger and could stop her.

A moment or two later – I felt no transition – White Me was once more imprisoned with Pink Me in one body, and there they have dwelt as oil and water ever since.

A moment's thought shows that this experience makes good sense. We all change through a number of levels of maturity from the cradle to the grave. 'I' am not now the person I was at six or twelve or eighteen, yet in a sense I feel that I am more 'myself' now than I was at eighteen. Past 'selves' have been discarded: yet at six and twelve and eighteen I was also quite convinced that the self I was aware of was the 'real me'. It seems logical to assume that even at fifty-six the self I am aware of is not the 'real me'. I am inclined to feel that if I could live to be two hundred and keep the full use of my faculties I might develop into something more like the 'real me', but the present 'me' is certainly not it.

What seemed to happen to Rosalind Heywood was that as a psychic, she was able to separate momentarily into 'present me' and 'real me'. Without the benefit of such an experience most of us assume that 'present me' *is* 'real me'. We should note that Rosalind Heywood's Pink Me was 'a totally self-regarding little animal entirely composed of appetites' – that is of emotions. She corresponds roughly to what in an earlier chapter we labelled 'the emotional body', while White Me was the mind or intellect.

There are other such experiences of 'separation' in the literature of paranormal research. In *The Personality of Man* G. N. M. Tyrrell cites a number of cases, including one of a soldier in the Great War who, in a state of intense physical stress, separated from his physical body. He then watched his body go on talking to a companion who later said he had chatted with great wit and humour. This seems to be quite clearly an example of the 'two selves'.

Tyrrell also goes on to cite the case of Sir Auckland Geddes, already described (p. 196). And in this case we encounter another interesting clue to the nature of dual consciousness. As his body became paralysed Geddes felt that his 'consciousness was separating from another consciousness which was also me'. One consciousness was attached to his body while the other was attached to his ego. He also noted that his body consciousness showed 'signs of being composite, that is, built up of "consciousness" from the head, the heart and the viscera'. Then these various 'organ consciousnesses' became more individual as body-consciousness began to disintegrate and ego-consciousness found itself outside the body. Ouspensky made the same observation during his states of 'experimental mysticism' when he noted that each organ of his body seemed to have its own individual consciousness, with which he could communicate. We may also recall Jack Seale's comment as the effects of his snake bite began to wear off: 'normal consciousness returned *in layers*' [my italics]. His body had been totally paralysed: in fact it was 'dead'. It seems probable that the 'layers' corresponded to the various 'organ consciousnesses' described by Geddes and Ouspensky.

It seems, then, that there is an overwhelming body of evidence for 'divided consciousness' or the existence of 'two selves'. And this to a large extent undermines the objection that my everyday self has no experience of being independent of the body. If the consciousness of 'real me' is inextricably blended with the various 'consciousnesses' of the body and emotions, that is exactly what we would expect. It is admittedly difficult for me, as I sit in my chair, to grasp that the 'me' who looks out of my eyes is not the 'real me'. But a little reflection shows me that I am mistaken. I experience a certain amount of eyestrain, the result of several hours' typing, and some physical fatigue, and I look forward to taking my dogs for a walk in the woods and picking blackberries: my present consciousness is narrow and stressful and I am aware that my tiredness is turning me into a kind of robot. This is not *real* consciousness, and the 'me' I am aware of is not the real me.

On the other hand the evidence presented in this chapter points to some strange conclusions. We talk about 'my consciousness' as if it were a unity, but if Geddes is correct it may actually be a whole collection of 'consciousnesses' including those from the head, the heart and the viscera. And 'my' consciousness may be capable of being present in more than one place at once – as Rosalind Heywood discovered. And what of those curious experiences of the 'double' described by Yeats and Beard and Carrington? Yeats's double talked to his student friend while Yeats, several hundred miles away, was unaware of what was going on. But unless the double was some kind of psychic imposter we must presume that *some* level of Yeats's mind knew what was going on and that it was only 'everyday Yeats', like Janet's hysterical patient, who was unaware.

In his last poem, 'Under Ben Bulben', Yeats wrote about how 'when a man is fighting mad . . .'

Something drops from eyes long blind,
He completes his partial mind . . .

We all know that sensation – the 'holiday feeling' – when 'normal consciousness' seems to expand to something far wider and richer, and our delight in the experience is undermined by a troubled recognition that we ought to be able to *grasp* this once and for all, and never again allow ourselves to be trapped in the poverty-stricken consciousness of every-day life. It is difficult to know exactly what we can do about it – except remain persistent and keep trying. But these insights at least make us aware that everyday consciousness is not 'real consciousness'. The jazz musician Mezz Mezzrow said about the first time he smoked opium, 'Lights came on all over my body where I didn't even know I had sockets.' And the same thing happens to consciousness in moods of

209

optimism and intensity, when 'lights' come on in distant reaches whose existence we had not even suspected. If Yeats had been in this state when he 'appeared' to his fellow student he might well have been aware of the conversation. And this in turn suggests that the part of us that can gain access to the 'information universe' of psychometry or precognition is some aspect of us which is concealed from everyday consciousness.

It should be possible to see that this theory covers every subject that has so far been discussed in this book: mystical experience, Faculty X, psychometry, 'time-slips', dowsing, precognitions (admittedly the most difficult topic considered), synchronicities, astral projection, *doppelgängers* and so on. It seems in fact to be the comprehensive theory of the paranormal that was so obviously lacking in the earlier researchers like Myers and Flammarion (although Myers made a very creditable attempt in *Human Personality and its Survival of Bodily Death*). This was my own view, as I saw it beginning to emerge in books like *Mysteries, Frankenstein's Castle* and *Access to Inner Worlds*: that the simple, straightforward answer to all the mysteries of the paranormal was the 'hidden power' inside all of us. Civilization has in effect turned us all into 'hysterical patients' whose left hand is not aware what the right is doing and whose brains are equally divided. The recognition that we actually possess these powers is the first step towards developing them.

Subject to certain qualifications, I still believe this to be true. But the qualifications – as will be seen – have turned out to be far more important than I originally expected.

Part Two

Powers of Good and Evil

1

The Search for Evidence

I have so far been able to present this material in a fairly impersonal and logical manner. Now it becomes necessary to speak again of my own involvement in the 'search for evidence'.

In the opening chapter I explained how my interest in the 'occult' was a natural development of an interest in mystical experience. And the interest in mystical experience was in turn a development of my interest in those curious states of happiness and affirmation that Chesterton called 'absurd good news'. In this state one thing is fundamentally clear: that our ordinary consciousness is bedevilled with certain errors or fallacies that have the effect of making life seem dull and ordinary. The demon Screwtape told his nephew Wormwood, 'Thanks to processes which we set at work in human beings centuries ago, they find it all but impossible to believe in the unfamiliar while the familiar is before their eyes. Keep pressing home on him the *ordinariness* of things . . . .'

Now this inability to believe in the unfamiliar while the familiar is at hand is, quite simply, a form of hypnosis. 'Familiarity' makes a few mysterious passes in front of our eyes: our minds go blank, and the world is suddenly 'ordinary' and rather boring. And our response to ordinariness is to sink into a state of passivity: it seems self-evident that it is not worth making any effort. Most people spend their lives in the 'hypnotized' state, and die wondering why they were born in the first place.

This explains why the romantics of the nineteenth century made such frenzied efforts to escape from 'ordinariness', even if it meant becoming alcoholics, drug addicts or suicides. Rimbaud wrote, 'I say that one must be a *visionary* – that one must make oneself a VISIONARY.' And he spoke of a 'reasoned derangement of the senses': 'I accustomed myself to simple hallucination: I really saw a mosque in place of a factory, angels practising on drums, coaches on the roads of the sky, a drawing room at the bottom of a lake. . . .'

But the real aim of all the romantics was to achieve those moments when consciousness seems to heave a sigh of relief and expand into a marvellous sense of the sheer richness of things: when it becomes aware – as Hesse's Steppenwolf puts it – of 'Mozart and the stars'. In this sense we are all romantics: the romantic impulse is one of the most fundamental drives of the human race. We make the mistake of thinking that we enjoy holidays because they allow us to recuperate, to recruit our

213

energies. This is untrue. We enjoy holidays because they *fill us with courage*. They remind us that the world is a richer and more interesting place than we had come to believe, and that the stakes we are playing for are unbelievably high. Ordinary consciousness tends towards depression, which is another name for discouragement. By making us again aware of the sheer variety of the world, holidays fill us with new courage and determination. Whenever we experience this feeling it suddenly seems that it would be absurdly easy to use it to change our lives. It all seems so obvious that it is difficult to see where the problem lies. All we have to do is to *remember* this insight, to refuse to be taken in by the ordinariness which we now know to be a deception. Yet somehow this simple lesson is appallingly difficult to put into practice. A single snap of the hypnotist's fingers and we are back in a state of yawning passivity.

This was the problem at the heart of my first book *The Outsider*. People who have glimpsed this freedom are no longer contented to accept 'ordinariness' as inevitable. They struggle and worry and fret, and seem permanently dissatisfied with their achievement. Their friends and relatives find it hard to understand what is the matter with them; they seem determined to make themselves unhappy and uncomfortable. I pointed out that in earlier centuries such people were tolerated as religious 'Outsiders'. St Augustine's *Confessions* and the Journals of George Fox describe the same deep self-dissatisfaction that we find in more recent 'Outsider' documents like Amiel's Journals and the novels of Dostoevsky. It also seemed clear that if some of the romantic 'Outsiders' had spent less time indulging in self-pity and more in trying to achieve some kind of self-discipline, they would have stood a better chance of surviving.

By the time I wrote *Religion and the Rebel* I had discovered the work of Arnold Toynbee, and it reinforced my conviction. Toynbee called the 'Outsiders' 'the creative minority' and spoke of a mechanism of 'withdrawal and return'. The religious 'Outsider' used to retreat into the wilderness and emerge finally with his own 'message from God'. Such men not only made an impact on their society; they often changed its entire direction. The gradual erosion of religious faith – due to the rise of science – meant that modern 'Outsiders' became more than ever a prey to 'ordinariness' and the lack of self-confidence it entails. Toynbee, who was deeply religious, hoped for some kind of great revival of Christianity; although he was realistic enough to recognize that it was unlikely. He concluded that all he could do was to 'cling and wait'.

To me, it seemed self-evident that some religious revival was not the answer. For better or for worse (probably for better) people have outgrown Christianity, and the movement of history suggests that the same will happen to the other major religions. But that is no cause for pessimism. The essence of religion has always been the feeling of 'absurd good news', not the dogmas of the theologians, so the essence of religion remains unaffected. The problem is how to grasp this essence. Besides, the decline of religion was not due to some demonic conspiracy but to the fact that human beings were learning to think for themselves. It would obviously be no solution to try to put back the clock. In which case the only clear alternative is to go forward in the same direction. We have to learn to think more, not less.

The next major clue came in 1959 when I received a letter from the American psychologist Abraham Maslow. Maslow felt that Freud and his followers had 'sold human nature short', and his own investigations had led him to conclude that there were 'higher ceilings of human nature'. His major key was the concept of the 'peak experience', by which he meant precisely what Chesterton meant by the feeling of 'absurd good news'. Peak experiences, he insisted, were not 'mystical'; they were simply a kind of bubbling-over of sheer vital energy and optimism and a recognition that the world is not 'ordinary' but exciting and strange. I was much impressed by his example – cited earlier – of the marine who had come back from years in the Pacific, and who had a peak experience when he saw a nurse back at base. He said that it suddenly struck him with tremendous force that *women are different from men*. He said that men take women for granted, as human beings like themselves, whereas the truth is that they are almost mystically different.

Maslow made the important observation that *all* healthy people seem to have peak experiences with a fair degree of frequency. This deepened in me the insight that the main trouble with 'Outsiders' is that they tend to shrink from their own experience and to accept it half-heartedly. If we could grasp the lesson of the 'holiday experience' we would get on with what we have to do with cheerful determination, which would have the effect of reinforcing the lesson of the 'holiday experience' and making it still easier to put into practice. Maslow made an important observation that confirmed this: as his students talked among themselves about peak experiences, they began having more of them. I noted the lesson: the best way to induce peak experiences is to recall past peak experiences and to try to recreate their very essence, the feeling of delight and courage.

It can be seen that Yeats was talking about a peak experience when he wrote:

Something drops from eyes long blind,
He completes his partial mind,
For an instant stands at ease,
Laughs aloud, his heart at peace. . . .

The peak experience is essentially an experience of 'completing the partial mind'.

I have described in the opening chapter how as I came to research *The Occult* I became increasingly convinced of the reality of the 'paranormal'. I defy anyone to make a serious study of the subject and not to end up totally convinced. Scepticism is only another name for a certain lazy-minded dogmatism. And as I wrote the book it became quite clear that 'occultism' is simply a recognition of man's 'hidden powers' – that is, a recognition that everyday consciousness is merely the 'partial mind'. At the same time I realized what had always repelled me about spiritualism and 'occultism'. The 'believers' treat them as a religion, something towards which they direct their faith – generally another name for credulity. Their attitude is essentially passive. The result is that their credulity is reinforced, and they are further than ever from thinking for themselves. What attracted me about 'occultism' was the same healthy element that lies at the heart of religion – that obsession with the mystery of human existence that created saints and mystics rather than 'true believers'.

The next major clue came from that curious byway of psychology, the study of multiple personality. It had fascinated me ever since I came across the Christine Beauchamp case in a popular book by Dingwall. In 1898 Dr Morton Prince of Boston began treating a girl called Clara Fowler for nervous exhaustion. One day he decided to hypnotize her and to his astonishment, a completely different personality emerged under hypnosis, a bright, mischievous child who called herself Sally. She insisted that she was not Clara (or Christine, as Prince preferred to call her in his book about the case) although they shared the same body. Sally was tough and healthy and found it hard to understand why Clara was so feeble. Eventually a third personality appeared under hypnosis, a self-possessed, schoolmistressy girl whom Prince called B-4. It gradually transpired that B-4 had first made her appearance when Clara had a bad shock.

She was a nurse at the time, and a friend of her father's named William Jones had come to call on her at the hospital. Finding a ladder outside, he had put it against Clara's window and climbed up. The sight of Jones' face peering through her first-floor window had given Clara such a bad shock that she went into a nervous decline, and B-4 suddenly appeared and took over.

Sally and B-4 loathed one another, and Clara herself had no suspicion of the existence of either. Unfortunately Prince had let a genie out of the bottle when he 'released' Sally. Being stronger than Clara, Sally could push her out of the body – out of the driving seat, so to speak – and do as she liked. She loved playing practical jokes on the timid Clara, such as taking a long walk in the country then vacating the body and leaving poor Clara to walk back home. On one occasion Sally even went off to another town and got a job as a waitress. During these pranks Clara suffered total amnesia, and would wake up to find herself having to cope with some embarrassing situation.

Prince achieved some kind of success by finally integrating Clara and B-4 under hypnosis. Yet, as he admitted years later, he never wholly succeeded in getting rid of Sally.

A case like this seems to defy all common sense: it certainly seems to defy all our comfortable, logical notions about what it means to be an 'individual'. Of course it is not difficult to understand the vague outline of Clara's illness. She was always a timid sort of person. When she was thirteen her mother had died an unpleasant death and her father, an irresponsible alcoholic, was largely to blame. An experience like that is enough to make anyone decide that they do not want to face life. It is conceivable that Clara left home because her father was sexually interested in her: she never said as much, but we know that the majority of contemporary cases of multiple personality are caused by sexual abuse in childhood. (A recent study of multiple personality by the Institute of Noetic Sciences in California, directed by Brendan O'Regan, concluded that *all* such cases have their origin in childhood sexual abuse.)

Clara Fowler placed all her affection and trust in the family friend William Jones, who seemed to be everything that her father was not. But he also seems to have conceived designs on her, and when he appeared outside her window – somewhat the worse for drink – and later made suggestive remarks, her courage collapsed completely and B-4 suddenly appeared and took over. But why should another 'person' take over? Most people who allow themselves to become defeated by some traumatic experience simply have a nervous breakdown. Does the answer lie in the observation that we seem to become different persons at different stages in our lives? Is it possible that Clara *was* Sally when she was six years old, but that she then became nervous and shy so that Sally remained suppressed?

Dozens of other recorded cases of multiple personality make it clear that there is no simple answer. The mystery seems to defy all our normal criteria of individuality. Perhaps the most famous case was the one recorded by Thigpen and Cleckley in their book *The Three Faces of Eve*. Eve White (whose real name was Christine Sizemore) was a colourless young married woman who came to see the doctors because she was suffering from headaches and blackouts. She returned one day and told them that her husband was enraged because she had been on an expensive shopping spree and bought a lot of sexy clothes, yet she had no recollection whatever of doing so. And one day as she was talking to Dr Thigpen, another Eve made her appearance: a sophisticated, self-confident, brash young woman who smoked, drank and liked virile men. (The original Eve was a rather priggish young woman and a born-again Christian.) Apparently Eve Black had made her first appearance when Christine was six years old: after a blackout she came to and found herself being beaten for attacking her twin sisters as they lay in their cot. It was her 'other self' that had done it.

Christine Sizemore's case has many parallels with that of Clara Fowler, down to the appearance of a third personality, Jane, who was more sensible and integrated than the other two. Even the outcome of the case was similar. Thigpen thought he had cured Christine by integrating the three personalities, but in her later book, *Eve*, Christine Sizemore

217

revealed that the problem had returned in a more virulent form and a whole host of new personalities had appeared – about thirty in all.

One of the oddest features of the case is that the two Eves had different physical characteristics. Eve Black was allergic to nylon – it brought her out in a rash: as soon as Eve White took over the rash disappeared. When one personality was under anaesthetic another took over and 'she' promptly awoke.

Another curious feature of the case is that Eve White was 'psychic'. When she was a child her sister became ill, apparently with pneumonia. In a dream Christine saw Jesus, who told her that her sister had diphtheria, not pneumonia. She told her parents the next day and they sent for the doctor, who confirmed the diagnosis and obtained the necessary drug from fifty miles away. A few hours' delay would have cost the child's life. As an adult Christine had a vision of her husband being electrocuted at work: she persuaded him to stay at home. The man who took over his job was electrocuted. When her daughter was to be inoculated against polio a presentiment made her try to prevent it. She was overruled and her daughter almost died from a bad batch of vaccine. On a drive through the mountains she begged her husband to stop the car and check the wheels: a rear trailer wheel was so loose that it was about to fall off at any moment.

The obvious question raised by such a case is whether the 'dual personality' phenomenon has any connection with the *doppelgänger* phenomenon discussed in the last chapter. An example will clarify the point. In a celebrated case a Mrs Butler, who lived in Ireland, dreamt repeatedly of 'the most enchanting house I ever saw'. She and her husband decided to move to England and inspected many properties around London. One day they went to look at a house in Hampshire and Mrs Butler recognized it as her dream house. She was so familiar with it that she was able to show the housekeeper around the premises and describe every room before they entered it. The price of the house was absurdly low, and when they went to see the agent he told them why. 'The house is haunted.' But, he added, 'you need not be concerned. You are the ghost.' He had recognized her from the owner's precise description. Rudyard Kipling came upon a similar case, of a house 'haunted' by a former occupant who brooded upon it obsessively, and dramatized it in a story called 'The House Surgeon'. But if a *doppelgänger* can appear elsewhere without its owner being aware could it not perhaps also 'take over' the body if the owner was in a state of nervous depression and low vitality?

Speculations like these seemed to me an important step towards creating some comprehensive 'Newtonian' theory of 'the occult'. But just as I began to feel I was making some progress I came upon the extraordinary Doris Fischer case, which introduced a new complication. Doris (whose real name was Britta L. Fritschle) had a childhood not unlike that of Clara Fowler, with a drunken father and a mild,

218

uncomplaining mother. Her first 'split' occurred when her father snatched her from her mother's arms and threw her on the floor. The girl who sat up was no longer Doris but a personality who claimed to be a spirit. For the sake of simplicity, I will call her Ariel. Ariel was immediately succeeded by a mischievous child who resembled Clara Fowler's Sally. And from then on Doris's life was made a misery by Margaret's endless practical jokes. Doris would promise not to go swimming in the river, then would 'wake up' to find herself returning home with wet hair. When Doris reached out for a piece of cake Margaret would take over and gobble it down. But Margaret allowed Doris to share the body. Sometimes the two of them would hold conversations using the same mouth: but although Margaret seemed to be able to read Doris's mind, Doris would never know what Margaret was about to say until the words came out of her mouth. *That* was an interesting complication. *Doppelgängers can* behave like independent entities, but this seemed ridiculous.

Doris, like Christine Sizemore, had flashes of clairvoyance. One day at work she had a vision of her mother: she rushed home and found her suffering from pneumonia. Twelve hours later she was dead. And as Doris sat by the body her drunken father staggered in and without even noticing that his wife was dead, slumped into bed and fell asleep. At that moment Doris 'split' again. The newcomer had no memory and no personality: she was virtually a newborn baby. And as she 'grew up' she developed into a dull and lifeless young woman. A year later Doris fell on the back of her head and yet another person appeared, this time an even duller personality who seemed to be little more than a memory circuit, a kind of tape-recorder. Doris was now virtually a family inside the same body.

The interesting thing was that they formed a kind of hierarchy. Ariel – the 'spirit' – could read the minds of the other four and knew all about them. Margaret, the next down the 'ladder', knew about the three below her but not about Ariel, who was above her. Doris knew about the two below her but not about Margaret and Ariel (except when they chose to communicate). Ariel used to get angry at the way Margaret often 'pushed' Doris out of the driving seat and took over. And one day, when it had just happened, Ariel pushed Margaret out of the driving seat. This was how Margaret came to realize that there was somebody else in the body besides the 'people' she knew about.

Eventually Doris became acquainted with a kindly Pittsburgh doctor, Walter Franklin Prince (the same man who later tested Maria de Zierold with the sea bean). He allowed her to move into his house as a kind of adopted daughter, and she steadily improved. He observed with amazement the complex relationships between this odd 'family'. Sometimes two of them shared the body and would answer Prince's questions alternately. As Doris became more confident and healthy the lower personalities gradually faded out. The girl who had started as a newborn

219

baby now began to revert to childhood until she could only prattle. She and Prince took a final walk together then she 'died'. The 'tape-recorder' personality also faded out. As Doris's confidence and strength grew Margaret also began to grow back towards babyhood. At last she went blind and 'faded out'. Now only Ariel remained. But she had always taken care never to interfere in Doris's life – in fact Prince was inclined to accept her statement that she was a spirit. Later she actually took charge of Doris and escorted her to New York, where Doris had some sittings with a famous medium. Margaret appeared at one of these sittings and when asked about her after-life replied drily, 'I never had a life before: how can I have an after-life?' (Sadly, Doris was shattered by Prince's death in 1934 and died in a mental home.)

The Doris case made me realize that the simple *doppelgänger* theory of multiple personality had to be abandoned; but in favour of what? If Margaret was an 'alternative' Doris then how could she occupy the same body at the same time, and hold conversations? In some sense at least Margaret was a separate person. And even Prince believed that Ariel was a separate person. But it was in 1973, when I was preparing to begin *Mysteries*, a sequel to *The Occult*, that I had an interesting new insight into the problem. It came through an experience which at the time seemed quite shattering: a sudden spate of panic attacks which brought me very close to nervous breakdown. I was greatly overworked at the time, writing a series of articles on crime for an encyclopaedic work called *Crimes and Punishment*, of which I was an associate editor. The publishers wanted the articles at the rate of seven a week – each one about 3,000 words – and soon increased their demand to ten a week: that entailed writing the equivalent of a full-length book every three weeks. I ploughed on, refusing to be discouraged, but the strain was enormous. It was brought to a climax after two young journalists came to interview me and kept me up until the early hours of the morning. I woke up a couple of hours later feeling hot, sticky and hung-over and began worrying about the sheer amount of work I had to do. As I began to feel obsessively tense and worried I was tempted to go down to my typewriter and begin work immediately – but I realized that this would be the worst thing I could do. I tried to suppress the anxiety by sheer will power – and suddenly felt a surge of panic, a flood of adrenalin into the bloodstream. My heart began to beat at twice its normal speed and I was afraid I might be having a heart attack. I got up and spent an hour in the sitting room trying to reason myself out of it. Finally I climbed into bed and lay awake struggling with the panic and wondering if I was going insane. In the morning I felt exhausted and shattered. But I made a determined effort to exorcize the experience by writing an account of it, which became the opening pages of *Mysteries*.

In retrospect I can see precisely what happened. Human beings are called upon continually to face problems and difficulties, and to overcome them. When they succeed they feel a surge of optimism that doubles their

220

strength. When they fail they experience a feeling of discouragement that halves their strength. Then we seem to shrink from life and to lose all desire to summon up courage and vitality. Every time we try to envisage the future we foresee disaster and further defeat. Suddenly all life seems a hopeless struggle; we understand precisely what Emily Brontë meant when she asked:

Does the road wind uphill all the way?

Once we have sunk into this state of pessimism the problem is suddenly complicated by self-doubt. It is bad enough to be faced with what seems an endless succession of difficulties. It is far worse to feel that it is not even worth making a start on them because all life is futile. Logic tells you that you cannot lie down and refuse to move: you have a home and family to support. Yet this conviction is continually undermined by a demon inside you that whispers, 'It will all be wasted effort anyway . . . .' And when you take yourself by the scruff of the neck and say, 'You've got to go on, whether you like it or not,' there is a terrible sinking feeling, as if you are a horse beaten and spurred beyond endurance. Something inside you wants to burst into tears and turn its back on life.

All this enabled me to understand clearly the kind of misery and discouragement that had turned Clara Fowler and Doris Fischer into multiple personalities. But how did it explain those 'other selves'? In a sense the answer was obvious, for here was I, basically self-divided, with one rational self trying to keep order and drive myself to work and a non-rational or emotional self – perhaps even more than one – doing its best to foment a rebellion. It was horribly easy to imagine my rational self being permanently overthrown. Was that what had happened to Clara Fowler when she saw Jones's face at the window, and to Doris Fischer when her drunken father hurled her to the floor?

The worst times were at night. If I began to think about that unpleasant pounding of the heart it immediately began – as we itch if we think about itching. This in turn would induce a sudden flash of fear, as if the solid ground had turned into shifting sands. Then it was necessary to distract myself – to turn over, scratch my nose, anything. The fear would rise in me like milk boiling over, increasing by a process of negative feedback. Suddenly the normal security I took for granted would seem an illusion. Yet even on the second night I discovered the way to master the panic. I simply had to wake myself up fully – if necessary get out of bed and go to the lavatory. As soon as I was wide awake it was as if some more sensible level of my being had become aware of what was happening. Like a schoolmistress entering a room of squabbling children it clapped its hands and there was instant silence.

But what precisely *was* this 'schoolmistress effect'? It was as if some *higher* level of my personality had stirred into activity – the equivalent of Clara's B-4 and Christine's Jane. And so my experience of panic attacks

221

seemed to generate an insight into the mechanism of multiple personality.

The trouble with these attacks was that they wasted so much vitality; I felt permanently tired. Nevertheless I pressed on with my work for *Crimes and Punishment*, realizing that work was the best form of therapy. And one day, quite suddenly, I grasped the basic issue. The experience sounds utterly trivial yet it enabled me to begin to win the battle against the panic. It was five o'clock one afternoon and I had to take some letters to the post-box at the end of our lane. It seemed an utterly pointless, boring activity, but I knew it had to be done so I clambered into the Land-rover and drove down the lane. At the end of the lane I stopped the Land-rover before venturing out on to the wider road, and as I did so a car shot past so close that it almost removed my bumper. It made me realize that if I had been slightly more bored and indifferent I might have braked a split second later and caused a collision.

Now the truth is that it was not a *very* close thing. Yet it was enough to bring a flash of insight. My problem was simply that I had become self-divided. My sensible rational self could see that I had to do a great many necessary tasks – like taking letters to the post. My emotional self heaved a groan of boredom and dug in its heels. So my rational self had to drag it along behind like some kind of anchor, and every task cost twice as much effort. What made it worse was that *I* sympathized with its reluctance, for I agreed that going to the post-box was just a dreary chore. And that, of course, was the problem. The near accident made my rational self realize that this boredom could be an expensive self-indulgence. If there *had* been a collision it would have involved me in a hundred times as much effort as going to the post. And as soon as I used my imagination to conjure up the endless inconvenience of exchanging addresses and insurance companies and getting the Land-rover repaired I instantly felt a surge of relief that it hadn't happened. And my rational self turned on my emotional self and said irritably, 'You see, you bloody idiot, the problems you cause by dragging your heels all the time?' And the emotional self dropped its eyes and looked abashed. And for the rest of that day it behaved extremely well.

From then on the attacks began to fade – although it was several months before they vanished entirely. In retrospect I realized that what had seemed an entirely pointless and horrible episode had been, in fact, one of the most valuable experiences of my life. To begin with the long struggle to control the anxiety meant a far greater command over my spontaneous reactions. If someone dropped a plate on the floor, I didn't even start; if someone bored me, my eyes no longer betrayed my feelings. But what was far more important was the insight into the stupid behaviour of the emotional self. This is not confined to panic attacks and states of nervous depression. Since we all spend our time doing a great many things that we do not really want to do, we all waste an immense amount of energy overcoming the 'reluctance' of the emotional self.

Every time the sun goes behind a cloud the emotional self heaves a groan of discouragement and the heart sinks. And this is why, as William James said, 'most of us feel as if a sort of cloud weighed upon us, keeping us below our highest notch of clearness in discernment, sureness in reasoning, or firmness in deciding.' For we allow ourselves to be *taken in* whenever the emotional self sighs with boredom and says, 'Is it really worth the effort?'

This also explains, of course, Maslow's observation that healthy people are always having peak experiences. Because they are highly motivated they put far more effort into living and receive a far richer return than people who have to drag the emotional body behind them like a badly-behaved child. They can *see* the fallacy behind the feeling that things are 'just not worth the effort'. They go through life in a state of optimistic expectation. When the sun comes out it merely confirms their feeling that life means well by us; but when the sun goes in they accept it as a part of life's interesting variety.

Obviously this is what is fundamentally wrong with the human race. Psychiatrically speaking we are all neurotics, if by neurotic we mean that we 'live far within our limits' – that we all possess powers which we habitually fail to use. Is it surprising that most of us fail to catch a glimpse of our 'hidden powers' when we are not even capable of making proper use of our ordinary vital energies?

It seemed to me fairly clear that the first step towards reactivating these 'hidden powers' would be to make a determined effort to overrule the habitual 'reluctance' of the emotional self and to maintain a higher level of optimism. And in fact this insight had often been confirmed by experience. I had frequently noted that I became accident-prone when I had allowed myself to become tired and discouraged, and that some instinct for avoiding accidents seemed to be aroused when I was feeling fully alive. I remember a Monday morning when I had driven into our local fishing village, Mevagissey, to collect the cleaning lady from the bus. My mind was seething with ideas which I intended to get on to paper the moment I arrived home. The end of our narrow private lane joins the public road at an acute angle, and it is necessary to slow down and change into a lower gear to negotiate it, then to accelerate up a slope. As I was about to do this the thought entered my head, 'What if the post-van is coming down the lane?' In all our years in the house I had never met the post-van in the lane. Nevertheless I slowed down as I turned the corner. And the post-van stopped within an inch of my bumper.

In California I had a chance to test the hypothesis again. I had spent the morning lecturing at a university in Los Angeles and had agreed to meet my wife and children in Disneyland. I had forgotten just how big the place is. When I arrived around midday the crowds were enormous, and my heart sank. But I had just given a good lecture and was feeling confident and optimistic. So I deliberately relaxed and told my feet to go and find them. They took me a hundred yards down the road and turned

223

left. My family were eating at a Mexican food stall a few yards away. Again I felt that success was due to my state of mind – a certain relaxed optimism.

In *Mysteries* I tried to apply these lessons in my theory of the 'ladder of selves'. Physically speaking we all evolve through a number of stages between birth and death – Shakespeare's 'seven ages of man'. But it also seems obvious that we evolve through a series of personalities. How often have we met a child after several years and been amazed that he no longer seems to be the same person? But our personal evolution is not as inevitable as our physical growth: it is the result of effort. If life becomes too difficult we cease to make efforts and cease to evolve. This, it seemed to me, is what had happened to Clara Fowler and Doris Fischer and Christine Sizemore. They remained stuck on a fairly low rung of the 'ladder of selves' and the 'other side' had revolted and tried to seize control.

It was a good theory, and I still feel that it is fundamentally correct – that our personal evolution is a matter of effort and optimism. But it still left a number of basic problems unexplained. Why are the personalities often so completely different? Flora Rheta Schreiber's *Sybil* is about another sexually-abused child who later split into fourteen different personalities, including a writer, a painter, a musician, a builder and a carpenter. Some liked one another, others loathed each other: they behaved exactly like a real family. The oddest thing of all is that medical tests showed they all had different brain patterns. Yet brain patterns are as individual as fingerprints.

An even stranger case came to light in 1977. A young man named Billy Milligan was arrested for rape. Psychiatric examination revealed that Billy was a multiple personality – again as a result of childhood abuse – who was a compound of twenty-three different people. One of these was a Yugoslav who spoke Serbo-Croat, a language Milligan had never learned. The personality who had committed the rapes was actually a lesbian. Daniel Keyes' book *The Minds of Billy Milligan* finally made it quite clear that my theory of the 'ladder of selves' simply failed to cover the highly complex facts.

But what was the alternative? It was not until I had finished *Mysteries* that I came upon the strangest – and apparently most absurd – theory that I had encountered so far. It was in a book with the unpromising title *The Secret Science Behind Miracles* by Max Freedom Long. But it soon became clear that Long was a careful investigator and that the book was based upon long experience of its subject – the Kahunas, or magician-priests, of Hawaii. Long came to Hawaii as a young school-teacher in 1917 and soon became intrigued by references to the old Huna religion, which had been displaced and outlawed by Christianity. He was particularly fascinated by a sinister practice known as the death prayer. When a man had been cursed by the death prayer he began to experience a prickling sensation in his feet, which gradually became numb: the numbness then spread upward until he died. It sounded absurd, but when Long checked at the Queen's Hospital in Honolulu he found that there were usually one or more victims per year and that they all died, in spite of medical aid. He also heard an apparently absurd story about a Christian minister who learned the death prayer and used it to kill a Kahuna magician. Long went to the trouble of investigating the story and was able to read the minister's diary, in which he described how he had finally decided to take drastic action as members of his flock died off one by one.

Little by little Long succeeded in compiling a dictionary of Huna words and deduced from them something of the philosophy of the Kahunas. Their most basic belief, apparently, was that man does not have one soul, but three. One of them is called the low self, dwells in the solar plexus and corresponds roughly to what Freud called the unconscious. Next there is the middle self, which is our normal human consciousness. Lastly there is a high self which is as much *above* everyday consciousness as the low self is below it. This is the self which is capable of clairvoyance and precognition.

I recognized immediately that although this sounded absurdly complicated, it corresponded closely to some of my own conclusions about paranormal powers. The distinction between the low self and the middle self sounds very much like the distinction between Hudson's subjective and objective minds or the left and right cerebral hemispheres – the middle self certainly corresponded precisely to our left-brain personality. As to the high self, it seemed to fit my hypothesis about a part of us that has direct access to 'the information universe'. Frederick Myers had called it 'the subliminal mind', and in his introduction to Myers' classic *Human Personality and Its Survival of Bodily Death* Aldous Huxley had explained it by describing it as a kind of 'attic' of human consciousness, as far above the everyday living quarters of the personality as the Freudian basement is below it. So Long's threefold division of the human mind struck me as obviously plausible. I was willing to pay respectful attention to anything else he had to say.

Long was finally able to obtain more detailed knowledge of Kahuna doctrines from a doctor, William Tufts Brigham, who had been studying them for years. According to Brigham, low selves or low spirits may become separated from the middle and high selves after death. And they can be used by Kahuna magicians for evil purposes – such as causing death. Brigham had had direct experience of this. On an expedition up a mountain a Hawaiian boy became ill and showed symptoms of suffering from the death prayer. When questioned the boy revealed that before he left his native village the local Kahuna had warned him that if he ever worked for the hated white men he would die. He had forgotten the threat until now. The natives regarded Brigham as a magician in his own right, and he felt that he had to make some effort to save the boy. Standing above him he addressed the 'spirits' who were slowly paralysing his body, praising and flattering them and declaring that the boy was an innocent victim and that the man who deserved the blame was the Kahuna who sent them. For a full hour he kept his mind concentrated upon this idea. Then, suddenly, the tension vanished and the boy said he could feel his legs again. The paralysis soon vanished completely. But when Brigham made enquiries at the boy's native village he learned that the Kahuna was dead. He had come out of his hut in the early hours of the morning and told the villagers that the white magician had redirected the spirits, and that since he had failed to take any ritual precautions he must bear the consequences. A few hours later he was dead.

So according to Brigham the Kahunas performed their magic by means of spirits. And Long seemed to believe that the Kahuna system of psychology offered a satisfactory explanation of the mystery of multiple personality. He begins by describing one of the earliest known cases of dual personality, a girl named Mary Reynolds who woke up one morning in 1811 to find that she had lost every vestige of memory – she was exactly like a newborn child and had to be taught to speak all over again. Five weeks later the original Mary woke up with no memory of what had happened. And for the rest of her life the two Marys alternated in the same body, so that her relatives never knew which of them would open her eyes in the morning. Moreover the two Marys were opposites in character. The original Mary was a dull girl, prone to nervous depression; Mary Two, like Sally Beauchamp, was merry and mischievous. Mary One hated nature; Mary Two loved it . . . .

After describing the Christine Beauchamp (Clara Fowler) case, Long goes on to speak of a case which he had heard described by a certain Dr Leapsley, who lived in Honolulu.* It concerned the twenty-eight-year-old daughter of a California attorney. From the age of four she had been subject to changes of personality similar to those of Mary Reynolds. This happened regularly every four years. The secondary personality had been a 'baby' when it first arrived, like Mary Two. Neither personality had any knowledge of the other or of what happened when the other was 'in the body'. So when the original inhabitant of the body woke up at the age of eight she had no memory of anything that had happened since she was four. At the age of twelve she 'fell asleep' again, and woke up to find herself sixteen . . . . The primary personality was quiet, studious and shy; the secondary personality was an aggressive tomboy.

Dr Leapsley and two colleagues were called in and were able to gain her trust and place her under hypnosis. The secondary personality was ordered to leave the body, but this (predictably) had no effect. The doctors tried ordering the two personalities to amalgamate, but still nothing happened. Then one day when the girl was under hypnosis she went into a deep trance from which she could not be awakened. Suddenly a third voice spoke from her mouth. It had a distinctly masculine quality – it almost seemed to be the voice of an old man. This personality seemed

*Nicholas Clark-Lowes, the librarian of the Society for Psychical Research, informs me that Dr Leapsley appears in their records as Dr James H. M. Le-Apsley MD, who in 1922 lived in Pasadena, California and who moved to Honolulu in 1928. His last appearance in the SPR records is in 1949.

to know all the details of the lives of both girls. And in answer to the doctors' questions it explained that it was their 'guardian' and that they were, quite literally, two different girls who were using the body.

The doctors argued that the girl's life was being ruined by this alternation of personalities: she was unable to marry or live a normal life. The guardian disagreed with them. The purpose of life, it said, was personal evolution, and the girl *was* learning and maturing, even though she had to share her body with a stranger.

Finally, in desperation, one of the doctors told the guardian that unless the secondary personality agreed to go away they would keep the girl hypnotized indefinitely. To this the guardian replied that unless they accepted the present situation it would withdraw both girls and leave them with a corpse. The doctors knew they were beaten, and the girl continued to live as a dual personality.

For Long the case was a proof of the Huna belief in the high self, the superconscious mind: the guardian, he says, was the girl's superconscious. The secondary personality, according to Long, was an 'invader', an independent spirit.

Most people will reject this view out of hand. Science and common sense seem to agree that personality has a great deal to do with the body. Professor John Taylor states, 'We recognize personality as a summation of the different contributions to behaviour from the various control units of the brain.' And it is true that a person with a brain tumour may begin to behave in a completely uncharacteristic way: if, for example, the tumour presses on the amygdaloid nucleus the gentlest person may become aggressive and violent. Yet it must be admitted that even in these cases the *basic* personality remains unchanged: there is nothing like the complete alteration of personality that occurred with Clara Fowler or Billy Milligan. The various photographs of Doris Fischer's personalities in the article by Walter Franklin Prince* make them look like different people.

Yet the notion that the mind and the brain are two quite different entities has begun to gain a foothold in modern science. Dr Wilder Penfield is one eminent brain physiologist who reluctantly came to this conclusion. It was Penfield who, in 1933, discovered that a person can be made to re-live past memories in total detail by stimulating a part of the brain – the temporal cortex – with an electric current. Penfield's outlook was basically reductionist: he believed that consciousness is a product of the brain as heat is a product of fire. But an experiment performed in 1959 changed his mind. The patient was wide awake and his brain was being stimulated by an electric current so that he experienced a kind of mental film of his childhood: yet while this was going on he was also fully conscious of the room around him. So two 'streams of consciousness' were flowing simultaneously without mingling. This convinced Penfield that, 'The patient's mind . . . can only be something quite apart from the

*Journal of Abnormal Psychology, 1916.

neuronal reflex action.' Much the same view is taken by Sir Karl Popper and Sir John Eccles in their classic work *The Self and Its Brain*, as the very title implies. But if the mind – or self – exists *apart* from the brain (and body), then what characteristics does it possess? Is it merely some anonymous 'life force' which has no more individuality than heat or light? That is possible, for when my mind goes blank my personality seems to disappear. Yet every mother knows that her babies show signs of personality long before they can do anything but drink milk and sleep. So perhaps my personality is merely inactive when my mind goes blank. And if the mind – or personality – can exist apart from the body, then this is a return to the religious notion of the soul and of life after death.

I must admit that this was a step that I found myself very reluctant to take. This is not because I am disposed to reductionism – the belief that life can be explained entirely in material terms – but because it has always seemed illogical to me to believe something we cannot prove. In *The Outsider* and subsequent books I took no interest whatsoever in the problem of life after death: it seemed to me unimportant. In fact it seemed downright irrelevant. The basic questions of existential philosophy are 'Why are we alive? What are we supposed to do now we are here?' To reply, 'Don't worry – there is another life after this one,' amounts to begging the question. Even in *The Occult* I was inclined to steer clear of the questions. I consulted one friend, Professor G. Wilson Knight, who was a spiritualist, and he provided me with some interesting material which seemed to suggest that his mother was able to communicate with him after death. But I remained basically unconvinced – or perhaps a better word would be uninterested.

Yet I must admit that the evidence for reincarnation struck me as very powerful indeed. The famous case of Shanti Devi, the Indian girl who claimed to have lived a previous life in the town of Muttra, was studied by Professor Hemendra Bannerjee, a psychologist at Rajasthan University, who was convinced of its genuineness. Shanti Devi, born in Delhi in October 1926, began to describe this previous life in detail when she was four. Her husband, she said, had been a cloth merchant named Kedar Nath Chaubey. A school principal who tried writing to the address she gave in Muttra was startled to receive a reply from Kedar Nath. A cousin of Kedar Nath's who hurried to Delhi was immediately recognized by Shanti Devi. And when the nine-year-old girl was finally taken to Muttra she recognized relatives and was able to direct the carriage around the town. In Kedar Nath's house she led them to a spot where she said she had buried money in a tin; the tin proved to be empty, but Kedar Nath admitted that he had taken the money . . . .

Even more startling is the case of Jasbir Lal Jat, recorded by Professor Ian Stevenson, author of *Twenty Cases Suggestive of Reincarnation*. In 1954 three-year-old Jasbir died of smallpox, but before he could be buried he stirred and returned to life. But the new personality was quite unlike the old one: the new Jasbir claimed to be someone called Sobha Ram who

228

had died in Vehedi at the same time as Jasbir as a result of a fall from a cart. He said he was of Brahmin caste and made difficulties about his food. The family dismissed his claims as childish imagination. When Jasbir was six a Brahmin lady from Vehedi came to Jasbir's village and he declared that she was his aunt. Taken to Vehedi, Jasbir showed the same kind of intimate knowledge as Shanti Devi had shown of Muttra. His relatives were finally convinced that Jasbir and Sobha Ram were the same person, and the reader of Professor Stevenson's well-documented account feels much inclined to agree. In that case it would seem that Sobha Ram 'moved into' Jasbir's body more or less at the moment of death, or soon after.

The problem with such cases is of course that the investigators get there long after it has taken place and therefore have to rely on witnesses who may or may not be lying. But in at least one of his cases Stevenson eliminated this possibility by actually introducing the two families concerned. In Lebanon in 1964 Stevenson heard about a man called Mohammed Elawar, a Druse who lived in the village of Kornayel ten miles east of Beirut. His son Imad had been born in 1958, and the first word Imad had uttered when he learned to speak was a woman's name, 'Jamileh'. Then Imad began speaking about his past life as a man called Bouhamzy and insisted that he had recognized one of Bouhamzy's relatives in the street. Imad said that Mouhamzy lived in the town of Khriby, twenty miles away, and gave details of the house and of his relatives.

In spite of all this, Imad's father was too lazy to check on his son's story. So Stevenson decided to do it for him. He first interviewed Imad and collected details of his life as Bouhamzy, then went to Khriby and talked to Bouhamzy's family. Introduced to Bouhamzy's family, the six-year-old boy not only showed intimate knowledge of his 'relatives' but astonished them by behaving and sounding like Bouhamzy. Fifty-one out of fifty-seven statements made by Imad about Bouhamzy proved to be correct. (Occasional incorrect statements seem to be due to a blurring of memory: for example he said he had five sons when in fact it was Bouhamzy's brother who had five sons.) 'Jamileh' proved to have been Bouhamzy's mistress. As Stevenson pointed out, the possibility of fraud was remote: it would have involved the deliberate collusion of seventeen people who had no reason to lie.

Perhaps the strangest case of all is that of Lurancy Vennum, a thirteen-year-old girl from Watseka, Illinois, who had a fit in July 1877. After this she became prone to fall into trances during which she was apparently 'taken over' by a number of disagreeable personalities. A doctor, W. W. Stevens, went to see her and talked to two of these personalities, Katrina Hogan and Willie Canning. When he placed Lurancy under hypnosis the girl declared that she had been possessed by evil spirits and that at present there was a spirit called Mary Roff in the room. A Mrs Roff, who was also present, said, 'That's my daughter.'

229

Lurancy then declared that she would allow Mary to 'possess' her for a while. And the next day she was claiming to be Mary Roff. When taken to the Roff household she revealed an intimate knowledge of its inhabitants that Lurancy, who had been born only a year before Mary had died in 1865, could not have acquired. On the way there they passed the house where Mary had formerly lived – the family had moved since – and Mary had to be persuaded that it was no longer her home. She later greeted her relatives by name and recognized her old Sunday school teacher. Mary went on to describe hundreds of incidents in her early life, all in such detail that any doubts were soon forgotten. The evidence was later presented in detail by Richard Hodgson, the member of the Society for Psychical Research who had 'exposed' Madame Blavatsky, but who was totally convinced of the genuineness of this case.

Mary Roff explained that 'the angels' would only allow her to stay for three months. At the end of that time she took leave of her family and walked back to Lurancy Vennum's home. On the way Mary vanished and Lurancy again took over. Lurancy later married a farmer, but Mary continued to drop in to talk to her parents. When Lurancy had a baby Mary put her into a trance so she would not suffer the pangs of childbirth.

Richard Hodgson's account concludes, 'I have no doubt that the incidents occurred substantially as described in the narrative by Dr Stevens, and in my view the only other interpretation of the case – besides the spiritistic . . . is . . . secondary personality with supernormal powers.' This, indeed, is the view that most sensible people would prefer: that Lurancy was a case of multiple personality and that extraordinary powers of telepathy enabled her to read the minds of Mary Roff's family and convince them totally that they were speaking to their daughter. But is this as plausible as the 'spiritistic hypothesis' that Mary's spirit survived after death and was able to 'take over' the body of Lurancy Vennum? That depends, obviously, upon whether you feel inclined to accept the view that the mind can survive death. And in the Lurancy Vennum case the two explanations make equally good sense. But if we also take into account cases like that of Shanti Devi, Jasbir Lal Jat and Iman Elawar, the multiple personality explanation is seen to be inadequate. On the whole it begins to look very much as if the mind survives death.

Before we allow ourselves to be convinced, however, it is worth taking into account an alternative view advanced by Thomson Jay Hudson and William James. Hudson devotes a number of pages in *The Law of Psychic Phenomena* to what he prefers to call 'dual personality', and concludes that it is simply evidence for his theory of the ' two minds'. He cites a case that had recently caused a sensation in America, that of the Rev. Ansel Bourne, a Baptist minister of Rhode Island who in January 1887 withdrew five hundred dollars from his bank and disappeared. Two months later Bourne 'woke up' to find himself running a shop in Norristown, Pennsylvania. Apparently he had rented the shop and stocked it with sweets and fruit, and had been living quietly under the name of A. J. Brown. It sounds very much as if Bourne had simply decided to take a holiday from his wife, but everyone who examined him, including William James, was totally convinced of his honesty. Hypnotized by James, Bourne's secondary personality emerged instantly and described exactly what he had been doing during the past two months. He explained, among other things, that he had left home because there was 'trouble back there' and he wanted a rest. A. J. Brown seemed to be a rather weak character who told James,'I'm all hedged in – I can't get out at either end.' James's conclusion was that Ansel Bourne had fallen into a spontaneous hypnotic trance to escape from his problems and had given himself a kind of dream identity. Hudson agreed, adding that this was a case in which the subjective mind had decided to take over, as it does in normal hypnosis.

How far does this theory fit the facts? The answer is that on the whole it fits them very well. Consider Hudson's case of the young man who held a long conversation with Socrates under hypnosis. If the hypnotist had suggested that Socrates was inside his head, or that he *was* Socrates, then he would have become in effect a dual personality. If the hypnotist had then gone on to suggest that he was also Kant, Hegel and Marx, he would have become – temporarily – a multiple personality. The self-hypnosis theory would also explain Clara Fowler, Doris Fischer, Christine Sizemore and even Billy Milligan. Milligan's sub-personality that could speak Serbo-Croat might have learned it unconsciously by overhearing it, like the girl cited by Coleridge who spoke Latin, Greek and Hebrew. It is a little more difficult to explain how Sybil could have a number of distinct sets of brainwave patterns, but Hudson would undoubtedly reply that the powers of the subjective mind are far greater than we realize. The conclusion is that it *is* possible to explain most cases of multiple personality in terms of Hudson's theory of the 'two minds'. (We shall reserve some of the cases that refuse to fit the theory for a later chapter.)

Hudson went further. At the time he was writing, hundreds of thousands of Americans worshipped at spiritualist churches. This had come about as a result of a series of strange events that took place in Hydesville, New York in 1848, when the Fox family home was invaded by a poltergeist – a banging ghost. Its loud banging noises were unintelligible until a neighbour asked it to use a code of one rap for no, two for yes, whereupon it explained that it was the spirit of a pedlar who had been murdered by the previous tenant and buried in the basement. (When the basement was excavated half a century later human bones and a pedlar's tin box were discovered.)

When the two teenage daughters of the Fox family moved into the homes of relatives the disturbances followed them: the 'spirit' began to behave like a conventional poltergeist, throwing things around and attacking people with pins. And one day, using an alphabetical code, the

231

spirit spelled out the words, 'You must proclaim this truth to the world.' The result was the setting up of the first spiritualist church in Rochester, NY. The rest of the country quickly followed suit. Suddenly hundreds of people discovered that they were 'mediums'. In darkened seance rooms all over America ghostly hands stroked the heads of the audience and accordions and trumpets floated in the air and played mournful melodies. For some odd reason the Fox sisters had started a spiritualist explosion, and within twenty years it had spread to every civilized country in the world.

Understandably, scientists found it all infuriating, a return to mediaeval superstition. Yet although there were undoubtedly dozens of fraudulent 'mediums' (the word meant an intermediary between this world and the next) there can be no possible doubt that a very large percentage of the manifestations was genuine. This is why, in 1882, Frederick Myers and a small group of Oxford intellectuals decided to set up a Society for Psychical Research to try to discover once and for all whether human beings survived their deaths.

Hudson's contribution to the argument, in the early 1890s, was to admit that the phenomena were amazing and then to insist that they could all be explained in terms of the subjective mind. For Hudson the 'spirits' were quite simply the creation of the subjective mind – like the 'spirit' of Socrates which had conversed so brilliantly that many people thought it might well be genuine. 'The man who denies the phenomena of spiritism today is not entitled to be called a sceptic: he is simply ignorant . . . . I shall indulge in the hope, however, that by explaining the origin of the phenomena on rational principles, and thus removing them from the realm of the supernatural, those who now assume to be sceptical may be induced to investigate for themselves.' He admits that as a Christian, he believes that the soul survives death, but says that this has nothing whatever to do with spiritualism, which is entirely a matter of the strange powers of the subjective mind. He does not explain by what strange ability the subjective mind can make a trumpet float through the air and play tunes, but he has no doubt that it is possible.

Ironically enough Hudson's explanation of poltergeists came to be generally accepted several decades after his work had been forgotten. From a fairly early stage investigators observed that there was usually a child or an adolescent in the house where poltergeist phenomena took place. In 1900 Professor Cesare Lombroso – a determined sceptic who had been converted to spiritualism by the sheer weight of evidence – went to investigate a poltergeist in a restaurant in Turin. As he stood in the cellar empty bottles began spinning on the floor and shattered against a table, and another half dozen rose gently from the shelves and smashed on the floor. As Lombroso and the proprietor went back upstairs they heard another bottle shatter behind them.* Lombroso observed that there

*The case is described at length in Lombroso's *After Death – What?* and in my book *Poltergeist, A Study in Destructive Haunting* (1981).

232

was a young waiter, an unusually tall lad of thirteen. His tallness suggested that his body was being flooded with growth hormones, including those that intensified his sexual awareness . . . . At Lombroso's suggestion the boy was dismissed, and the disturbances ceased immediately.

It was not until the 1930s that the notion that poltergeists were connected with sexually-disturbed adolescents began to gain wide currency. This was largely the work of the Hungarian psychoanalyst Nandor Fodor, who had arrived in America in his late twenties and become simultaneously fascinated by psychical research and psychoanalysis. At his first seance, at the home of the well-known medium Arthur Ford, Fodor was convinced that the dead could communicate with the living. After the voice of the medium's 'control' began to speak – a control being a spirit who acts as Master of Ceremonies – Fodor made the rather unreasonable request that he would like to speak to someone who spoke Hungarian. The astonishing result was that a voice that claimed to be Fodor's father proceeded to address him in good Hungarian, pronouncing the word 'journalist' with a German accent just as Fodor's father did. The spirit declared that he had died on 16 January. (This proved not quite correct: Fodor's father had been buried – some years earlier – on 16 January.) And he prophesied – correctly as it turned out – that Fodor's Uncle Vilmos would go blind.

It was Fodor who, as a psychoanalyst and a psychical researcher, first popularized the notion that a poltergeist is yet another manifestation of repressed sexual energies. And it is undoubtedly true that some of the most famous poltergeist cases have involved adolescents who have just reached puberty. The Esther Cox case, which became famous as 'the Amherst Mystery', took place in Nova Scotia in 1878. It began when twenty-two-year-old Esther escaped an attempted rape by her boyfriend, who then fled the area. Esther became depressed and disturbed. One night her bedclothes began flying around the room, her pillow inflated, then she herself began to swell like a balloon. There was a loud explosion and she 'deflated'. As she lay there an invisible hand scratched on the wall above her bed, 'Esther, you are mine to kill.' The raps continued for hours. This poltergeist continued to persecute Esther for several months: furniture moved around, fires were started spontaneously and metal objects stuck to her as if she were a magnet. When a barn caught fire and Esther was jailed for arson the manifestations suddenly ceased.

This and many other similar cases seem to support the view that a poltergeist is simply a manifestation of the sexual energies of a disturbed adolescent or a kind of juvenile delinquent in the unconscious mind – or the right side of the brain. The fact that Esther's manifestations ceased after she was jailed for four months seems to indicate that her unconscious mind finally decided to stop playing jokes. This was my view of the case when I presented it in *Mysteries*, and my feelings were confirmed by a more recent case that I presented on BBC television in 1976.

In 1967 the office of a lawyer in Rosenheim, Bavaria, became the scene of a number of violent poltergeist disturbances. Light tubes shattered, pictures turned on the walls and a heavy filing cabinet was moved as if it weighed only a few pounds. Moreover the telephone bill was enormous because hundreds of calls had apparently been made to the talking clock – more calls than were physically possible in the time available. The 'poltergeist' was apparently getting straight through the relays. A well-known professor of parapsychology from Freiburg, Hans Bender, went to investigate the case and soon observed that the disturbances only took place when a young girl named Anne-Marie Schaberl was in the office. Anne-Marie was a country girl who was unhappy working in a town; her family life had been difficult – her father was a strict disciplinarian – and she was mistrustful and tense. Bender took her back to his laboratory to try various tests for extra-sensory perception and she showed remarkable telepathic abilities. And while Anne-Marie was in Freiburg the disturbances stopped. So she was sacked from the job and the disturbances in the office ceased. But they continued at the mill where she found work: when someone was killed in an accident Anne-Marie was blamed, and she left. Her fiancé broke off his engagement to her because she had such an extraordinary effect on the electronic scoring equipment at his favourite bowling alley. Finally she married and had a child, and the manifestations ceased.

Anne-Marie had no suspicion that she was the cause of the disturbances in the lawyer's office: indeed when I met him during the course of the programme Professor Bender told me that one of the first rules of poltergeist investigation is not to tell the 'disturbed adolescent' that he – or she – is the real cause of the disturbances, for it usually terrifies them.

In 1980 I heard of a poltergeist haunting that was even more astonishing than the Rosenheim case. It had taken place in Pontefract in Yorkshire and I heard about it from a friend of the family concerned, who seemed to think that it might make a book rather like the best-selling *Amityville Horror*. The poltergeist had, it seemed, wrecked practically every breakable item in the house and made such loud drumming noises at night that neighbours gathered in crowds to listen. But in this case a number of people concerned had apparently also seen the poltergeist, which took the form of a monk dressed in black. The friend of the family who contacted me was also interested in local history and told me that his researches had revealed that there had once been a gallows on the site of the house, and that a Cluniac monk had been hanged there for rape in the time of Henry VIII.

The story sounded almost too good to be true. But before deciding to write about it I asked a friend who lived in the area, Brian Marriner, to go and investigate. He wrote me a long letter in which he outlined the story of the haunting, and I was left in no doubt that this was a genuine case, not a hoax. The daughter of the family, Diane Pritchard, had been dragged upstairs by the throat by the 'Black Monk' and thrown out of bed repeatedly. But the ghost also seemed to have a sense of humour. When Aunt Maude, a determined sceptic, came to see for herself, a jug of milk floated out of the refrigerator and poured itself over her head. Later what looked like two enormous hands appeared around the door: they proved to be Aunt Maude's fur gloves. As the gloves floated into the bedroom Mrs Pritchard asked indignantly, 'Do you still think it's the kids doing it?' Aunt Maude burst into 'Onward Christian Soldiers' and the gloves proceeded to conduct her singing, beating in time.

Having studied Brian Marriner's report on the case I concluded that there was not enough material there for a full-length book, but it would make an admirable centre-piece for a book on the poltergeist, on which there is an immense amount of well-authenticated material. Poltergeist cases seem to be among the most frequent of paranormal events – at any given moment there are probably thousands of them going on all over the world and there is likely to be one going on within a dozen miles of where you are now reading this book. This, I concluded, is because the world is so full of sexually disturbed adolescents. I sketched out an outline of a history of poltergeist phenomena and submitted it to my publisher, who wrote back to say he liked the idea. Then, accompanied by my wife, I set out for Yorkshire to investigate for myself.

On our way to Pontefract we stopped for a night at the Hayes Conference Centre in Swanwick, Derbyshire, where I was to lecture at a conference on the paranormal. The following afternoon, just as we were about to leave, someone mentioned that Guy Playfair was due to arrive in half an hour. He and I had corresponded but had never met. So although I was anxious to get on to Yorkshire I decided to stay around for another half hour to introduce myself. It proved to be one of those fateful decisions that exercise an immeasurable influence on the future.

Guy, I knew, had spent some time in Rio de Janeiro, where he had joined the Brazilian equivalent of the Society for Psychical Research and studied the local version of black magic, *umbanda*. I knew this book *The Indefinite Boundary*, a scientific study of the paranormal, and was impressed by its logic and detachment. I was just as impressed by Playfair himself, a quietly-spoken man whose modest utterances nevertheless carried total conviction. For half an hour or so we talked about ley lines, animal homing and telepathy. Then, just as it was about time to leave, I told him I was writing a book on the poltergeist and asked his opinion. He frowned, hesitated, then said, 'I think it's a kind of football.' 'Football!' I wondered if I'd misheard him: 'A football of energy. When people get into conditions of tension, they exude a kind of energy – the kind of thing that happens to teenagers at puberty. Along come a couple of spirits, and they do what any group of schoolboys would so – they begin to kick it around, smashing windows

235

and generally creating havoc. Then they get tired and leave it. In fact the football often explodes, and turns into a puddle of water.'

'So you mean a poltergeist is actually a spirit?'

'That's right. I'm not saying there's not such a thing as spontaneous psychokinesis. But most poltergeists are spirits.' And he advised me to read the French spiritualist Allan Kardec.

I must admit that I found this notion hard to swallow. Ever since making the programme on the Rosenheim case I had taken it for granted that poltergeists are some kind of strange manifestation of the unconscious mind. I was not sure where the energy came from, but suspected that it was from the earth itself. I had seen a dowser standing above an underground spring, his fingers locked together and his hands pumping up and down so violently that the sweat poured down his face: he was obviously unable to stop himself while his hands were together. And at a dowsing conference I had been introduced to an old lady who sometimes picked up a large fallen branch and used it as a dowsing rod. Suspended in one hand, it would swing from side to side like a huge voltmeter needle. It seemed to me highly likely that the energy used by the poltergeist flows from the earth via the right brain of the disturbed adolescent. And now Guy Playfair was advising me to abandon these carefully constructed theories and return to a view that sounded like crude mediaeval superstition.

The following afternoon we arrived at the home of Joe and Jean Pritchard in Pontefract. It was the typically neat home of an upper-working-class family. Their nineteen-year-old son Phillip was at home, and during the course of the afternoon their daughter Diane came over with her husband to join us. These two had been the unconscious cause of the events that had caused a local sensation in 1966. I asked how the disturbances had begun. 'With these pools of water on the kitchen floor.' Joy and I looked at one another. 'Can you describe their shape?' Mrs Pritchard shook her head. 'They were just neat little pools – like overturning an ink bottle.' This, according to Playfair, was a description of the pools of water created by the explosion of the 'energy football'. He said it was almost impossible to make them by pouring water on the floor – from a jug for example – because it splashes. These pools look as if a small cat has placed its behind close to the floor and urinated. I began to feel that there might be something in his spirit theory after all.

Mrs Pritchard said that as fast as they mopped up the pools they reappeared elsewhere. But waterboard officials could find no leak. And when the tap was turned on green foam rushed out. Then the button of the tea dispenser began to move in and out, covering the draining board with dry tea leaves; lights switched on and off and a plant-pot somehow found its way from the bottom to the top of the stairs.

This first set of manifestations occurred in 1966 and Phillip was obviously the focus since Diane was away on holiday at the time. Two days later, they ceased. But when they began again in 1968 Diane – now fourteen – had become the focus. The ghost seldom paid a visit during the day, when she was at school. But in the evening the racket would start – usually a noise like a child beating a big drum – and ornaments would levitate across the room while the lights turned erratically on and off. Yet the poltergeist did not seem malicious – rather an infuriating practical joker. After a tremendous crash all the contents of the china cabinet were found scattered around the sitting room, yet not one was even cracked. When the vicar came to try to exorcise the poltergeist and told the family that he thought their trouble was subsidence, a candlestick rose from the shelf and floated under his nose. The exorcism was unsuccessful.

Diane found it frightening, yet less so than might be expected. She always had a kind of inward notification when the pranks were about to start. Hurled violently out of bed with the mattress on top of her, she was unhurt. When the hall stand – made of heavy oak – floated through the air and pinned her down on the stairs (with a sewing machine on top of it for good measure) she was unable to move and the family were unable to budge it, yet she was not even bruised. When the ghost – whom they called Mr Nobody – hurled the grandfather clock downstairs so that it burst like a bomb, no one was anywhere near.

At a fairly late stage in the haunting the ghost began to show itself. Jean and Joe Pritchard awakened one night to see a dim figure standing in the open doorway. Their next-door neighbour was standing at the sink when she felt someone standing behind her: it proved to be a tall figure in a monk's habit with a cowl over the head. It looked so solid and normal that she felt no alarm: then it vanished. Another neighbour, Rene Holden (who was a bit psychic), was in the Pritchards' sitting room when the lights went out. In the faint glow of the streetlamp that came through the curtains she saw the lower half of a figure dressed in a long black garment.

The haunting was nearing its climax. One evening when the lights went out Diane was heard to scream: the family rushed into the hall and found her being dragged up the stairs. The ghost seemed to have one hand on her cardigan, which was stretched out in front of her, and the other on her throat. As Phillip and Jean Pritchard grabbed her the ghost let go, and they all tumbled down the stairs. Diane's throat was covered with red finger-marks yet Mr Nobody had not exerted enough pressure to hurt her. Soon after this Jean Pritchard came downstairs to find the hall carpet soaked in water; on the wet surface there were huge footprints.

One day Phillip and Diane were watching television when they both saw the Black Monk – or at least his shape – silhouetted on the other side of the frosted glass door that led to the dining room. As Phillip opened the door they saw his tall, black shape in the process of vanishing. It seemed to disappear into the kitchen floor. And that was the end of the Pontefract haunting. Mr Nobody disappeared and has not been heard from since.

I spent the whole of that Sunday afternoon listening to recordings of the poltergeist making violent banging noises, and questioning the family and

237

neighbours. I also read the accounts contained in the local newspapers at the time. There could not be the slightest reasonable doubt that the haunting was genuine: there were too many witnesses.

Even if I had not met Guy Playfair some of the features of the case would have puzzled me. This poltergeist behaved more like a ghost, and its connection with the former Cluniac monastery and the local gallows was fairly well established. In that case the theory that it was a really a kind of astral juvenile delinquent from Diane's unconscious mind seemed absurd. Besides, as Diane described her feelings as she was pulled upstairs by Mr Nobody I experienced a sudden total conviction that this was an independent entity, not a split-off fragment of her own psyche. When I left the Pritchards' house that afternoon I had no doubt whatever that Guy Playfair was right: poltergeists are spirits.

It was an embarrassing admission to have to make. With the exception of Guy Playfair there is probably not a single respectable parapsychologist in the world who will publicly admit the existence of spirits. Many will concede in private that they are inclined to accept the evidence for life after death, but in print even that admission would be regarded as a sign of weakness. Before that trip to Pontefract I had been in basic agreement with them: it seemed totally unnecessary to assume the existence of spirits. Tom Lethbridge's 'tape-recording' theory explained hauntings; the unconscious mind theory explained poltergeists; and the notions of 'double consciousness' and the 'information universe' combined to explain mysteries like telepathy, psychometry, even precognition. Spirits were totally irrelevant. Yet the Pontefract case left me in no possible doubt that the entity known as Mr Nobody was a spirit – in all probability of some local monk who died a sudden and violent death, perhaps on the gallows, and who might or might not be aware that he was dead. And I must admit that it still causes me a kind of flash of protest to write such a sentence: the rationalist in me wants to say, 'Oh come off it . . . .' Yet the evidence points clearly in that direction and it would be simple dishonesty not to admit it.

When I returned from Yorkshire I took a deep breath and plunged into the annals of poltergeist activity with the aid of the library at the Society for Psychical Research and the College of Psychic Studies. The picture that now began to emerge made me aware of how far my preconceptions had caused me to impose an unnatural logic on the whole subject of the paranormal. It was not so much that the conceptions underlying *The Occult* and *Mysteries* were wrong as that they were incomplete. And much of the evidence required to complete them had been staring me in the face from the beginning.

I began, on Guy Playfair's advice, by reading Allan Kardec.

2

The Truth About Magic

Allan Kardec was one of the first and most influential converts to spiritualism. Born in Lyons in 1804 Kardec's real name was Denizard-Hyppolyte-Léon Rivail, and he was descended from generations of lawyers and magistrates. He attended the school of the great educationalist Pestalozzi and soon revealed a brilliant and far-ranging intelligence. Like Ruskin or Carlyle in England, he was a born educator. By the time he was thirty he was the author of a French grammar, a work on arithmetic and a treatise on education. He gave immensely successful lectures on astronomy, chemistry, physics and anatomy and became a member of many learned societies. He was also fascinated by the great Mesmer, who had died lonely and discredited in 1815, at the age of eighty-one. In the 1850s most French doctors would have been afraid to confess an interest in mesmerism; it would have been tantamount to professional ruin. But Rivail had no need for caution; he was a famous savant with independent means and had no need to fear the malice of the coteries. So it came about that in May 1855, when he was fifty years old, he attended a hypnotic session with a certain Mme Roger who, in a trance, was able to perform apparently paranormal feats such as mind-reading. At that session Rivail met a Mme Plainemaison, who persuaded him to attend a seance at her house. There this disciple of the French encyclopaedists was astonished to see tables dancing and moving around the room. (It had been seven years since the manifestations in the home of the Fox family in New York and spiritualism had already become the latest craze all over Europe.)

It was in the home of Mme Plainemaison that Rivail met a M. Baudin, who told him that his two daughters practised automatic writing. They were apparently rather frivolous young ladies, fond of dancing and parties. But when Rivail asked them questions, their hands raced across the paper and produced answers that were far beyond the intelligence of the attractive amanuenses. Asked, 'Is density an essential attribute of matter?' the disembodied intelligence replied, 'Yes, of matter as understood by you, but not of matter considered as the universal fluid. The ethereal and subtle matter which forms this fluid is imponderable for you, and yet it is none the less the principle of your ponderable matter.' When the communicator was asked why its replies were so much more profound than anything so far transmitted to the young ladies, it explained that spirits of a much higher order had come expressly for him, to enable him to fulfill a religious mission.

When Rivail had accumulated a vast amount of information, he was told that he should publish it using the pseudonym Allan Kardec – both names that he had borne in previous incarnations. *The Spirits' Book* was a widespread and immediate success, one of the first – and perhaps one of the most important – of the classics of spiritualism.

The philosophy of *The Spirits' Book* is certainly remarkably profound and consistent. The universe is permeated by a vital principle, but 'life' means the union of spirit and matter. This vital principle, or fluid, sounds like Mesmer's 'magnetic fluid'. When it is blocked, the result is ill health. The universe is also permeated with disembodied intelligences, and human beings are such intelligences confined within a body. But the purpose of their existence as human beings is a certain evolution. When the body dies, the spirit is eventually reincarnated in another body. In the meantime, depending upon its state of evolution, it may wander around, unaware of its condition. Such immature spirits may be responsible for various forms of mischief such as poltergeist effects, or they may turn up at seances and talk nonsense. Such a spirit, Kardec learned, had been the cause of violent poltergeist disturbances in the Rue des Noyers, when objects had been hurled around and every window had been smashed. The culprit in this case was a drunken rag-and-bone man who had been dead for fifty years and who was getting his own back on people for treating him without respect during his lifetime. He obtained the necessary 'magnetic energy' from a servant girl in the house: the poor girl was quite unaware that her energies were being drained and was more terrified than anyone of the 'ghost'. The rag-and-bone man qualified as a low spirit, one of those who are trapped in the material world and addicted to mischief. More evolved second degree spirits experience only a desire for good, while perfect spirits have reached the peak of their evolution. To some extent the spirit can choose the trials it will undergo in its next life: these are chosen for the purpose of evolution. (Rudolf Steiner had once remarked, 'Never complain about your lot, for you chose it before you were born.') Kardec's informants also stated that man is a fourfold being, consisting of body, vital principle ('aura'), intelligent soul and spiritual soul – the same divisions that can be found in Steiner and Friederike Hauffe, the 'Seeress of Prevorst'.

In spite of its success *The Spirits' Book* was soon causing severe controversy in the French spiritualist movement. Generally speaking spiritualists do not accept the doctrine of reincarnation, which lies at the heart of Kardec's doctrine. Kardec's main rival as a channel of 'spiritual' information was a man named Alphonse Cahagnet, who obtained his information about the next world through a somnambule (hypnotic subject) named Adèle Maginot, who said nothing about reincarnation. The French spiritualist movement soon split into two, and since Kardec was to die in 1869, sixteen years before Cahagnet, his own doctrines were the first to be generally rejected. But *The Spirits' Book* and its successor *The Mediums' Book* made their way across the Atlantic to Brazil, where a powerful spiritist religion already flourished (based, to some extent, on voodoo) and where they became religious classics, held in almost as much esteem as the New Testament. Spiritism (or Kardecism) is still Brazil's most widespread religious belief. And it was there that Guy Playfair came upon it when he arrived in Rio de Janeiro in 1961.

In *The Flying Cow* Playfair has described his own startling introduction to spiritism. Suffering from some minor stomach ailment, he was taken by a friend to see a healer named Edivaldo Silva who gave him some pills and told him to come back for an operation. Lying on the table was an old man whose abdomen had been ripped wide open, exposing his entrails. Yet a few minutes later the old man was being helped out by his wife, and Playfair was told to lie down. Moments later Playfair felt a distinct plop as Edivaldo's hands entered his stomach, which suddenly felt wet all over as if he was bleeding to death. He experienced a tickling sensation and a smell like ether. Then he was told it was over: someone slapped on a bandage and he was helped out of the room feeling strangely stiff and rather weak. He took a taxi home. The next day he felt normal again. A few months later the stomach complaint was still not entirely cured and he went through the whole thing again: on this occasion he felt as if there were two pairs of hands inside him. Then he was told he could go. This time the pains (presumably caused by an ulcer) vanished for a year. Playfair began to spend all his spare time in Edivaldo's surgery, watching him plunge his hands inside people's bodies and then leave the flesh intact after the operation.

For the unprepared reader this part of Playfair's narrative sounds so preposterous that it is bound to raise suspicions that he is either (a) mad (b) a liar or (c) hopelessly gullible. Fortunately I was not entirely unprepared. While writing *The Occult* I had come across Pedro McGregor's book *The Moon and Two Mountains*, an important study of magic and spiritism in Brazil which preceded *The Flying Cow* by nine years and which spends a whole chapter discussing José Pedro de Freitas, better known by his nickname Arigó, the simple one. In 1958, Arigó claimed, he had been 'taken over' by the spirit of a German surgeon who had been killed in the First World War: now he was performing complicated operations like removing tumours with a kitchen knife, a scalpel, scissors and a pair of tweezers. I had quoted a passage in which a number of eminent doctors witnessed Arigó thrusting scissors and scalpels into the vagina of a young woman who was suffering from a tumour in the womb: the witnesses noticed that Arigó was holding only one handle of the scissors, yet the other moved in and out as he cut. After Arigó had said, 'Let there be no blood, Lord', the bleeding had stopped and Arigó had removed the tumour and sealed the cut by pressing its edges together with his fingers.

Arigó was to die in a car crash in 1971, but not before a team of

241

American doctors and scientists had been to his village to witness his operations. What they saw has been described by John G. Fuller in a book called *Arigó – Surgeon of the Rusty Knife*, and it describes so many of these operations and cites so many eminent witnesses that the reader finally becomes slightly punchdrunk. By the time I read the book I had become a friend of two of the scientists – Andrija Puharich and Ted Bastin – and so had their first-hand confirmation. I had also seen the amateur film that Ted Basin made of Arigó, which showed him thrusting a penknife into the eyes of two patients and extracting a lump of pus. Compared to the things described by Fuller it was rather disappointing, but I could not share the view of two companions at the showing, the late Dr Christopher Evans and the magician 'the Amazing Randi', that the whole thing was a fake. It was true that a film such as this was no final proof of Arigó's genuineness, but unless all the other witnessed accounts were part of a conspiracy then it was 99 per cent certain that Arigó was genuine (he had in any case nothing to gain from fraud since, like Edivaldo, he charged nothing), in which case it followed that the operations on the film were genuine too.

As I read Guy Playfair's account I could suddenly see the essence of the problem of 'the occult'. To someone like Playfair or Bastin or Puharich, who have actually witnessed such things, it is self-evident that if they contradict medical theory, then medical theory must be wrong. And people like myself, who have not actually witnessed the phenomena but have read about them and talked to obviously honest people who *have* witnessed them, are also struck with a conviction that such things really happen and that therefore the world of the paranormal is a reality, not some fairy tale. But sceptical scientists living in London or New York have already concluded that the paranormal does not exist because it *cannot* exist. Almost without exception they would not take the trouble to go and see a psychic surgeon even if one lived round the corner: they tell you wearily that they know nothing will happen, or that if it does it will be trickery. All they *are* prepared to do is to consider the evidence at second hand, preferably in some easily digestible form, for they all lack patience, and then think up objections. And the result of their deliberations is then accepted by the rest of the scientific community as the unbiased conclusions of hard-headed scientists. In fact it is little more than a regurgitation of the opinions they have been expressing for years, opinions which are change-proof because the scientists have no intention whatever of studying the evidence.

One of the chief culprits, Christopher Evans, was an old friend and colleague – we had even edited a series of books together – and I found 'the Amazing Randi' likeable and plausible. The leading American sceptic, Martin Gardner, was also an old friend. (No longer, alas: he became increasingly bad tempered at my criticisms and finally broke off the correspondence.) But once it had become clear that they were entrenched in a kind of lazy dogmatism then it was obvious that they simply had no right to pronounce on the facts; they really had nothing whatever to say, except to repeat their old convictions, which, however sincerely held, were quite irrelevant as evidence. I could only endorse the irritable comment made by the American researcher Professor James Hyslop, who remarked, 'I regard the existence of discarnate spirits as scientifically proved and I no longer refer to the sceptic as having any right to speak on the subject. Any man who does not accept the existence of discarnate spirits and the proof of it is either ignorant or a moral coward. I give him short shrift, and do not propose to argue with him on the supposition that he knows nothing about the subject.' And whether such waspishness is scientifically defensible or not, I understand just how Hyslop felt – as, no doubt, do most readers of Guy Playfair's account of his own experience of 'psychic surgery'.

In fact for Playfair this was only a beginning. He joined the IBPP – Brazilian Institute for Psycho Biophysical Research – moved to Sao Paolo, and studied more psychic surgeons. Then he heard of a case of poltergeist haunting and agreed to look into it for the Institute. In October 1973 he sat in the home of a divorced Portuguese woman reading Frank Podmore – the highly sceptical investigator of the Society for Psychical Research – on poltergeists and waiting for something to happen. It all began as he was falling asleep: a series of loud bangs that shook the house yet failed to cause things to vibrate as bangs normally do. In fact laboratory analysis has shown that poltergeist bangs seem to differ from ordinary bangs. Shown on a graph an ordinary sound has a curve that rises and falls like a mountain: spirit bangs begin and end abruptly, like cliffs. Later a footstool bounced down the stairs, a drawer full of clothes was shot out into the yard and a pillow was pulled from under the head of Nora, the daughter-in-law of the house. Again and again Playfair noticed that such things seemed to happen when people were falling asleep or waking up: he assumed that this was simply clever timing, to avoid observation. But Mavromatis's investigations into hypnagogic states suggest another explanation. If the twilight state between sleeping and waking makes human beings more 'psychic' (i.e. allows them entry into another condition of being), then it may be a two-way door that also allows the denizens of the psychic realm to invade the physical world.

Once the IBPP team was convinced they were dealing with a genuine poltergeist and not with a mischievous child or malicious adult, they took steps to get rid of it. The Pritchard family of Pontefract had sent for the vicar, unaware that exorcism is quite useless in poltergeist cases. (This, Kardec explains, is because poltergeists are not evil spirits but merely mischievous practical jokers.) The Brazilians, more experienced, know that the best way is to use mediums to contact the spirit. A team of four mediums came to the house, and although they failed to 'make contact' they asked their own 'spirit guides' to persuade the poltergeist to go elsewhere. For two weeks it looked as if this had worked: then the manifestations began again. (The poltergeist had a nasty habit of starting small fires.) So the family decided to take the ultimate step. They called in a *candomblé* specialist – *candomblé* being an African-influenced cult allied to voodoo. The *candomblé* team spent several days burning incense and invoking their own spirits to drive away the poltergeist. And this apparently worked: when Playfair checked three months later, all was silent.

At this point in his narrative Playfair makes a statement that would undoubtedly cause raised eyebrows among the members of the Society for Psychical Research:

> Hernani Guimaraes Andrade, the spiritist scientist; Father Carlos, the Catholic professional exorcist; and the young *candomblé* father-in-sainthood have one view in common. They are convinced that poltergeists are the result of black magic, except where the premises rather than the people are being haunted.
>
> 'In every case of person-directed poltergeist activity where I have been able to study the family background,' says Mr Andrade, 'there has been evidence that somebody in the house could be the target of revenge from a spirit. It may be a former lover who has committed suicide, a jealous relation, a spiteful neighbour, or even a member of the same family bearing some trivial grudge. Any Brazilian is well aware that this country is full of backyard *terreiros* of *quimbanda* (black magic centres), where people use spirit forces for evil purposes.'

For anyone educated in the West this seems a breathtaking statement, startling in its absurdity – nothing less than primitive superstition. Playfair's experiences in Brazil convinced him that it is the literal truth, as Max Freedom Long's experiences in Hawaii had convinced *him* that poltergeists (low spirits) can be used for malevolent purposes. In fact when Playfair read Max Freedom Long's *Secret Science Behind Miracles*, he recognized immediately that Long and Andrade were in fundamental agreement about spirits. According to the Hunas, man's three 'souls' may be separated at death. The low self, which possesses memory, may be persuaded to commit mischief by a magician-priest or a practitioner of black magic: these are poltergeists, the spirits used in the death prayer. If the middle self becomes detached it becomes a ghost, a mindless wanderer around the scenes of its past life, for it has no memory.

In the case of the Portuguese household the *candomblé* specialist was of the opinion that this was a case of black magic, and the IBPP was inclined to agree. The case had been going on for six years, ever since Nora had married the son of the household. Family members had received hostile telephone calls; photographs of one of the daughters, stitched with thread, had been found on the floor – a sign of witchcraft; the family had changed houses three times during the haunting, and Nora had attempted

244

suicide twice. Most poltergeist hauntings last only a short time – perhaps, as in the case of the Black Monk of Pontefract, a few months. For a case to continue unabated for six years it seems that the entity needs to have some purpose apart from its own juvenile sense of mischief. That purpose, according to the IBPP, can only be provided by a black magician – probably, as Andrade says, some 'backyard *terreiros*' who will cast spells for payment.

In his book *Drum and Candle* Playfair's friend David St Clair has described his own experience of being 'bewitched'. For eight years he had lived in a pleasant Rio de Janeiro apartment, served by a pretty brown-skinned maid named Edna. She was, he assures the reader, nothing more than a maid. Finally, when St Clair decided it was time to leave Brazil, he gave her six months' notice. Suddenly everything began to go wrong: the book he was working on jammed firmly; his publisher rejected it; an inheritance failed to materialize; a love affair went wrong; he fell ill with malaria. His plans for moving to Greece had to be shelved.

Then a psychic friend stopped him in the street and told him that someone had put a curse on him: 'all his paths had been closed'. In fact it seemed to be general knowledge in *umbanda*, (voodoo) circles. St Clair's suspicions finally came to rest on his pretty maid Edna. It was true that she was a Catholic who claimed to disapprove of *umbanda*, but when St Clair learned that a curse could be invoked by using some personal item of his clothing he recalled that his socks had been disappearing recently, and that Edna had claimed they had blown off the line. He told Edna that he wanted to go to an *umbanda* session. After much protest she agreed to take him.

Towards midnight the ritual dance began. Then the *umbanda* priestess came in and danced as if possessed. After some ceremonial drinking of alcohol – a mouthful of which she spat in St Clair's face – a medium was asked who had put a curse on him. The reply was, 'The person who bought him here. She wants you to marry her or buy her a house with a piece of land.' Then Edna was ordered to leave, after which there was more ritual drumming and dancing to lift the curse. Finally the priestess told him, 'Now you are free.'

Immediately afterwards St Clair's luck changed: money came in, the book was accepted, the love affair restarted. But Edna herself became seriously ill with a stomach growth. An *umbanda* priest whom she consulted told her that the curse she had put on St Clair had rebounded on herself and would continue as long as she stayed with him. At this point Edna admitted that she had tried to make him marry her by means of black magic: she then walked out of his life, acknowledging that she had brought her misfortune on herself.

When St Clair had come to Rio he had been astonished by the superstitions of his intellectual friends. He tells of seeing a clay statue of the devil surrounded by burning candles on the pavement in a main avenue: when he leaned forward to touch it a friend pulled him back,

245

saying, 'It's *despacho*,' an offering to a spirit. 'You surely don't believe all that stuff?' asked St Clair incredulously. His friends replied that they didn't – but still would not allow him to touch. After this St Clair saw many such pavement offerings. And he noticed that even starving beggars would not touch offerings of cooked chicken, and dogs would sniff them and back away.

Playfair was intrigued by a case that seemed to show that contrary to the usual assumptions, poltergeists *do* sometimes commit lethal mischief. In December 1965 a Catholic family living in the small town of Jabuticabal were visited by what Playfair calls 'one of the most persistently malevolent poltergeists in history'. It began with stone-throwing – or rather brick-throwing. A spiritist named Volpe came to survey the situation and decided that the focus of the activity was a pretty eleven-year-old girl named Maria José Ferreira, a natural medium who was unconsciously lending the spirits her energy. He took the girl into his own home and soon bricks were flying around there too. But at this stage the spirits seemed fairly amiable: if Maria asked for a flower or a piece of candy it appeared at her feet. Then the honeymoon period came to an end and the spirits began hurling glasses, plates, flower vases and other items around the house. While Maria was asleep there were apparent attempts to suffocate her by placing cups or glasses over her mouth, and an attack in the genital region suggested an attempt at rape. Then the poltergeist began sticking needles into her left heel, and the fact that she was wearing shoes and socks made no difference: one day fifty-five needles were removed at the same time. When the foot was bandaged the bandages were wrenched off without being untied. One day at school her clothes began to smoulder from a burn that looked as if it had been made by a cigarette. Finally the Volpes took her to an *umbanda* centre where a 'spirit' came and spoke through Chico, Brazil's best-known medium. It declared that Maria had been a witch in a previous life and that many people had suffered through her – including the spirit itself, whose death she had caused. Pleas were ignored, and although the more painful attacks ceased the poltergeist continued to throw fruit and vegetables around. Finally Maria died from drinking ant killer in a soft drink. Whether it was suicide or whether the spirits introduced the poison was never established.

When Playfair had finished reading Maria's file he asked Andrade why it was that such cases always seemed to happen in the backwoods to uneducated people. Andrade shook his head and took a file from his drawer: 'Look at that.' The story was so incredible that Playfair decided to double-check and went to meet the girl involved. She was a Catholic with a master's degree in psychology, and Playfair calls her Marcia F. Marcia had incurred the wrath of the spirits by picking up an offering made to the sea goddess Yemanjá. It was a small plaster statue of a woman with most of the paint washed off it, and when Marcia found it on the beach near Santos she decided it would make a nice ornament for the apartment she shared with another girl. A few days later Marcia was violently ill with food poisoning. Then she began spitting blood. A holiday with her parents was pleasant and uneventful – the statuette stayed behind on the mantlepiece. But when she returned the pressure cooker blew up and burned her face and neck. The oven exploded, shooting out a sheet of flame towards Marcia; a gas fitter could find nothing wrong with the gas pipes.

Marcia began to experience suicidal impulses – an impulse to fling herself before oncoming cars and out of a window. A voice inside her seemed to be urging her to throw herself out. Then she became aware of the presences. They came at night and entered her bed: she felt hands touching her all over. Then a male presence climbed on to her and she felt a penis entering her. She tried without success to push him away. But the 'incubus' – as such spirits were known in the Middle Ages – came for several nights.

Finally Marcia did what she should have done a long time before and went to an *umbanda* centre. When she mentioned the statue she was told to go and throw it back into the sea, where she had found it. After that life returned to normal. It was only after she had been to the *umbanda* centre that Marcia noticed something that shook her. The burns on her face and neck corresponded precisely to the areas of paint left on the neck of the statue. A patch of TB which had showed up on the X-ray plate after she began spitting blood corresponded to another patch of paint on the statue's back. The only other paint on the statue was one piercing blue eye: Marcia preferred not to think about that.

As I read these stories in Playfair's *Flying Cow* and *The Infinite Boundary* I felt exactly as he must have done as he investigated them: that they are *so* preposterous that normal, sensible people can never accept them. That is one of those strange and persistent facts about 'the occult': it somehow *never* lends itself to general consumption. The facts are always just that little bit *too* absurd to fit into our picture of things. Human beings *can* be persuaded to widen their mental boundaries, but it has to be done little by little: whatever the New Testament says to the contrary, they will swallow a gnat but not a camel. When Frederick Myers and Professor Henry Sidgwick decided to found a society for psychical research in 1869 they felt that it surely ought to be possible, with modern techniques of scientific research, to decide once and for all whether spiritualism was based on fact or nonsense. But they quickly discovered that the paranormal has its own equivalent of the uncertainty principle. A psychical investigator can establish the reality of the paranormal beyond all doubt – in private. But as soon as he tries to drag his evidence into the light of public scrutiny it melts away like ice in the sun. And if in despair he shouts, 'Please stop playing games and give me some *public* evidence!' the practical joker replies blandly, 'But *of course*, my dear fellow – how about his?' and presents a 'proof' so preposterous that no one will take it seriously – such as surgeons tearing open stomachs with their bare hands and pulling out tumours, or mediums who, like Daniel Dunglas Home, float out of one second-floor window and in at another, or wash their faces in red-hot coals.

I suspect I know why this is so. Eileen Garrett once warned that 'communication with the "other world" may well become a substitute for living in this world.' But this world ought to have priority. The greatest question of human existence is why we are here and what we are supposed to do now we *are* here. To say that we shall go on living after death is simply no answer. This is why all mentally healthy people experience an instinctive dislike of looking too closely into spirits and ghosts. Yet a totally pragmatic society would also be counter-productive, for a lifelong obsession with material security also begs the real question. So presumably the head of the Supernatural Civil Service has issued a directive to the Department of Diplomatic Contacts with Earth stating that the evidence must either be kept ambiguous, or so absurd that no one will believe it anyway. Poltergeists and psychic surgeons are sufficiently outlandish; so are synchronicities, provided they are rare enough to be dismissed as chance or outrageous enough to be simply unbelievable. But anything more credible is to be strictly avoided.

In fact when I looked back on my own interest in the paranormal I recognized every sign of the same reluctance and resistance that now irritates me in sceptics. I had accepted the commission to write *The Occult* solely because I needed the money. I would not have been too upset to discover that the whole thing was merely a proof of human gullibility. Instead I was overwhelmed by the sheer consistency and variety of the evidence. Before I was a tenth of the way into the book I knew beyond all doubt that telepathy, precognition and clairvoyance take place. Yet although I wrote sections on reincarnation, life after death and poltergeists, I still preferred to keep what I called an 'open mind' about them – meaning really that I preferred to remain ambivalent. When I came upon Tom Lethbridge's 'tape-recording' theory about ghosts I was glad to incorporate it into *Mysteries*. I had no doubt whatever that poltergeists are a manifestation of the unconscious mind, that 'demoniacal possession' (as in the famous case of the nuns of Loudun) was a matter of sexual repression, and that witchcraft and magic were simply old-fashioned names for the 'hidden powers' of 'the other self'. It was a neat little package and I felt justly proud of it.

A few doubts began to insinuate themselves when I began to look more closely into witchcraft and magic. In *The Occult* I had taken it for granted that witches are unfortunate old ladies who happen to possess certain odd powers – of healing, for example – and who are consequently regarded with superstitious fear by their neighbours. This view seems to be supported by the fact that the first secular witchcraft trial, which took place in Paris in 1390, was of a woman called Jean de Brigue who had cured a man named Ruilly when he was on the point of death. She insisted that she was not a witch but had simply used charms which included, 'In the name of the Father, the Son and the Holy Spirit.' (I had myself investigated some local wart-charmers whose 'charms' worked. They told me that they simply repeated a text from the Bible which had been passed on to them by another wart-charmer.) Under torture Jean de Brigue confessed to having sexual intercourse with her demonic familiar and to trying to kill Ruilly by witchcraft at the request of his wife. (It is not quite clear why she then saved his life.) Both she and the wife were executed.

I had always been fascinated by the strange case of Isobel Gowdie, a Scottish farmer's wife who in 1662 quite suddenly and voluntarily decided to confess to being a member of a witches' coven and having sexual intercourse with demons. She claimed that a 'grey man' whom she had met on the downs had persuaded her to become a witch, and that she had been baptized the same evening and had joined a coven of other witches. After this she was able to transform herself into a hare or cat. The Devil himself used to flog the naked witches with a broomstick and often violated Isobel with an immense scaly penis, which produced pangs as excruciating as childbirth yet immensely pleasurable – his sperm was as cold as ice. He sometimes possessed her as she lay in bed beside her sleeping husband.

In my analysis of this case I wrote,

> The picture that emerges is of an imaginative and highly-sexed girl being driven half insane with frustration, until she evolves a whole fantasy about the powers of evil . . . . Her sexual perversion develops until it becomes a kind of sweet poison, made all the more potent by the rigid Presbyterianism, the Calvinistic Bible-thumping, that dominates the community . . . . After fifteen years of this she is suddenly seized by a terrifying, an almost unthinkable idea . . . . Why not make her fantasy *public*, shatter everybody by telling them what has been going on in their stolid, sabbatarian community? . . . They strip her and search her minutely for devil's marks, and she finds it all deliciously voluptuous.

And in due course, she and her fellow 'witches' are all executed. (We have no record of Isobel's execution but it seems a reasonable certainty.)

The problem with this theory is that the other accused women also confessed. The natural assumption is that this was under torture, but the detailed court records make no mention of torture.

The same problem arose in another celebrated case, that of the North Berwick witches. This again looked like a case of a naturally gifted 'healer' who was tortured by a superstitious bigot until she implicated various other women. David Seaton, the deputy bailiff of Tranent (near Edinburgh), grew suspicious about the nocturnal movements of a young servant girl, Gilly Duncan, who had a reputation for curing sickness. He crushed her fingers in a vice, twisted a rope round her throat and examined her for devil's marks. Finally she confessed to being a witch and implicated the local schoolmaster, John Fian, an elderly gentlewoman named Agnes Sampson, and two more well-connected ladies named Barbara Napier and Euphemia Maclean. Under torture they confessed to being involved in a plot to drown King James I by raising a storm that almost wrecked his ship when he was on his way to Oslo to collect his future bride, Anne of Denmark. King James understandably took a keen interest in the affair, but when Agnes described how the witches had sailed in sieves to North Berwick then performed their black magic rituals in a church under the direction of the Devil, he suddenly decided it was all nonsense. At this point however Agnes whispered in his ear some words that he had spoken to Anne of Denmark on their bridal night in Oslo, and the king changed his mind. John Fian also confessed under torture, his leg crushed by 'the boot': but twenty-four hours later he escaped and made his way back home. Recaptured, he withdrew his confession, claiming that it had been obtained by torture; and although his nails were pulled out and his legs again crushed in 'the boot', he continued to deny everything and was finally burned, like Agnes Sampson and Euphemia Maclean. Barbara Napier escaped on the grounds that she was pregnant and was finally released.

In his *Encyclopaedia of Witchcraft and Demonology* Russell Hope Robbins takes the view that the whole 'witchcraft craze' was a matter of absurd superstition, and has some of his harshest words to say about the inquisitors of the North Berwick witches. Yet there are certain matters that demand explanation. Why did Agnes Sampson tell the king about the words he spoke to Anne of Denmark on his wedding night when he had already decided that the witches were 'all extreme liars'? She was condemning herself to death. Robbins makes the odd comment that 'the only witness of this extra-sensory perception was James himself; and a fanatic could be easily persuaded, particularly when a possible plot against his life was introduced.' But that fails to explain why Agnes *did* whisper in his ear and make him change his mind. Robbins also ignores the fact that John Fian had been secretary to the Earl of Bothwell, who is believed to have been plotting to kill King James (Bothwell would have been heir to the throne). And Bothwell in later life acquired a reputation of dabbling in black magic. There was good reason for Fian to be involved in a witchcraft plot to kill the king. And it may be significant that the three other accused witches were all gentlewomen, related to the nobility, not just poor old hags as in the Isobel Gowdie case.

Robbins fails to explain another oddity. *After* his original confession, obtained under torture, Fian volunteered the information that the devil had visited him in his cell that night. Since he was in no danger of being tortured again this seems an odd thing to do. Perhaps Fian was crazed with the pain of his crushed leg? But if the leg was so badly crushed then how did he escape and make his way home? Robbins explains this by suggesting that this escape was pure fiction, yet there is no evidence for that view.

On re-reading *The Occult* it struck me that I *had* accepted the evidence for African witchcraft and quoted stories to confirm it. My friend Negley Farson told me that on several occasions he had seen a witch-doctor conjure rain out of a clear sky. Another friend, Martin Delany, described how a Nigerian witch-doctor had assured his European company that the torrential rain that had lasted for weeks would stop in time for a staff garden party. The rain stopped just before the party was due to start and started again immediately after it finished. Martin Delany had told me some other very strange stories of African witchcraft, which I had cited in my book on Rasputin. So why could I accept that an African witch-doctor could control the weather but insist on regarding the North Berwick witches as innocent? By the time I wrote a second small book about the paranormal, *Strange Powers*, shortly after *The Occult*, I had recognized this inconsistency and pointed it out in that book.

In 1926 the Reverend Montague Summers had caused a sensation with his work *The History of Witchcraft* in which he set out from the assumption that 'black witchcraft' was a reality and that many of the women who were burned at the stake were guilty as charged. H. G. Wells was so shocked that he launched a vituperative attack on the book in the *Sunday Express*. Many reviewers took the view that Summers was merely trailing his coat for the sake of publicity. This was untrue: Summers believed that witches may possess real powers, and that these powers are dependent on 'forces of evil'. In *Strange Powers* I concluded that 'the truth probably lies somewhere midway between Summers's total acceptance of black witchcraft and Robbins's total scepticism.' Seven years later, after reading Max Freedom Long, Allan Kardec, David St Clair and Guy Playfair, I began to feel that the truth lay closer to Summers than to Robbins.

Yet in a basic sense this change of viewpoint made very little difference. I continued to believe – as I still believe – that the 'occult' or paranormal is about the hidden powers of human beings, not about spirits. But acceptance of the reality of spirits made me rather less dogmatic about individual cases. At the time I was making the Rosenheim programme at the BBC in Bristol a girl approached me in the canteen and asked my advice about her flatmate, who was the focus of a poltergeist outbreak. Her clothes were hurled all over her locked bedroom, her possessions were damaged and on one occasion her coat had burst into flame. I assured the girl that poltergeists were manifestations of the unconscious mind and asked if her friend suffered from psychological tensions or sexual problems. When she admitted that this was so, I said, 'There – you see!'

Soon after the Rosenheim programme I received a letter from a clairvoyant who called herself Madame Rose. She told me that she had held a 'sitting' in Rosenheim and had been in contact with a spirit that claimed to be responsible for the poltergeist outbreak. It was a girl who had been murdered during the course of the war and whose body was still in a secret grave. She had been trying to use Anne-Marie to draw attention to herself, to persuade someone to have her reburied in hallowed ground. I replied politely to Madame Rose but had no doubt whatever that she was talking nonsense. After writing *Poltergeist* I changed my mind and decided to contact her again. A German friend who spends her winters in Munich agreed to go to Rosenheim and look for some documentary evidence of the existence of the murdered girl. If this proved to exist then we would ask Madame Rose's assistance in trying to find the body. To my surprise Madame Rose now proved to be totally uncooperative. Yet that should not have surprised me: if we *had* traced the girl's existence, then located her body, it would be positive proof of the reality of the paranormal – and that would have been a violation of the directive from the head of the Supernatural Civil Service stating that such matters must remain in a state of misty ambiguity.

Soon after writing *Poltergeist* I encountered a case that might have been reported by Guy Playfair. A young married woman wrote to ask my advice about an unpleasant experience in Brazil. She began to suspect that her husband was having an affair with a native woman. A stranger who claimed to be a clairvoyant stopped her in the street and told her that she was a victim of a *trabalho* ('job' or spell). Then, as for David St Clair, life became a nightmare of frustrations with 'every alley blocked'. Lying in the bath, she was amazed to see her wedding ring slipping from her finger. It was a fairly tight fit and the water should have made her flesh swell, yet it slid off and fell into the water. She decided not to pull the plug out – in case the ring went down – but to drain the bath with a saucepan. When the bath was empty there was still no sign of her ring. One day, convinced that her husband was about to leave her, she obeyed a sudden impulse to go and talk to him at work and beg him to make up. Oddly enough it worked, and their differences were resolved. Back home, immensely relieved, she decided to have a bath. And as she sat in the warm water she decided that she might as well wash her knickers. As she did so her wedding ring fell out of them.

A year earlier the story would have baffled me and I would probably have made vague pronouncements about 'apports' or poltergeists. Now I was able to tell the young woman precisely what Guy Playfair would have told her: that the 'other woman' had determined to make the husband desert his wife and had gone to some 'backyard *terreiros*' or *umbanda* specialist and paid good money to have a spell cast. The specialist, in turn, would perform the correct rituals and make offerings to the low spirits – including food, alcohol and tobacco – and the spirits would do their best to carry out the instruction. Fortunately, as Playfair remarks, these spirits seem to need very precise conditions in which to carry out their tasks, and meet with many obstructions. And the successful outcome of this particular case may be explained by a remark of Playfair's mentor Hernani Andrade: 'To produce a successful poltergeist, all you need is a group of bad spirits to do your work for you, for a suitable reward, and a susceptible victim who is insufficiently developed

252

spiritually to be able to resist.' The wife's decision to make a direct appeal to her husband seems to have short-circuited the *trabalho*. When I talked to her she was living happily in England with her husband.

It is, I agree, difficult for normal, sensible people to accept this notion of spirits. Most of us have never encountered a ghost during the course of a lifetime and are never likely to. So ghosts are, quite simply, an irrelevancy. And since most children spend a great deal of time being quite unnecessarily afraid of the dark it is probably just as well that belief in spirits is not a basic part of our culture. The fact remains that anyone who will take the trouble to study the evidence will concede, regretfully, that there are such things as spirits and that under certain conditions, they can impinge on human existence. And when Montague Summers declared that modern spiritualism is a revival of mediaeval witchcraft, he was being strictly accurate. Summers admits that many of the men and women burned during Europe's three centuries of witchcraft madness were innocent. But he also insists that witches *made use of* spirits and 'demons' to perform their magic. And the evidence gathered by Playfair and Max Freedom Long makes it practically certain that he was correct.

Rudolf Steiner has an interesting notion – which we may take or leave according to our inclination – to the effect that man has been through various distinct stages of evolution, each of which began and ended in a particular year. At the time of Jesus, he says, man was launched on to a new stage of evolution in which he finally developed a conscious ego, an 'I' which could make its own choices. Before that he had been essentially a communal being whose identity was bound up with the group. In this earlier stage there was no clear distinction between the human world and the world of spirits, and shamans and 'witches' (or witch-doctors) took the world of spirits for granted. This faded away in the new epoch of the 'intellectual soul' (as Steiner calls it). And when, in 1413, the age of the 'intellectual soul' gave way to the age of the 'consciousness soul', man virtually lost contact with the invisible world. The new spirit gave rise to experimental science and has finally led to an age in which the invisible world has been totally forgotten.

This view undoubtedly contains a hard nugget of symbolic truth. There can be no doubt that modern man has become increasingly a 'split brainer' who has lost contact with his intuitive half, and that primitive peoples are far more naturally intuitive – and 'psychic'. In *The Occult* I cite an article by Norman Lewis which I found in a Sunday colour supplement. Lewis had gone to study the Huichol Indians of the Mexican Sierra Madre and had been fascinated by the way they took powers of extra-sensory perception for granted. While Lewis was there the *shaman* Raymond Medina, visiting a village called San Andreas, had sensed death, and walked up to a locked house. The corpse of a murdered man was discovered in the roof. Even the local Franciscan missionary fathers accepted the ability to solve crimes by ESP as a natural part of life.

If Steiner is correct then the 'witchcraft craze' began at exactly the

253

same time that man changed from 'intellectual soul' to 'consciousness soul' and the last vestige of that sense of 'invisible worlds' vanished from western Europe. Witches ceased to be accepted as a natural part of life, as the huichols still accept *shamans*, and became a symbol of evil, of intercourse with demonic powers. And faced with persecution many witches no doubt used their mediumistic powers – for that is what it amounted to – to cast spells and torment their tormentors.

The rationalization of witchcraft entered a new phase with the publication of Margaret Murray's book *The Witch Cult in Western Europe* (1921) and its successors *The God of the Witches* and *The Divine King in England*. Margaret Murray was an archaeologist who spent the First World War in Glastonbury studying the King Arthur legends and old witchcraft trials. Starting from the assumption that witches were poor old women who were persecuted for their delusions about the Devil, she was suddenly struck by the 'revelation' that they were really members of an ancient religious cult that pre-dated Christianity and worshipped the powers of nature. Their priest, she suddenly realized, was simply a primitive *shaman* dressed up in an animal skin with horns – like the drawings on the walls of Cro-Magnon cave dwellings. Being a fertility cult it naturally laid heavy emphasis on the phallus and sexual intercourse – another reason that it horrified the Christian Church. Witches, according to Margaret Murray, were simply worshippers of the goddess Diana who still practised their fertility rites in country areas.

To some extent she was undoubtedly correct. But in the excitement of her insight into the pre-Christian religion she went too far and decided that all tales of black witchcraft were pure invention. She even went on to declare that dozens of famous historical characters like William Rufus, Joan of Arc and Gilles de Rais were really members of the old religion who allowed themselves to be ritually sacrificed as kings were once sacrificed to ensure a good harvest. Half a century later Professor Norman Cohn went back to many of the original documents cited by Margaret Murray and discovered that she had been guilty of considerable distortion to support her arguments. Where she had left leader dots to indicate that something had been left out there were often wildly improbable events, like Isobel Gowdie's descriptions of sexual inter-course with the Devil or Agnes Sampson's description of sailing to sea in a sieve. Cohn of course had no doubt that the whole 'witchcraft craze' was sheer delusion. In fact his criticism of Margaret Murray tends to show that the Rev. Montague Summers may have been closer to the truth than his contemporaries thought.

But what *can* we make of these absurd descriptions of satanic orgies and witches' sabbats? Playfair's investigations into 'the psi underworld' indicate that Isobel Gowdie's confession of having sex with a 'demon' may have been factually correct. And this receives unexpected support from the contemporary psychologist Stan Gooch, whose first book, *Total Man*, published in 1972, argued that man's darker, more instinctive being resides in the area of the brain known as the cerebellum, the 'old brain' which man inherited from the animals. But in that otherwise academic book Gooch also admitted casually that he had once attended a seance at which he suddenly lost consciousness: when he awoke he discovered that several 'spirits' had spoken through him. In a later book, *The Paranormal* (1978), Gooch goes on to describe his subsequent experiences as a medium and his increasing interest in the paranormal. But in books like *Personality and Evolution, The Neanderthal Question* and *The Double Helix of the Mind* (which rejects the split-brain hypothesis in favour of his own cerebellum theory), his approach remains cautiously scientific even when challenging the accepted wisdom. So his 1984 book *Creatures from Inner Space* caused astonishment and consternation among reviewers. It begins by describing the experiences of an ex-policeman, Martyn Pryer, who began trying to induce hypnagogic states as he lay in bed and who soon found himself being 'attacked' by some invisible entity which lay on top of him. And one night, when the entity seized him from behind, he realized that it was a woman who wanted him to make love to her. He lay there, paralysed, until it faded away. Gooch then goes on to quote the experiences of an actress named Sandy who was interested in 'the occult'. She woke up one night to find that a spotlight in the corner of the ceiling had apparently changed into an eye, and she felt a weight lying on top of her. Soon it began to move gently, and she felt pressure on her vagina. Part of her was quite willing for the lovemaking to proceed; another part rejected it. She struggled and eventually broke free: when she went to the bathroom she found that her mouth was full of half-dried blood although there was no sign of a nose-bleed.

At this point Gooch goes on to describe his own experience of a succubus (the female equivalent of an incubus). Lying quietly in bed one morning he became aware of another person in the bed with him – a female. Without opening his eyes he was aware that it was a composite of various ex-girlfriends, including his previous wife. As his conscious interest in the situation got the better of him, the creature faded away. But he admits, 'on subsequent occasions . . . the presence of the entity was maintained, until finally we actually made love.'

In fact Gooch goes on to conclude that entities like these are not real (in the sense of being genuine spirits) but are creations of the human mind. He cites at length the case of Ruth, described in a book by Dr Morton Schatzman* At the age of ten Ruth had fought off a rape attack by her father. After she married and moved to England she had dreams of actually being raped by him. Then she began having hallucinations of him, or she would hear him walking around the house. He continued to intimate that he wanted to make love to her. Then the father began to appear to her in Schatzman's consulting room, and Schatzman was able to hold conversations with him through the medium of Ruth. Little by little Ruth realized that she could control her apparitions – she was even

*Morton Schatzman, *The Story of Ruth*, (1980).

255

able to produce two Schatzmans. What she was doing was literally self-hypnosis. A good hypnotist can make his subject see 'apparitions' as Dr Carpenter made the young American see Socrates, and psychological tests prove beyond all doubt that the hypnotized subject really sees a solid, three-dimensional being. On a later occasion Ruth created an apparition of her husband – for whom she had formed an aversion – in bed, and went through a full act of sexual intercourse with it, ending as it ejaculated inside her. Ruth's recognition that she could control her hallucinations finally led to her cure.

Gooch's argument is certainly plausible and serves to remind us that our 'hidden powers' are far greater than we normally recognize. But then Gooch is also convinced that the poltergeist is 'an extension of some form of living energy projected by the nervous system' – in other words a manifestation of the unconscious mind. In my view Playfair is correct, and there is overwhelming evidence that most poltergeists are spirits. A subsequent book, *This House is Haunted* (1980), is an account of Playfair's own investigations at a house in Enfield (north of London) where a particularly destructive poltergeist caused problems for more than a year. The focus on this occasion seemed to be the eleven-year-old daughter of the family, Janet. In December 1977, five months after the disturbances began, the poltergeist began to make whistling and barking noises and then began to speak. It at first identified itself as Joe, then later told the investigators, 'I am Bill Haylock and I come from Durant's Park and I am seventy-two years old and I have come here to see my family but they are not here now.' (I have the tape-recording of these sessions: the voice sounds oddly jerky and mechanical, like a record I possess of an 'electronic brain' singing 'Daisy, Daisy'.) When Guy Playfair asked, 'Do you know you are dead?' he was told to 'fuck off'. Investigation revealed that the Joe referred to was a Joe Watson who had lived in the house, and that Bill Haylock had been a local resident who was now buried in the graveyard, Durant's Park.

Playfair commented of the various entities that manifested themselves in the house, 'It looks as if we had half the local graveyard at one time or another.' The 'haunting' was finally ended by a Dutch medium, Dono Gmelig-Meyling, who persuaded the entities that they were dead and ought to stop tormenting the Harper family. The Enfield case powerfully supports Playfair's view that poltergeists are 'earth-bound spirits' who are often unaware that they are dead.

This does not mean, of course, that Gooch is incorrect to believe that his own experience with a succubus was some kind of manifestation of his own unconscious mind. But it certainly means that Gooch is mistaken to believe that *all* such experiences can be explained in these terms. If it is unlikely that Diane Pritchard's unconscious mind dragged her upstairs and made bruises on her throat, then it is also unlikely that the unconscious mind of Marcia F., the lecturer in psychology, created the entity that raped her as she lay paralysed in bed.

It seems likely that we shall never know what really happened at witches' sabbats, or whether the entity that made love to Isobel Gowdie was a genuine incubus or a product of her unconscious mind. But it *does* seem safe to say that witchcraft in mediaeval Europe was probably a great deal like witchcraft in modern Brazil, and that it would be a mistake to dismiss it entirely in terms of superstitions and delusions.

3

The World of Spirits

In *Memories, Dreams, Reflections* Jung reveals that he has come to admit the reality of life after death and describes one of the experiences that finally convinced him. One night he was lying awake thinking of a friend whose funeral had just taken place. 'Suddenly, I felt he was in the room. It seemed to me that he stood at the foot of my bed and was asking me to go with him. I did not have the feeling of an apparition: rather, it was an inner visual image of him.' Jung asked himself whether this was a fantasy, then decided that he might as well – for the sake of experiment – assume that it was real. Thereupon his friend beckoned him to the door. In imagination (and it must be remembered that Jung had a highly developed faculty of 'active imagination') Jung followed him to his house next door. In the study his friend climbed on a stool and showed Jung the second of five red books on a high shelf. The next morning Jung called on the man's widow to ask if he could go into his friend's study. There was the stool that he had seen the night before and, near the ceiling, the books with the red bindings. Jung had to stand on the stool to read the titles. The book indicated was a novel by Zola with the title *The Legacy of the Dead.**

Citing this experience, Gooch declines to accept it as proof of life after death, pointing out that our minds have the power to obtain paranormal information by other means. But he then mentions a case that he regards as *almost* watertight. It was described in a book called *Life Without Death?* by Nils Jacobsen. In 1928 Jacobsen's uncle was run over by a lorry. The lorry slammed him against a wall and he died three days later without regaining consciousness. Six years later, at a seance in England, the medium told his father that his dead brother was present. The brother then described the accident that had killed him and added that he had not died of an injury to his skull, as his family had always assumed, but that 'it came from the bones'. Years later Jacobsen realized that he could check the hospital records, and did so. The post mortem report showed that his uncle had not died of a skull fracture, but from a brain embolism caused by a blood clot from the bone – lower-bone thrombosis.

The loophole in this story, says Gooch, is that the surgeon who performed the post mortem must have known the truth. So the 'information' *was* available in someone's mind and might have reached

*Carl Jung, *Memories, Dreams, Reflections*, p. 289.

the medium's mind through this source. It is true that this is remotely possible but it seems so far-fetched that it is hard to take seriously – like believing that the road from London to Southend goes via the North Pole. We have to suppose that the medium obtained the facts of the accident from the sitter's own mind and then somehow contacted the mind of the surgeon to find out what really happened. On the whole it is simpler to believe that Jacobsen's uncle survived death.

The truth is that these stories, and thousands more like them, are parts of a jigsaw puzzle that build up into an overwhelmingly convincing picture, and the general purport of this picture is that the human soul, or spirit, is independent of the body, and can survive the death of the body. Again I must admit to a certain embarrassment in writing these words, for in a very real sense I couldn't care less whether human beings survive their death. My own increasing conviction that the mind can survive death has not tempted me to become a spiritualist – that is to attend seances or read spiritualist newspapers. And when I am not actually writing books about 'the occult' I am inclined to ignore it altogether and read books on philosophy, science and history. Yet whenever I return to the subject I am again overwhelmed by the sheer consistency of the evidence. And where 'survival' is concerned I cannot believe, like Stan Gooch, that we can explain the evidence in terms of telepathy. Where, for example, is there room for telepathy in the following experience described by Wilbur Wright:

In early 1941 I was stationed at RAF Hemswell, Lincoln, as a ground engineer. I returned from leave by bus late one Sunday evening completely out of cigarettes, and all the canteens were closed. But I remembered I had left some cigarettes in the hangar and walked down in the black-out, entering the hangar through the central steel doors at the front. The aircrew room was on the right, where flying personnel of 61 Bomber Squadron kept their flying clothing. I heard a noise from the crew room, and opened the door to investigate it. It was in total darkness and I switched on the light: the black-out curtains were in position and I saw a figure in uniform groping in one of the lockers. He was wearing a flying helmet, a leather fur-lined jacket, black knee-length flying boots, and I recognized him as Leading Aircraftsman Stoker, a mid-upper gunner on the Hampden bomber, who had to fly with the hood open to look for attacking fighters. (This was before all aircrew had sergeant rank to gain improved treatment for POWs.)

I said, 'Hey, Stoke – what are you doing?'

He replied irritably, 'I can't find my bloody gloves.'

'Well, that's your problem,' I said. 'Put out the lights when you go.'

He made no reply to that, and I entered the hangar, found my cigarettes and went back to my billet. Next morning I went to

259

breakfast, and as always happened, I asked the man next to me what had been happening during my week's absence.

'Very dodgy two nights ago,' he said. 'They went mine-laying in the Dortmund Ems Canal and we lost McIntyre and his crew, hit at low level by flak, rolled and went straight in. The mine went off – they had no chance.'

'My God,' I said. 'That chap Stoker had a lucky escape, then!'

'Stoker? Oh, he went in with the rest. There was trouble before they took off – he couldn't find his flying gloves and he could have frozen to death with the rear gun hatch open. He was moaning all the way out to the transport.'

I said nothing, but this preyed on my mind, and two days later I reported sick, told the MO what had happened. He said he believed me, but he gave me some pills to make me sleep, and as time went on the shakes stopped and I forgot about it. Looking back, the most remarkable aspect was that the air gunner looked perfectly normal to me. His clothing creaked as usual when he moved, his face was worried but in no way remarkable, and it was only later that I realized that he had been groping round in his flying-clothing locker in pitch darkness.

I took the advice of the Medical Officer on the Station and told the story to nobody else. He asked me to write an account of it in longhand, which I did on the back of a sheet of Station Routine Orders and gave it to him. Ever since I have wondered how many of these things we see in broad daylight, regarding them as normal living human beings. As I see it, there is no way to distinguish them from a living breathing person.

A number of interesting points emerge in this narrative. The first is that Stoker was obviously able to open his locker door and was therefore, in some sense, solid. This disposes of the theory that perhaps he was a 'telepathic projection' of someone else on the station who happened to be thinking about Stoker at that moment. The second is that Stoker obviously believed that he was alive. The third is that he looked and acted exactly like a living person. The notion that ghosts are semi-transparent and look and behave in a 'ghostly' manner is an old wives' tale. What would have happened if Wright had tried to shake hands with Stoker is difficult to say, but in all probability he would have felt perfectly normal and solid. In their book *Apparitions* Celia Green and Charles McCreery devote a whole chapter to touch and pressure in which there are several cases in which people have shaken hands with ghosts. 'His hand was not icy cold like that of a corpse,' says one man who shook hands with an apparition of his father, 'it was only cool.' And in another well-known case from the records of the SPR, Lieutenant J. J. Larkin was writing letters when the door opened and his friend Lieutenant David McConnel shouted, 'Hello boy!' Larkin heard a few hours later that

McConnel had crashed at roughly the time he had seen him. His ghost seems to have had no problems opening a door and holding a brief conversation.

Stories already cited about *doppelgängers* seem to suggest that one of our 'hidden powers' is an ability to project a more or less solid image of ourselves to other places. As often as not this seems to be done unconsciously: Celia Green cites a report of a woman who was knitting as she listened to a talk on the radio when her husband (who was in fact at work) entered the room and touched her under the chin. His hand was icy cold. Then he disappeared.* However the novelist Theodore Dreiser has described how, after eating dinner at Dreiser's house, his fellow novelist John Cowper Powys told him that he would appear to him later that night. Two hours later, as he sat reading, he looked up and saw Powys standing by the door. The apparition vanished as Dreiser went towards it.† Powys later refused to explain how he did it but it seems certain that he had learned the same odd 'trick' as the student Beard.

In the circumstances it seems highly likely that persons on the point of death are able to exercise this faculty of 'projecting the double' by means of thought: in other words that apparitions of the dying seen by their relatives are not 'ghosts' in the normal sense of the word – i.e. spirits of the dead – but something more like a mental television picture. In some cases this 'picture' is solid enough to open doors or shake hands, which seems to argue that scientists like David Bohm and John Wheeler may be correct to believe that reality is to some extent a mental construct (a theme to which we shall return in the final chapter). But what seems equally obvious is that if Leading Aircraftsman Stoker could still project his image two nights after his body had been blown to pieces, then the 'image-projecting' part of his mind must have been operating normally, which could hardly have been possible unless it had survived his death.

In 1979 the mind's survival of death was even recognized in an American courtroom. The occasion was the trial of a man named Allan Showery for the murder of a Filipino nurse, Teresita Basa. She was stabbed to death in her apartment in Evanston, Illinois, on 21 Feburary 1977. Medical evidence indicated that the forty-eight-year-old nurse had let a man into her apartment and that he had encircled her neck from behind in a Japanese half-Nelson and rendered her unconscious: then he had stripped her and stabbed her between the ribs with such force that the knife went right through her. He left her in a position that suggested rape to confuse the investigation (his real motive was robbery), then set the place on fire.

Two weeks later, in the Edgewater Hospital where Teresita Basa had worked, one of her colleagues remarked to another Filipino, a respiratory therapist named Remy Chua, 'Teresita must be turning in her grave. Too bad she can't tell the police who did it.' And Remy Chua replied seriously, 'She can come to me in a dream. I'm not afraid.' Later that day, as she was

*Celia Green and Charles McCreery, *Apparitions*, p. 102.
†The story is told more fully in *The Occult*, pp. 54–5.

dozing in the locker room, Remy Chua opened her eyes to see Teresita Basa standing in front of her. She ran out of the room in a panic.

Remy Chua began to dream of the murder and of the killer, whom she then recognized as a black hospital orderly named Allan Showery. And one day, as she lay on her bed, a voice spoke through her mouth saying, 'I am Teresita Basa. I want you to tell the police. . . .' The voice spoke in Tagalog, the native language of the Philippines. Her husband heard the words although Remy Chua remembered nothing when she recovered from her trance. They decided to do nothing about it. Two weeks later 'Teresita' came back and spoke through Remy Chua's mouth again, this time naming her killer as 'Allan'. A few days later she named him as Allan Showery, and said he had stolen her jewellery and given it to his girlfriend – she even gave the telephone number of someone who could identify the jewellery. She claimed that 'Al' had come to fix her television and killed her.

Finally the Chuas called the police. They were unconvinced and it was several days before they questioned Showery, who admitted promising to repair Teresita's television but claimed he had simply forgotten. However when the police questioned Showery's live-in girlfriend Yanka and asked her if he had ever given her jewellery, she showed them an antique ring that he had given her as a 'belated Christmas present'. The police called the number that Mrs Chua had spoken in her trance and two of the victim's cousins came to the station and identified the ring as Teresita's. They also identified some other jewellery that had belonged to her. Faced with this evidence Showery broke down and confessed.

At the trial in January 1979 the defence argued that the case should be dismissed on the grounds that the evidence had been – apparently – provided by a ghost, and implied that ghosts were untrustworthy. Judge Frank W. Barbero overruled the objection. But the jury obviously had its doubts and confessed to being hopelessly deadlocked. At a second trial a month later, however, Showery changed his plea to guilty and was sentenced to fourteen years in prison.

Stan Gooch might well argue that this case also has loopholes. The Chuas worked in the same hospital as Teresita Basa. Remy Chua may have suspected Showery – or even obtained paranormal knowledge of the murder – and found this way of conveying her suspicions. She might have obtained all her information – about the jewellery, the television repair motive, the girlfriend – from Showery's mind. But how could she have obtained the telephone number of the cousins who could identify the jewellery from Showery's mind? Although she often spoke to Teresita when their shifts overlapped they were not close friends, and she had no reason to know the telephone number. Only Teresita could have provided it.

England has never had its own equivalent of the Basa affair but the case of Eric Tombe – which took place in 1922 – has some curious parallels. Tombe, an ex-army officer, was shot in the back of the head by his crooked business partner, Ernest Dyer, at the racing stable they ran together at Kenley, Surrey. Dyer concealed the body in a cesspit and 'disappeared'. Soon after the murder Tombe's mother – the wife of the Rev. Gordon Tombe – began to dream he was dead, and that his body was down a well with a stone slab over its mouth. She had never been to the racing stable at Kenley and did not even know of its existence: her husband finally tracked it down when trying to find his son. But as the dreams about the corpse in the well continued, the police decided to humour her and search the stud farm at Kenley. There was no well but there *were* four cesspits, each covered with a heavy slab. Eric Tombe's body was found in one of these, hidden in a recess. The murderer – of whose existence the Tombes had also been unaware – had meanwhile moved to Scarborough, where he lived precariously by passing dud cheques. When the police came to question him about one of these he pulled out a revolver and killed himself – probably believing they had come to question him about the murder.

Tombe had been killed from behind, the back of his head blasted off by a shotgun, so he could not have conveyed knowledge of the murder by telepathy as he was dying. Ergo: it is hard to avoid the conclusion that Eric Tombe survived his death and caused his mother to dream of where he was buried.

Both these cases are fundamentally about mediumship. Mrs Chua first became aware of Teresita Basa when she was dozing and felt that someone was trying to communicate with her. She had already expressed her willingness to be 'taken over' by her fellow Filippino. Once Teresita Basa had succeeded in 'getting inside her', so to speak, she was able to take over when Remy Chua was dozing or asleep in bed. Eric Tombe's mother also learned of the murder when she was asleep: in a sense she had also become a medium.

It reminds us that mediumship could be regarded as a form of 'possession'. The medium goes into a trance, not unlike a hypnotic trance, and is 'taken over' by a 'spirit guide' who acts as master of ceremonies, or by 'spirits'. But this in turn may remind us that cases of multiple personality also look like a form of 'possession'. Mary Reynolds fell into a twenty-hour sleep and woke up 'possessed' by another personality. Clara Fowler was hypnotized when Sally took over. Doris Fischer was momentarily unconscious, having been thrown to the floor by her father, when the first of her multiple personalities took over. Pierre Janet was hypnotizing a girl called Lucie when she plunged into such a profound sleep that it was impossible to wake her: when she finally awoke she was another personality. In 1877 a French youth named Louis Vivé began having epileptic attacks after being bitten by a viper: after an attack lasting fifteen hours he became another personality – a rebellious criminal who was completely unlike the timid and quietly-spoken Louis of earlier days. Vivé became one of the most famous cases of dual personality in the late nineteenth century. (Max

263

Freedom Long makes the astonishing statement that 'epilepsy is the result of habitual attack by disembodied low spirits who are able to overcome the resident low self of the afflicted individual and absorb the vital force from his body in a matter of a few minutes.')

It is also worth mentioning that when Kardec questioned the 'spirits' about 'possession' he was told that human beings can be influenced by spirits to a far greater degree than we suppose: they often influence both our thoughts and actions. Low spirits cannot actually take over a body since it is the property of its original occupant. Yet they can, either through the co-operation or weakness of that occupant, exercise total domination: this, said Kardec's informant, is the real meaning of 'possession'.

The classic modern study of a case of possession is Aldous Huxley's *The Devils of Loudun*, which describes how a convent of Ursuline nuns in Loudun began to writhe, twist and blaspheme and generally behave as if 'possessed by demons'. The local parish priest, Father Urbain Grandier – also known as something of a Don Juan – was called in to exorcize them: soon they were accusing him of being responsible for their possession. Grandier was tortured, condemned to death and burnt alive. Huxley has no doubt whatever that the nuns were in the grip of sexual hysteria and that the case can be understood in entirely Freudian terms. Discussing it in *The Occult* I was in total agreement with this judgement, writing, ' . . . one can be quite certain that the "demons" were non-existent in the ordinary sense, but the possessed nuns believed in them. . . . The antics of the nuns went no further than blaspheming, making lewd suggestions and rolling on the ground in a way that displayed the part of the body that was the root of the trouble.'

Yet the truth is slightly more complicated than that. It was not only the nuns who were possessed, but also the priests who tried to exorcize them. And it seems highly unlikely that this was merely a case of contagious hysteria. Father Lactance, a sadistic fanatic who deliberately broke his promise that Grandier should be strangled before being burnt, began seeing and hearing things within weeks of Grandier's horrible death then began frothing at the mouth and screaming blasphemies; he died a month after the execution. Then Dr Mannoury, the surgeon who had pricked Grandier all over and claimed to find 'Devil's marks' (spots that were numb because they had been touched by the Devil), began seeing Grandier's ghost, and died insane. Father Tranquille, a Capuchin inquisitor who had gone to Loudun convinced that the Church would protect him, became possessed at intervals after Grandier's death but finally succumbed four years later, when he would writhe on the ground, cursing, hissing, barking and neighing. As he lay dying the devils left his body and entered that of a friar kneeling in prayer and *he* began to writhe and blaspheme.

The final victim of the devils was the Jesuit mystic Father Jean-Joseph Surin, who came to Loudun four months after Grandier's death, in

December 1634, to exorcize the nuns who were still possessed. A man who was inclined to obsessional neurosis, he was the ideal victim for the possessing spirits, who soon entered his body. In a letter to a friend he described how 'the alien spirit is united to mine, without depriving me of consciousness or of inner freedom, and yet constituting a second "me", as though I had two souls, of which one is dispossessed of my body . . . and keeps its quarters, watching the other, the intruder, doing whatever it likes.' When he tried to make the sign of the cross the 'other soul' would twist his hand aside or push the fingers between his teeth and bite them savagely. Meanwhile the nuns would continue to give astonishing public performances: a young nun named Sister Claire would roll on her back masturbating and shouting, 'Come on, fuck me.' All Surin's exorcisms proved useless. And Surin himself suffered periodic attacks of insanity and 'possession' for the next twenty-five years: only in the last five years of his life was he free. Reading his own account of his illness it is hard not to feel that Kardec's *Spirits' Book* explains it rather better than Huxley's *Devils of Loudun*.

Walter Franklin Prince himself encountered a curious case of 'possession' in 1922. A wealthy and cultured woman whom he calls Mrs Phyllis Latimer (a pseudonym) told him that she was 'obsessed'. The 'spirit' in question was her cousin Marvin, who had died two years earlier. A few days after his death she began to hear his voice telling her that he was going to make her suffer and that he had a reason for this. Soon the voice began speaking inside her head, telling her that she had made him suffer. She was unable to recall any injury that she had ever done him and begged him to tell her what he meant. Finally he told her how one day, shortly before his death, she had left the room while in the middle of writing a letter: he had read the letter and found a remark about himself that offended and upset him deeply. Now reminded of it, Mrs Latimer recalled the letter and the remark that had caused so much trouble.

Cousin Marvin seemed to have remarkable knowledge of the future: he would tell her with glee of things that people would do to make her miserable, and they always happened as predicted. During a domestic crisis the voice told her that a certain person would offer to help her but that the promise would not be kept. Again he proved to be accurate. The voice also reproached her for not even sending flowers to his funeral. She protested that she had sent roses, but on enquiring she found that they had not been put on display.

Prince's first assumption was that Phyllis Latimer was suffering from paranoia – delusions of persecution – and his own acquaintance with such cases, where the delusions of persecution were accompanied by auditory hallucinations, convinced him that there would be no hope of a cure. But his friend James Hyslop of the American SPR had believed that there *is* such a thing as possession by an ill-disposed spirit, and Prince decided to act upon this theory. (He was almost certainly being disingenuous. His paper on the case* makes it sound as if he is an orthodox psychotherapist with no belief in 'spirits', yet we know from his account of the Doris Fischer case that he accepted Ariel as a spirit.) So, like Max Freedom Long's Dr Brigham, Prince decided to talk to the 'spirit' and see if it could be persuaded to leave Mrs Latimer alone. Assuming that cousin Marvin could hear him, Prince explained that he wished to talk as one gentleman to another, then went on to point out that as well as possessing his cousin, Marvin was also being possessed *by* her – that is, by his obsession for revenge. And after a great deal more persuasive talk in this vein Prince went on to suggest that purely as an experiment, Marvin should try thinking charitably about his cousin Phyllis and see whether this would not free him from the hatred that now tormented him.

Two nights after this Mrs Latimer dreamed that her dead mother came to her and told her, 'We heard what the man said. I will take care of Marvin.' She continued to hear the voice after this but it no longer expressed hatred. Following Prince's instructions, Mrs Latimer declined to answer. Finally one day she allowed the voice to speak to her. It told her that because Marvin had died with resentful thoughts about her he had been unable to escape from them. When he started persecuting her, he said, 'others had joined in' and urged him on. Now he had taken wiser advice and was going to leave her. Not long after this all her inner tensions vanished and she felt free again.

It is of course possible that this is a simple case of paranoia: but a number of points in Prince's account suggest that he does not think so. He mentions that Mrs Latimer had no idea of why her cousin should feel resentment against her, and had to be reminded of the letter. If she had actually recalled writing the letter and guessed that her cousin had read it when she was out of the room, it might well account for her paranoia, but not for her insistence that she had no idea of why Marvin should dislike her. Marvin's ability to foresee the future might also be explained naturally if his 'spirit' was merely a figment of her imagination: but Prince's account suggests he thinks there was more to it than that, and so does the incident of the roses that were not displayed at the funeral. Finally there is Prince's comment that he has never yet succeeded in curing a case of paranoia accompanied by hallucinations: it is hard not to feel that the successful conclusion of the case is intended as a hint to the reader that he believes this to be one of these rare cases where a person's belief that he is being tormented by 'invisible intelligences' 'has a basis in corresponding fact'.

Dr James Hyslop, whom Prince mentions, had come to believe that possession can be genuine through a rather curious case. In 1907 a goldsmith named Frederic Thompson came to see Hyslop, who was president of the American Society for Psychical Research from 1905 until

*'The Cure of Two Cases of Paranoia', Bulletin 6 of the Boston Society for Psychical Research, December 1927.

1920, the year of his death. Thompson had met the American landscape painter Robert Swain Gifford once or twice. In January 1905 he had unexpectedly been possessed by the urge to draw and paint, and later discovered that these compulsions had started at the time of Gifford's death in New York. Now he heard Gifford's voice urging him on and had visions of landscapes. Hyslop consulted his friend Dr Titus Bull, a neurologist who also happened to be interested in psychical research: Bull referred him to two other neurologists, who had contradictory opinions on the case. Then Hyslop learned that mediums were receiving messages from an entity that purported to be the late Robert Swain Gifford and who claimed that he *was* influencing Thompson. It began to look very much as if Thompson really might be 'possessed' by the dead painter. Thompson painted in Gifford's style although he had no artistic training, and when Hyslop looked at some of Gifford's final sketches, made shortly before his death and never exhibited, he was amazed to find that they were identical to some of Thompson's. Moreover Thompson painted pictures of places he had never been to, and when Hyslop went to the New England swamps and coastal islands where Gifford used to paint he immediately recognized landscapes drawn by Thompson. That finally convinced Hyslop that this was a genuine case of possession, not of mental illness.

In fact William James had reached the same conclusion. After all, if a medium can be possessed – temporarily – by spirits of the dead, then is it not conceivable that other people might be? For the remaining thirteen years of his life Hyslop studied cases of 'possession', and when he died he asked Dr Titus Bull to take over where he had left off.[*]

Unfortunately most of Bull's records have apparently been lost, but accounts of two of his most remarkable cases survive. One concerned another man who was apparently possessed by the spirit of a dead artist. C.E., as Bull calls him, had been a wreck since he had been 'taken over' by the spirit of an Austrian painter, Josef Selleny, who had been a friend of the Emperor Maximilian. He was suffering from premature senility, epileptic attacks and incessant sexual broodings. (We may recall Long's assertion that epilepsy is due to attacks from low spirits who drain the subject's vital energy like a vampire.) He had even been in an asylum. C.E. had apparently been hospitalized for a head injury, which might explain his 'madness' – or how a psychic entity had succeeded in 'possessing' him.

Bull had reached the same conclusion as Hyslop: that if someone was 'possessed' by an ill-disposed spirit then the best solution was to persuade well-disposed spirits to help get rid of it. (Of course in some cases, like that of Robert Swain Gifford, the possessing spirit was not actually ill-disposed and only had to be persuaded to leave.) For this purpose Bull used specially trained mediums, one of whom, Mrs Conklin,

[*]I must express my indebtedness to the chapter on 'The Work of Dr Titus Bull' in *The Infinite Boundary* by D. Scott Rogo, and to D. Scott Rogo himself for providing me with additional information.

he had found in a madhouse and cured by exorcizing her. One of his mediums now researched C.E.'s story to find out whether Josef Selleny was a creation of his imagination. The answer was no. After much research she discovered that Selleny actually existed – although he was hardly known outside Austria – and that he had indeed been a friend of the Emperor Maximilian. C.E. could not read German, so it looked as if this was a genuine case of possession.

When the mediums got to work on 'dispossessing' C.E. they soon discovered that Selleny was only one of many spirits. The main one was a Muslim priest who defended himself against the attempts to throw him out by calling on the spirit of a young man: but eventually, after more than thirty sittings, C.E. was cured.

Another case – Bull calls the patient K.L. – concerned a manic depressive woman of thirty-seven. Her problems began when she was terrified by a thunderstorm as a child: her nurse had locked them both in a closet and prayed for help. Later an attempted rape had further undermined her self-confidence. Now she alternated between profound depression and fits of manic rage.

The sittings apparently revealed that the main 'possessor' was the nurse who was responsible for the original neurosis. She was not ill-disposed – only inclined to continue to dominate the patient and look after her affairs. Asked to go away and leave K.L. in peace she replied, 'I do not know whether I will or not.' But she was finally convinced that she ought to leave. Other possessors were less tractable: one of them declared, 'She is mine and I am going to keep her. You keep out of this.' But when the medium's controls intervened and told her they could break her in two if they wanted to, she changed her mind and left. Eventually only one entity remained, and she had become an 'obsessor' by accident. She was a woman whose lover had abandoned her to die of venereal disease and was still in a mentally confused state. When Bull explained her situation to her she left voluntarily. After she had left K.L. ceased to be troubled by irritations in the genital area. The treatment was totally successful: two years later she wrote to Dr Bull, 'I have never felt so well and happy in my life.'

It must be acknowledged that in most such cases there is bound to be a strong suspicion that no matter how convincing the evidence for possession, the real culprit is the patient's subjective mind producing – as James says – a kind of unconscious self-hypnosis. Yet there are some cases which leave no possible room for doubt. One such was witnessed in Casablanca by Dr Natalie Monat, now practising in Alexandria, Virginia.* She has described how, in 1943, she was approached by a rich dry goods merchant whom she calls Mohammed Sayed, who told her that his son had been possessed for the past two months. The basis of the problem was Sayed's own strictness as a father: his son was terrified of him. The boy, who was eighteen, had stayed out late one night and got

*Reprinted in *Exorcism – Fact Not Fiction*, edited by Martin Ebon.

drunk. In the early hours of the morning his mother heard him creeping through the house and going into the bathroom. When she knocked on the door – which was locked – a shrill woman's voice answered, 'Don't call me your son. I am your daughter because I am using your son's body.' From then on their son behaved and sounded like a woman. Dr Pierson, a Casablanca psychiatrist, concluded that the boy had been so afraid of his father's anger that he had had a nervous breakdown. On the doctor's advice the youth was placed in a mental home. But since he had shown no improvement they had just brought him home.

The boy/woman spoke not only modern Moroccan Arabic but also an incomprehensible language that they could not understand. However one day the boy's tutor heard 'her' speaking and recognized the language as Egyptian, the language spoken in ancient Morocco. Since the tutor himself could speak Egyptian he engaged 'her' in conversation and learned that she was a girl who had died at the age of eighteen many years before; she resented dying so young and had been looking for another body for a long time. Then she found the boy, 'whose own spirit was loosely anchored to his body due to the influence of a few drinks and his fright of [his father's] anger', and threw him out of his own body, much as Margaret used to dispossess Doris Fischer. She violently resisted all the tutor's attempts to persuade her to leave the young man.

The tutor knew of a witch who lived in the south: the merchant sent for her. She drew a circle round the youth and asked them to pray with her. The boy was unable to cross the chalk line and screamed with rage while they prayed. The woman – who was obviously a medium – addressed the spirit in a more and more imperative manner, using various strange incantations. The girl's voice continued to scream, 'No! I shall never leave the body.' But eventually the boy collapsed in a kind of fit, his mouth foaming. Then there was a howl of rage and despair and the boy became unconscious. The tutor restrained his mother from rushing to him. A few minutes later he opened his eyes and asked dazedly, 'Why am I sitting on the floor? Why are you all staring at me?' The possession was over.

Such cases sound preposterous: yet by the time I came to research *Mysteries* in the mid-1970s I had come across so many of them that it was impossible to ignore them. One of the oddest was told to me by the head of BBC television drama, Bill Slater. In the early 1950s, when he was a drama student, he had attended a party where the guests began to experiment with an ouija board – an inverted glass with a circle of letters around it. The glass moved around the table at an incredible speed, spelling out answers to questions so quickly that it seemed unlikely that the guests were pushing it. Bill Slater made some facetious remark which the glass seemed to resent: asked if it would like anyone to leave the circle it shot unmistakably towards him. He went off to flirt with a pretty girl.

That night, in his room, he woke up with some 'presence' sitting on his chest and apparently trying to take over his mind and body. He concentrated his energies and fought back: the struggle seemed to go on for about twenty minutes. During this time there was a feeling of paralysis and he was unable to speak. At last he was able to cry out, and his room-mate woke up and switched on the light – 'to find me', says Slater, 'well-nigh a gibbering idiot'. This was his one and only encounter with the 'supernatural'.

All this sounds rather frightening – so much so that we may feel that even if possession really *does* take place it might be better not to talk about it. After all, mentally-ill people have enough problems without worrying about evil spirits. But the view of Hyslop, James and others who have accepted the possibility of possession is that it is rare, because there are 'barriers' between the human world and the world of 'discarnate entities'. Most mediums are also firmly convinced that every human being possesses his own 'guardian spirit' and that other well-disposed entities also act as policemen to prevent incursions.

As we have seen, the psychiatrist Wilson Van Dusen, whose views were quoted in chapter six, came to the conclusion that not all patients who 'heard voices' were suffering from hallucinations. In his book *The Presence of Other Worlds*, a study of Emanuel Swedenborg, Van Dusen goes rather further than this. The chapter called 'The Presence of Spirits in Madness' begins with the words, 'By an extraordinary series of circumstances I seem to have found a confirmation for one of Emanuel Swedenborg's more unusual findings: that man's life involves an interaction with a hierarchy of spirits. This interaction is normally not conscious, but perhaps in some cases of mental illness it has become conscious.' He describes how, working in the Mendocino State Hospital in California in the 1960s and examining thousands of mentally-ill patients, he began to notice the similarity between their hallucinations and Swedenborg's description of 'spirits'. Like Kardec, Swedenborg states that there are two types of spirit, low and high, and that low spirits are basically the earth-bound spirits of the dead.

Van Dusen's breakthrough came one day when he asked a patient suffering from hallucinations if he could talk to the 'spirit'. From then on he made a habit of engaging the hallucinations in conversation as often as possible and found that it immensely enriched his psychiatric experience. In some cases psychotics had been so overcome by their hallucinations that the two had blended and they were unable to distinguish: 'the ego had been overrun with alien forces.' But patients who were still able to see their hallucinations as objective realities were able to provide invaluable insights.

Van Dusen soon observed that the hallucinations seemed to come in two varieties, and that they acknowledged that they belonged either to the 'higher' or 'lower order'. Lower order voices seemed stupid and malicious, 'similar to drunken bums at a bar who like to tease and torment for the fun of it'. They found out a patient's weak point and then

270

worked on it interminably. They threatened disaster and death, or allowed the patient to hear voices plotting his death. Significantly, they seemed to have no identity and no memory (or no memory that they would acknowledge). They were often violently anti-religious, which seems to suggest that they may have been identical with the 'spirits' who possessed the nuns of Loudun. Van Dusen also discovered that they were quite willing to accept identities suggested to them – which may again help to explain why so many 'possessing entities' in the past insisted that they were demons. On the other hand the higher-order spirits were helpful and considerate: they respected the patient's individuality and made no attempt to 'invade'.

It struck Van Dusen as extraordinary that hallucinations should fall so neatly into these two categories: after all one might expect psychotic patients to believe they were tormented by birds, animals, perhaps even machines or hat stands. Yet this was not Van Dusen's experience. As we have seen the experiences of patients sounded strangely like Swedenborg's high and low spirits, or the 'demons' described in the literature on possession and witch trials: one woman declared that her sexual experiences with a male spirit were far more pleasurable and 'inward' than normal intercourse.

Van Dusen's observations on high spirits seem to be supported by the curious case of the science-fiction writer Philip K. Dick. Dick's early work had a strong tinge of neurosis and pessimism. He was obsessed by the idea that each of us lives in an individual universe and that therefore there is no such thing as an objectively real world – a dangerous notion that can obviously undermine our 'reality function'. In an interview with fellow writer Charles Platt, Dick described how as a child he saw a newsreel of a Japanese soldier hit by a flame-thrower and burning like a torch, and how he was dazed with horror as the audience cheered and laughed. He continued to be obsessed by pain and suffering and finally, in his forties, reached a 'trough' in his life when he saw only inexplicable suffering. At this point, he says, 'my mental anguish was simply removed from me as if by a divine fiat. . . . Some transcendent divine power which was not evil, but benign, intervened to restore my mind and heal my body and give me a sense of the beauty, the joy, the sanity of the world.' It sounds as if some unconscious 'will to health' had intervened: but Dick is emphatic that it was more than this. In 1974 (when he was forty-six) he experienced 'an invasion of my mind by a transcendentally rational mind, as if I had been insane all my life and suddenly I had become sane.' This rational mind,

' . . . assumed control of my motor centres and did my acting and thinking for me. I was a spectator to it. It set about healing me physically, and my four-year-old boy, who had an undiagnosed life-threatening birth defect that no one had been aware of. This mind, whose identity was totally obscure to me, was equipped with

271

tremendous technical knowledge – engineering, medical, cosmological, philosophical knowledge. It had memories dating back over two thousand years, it spoke Greek, Hebrew, Sanskrit. There wasn't anything it didn't seem to know.

It immediately set about putting my affairs in order. It fired my agent and my publisher. It remargined my typewriter. It was very practical: it decided that the apartment had not been vaccuumed recently enough; it decided I should stop drinking wine because of the sediment . . . . It made elementary mistakes such as calling the dog 'he' and the cat 'she', which annoyed my wife, and it kept calling her 'ma'am'.

. . . I made quite a lot of money very rapidly. We began to get cheques for thousands of dollars – money that was owed me, which the mind was conscious existed in New York. . . . And it got me to the doctor, who confirmed the diagnoses of the various ailments that I had . . . . It did everything but paper the walls of the apartment. It also said it would stay on as my tutelary spirit. I had to look up 'tutelary' to find out what it meant.

Dick was later to describe the experience in his novel *Valis*. But his fellow science-fiction writers found it impossible to swallow: Ursula Le Guin told him she thought he was crazy. And the bewildered interviewer recorded, 'I can't suddenly believe that there really are extraterrestrial entities invading the minds of men.' Yet he admits that 'I do believe that something remarkable happened to him, if only psychologically. . . .' On the evidence of Dick's interview it is hard to decide whether the 'possession' was purely psychological or genuine – although the half million words that he wrote about his experience may eventually shed some light on it. (Dick died of a stroke in 1982.) But if Dick is correct in stating that the entity could speak Greek, Hebrew and Sanskrit and that it had memories dating back for two thousand years, this would undoubtedly be powerful evidence for regarding it as one of Swedenborg's 'higher order'. Which of course raises the interesting question of why such an entity should wish to help Dick tidy up his life. One possible answer is that by the early 1970s Dick had become one of the most widely admired science-fiction writers of his time and was therefore worth converting to the conviction that life is not a meaningless nightmare after all.

This notion of benificent possession is of course older than civilization. In his classic work *Possession, Demoniacal and Other* (1930) Professor T. K. Oesterreich concluded that the 'possession' of the Delphic Oracle in ancient Greece was a case of benevolent possession. Joseph Rock, a member of the National Geographic Society's expedition to Yunnan in 1928, described an extraordinary performance in which a *sungma* (a kind of medium) was possessed by the 'demon' Chechin. The *sungma* took his seat in the temple while the Tibetan monks chanted, rang bells and blew conch shells: he was wearing a tall iron hat strapped under his chin. When the spirit arrived his face swelled so much that the chin-strap split and blood trickled from his mouth and nose. Then the *sungma* was handed a Mongolian steel sword a third of an inch thick and proceeded to twist it into knots as though it were paper: presumably the spirit possessed the same kind of metal-bending powers as Uri Geller. He ended by performing a spectacular dance in a pile of burning straw, 'whirling like a demon' in the flames without getting burnt.*

Dr Titus Bull carefully concealed his belief in possession from his professional colleagues and ordinary patients. In recent years at least two American psychiatrists, Adam Crabtree and Ralph Allison, have shown a bolder spirit. Crabtree was a theological student in Minnesota when he came upon a pamphlet called *Begone Satan*, which described one of the most extraordinary cases of 'possession' on record.

In 1896, when she was fourteen, Anna Ecklund found herself unable to enter a church building, although she was a devout Catholic. She was troubled with fantasies of committing 'unspeakable sexual acts' and an impulse to attack holy objects. In her mid-twenties she asked for help, but the Church was sceptical and it was not until 1912 that an exorcism ceremony seemed to bring relief. In 1928 she was still suffering from attacks and Fr Theophilus Reisinger, a Capuchin monk from the community of St Anthony at Marathon, Wisconsin, decided to carry out a second exorcism at a convent in Earling, Iowa. As soon as he began the formula of exorcism Anna shot up from the bed – in spite of the vigilance of several strong nuns – and stuck on the wall above the door. As he continued the exorcism her howls and screeches brought the towns-people running to see what was happening.

Anna spoke in a variety of hoarse voices even when her mouth was closed, and when it was open her lips did not move. Her head swelled to the size of a water-pitcher and her face was fiery red. She vomited incredible quantities of foul matter – another sign of 'possession' (Fr Tranquille in the Loudun case had also vomited). If food had been sprinkled surreptitiously with holy water, she knew instantly. When the priest was reciting sections of the exorcism rite in German and Latin, 'the devil' would reply correctly in the same tongue. And a devil who called himself Beelzebub explained finally that they were tormenting her because her father had cursed her. Attempts to summon her now deceased father were finally successful, and he admitted that he had made many attempts to commit incest with her but she had resisted him: this was why he had cursed her and wished that devils would enter into her to entice her into sex. His ex-concubine also appeared and confessed to killing four of her children – probably in abortions. All this went on for twenty-three days, during which time several nuns had to be moved to another convent because of the disturbances and the pastor was involved in a strange car accident. Anna remained unconscious during most of the

*Quoted by J. Finley Hurley in *Sorcery* (1985), p. 191.

273

exorcism, but speaking in multitudes of voices. Then, on the twenty-third day, her body shot erect as if propelled by a spring, only her heels touching the bed. She collapsed on to her knees while a terrible voice repeated the names of the tormenting spirits until it died into the distance. At this point Anna opened her eyes and smiled.

The monk who had translated the pamphlet from the German was in the same monastery as Crabtree and was able to verify the details of the story. He naturally believed that Anna was contending with demons from Hell. But it seems far more likely that they were the same 'earth-bound spirits' that caused so much trouble in the Harper household in Enfield.

In 1969 Crabtree decided to leave the cloister and become a psychiatrist. He soon came to accept the reality of telepathy and clairvoyance. But it was not until 1976 that a colleague told him about a 'possessed' patient and he witnessed the phenomenon for the first time. He flatly declined to believe that he was witnessing anything 'paranormal'. But in the following year he began to encounter cases among his own patients. These finally led him to the highly unorthodox conclusion that living persons *can* be possessed by the dead – and, incredibly enough, by the living.

His first case was of a young woman whom he calls Sarah Worthington, who was referred to him by a colleague. Crabtree started by asking her if she had heard 'voices inside her head', and she admitted that she had. Then he persuaded her to go into a deep state of relaxation on the couch. Suddenly Sarah spoke in another voice, a stronger, more authoritative voice, declaring she was hot. Asked to name itself, the voice said it was Sarah's grandmother, Sarah Jackson. Her aim, she said, was to help Sarah. And the comment about being hot referred to a traumatic experience in Sarah Jackson's early married life when she thought her seven-year-old son was trapped in a blazing house. It became clear that Sarah Jackson – who claimed to have 'entered' her grand-daughter while she was playing the piano and was therefore in an 'open' state of mind – had as many psychological problems as her granddaughter, possibly more.

In the long run it turned out to be unnecessary to 'dispossess' Sarah Worthington. Now that she understood that the voice inside her was her grandmother she ceased to worry, and even came to derive a certain comfort from her grandmother's presence at the back of her mind. In this case the cure was effected simply by understanding what was happening.

In another case a social worker named Susan had been 'possessed' by her father, who had died in a car crash and who had been so sexually obsessed by his daughter that he used to creep into the bedroom when she was asleep to fondle her genitals. The possession was not deliberate: the car crash had left him in a state of confusion. Crabtree was able to persuade him to leave her alone.

Crabtree worked with a female colleague on the case of a girl called Jean who was obsessed by the memory of her mentally-retarded sister

274

Amy, who had died at the age of twenty. Jean felt a kind of 'alien mass' inside her which she had tried – unsuccessfully – to get rid of through bioenergetics. Now, lying on Crabtree's couch, the childish voice of Amy began to speak through her mouth. Amy told the doctors that she had first 'entered' Jean when she was five years old and had then 'lived through' her. 'She could go places and learn things that were otherwise impossible in her condition.' The family background was full of violent, negative emotions, so their 'partnership' was important.

Under Crabtree's instructions Amy 'looked around her' and observed a grey-haired, elderly man who told her that he had been appointed to be her teacher. It was hard to persuade Amy to go away and listen to her instructor, but eventually Crabtree succeeded – after a 'heated exchange'. Following this Jean continued to feel Amy as a vaguely benevolent presence, but the 'alien mass' inside her went away.

If we can accept that Jean was really 'possessed' by Amy and was not simply experiencing guilt about her – as she herself believed at one point – then the most interesting part of the case is the fact that Amy 'entered' her sister while both were still alive and was able to use her for the sake of vicarious experience. Presumably what happened was that she established some sort of telepathic contact which enabled her to share her sister's life.

The same thing seems to have happened in another extraordinary case, that of a university professor called Art who experienced 'inner storms' in which his mother's censorious voice expressed her dislike of his friends and his behaviour. His mother was alive and living in Detroit. In a state of deep relaxation, Art identified himself as Veronica, his mother. 'Art is mine and his life is mine.' She began to make harsh comments on a girl Art proposed to marry. She had always been a highly possessive mother and even in his teens would call him into her bed after her husband had left for work and tease him into a powerful state of sexual excitement. It was obviously this intense relationship between them – and his sexual interest in her – that had opened him to the 'possession'.

Veronica eventually admitted that this obsession with her son was good for neither of them. And when, still in Detroit, she developed a cancerous growth and needed an operation, the possessing entity agreed that this might be because dividing her energies between herself and her son had robbed her of vitality. At this point the 'possession' gradually faded away, while Art's mother in Detroit underwent an astonishing transformation: from being dull and withdrawn she began to lead an active social life. (It would be interesting to know whether Art's mother realized she was possessing her son, but Crabtree does not mention this.)

In the writings of Titus Bull, Crabtree came upon the interesting remark that dead ancestors can influence the lives of their descendants, the aim being to 'keep the mortal in line with family ideals'. Two of Crabtree's female patients seemed to illustrate what Bull meant – one an Italian, one an east European, both subject to a 'dark cloud' that made them subject to some 'external agency' – but both these cases could also be interpreted as ordinary neurosis. However in the case of a man called Mike Doan a strange entity emerged that seemed like the traditional leprechaun. Speaking in a strong Irish brogue it made witty and amusing remarks about Mike and his family. Eventually this character – who called himself Shamus – explained that he was one of Mike's ancestors. The family had originally been prosperous and successful, but then avaricious women had taken over and their meanness had finally led to poverty and misery. One day the menfolk of the family – probably drunk – attacked the women and subjected them to sexual humiliation, also desecrating a statue of the Virgin Mary. From then on they were convinced that they were accursed, and the guilt persisted down the centuries. Shamus, who had taken part in the 'crime', was burdened with guilt and was still dominated by 'the women'. When he had talked about the crime and his sense of guilt he was finally freed from the burden of sinfulness and Mike was freed from his presence. Both Crabtree and Mike Doan keep an open mind about whether Shamus was a real person or a creation of Mike's unconscious mind, but Crabtree insists that from the therapist's point of view it makes no difference: Mike's cure justifies the method.

Of all the cases cited by Crabtree the most normal and typical – from the point of view of psychical research – is that of a friend of Crabtree's named Pat who spent a weekend at the farm of a friend's grandparents and allowed herself to be drawn into automatic writing. She immediately went into a trance-like state and seemed to see a woman dressed in mauve, while her hand wrote 'Elizabeth Barrett Browning'. Other 'entities' caused her hand to write messages but it was not until she returned home that she began to hear 'Elizabeth's' voice inside her head, trying to persuade her to do more automatic writing and insisting, 'We need you.' She ignored it and tried to read, but experienced a sensation as if someone was pressing her face against hers. It took several days of ignoring the entity before it gradually departed and at last she thought she could see the woman receding.

Some of Crabtree's cases sound so preposterous that it is difficult to take them seriously, and he explains – perhaps defensively – that he feels the same but is nevertheless telling them exactly as they occurred. One young woman who showed signs of dual personality finally began to speak with the voice of an entity that identified itself as 'the coach' and assured the doctors that the young woman was totally within his control. After a great deal of questioning 'the coach' recalled that he had once been a human being. Little by little he was able to recall details of three lifetimes, in the last of which he had been horrifyingly executed by being thrown into a pit with a hungry python or boa constrictor; as he had died he had had an 'out-of-the-body experience' and had watched himself being crushed to death. (Describing this scene, the girl filled the room with shattering screams.) A kind of amnesia had supervened and the

276

coach became a bodiless entity wandering without memory and possessing several successive generations in the patient's family. After a month of intensive therapy the girl ceased to be on the point of nervous breakdown and 'the coach' departed. Whether or not it was a delusion of her unconscious mind, the treatment certainly worked.

The oddest case concerns an entity that seemed to possess a university history lecturer named Marius, who began to experience irrational impulses to kill his wife. He talked of a 'monster inside'. When Crabtree and a group of helpers eventually succeeded in exorcizing some of Marius's pent-up rage he was able to describe a scene in the remote past when 'half human' hunters had killed a bear with appalling sadism. While they did so some unspecified entity – a 'round hole in space' – absorbed the violence. One of the hunters had been 'possessed' both by the spirit of the bear and by the 'round hole'. After Crabtree's session with Marius 'the bear' departed but the 'round hole in space' remained. The next day Crabtree succeeded in speaking to this entity, which described itself as a non-human vortex which needed the energy of living beings for nourishment. When the group concentrated feelings of love and affection on Marius the entity complained of his discomfort at 'the white light'. In later sessions it recalled its experiences before it had come to earth and that it had not always been totally dark. Eventually it was persuaded to leave, and Marius experienced no more impulses to commit violence.

Obviously these cases must be accepted for what they are – studies of clinically disturbed individuals from which it would be unwise to draw general conclusions. Yet there is nothing in them that contradicts the conclusions reached by Guy Playfair as a result of his years in Brazil. One thing puzzled me: that Crabtree should have encountered so many cases of 'possession'. It sounded too good to be true, rather like Agatha Christie's Miss Marples who constantly stumbles across murders. The dozen or so possession cases that Crabtree cited were of course only a tiny fraction of his clinical experience, yet it still seemed odd, and when I entered into correspondence with him – as a result of writing an introduction to his book *Multiple Man* – I took the opportunity to ask this question. He replied that he had often pondered on this himself and wondered whether he was 'creating' the phenomenon in his patients. Another possibility was that he might somehow unconsciously 'draw' such patients to himself. But it seemed to him that the likeliest explanation was that the phenomenon is not as rare as might be supposed but usually goes unrecognized. He pointed out to me that another therapist, Ralph Allison, had also encountered a surprising number of cases of multiple personality in the relatively small area of Los Osos, California.

In fact I was not unfamiliar with the notion that mental – or even physical – illness may be caused by 'discarnate entities', for my old friend Dr Arthur Guirdham had written a book, *Obsession*, on precisely this subject. But then Guirdham is a firm believer in reincarnation, which has the understandable effect of making his ideas suspect in the eyes of his medical colleagues – he took care not to publish his unorthodox ideas until he had retired from medical practice.

Adam Crabtree and Ralph Allison are both working psychiatrists who had been forced to entertain their unusual hypotheses as a result of clinical experience. Allison's story is just as remarkable as Crabtree's. In *Minds in Many Pieces* he offers an interesting and amusing account of his early days as a psychiatrist. He began practising in Santa Cruz in the mid-1960s, when many of his patients were hippies suffering from drug abuse, alcoholism and a general feeling of meaninglessness. It was not until 1972 that he encountered his first case of multiple personality. Janette was a quiet, rather mousy woman who had been diagnosed as a schizophrenic with compulsive tendencies: she experienced impulses to kill her husband and children. In one hospital where she had been treated she had been raped by a group of orderlies who had then given her a pair of earrings to bribe her into keeping quiet. Allison sent her to another psychiatrist for a second opinion, and it was the other psychiatrist who told him that he had another *Three Faces of Eve* case on his hands: Janette had been walking about agitatedly, saying, '*She's* the one who's depressed, not me.' So the next morning Allison explained to Janette that he thought there might be another personality inside her body, persuaded her to relax deeply, then asked if he could speak to the 'other person'. Instantly Janette changed: her face hardened and she spoke in a grating voice, 'God, it's good to get rid of that piss-ass Janette.' This new personality identified herself as Lydia. And like Eve's alter-ego, she seemed to be the total opposite of the original personality. Asked what she considered fun she explained, 'Drinking, dancing, fucking', then moved into a provocative position. It struck Allison that perhaps the rape by the orderlies had not been entirely unprovoked.

Janette's problem turned out to be lack of affection during childhood. She hated her mother, and when her father, whom she adored, had been inducted into the army she felt he had abandoned her. She was delighted when he finally returned then shattered when her mother had another child, a son. At this point Janette retreated from life and the 'naughty' alter ego, Lydia, took over. Lydia even dropped her baby brother, hoping to smash his skull, but failed. The local minister tried to molest her sexually, and at the age of eleven she was raped by a boy of fourteen. Another girl called Marie now took over, but Marie was so stupid that she learned nothing and left school at sixteen to get a job as a waitress. Her first marriage – to a homosexual – had been a disaster.

Allison's main problem with Janette was that his patient was not really convinced that she *was* a multiple personality – or not enough to make her really want to get well. What finally made her make up her mind was an experience she had while driving home one day. Lydia had picked up a couple of drunken and particularly smelly beatniks. Janette took over,

278

and when she glanced around to see what was causing the smell she screamed and shot off the road into a ditch. From then on she was determined to get well.

Allison had a good idea. It was clear that part of Janette's trouble was her fear of life, which made her passive and called forth the aggressive Lydia. He persuaded Janette to lead a more active social life, to begin attending teacher-parent meetings. He also inaugurated a therapy to remove her dislike of having sex with her husband. As Janette became stronger and more outgoing, Lydia became weaker.

When she apparently rang Allison's office and left a message, Janette – who had no memory of doing it – assumed it was Lydia. But Lydia denied it. Janette now performed a remarkable experiment. She set up a tape-recorder, asked Lydia to 'come out', and proceeded to conduct a dialogue with her. It soon turned into a quarrel. At this point a third voice suddenly interrupted – the personality that had made the phone call and which called itself Karen. She seemed to correspond roughly to Clara Fowler's B-4, and was an altogether more mature and balanced person than the others. When Allison conducted psychological tests on Karen he found that unlike the others, she seemed to be completely normal. She was his first experience of what he came to call the 'Inner Self Helper', a part of the personality that does its best to integrate the others.

Eventually, with the help of Karen and his own 'self-expression therapy', Allison succeeded in integrating Janette's personalities. The cure even survived her subsequent break-up from her husband. 'She is coping as everyone else does, facing the ups and downs of life as a whole individual.'

What is so important about this case is that it leaves no doubt whatever that multiple personality *is* a 'coping mechanism' and not, as Max Freedom Long believed, a matter of 'possession'. This obviously explains why so many multiple personalities seem to complement one another – as if the alter egos are built up of the spare parts that the 'original personality' leaves unused. The conscious personality is the part of us that copes with the world, and it is basically composed of *decisions*. We decide, from moment to moment, how we will react to our present situation – like a schoolboy in class deciding whether to put up his hand to answer a question or keep quiet. The 'original self' of most multiple personalities – Clara Fowler, Chris Sizemore, Janette – has decided that the least troublesome strategy is to keep quiet. But other aspects of the self will inevitably feel frustrated by this play-it-safe situation, which stands in the way of personal development. When the pressures are serious enough and the original personality is weak and miserable enough, the alter-ego takes over . . . .

Yet is this the *whole* story? Allison's second case of multiple personality raised an element of doubt. Carrie Hornsby was an incredibly beautiful redhead whose good looks were her greatest misfortune. Like Janette she was rejected by her mother and upset when her father – who was in the army – apparently deserted her. Her first alter-ego came into being when she was four and a small boy sat on her chest until she almost suffocated. The creation of an alter-ego always seems to be a withdrawal mechanism, a retreat from some unpleasant situation, like an ostrich burying its head in the sand. This first personality was a boy, like her tormentor. Her masculine aspect developed as a result of associations with the lesbians hired by her grandmother as hands at the ranch: the grandmother hated men.

One night at the ranch Carrie was unable to sleep and decided to go for a moonlight ride to a nearby lake. There she ran into a group of motorcycle riders having a drunken party, and was gang-raped. Thereafter she was terrified of sex. When her high-school boyfriend told her that it was time she 'came across', she blacked out. When she regained self-awareness they were driving home, and she gathered from her boyfriend's comments that she had apparently enjoyed the sex. Later she married this boyfriend.

A doctor at the centre for the treatment of alcoholics where Carrie worked persuaded her to perform oral sex on him: this would happen with the doctor's wife typing just outside the door. He actually billed her for these sessions, and she paid the bills: the relationship was clearly sado-masochistic.

Carrie decided she needed treatment when she found herself walking up to her neck in the sea and had to swim back to shore. Under hypnosis in Allison's office the personality responsible for this episode emerged: a girl called Wanda who called Allison a fat-headed son of a bitch. Later a third personality, a small girl called Debra, appeared. She treated Allison as her father and his other multiple-personality patient, Janette, as her mother: this produced some embarrassing situations.

One day a friend of Carrie's – another nurse – approached Allison and told him a strange story. She was interested in ESP and telepathy and had attended a course with an instructor who claimed to be able to enter the minds of other people: he was able to do this merely from a detailed description of the person. After demonstrating his abilities successfully he attempted to 'enter' Carrie's mind. He immediately became worried and agitated and broke off the experiment. Later he confessed that he had encountered some sort of evil force and declared that a drug addict who had died a few years before had taken over Carrie's body: he said her name was Bonnie Pierce or Price.

Allison was deeply sceptical: he had been brought up as a rationalist and this sounded absurd. All the same he wrote off to various record departments to see if he could verify the existence of a Bonnie Pierce who had died in New York in 1968. He was unsuccessful. But as Carrie's condition grew worse he decided to try an unusual experiment: to exorcize her. He knew that she had dabbled in witchcraft in high school and that one of her boyfriends had been serious about black magic. It followed that Carrie herself might believe in the efficacy of exorcism and that it might cure her. She was placed under hypnosis but denied that Bonnie was present. A colleague who was also in the room suggested trying to place her in an even deeper trance. This worked. Now Carrie said there *was* a Bonnie inside her and that she urgently wanted to get rid of her. Allison now suspended a crystal ball on a chain above Carrie's head and commanded Bonnie to leave her body. He declared that the ball would swing until the spirit had left, and that when this happened Carrie should raise her finger as a sign that she was now free. To Allison's surprise the ball began to swing in a circle, although he tried hard to hold it still. Then it slowed down. At the same time Carrie raised her finger. When brought out of her trance Carrie confided that she had always felt there was a spirit inside her and that now she felt free of it.

However this failed to solve the problem of Wanda and the other personalities. Wanda hated Carrie: she used to slash her wrists and take overdoses of pills. Ultimately Allison's attempts at 'integration' were a failure. After violently attacking him and almost incapacitating four police officers and two ambulance men, Carrie was handcuffed and hospitalized. When she came out she committed suicide with an overdose of drugs and alcohol. Allison never found out whether Bonnie had been a real person or a figment of someone's imagination.

Like Adam Crabtree, Allison seemed to encounter more than his fair share of multiple personalities, raising the obvious question of how far his own expectations caused them to materialize. Yet in at least one case the classic symptoms confirm the correctness of his diagnosis.

A grotesquely overweight woman named Babs was sent to Allison after attempting suicide. Oddly enough it was Lila, another multiple-personality patient who had become Allison's assistant, who realized that Babs was suffering from the same disorder. And when Babs admitted that she had blackouts during which whole sections of her life were obliterated, and that she had once 'missed' an entire year of school, Allison felt certain that Lila was correct. Soon Allison had encountered Lenore, a negative and destructive personality, and Alice, another competent B-4 type. Not long thereafter another personality called Tammy emerged, a charming, self-confident person who seemed to know all about Babs and her problems: in fact Tammy was virtually a 'built-in therapist'. Babs, she explained, had become a multiple personality because of a miserable and loveless childhood and various traumatic experiences.

With Tammy's help the therapy seemed to be making excellent progress. Then one night Babs rang up in a state of desperation. She had just blacked out in church and insulted her best friend: now she was almost hysterical. On the spur of the moment Allison told her to lie down, put herself into a trance and summon Tammy. Then they were both to join in prayer for God's healing power to solve their problems. This expedient was rather too successful. When Allison was summoned the next morning by Babs's husband he discovered that Babs had turned

281

into a five-year-old child. And this new personality remained in control. Yet if Allison had recalled the Mary Reynolds case recorded by William James he might have taken some comfort. Mary Two was also virtually a new-born baby when she first appeared, yet she 'grew up' at an astonishing rate, learning to speak within a matter of weeks. This is what happened to Babs. She matured with remarkable speed. She and her husband went through a second courtship and married again, and when her memory returned fully she was at last an integrated personality.

Here again the diagnosis seems perfectly clear. Babs had 'created' the other personalities to cope with her problems, and she finally had to start from scratch and develop an undivided personality.

The case of Babs makes it quite clear once again that multiple personality *can* be explained as a coping mechanism, and that in such cases it is quite unnecessary to evoke Long's low spirit hypothesis to explain it. So it comes as something of a surprise for the reader of *Minds in Many Pieces* to learn that Allison ended by accepting that in certain cases, the 'spirit hypothesis' is the only one that works. His change of heart came when he was treating a twenty-four-year-old girl called Elise who had sixteen alter-egos and five 'Inner Self Helpers'. 'Each served a specific purpose in her life and each was created to handle a trauma that Elise herself couldn't face.' Once a person has learned to 'solve' a problem by creating an alter-ego it becomes the simplest method of avoiding any difficult problems.

One day, when Elise had been discussing the death of her grand-mother, she 'faded out' and a male who identified himself as Dennis took over. Close questioning of Dennis finally convinced Allison that he was not a normal alter-ego; he seemed to serve no purpose and Allison was unable to discover when he was 'born'. Dennis went on to explain that he stayed in Elise's body because he liked having sex with Shannon, another alter-ego. Shannon had been 'born' to cope with Elise's loss of her baby: now she returned every October and stayed until the anniversary of the baby's death the following March. She was emotion-ally strong and self-assured and Dennis had, apparently, fallen in love with her. When Allison asked how Dennis could have sex with her he explained that when other men made love to Shannon he slipped into their bodies and enjoyed it. He was not in the least sexually interested in Elise, although she and Shannon had the same body – a statement that brings a fascinating insight into the psychology of sex.

When Elise woke up she complained about Dennis and declared that none of the other personalities liked him. It seemed that when Shannon was having sex with a man of her choice Dennis would pinch her to let her know that he was enjoying it too. Elise's 'Inner Self Helpers' also confirmed that Dennis was not one of Elise's personalities but an interloper in the body. In a further interview Dennis explained that he had been a stockbroker named Julius who had lived in Louisiana and had been shot in the course of a robbery. Since then he had been wandering in and out of various male bodies, apparently under the guidance of someone who 'assigned' them – he was unsure about who this was. The chief 'Inner Self Helper' told Allison that Dennis had 'entered' Elise when she and her friends had been experimenting with black magic in her late teens: she had tried to induce Satanic possession and 'opened her mind'. Allison was also told that he could get rid of Dennis the next day but that he should stand well back in case Dennis entered his body. However when Allison placed Elise under hypnosis the next day yet another personality emerged: a woman called Michelle who declared that she hated God and had no intention of being driven out of Elise.

Allison took Elise – who had listened to tape-recordings of these other personalities – to a grassy spot in the hospital grounds. She collapsed on to the grass and began to scream, 'Get out of my body! Get out!' Another voice replied, 'I'm not going to leave.' Elsie cried, 'If there's a God, help me,' then became unconscious. When she woke up an alter-ego called Sandi took over, and Sandi described three dark-blue spheres leaving Elise's body. The next day the 'Inner Self Helper' said that Dennis, Michelle and another female spirit he had never met had all left Elise.

There was a further surprise to come. The 'Inner Self Helper' declared that Shannon was not an alter-ego but the spirit of Elise's dead baby. The baby would also have to be got rid of. One day, after another noisy session, Shannon told Allison that she would be leaving in a few hours. Elise woke up with amnesia. This slowly disappeared over the next few days, but Shannon never returned.

Allison goes on to describe another case that convinced him that there were 'spirits' involved. This was a girl called Sophia, and Allison's attempts at fusion of her personalities had been highly successful. Yet two personalities remained, girls called Mary and Maria who seemed to serve no purpose. Finally, under hypnosis, Sophia was regressed to her birth and stated that her mother had had triplets. The doctor, who had been her mother's lover, suffocated the first two but was interrupted by a neighbour before he could kill Sophia. The three spirits had been hovering over the babies' bodies, prepared to enter, and now two of them were 'homeless'. So Sophia invited them to share her body: they accepted gratefully.

It was Sophia who told Allison that she now no longer needed her two sisters. Allison put a bottle in each of her hands and placed her in a trance. He then ordered her to send Mary into one bottle and Maria into the other. After grunting and groaning, Sophia relaxed. When Allison tried to recall Mary and Maria he was unable to: they had gone.

Although Allison writes, 'Is there true spirit possession? I don't know,' the final pages of his book make it clear that he believes that there is. He goes on to describe five levels of 'spirit possession' which he has identified in his own practice. The first is compulsive neurosis, such as alcoholism – a dubious example that hardly seems to qualify as 'spirit possession'. Next comes multiple personality which, if Allison's 'coping' theory is correct, does not qualify either. The next level involves the invasion by the mind of another human being, as in Adam Crabtree's case of Art and his mother Veronica. Allison cites a case in which a Mexican woman complained of general depression, which had developed after her nephew had been killed in a car crash. It turned out that her sister – the young man's mother – blamed her for his death, and she and her own mother had been seen visiting a black witch and performing magical rituals. Under hypnosis the sister emerged and admitted that she was causing the nervous problems. Allison ordered her to leave and the 'exorcism' was apparently successful: the woman woke up relieved of her symptoms.

The fourth type of possession Allison defines as possession by a discarnate spirit. One of his patients experienced a compulsion to keep walking to the local harbour, during which time she lost consciousness of her actions. Under hypnosis a voice emerged that identified itself as the spirit of a woman who had been drowned when searching boats in the harbour, looking for her missing husband and children. She said she had taken over the woman's body to continue her search but agreed to leave the patient, who then ceased to experience the compulsion to walk to the harbour.

The fifth type of possession, says Allison, is by apparently non-human spirits. He describes a patient who had convulsive seizures after an accident at work, although his injuries were insufficient to explain the seizures in physical terms. Under hypnosis a voice claiming to be a 'devil' explained that it had entered the man when he was a soldier in Japan and an explosion in a burning house had hospitalized him. Allison consulted a local priest, who finally succeeded in banishing the 'devil' through the Church ritual of exorcism.

So in the final analysis Allison's conclusions support Adam Crabtree's, and both are consistent with Guy Playfair's observations about *umbanda* in Brazil and with the information that Kardec obtained from his 'spirits'. These conclusions will strike many people as rather disturbing – they seem to be a complete departure from Western modes of thought that have developed over the past two centuries, and a return to tribal superstition. In a sense this is undoubtedly true – but it is still not in itself any reason for rejecting them.

In a paper on the treatment of Multiple Personality Disorder (usually abbreviated to MPD) in Brazil* the parapsychologist Stanley Krippner reveals that the 'spirit hypothesis' is accepted by an increasing number of doctors and healers and that many of these cannot be dismissed as practitioners of *umbanda*. Eliezer Cerquiera Mendes is a retired surgeon; Carlos Alberto Jacob is an anaesthesiologist who taught in a medical school for many years; while Hernani Guarmaes Andrade – Playfair's mentor – is an engineer and founder of the Brazilian equivalent of the

*'Cross Cultural Approaches to Multiple Personality Disorder: Practices in Brazilian Spiritism.' *Ethos* (Journal of the American Anthropological Association), September 1987.

Society for Psychical Research. But the assumptions they seem to share is that Multiple Personality Disorder has three basic categories: (1) the 'retreat' of the primary personality due to some unbearable trauma: (2) 'possession' by 'earthbound spirits'; (3) 'possession' by one of the subject's own past incarnations. At the time he was interviewed by Krippner in 1985 Mendes had dealt with some 20,000 psychiatric cases and had diagnosed 300 of these as MPDs. In most of these cases the treatment consisted of an attempt to merge the various personalities: that is, Mendes assumed the 'splitting' to be due to trauma. The same treatment was sometimes appropriate in the case of 'obsession' by a previous personality: Mendes described a case of a twelve-year-old girl who became a tomboy at puberty and expressed dislike of her developing female anatomy. A 'superteam' of mediums reported that the girl had been a male in a previous existence and that her former personality had been evoked by the biological changes. After three months of treatment the male personality had merged with the female. But in a case described by Andrade in which the patient's alter-ego was her past life as a Spanish gypsy (who spoke an Iberian gypsy dialect), the two personalities simply had to learn to cohabit. In cases of 'obsession' by an earthbound spirit or by non-human spirits the usual solution was exorcism to expel the intruding entity.

A case described by Jacob also involved a gypsy alter-ego. A sixteen-year-old girl named Isabel had periods of amnesia during which she wandered the streets dressed in gypsy clothes and earrings (garments she normally liked to wear during carnival). Isabel's mother, a possessive and strong-willed woman, brought her daughter to Jacob for therapy. Under hypnosis Isabel recalled a past life as a French gypsy who had enjoyed a carefree life of travelling, singing and dancing. The gypsy had chosen her present incarnation as Isabel because she felt that the fight for independence in her new environment would add a certain strength to her character. Jacob proceeded to merge the two personalities and Isabel began to confront her mother and resist her possessiveness – to her mother's dismay. Yet in spite of this conflict Isabel reported that she was far happier than before . . . .

Krippner's attitude towards these theories is one of detachment: he notes simply that they seem to work and that from the doctor's point of view, this is all that matters. But we should also bear in mind that this is not a question of either/or. Like the Brazilian doctors, Allison and Crabtree are not denying that most cases of multiple personality are a form of psychological self-defence against some unbearable trauma: they are simply asserting that in their own clinical experience some cases fail to fit this category but *do* seem to fit the category of what used to be known as 'possession'. They are not attempting to overturn current psychiatric theories, only to broaden them. Their aims are therefore consistent with those of the present book. What I have attempted to argue is that in the course of becoming 'civilized' man has deliberately suppressed certain paranormal faculties – like Jim Corbett's 'jungle sensitiveness' – because he no longer needs them. But one unwelcome side-effect of this suppression is that he finds himself trapped in an apparently futile material world whose processes go on repeating themselves idefinitely. Jung explained why he felt this to be dangerous:

> The maximum awareness which has been attained anywhere forms, so it seems to me, the upper limit of knowledge to which the dead can attain. This is probably why earthly life is of such great significance, and why it is that what a human being 'brings over' at the time of his death is so important. Only here, in life on earth, where the opposites clash together, can the general level of consciousness be raised. That seems to be man's metaphysical task – which he cannot accomplish without 'mythologizing'. Myth is the natural and indispensable intermediate stage between unconscious and conscious cognition.*

At this point in the development of civilization the aim is to re-establish that ancient contact with the 'unconscious', the realm of myth. This realm of myth is also the realm of man's 'hidden powers'. What the last two chapters should have made quite clear is that whether we like it or not it is also the realm of 'spirits'. Ancient man believed in spirits not because he was a superstitious ignoramus, but because he often *saw* them. In that sense Voltaire and the French rationalists were completely wrong. Voltaire writes condescendingly in his article on superstition in the *Philosophical Dictionary*, 'All the Fathers of the Church without exception believed in magic. The Church always condemned magic, but it always believed in it; it didn't excommunicate sorcerers as madmen who were deceived, but as men who really had intercourse with devils.' And this, to Voltaire, was so preposterous that it was not even worth discussing. We can hardly blame Voltaire for taking what after all strikes us as a sensible attitude. The fact remains that we now possess factual evidence that enables us to go beyond Voltaire, and the evidence indicates that the world is a more strange and complex place than we assumed. Jung and Kardec seem to be in agreement on one fundamental point: that the road that will take us forward is also the road that will take us inward.

Memories, Dreams, Reflections, p. 288.

4

Visions

If man could return to that primitive 'visionary' state, what would the world look like? The autobiography of Eileen Garrett offers some interesting clues. As a four-year-old child she was lying in bed one morning and looking into the shadows when she noticed globules of light bursting at intervals in the beam of sunlight. They were egg-shaped light balls which seemed to be full of colours, and they swelled and exploded like bubbles. As they swirled around in the sunlight they also moved in a well-regulated pattern like a dance. She observed at the same time that the air was full of 'singing sounds'. As she stared at the 'bubbles' she felt herself drawn into their dance so that she seemed to be split up – 'as though divided into little pieces and each piece was located in a different place'. She began to develop this ability to project some 'fluid' part of herself into flowers and trees and rocks – and sometimes into people – so as to experience their identity.

This sounds like Wordsworth's description of childhood in 'Intimations of Immortality', with its sense of 'the glory and the freshness of a dream'. In fact we can all experience something like this in states of deep relaxation – even sinking into a warm bath. What happens is that in focusing on the joy of relaxing, we somehow side-step the left-brain ego, the personality, and simply see things as they *are* instead of seeing them from the viewpoint of their usefulness to ourselves.

Eileen Garrett was also aware of what she called the 'surrounds' of living creatures, which clairvoyants usually call their auras.

As a child I knew that the character of people depended on their *surrounds*. By the quality of light and colour they gave forth, I could judge their personality. Some people moved in grey shadows and some in glowing lights . . . . This was equally true for me of plants and of animals: I knew, according to the condition of the *envelopes*, when the vitality of trees and flowers was high or low . . . . I noticed how animals behaved towards each other . . . and I could tell that they sensed these *surrounds*. As a mouse reacts to the presence of a hawk before it sees its form, so did I know that all animals reacted to their enemies and friends, by means of these enveloping forms.

287

When she was four Eileen Garrett also became aware of the presence of three children in the garden of the farmhouse she lived in. These children seemed to be made entirely of the light that merely surrounds solid human beings. She was able to communicate with them without words, 'as I did with everything that was alive; for it seemed to me that I knew what the flowers and the trees were saying without the use of words.' Ralph Allison mentions that many of his multiple personality patients had imaginary playmates in childhood who seemed to them as real as solid human beings, and also that some of them could see auras around people. But then most of his multiple personality patients also possessed Eileen Garrett's strange ability to 'withdraw' inside herself. Aldous Huxley, describing his reactions after taking mescalin, speaks of the sense of intense *meaning* that seemed to radiate from everything he looked at – from a flower to a deckchair – as if they were somehow speaking to him. And Ouspensky has described how wandering around St Petersburg at night and practising 'self-remembering', he would feel that the houses were communicating with him. In reading such descriptions we assume that they are a manner of speaking, a kind of poetic licence. But in doing so we are failing to grasp the basic mechanisms of perception: our personalities *cut out* most of the meaning of the world around us; it becomes in a sense like a television set with the sound turned down. Clairvoyants like Eileen Garrett are simply seeing the world with the sound turned up. There is a sense in which their perception is far more normal than ours.

There are many different degrees of clairvoyance. Eileen Garrett possessed a high level; some people possess almost none at all. Sartre's novels, for example, reveal that he saw the world as a dull, solid reality that oppressed his senses. But most artists and poets possess a slightly higher degree than most people. The result is that when they are feeling fresh and wide-awake they sense a meaning that is exuded by everything that surrounds them. Most of them are inclined to believe that this is simply a pleasant illusion, a way of being drunk on one's own vital energy: in fact they are catching a glimpse of the world in its primitive 'visionary' state.

Whenever I visit a picture gallery I become aware that art is an attempt to communicate this sense of 'the meaning exuded by objects'. The artist who merely paints what he sees in front of him is no more than a journeyman. The genuine artist is struck by the 'interestingness' of lines and colours and wants to isolate them on canvas. He is in fact catching a glimpse of the world of the clairvoyant. There is a case for arguing that all artists are undeveloped clairvoyants or visionaries.

Albert Tucker is one of Australia's finest living artists. When I asked him whether he had ever had any paranormal experiences he replied, 'Very few.' Yet these few emphasize that he lives in a very different world from the rest of us – a world that is already halfway to that of Eileen Garrett.

The first 'paranormal' experience he could recollect happened at the age of about seventeen. Every night as he lay down to sleep a heavy weight would come and settle down on his leg – the weight of a human being which was rather soft and warm. As soon as he turned from his side on to his back the weight vanished. Oddly enough he knew exactly what his visitant looked like: he had a clear mental image of a small, short, plump elderly woman with frizzy grey hair and a brown coat. This continued for a number of weeks, then ceased. It has never happened since.

Not long after this Bert and his mother were eating lunch one day when there was an appalling crash from the next room – the whole house shook. Mrs Tucker said, 'Good God, the bookcase has fallen over,' and they both rushed into the room. There was no disturbance whatsoever. Puzzled but relieved, they went back to their lunch.

A few years later Albert Tucker had his only experience of clairvoyance or precognition. Walking along a street in the Melbourne suburb of Malvern, approaching a corner, he was startled by a powerful visual image that came into his mind. It was of the street he was approaching, and it stood still, like an arrested film, so that he could scan it in detail. Halfway down the street a man was standing talking to someone in a gateway: he was wearing a grey felt hat and a tweed overcoat with a very strong and marked herringbone pattern. And even though the man was halfway down the street Tucker could see every detail in the cloth of the coat, every warp and woof in the material. Seconds later he reached the corner, looked down the street, and saw the same man standing in the gateway talking to someone.

Ten years later Tucker was living in a rooming house in Powlett Street, east Melbourne, with his first wife Joy. The two single beds in the room were at right angles to one another. Just about to doze off to sleep Tucker was suddenly awakened by a loud crash at the foot of his wife's bed. He sat up and leaned on one elbow, then saw that his wife was sitting on the end of her bed. He assumed that she had got up to go to the bathroom and had kicked the dressing table. To his surprise his wife continued sitting on the bed and – as in the case of the man in the overcoat – he was aware of being able to see every detail of the material of her nightdress and every hair on her head. This struck him as odd since the faint moonlight hardly illuminated the room. As he was about to open his mouth to speak his wife vanished 'as if a light had been switched off'. At the same time the sound of stertorous breathing came from her pillow. Tucker went across to her and looked down: she was curled up in a foetal position, breathing so heavily that it sounded like gasping. Then, slowly, her breathing became normal again. In the morning he asked if she recollected any dreams: she said no. When he described what he had seen she was as bewildered as he was. Never having heard of the 'astral double' Tucker had no idea of what to make of the experience.

A later experience seems to belong in the same category as the episode of the man in the tweed coat. One evening Tucker was sitting watching television and waiting for his second wife, Barbara, to return home from a book launch; his Doberman pinscher, Gretel, was lying on the settee dozing. Suddenly they both heard the sound of Barbara's returning car; Gretel's ears went up and she ran to the door. The car went past the house to the garage; the tyres gripped on the gravel and the motor revved. He opened the door and looked towards the garage; no rear lights were visible and the garage light was not on. The dog raced up to the garage while Tucker walked to the end of the terrace. A few moments later Gretel came back looking bewildered. There was no car. They both went back indoors. Ten minutes later they heard the identical sounds; the tyres gripping on the gravel, the engine revving as the car passed the house. This time it was Barbara returning home. The previous time had been a kind of 'rehearsal', or what the Norwegians call a *vardoger* or forerunner – an event that seems to occur some time before it happens in reality.

But by far the strangest of all Tucker's paranormal experiences took place in the same room in east Melbourne where he lived with his first wife. One weekend Joy went away to see her mother, leaving Albert alone in the room for the first time in five years. He experienced an odd pang of nervousness at the thought of spending the night alone, which he assumed to be some throwback to childhood – he later wondered if it was a premonition. That evening he went over to see some friends in the adjoining suburb of south Yarrow. Some time towards midnight he set out to walk home, a distance of approximately a mile. As he strolled along the bank of the river he became conscious of a feeling of uneasiness – which he again attributed to the knowledge that he would be spending the night alone. The closer he drew to home, the stronger became the feeling of nervousness. It was so strong that he began to lecture himself on being infantile. Yet by the time he was close to home it had become a feeling of acute anxiety. This turned to fear, then to terror. As he turned into Powlett Street he was driven along by pure will, determined not to give in to a nameless dread that had no object. He went into the house and groped his way upstairs in the dark – there was only one light-switch at the bottom of the stairs – then switched on the light in his own room. As he stepped inside he was assailed by what he describes as 'a most revolting stench – I can only describe it as the kind of smell you've probably picked up yourself in zoos – a kind of wet, hot fur and acute animal stench.' He stood in the centre of the room, rigid with terror yet still fighting it as childishness, then noticed something on the coverlet of his bed. It was a dead mouse. (In fact the Tuckers had never seen a mouse in this house.) It was lying on the bed with its back legs spread out, and as he bent over it he could see drops of urine sprinkled along the coverlet for about a foot behind the mouse. He bent over and touched it with his forefinger. It was still as warm as if it were alive. 'All of a sudden, instantly, I knew that if I spent the night in the room I wouldn't see the morning – I knew that with inner and absolute certainty.' He turned round and went downstairs. As soon as he went into the street the terror vanished. He went back to his friends' house and spent the night on their sofa. The next morning he returned to the room. It was full of sunlight and the terror had evaporated.

Thinking about this later Tucker came to the conclusion that 'somehow an opening had been created through which demonic forces could emerge'. The landlady had an idiot son who was institutionalized: periodically he came home for the weekend, and he was at home that weekend, in the room directly below the Tuckers. Bert Tucker felt that it was his presence that had somehow 'opened the door' to the demonic entity. And what of the dead mouse? His conclusion was that he became a 'kind of battleground' between the evil forces and a force that was trying to preserve him. It was this 'guardian' force that had filled him with terror on his way home and which – recognizing that he was too stubborn to accept the warning – killed the mouse as he entered the room and finally convinced him that this was not some purely irrational fear.

These various episodes all seem so unlike one another that it is hard to see any overall pattern. Yet the first and most obvious thing that emerges is that Albert Tucker is naturally 'psychic', which means, quite simply, that he is to some extent aware of that 'invisible world' that *shamans* like Ramon Medina take for granted. He mentions that he became aware of this in his early teens but that there was nothing he could pin down as a 'paranormal event'. Like many artists he was probably a late developer, so the grey-haired lady who sat on his legs was simply taking advantage of the peculiar energies of adolescence. (Could it be significant that she vanished when he turned on his back, removing the pressure from the region concerned?) The same explanation applies to the thunderous crash: since it occurred only once it might be interpreted as the poltergeist saying farewell.

The 'vision' of the man in the tweed overcoat may be regarded either as clairvoyance or precognition. If it was clairvoyance then his mind was simply grasping something that was happening a few hundred yards away, as if the intervening fence and houses were non-existent. But in view of the later episode of the phantom car I am inclined to regard it as precognition. Because he was totally relaxed his mind was able, in some odd way, to scan the future. In that case we must assume that the whole episode took place inside his own head, and that if another person had been present in the room he would have heard nothing. The dog's response would in that case simply be a response to Tucker's own reactions, or possibly a telepathic rapport. The alternative explanation is that Barbara Tucker, driving home, imagined pulling into the drive and somehow 'projected' the event into her husband's mind. I have cited elsewhere* the curious case of the Rev. Mountford of Boston, who was standing by the window in a friend's house when he saw a horse and carriage arrive; his host also saw it. But when they reached the front door there was nothing there. The genuine carriage pulled up ten minutes later. But in the meantime the daughter of its occupants arrived, looking worried. She had been walking along the road when the carriage had passed her, and had wondered why her parents ignored her and drove straight past. In fact her parents were still sitting in front of the fire at home, resting before they set out. The likeliest explanation is that one of the parents had fallen into a doze or a revery and 'projected' the image of the carriage.

The mouse episode raises some interesting questions. No doubt Tucker was right in assuming that some unpleasant denizen of the spirit world had been able to 'find the door' into the physical universe by stealing the energies of the idiot son, and Tucker's own psychic sensitivity may have made him doubly vulnerable. The natural assumption would be that it was some ill-disposed 'low spirit' – that is, basically a poltergeist. But poltergeists seldom seem to show any genuine ill-will unless 'directed' by a malevolent human being. This entity seems to have been genuinely malefic in its own right. Moreover the smell of wet animal fur is the smell often associated with demons in witch trials. We must accept, at least as a possibility, that the demonic forces of mediaeval theology may have some real existence – even if, as Kardec insists, they are not permanently and irretrievably evil.

Albert Tucker is obviously an unwilling psychic who has no intention of developing his powers and no desire to do so. This may sound strange, since most of us would like to be able to foresee the future and contact dead loved ones. But being psychic also has its disadvantages: living 'between two worlds' can be a wearing experience. Anne Bancroft notes that when she was sixteen she 'became afraid and stopped it all'. Even Eileen Garrett experienced doubts about it. Describing her childhood 'reveries' she says, 'These were not the beginnings of my ability to withdraw from the world and live within myself. I think that I may have had that ability always, but as the practical outer world became more insistent in its demands I developed the faculty for shutting it out . . . in an instinctive struggle for self-preservation.'

The psychic experience seems to begin with a certain 'opening up', which brings with it an intense sensitivity to nature – Anne Bancroft's sense of a 'presence' in woods and fields, Eileen Garrett's ability to 'converse' with trees and flowers. Another remarkable psychic, Rosalind Heywood – of whom I have written at length elsewhere* – developed her childhood sense of 'presences' in the foothills of the Himalayas and cried herself to sleep with nostalgia when her family returned to England. It was then that she became aware of other 'presences' in her grandfather's house

*Afterlife, p. 141, quoted from Myers' *Human Personality and Its Survival of Bodily Death.*
†*Afterlife*, chapter 2, 'The World of the Clairvoyant'.

near Dartmoor: a female 'presence' in her bedroom (her mother later admitted to seeing the apparition of an old woman there) and other 'melancholy presences' in her aunt's home in Norfolk. Years later her aunt saw a portrait of a man in seventeenth-century dress and exclaimed, 'That's the man who's always trying to stop me going upstairs'. She was told that it was Oliver Cromwell, who had been unhappily in love with a girl who had once lived in her house.

We have noted that Eileen Garrett heard 'singing sounds' as she stared at the 'globules of light' in her room. Rosalind Heywood devotes a whole chapter of her autobiography *The Infinite Hive* to 'the Singing',

> ... a kind of continuous vibrant inner *quasi*-sound, to which the nearest analogy is the noise induced by pressing a seashell against the ear, or perhaps the hum of a distant dynamo .... It is far more evident in some places than in others: particularly so in a quiet wood, for instance, or on a moor or a mountain – clean wild places unspoilt by man. It is also clear in, say, a church or a college library, places where thought or devotion have been intense for years ....

In this last sentence she seems to be speaking about the 'information universe' and the fact that objects can 'record' the vibrations of the human mind.

Rosalind Heywood also makes it clear why this kind of 'openness' can be uncomfortable to live with. In such states the slightest sound or touch seems like an earthquake. She describes returning from a concert feeling so ecstatic that she lay down on the bed,

> ... to mull it over .... Almost at once the whole vivid soaring climax existed again, simultaneously, not in sound but to my inner eye in colour. I was swept up into it and up it until I emerged at the top into a vast and beautiful marble hall, oblong, with painted walls and the whole of the east end open to the night sky and the stars. While I was staring enthralled at these splendid surroundings my husband thought I looked odd and touched me gently. The effect of his touch was far from gentle: it forced me back sharply and painfully into my body ... and shaken and disappointed I told the poor man what I thought of him in no uncertain terms.

On another occasion she was trying to practise a little mind-reading in her bedroom and experienced a feeling 'like a glorified version ... of going under anaesthetic'. Then she was jerked back to the world by a series of agonisingly loud bangs: her husband was gently tapping on the door to ask if she was ready for breakfast. This clearly explains why it can be dangerous to suddenly 'awaken' a medium who is in a trance: if the medium happens to have a weak heart the result can be fatal.

Rosalind Heywood's 'openness' also made her aware of non-human presences. When she and her husband walked out on to Dartmoor in the dusk, 'the incredible beauty swept me through a barrier. I was no longer looking at Nature. Nature was looking at me. And she did not like what she saw. It was a strange and humbling sensation, as if numberless unoffending creatures were shrinking back, offended by our invasion . . . .' She decided that they ought to stand quite still and try to explain mentally that they came as friends. Then 'I seemed to feel their sigh of relief. . . . Our apology was accepted.' A few days later, facing the moor through an open window, she 'suffered an invasion. . . . It was as if, like ebullient children, a covey of little invisibles floated in at the window to say "Hullo!" and coax me to play with them.'

On a visit to the House of Commons she sat, relaxed, in the entrance to Westminster Hall 'and let the world fade out'. She found herself 'passing beyond the Singing' and into the presence of 'a profoundly wise and powerful Being who I felt was brooding over the Houses of Parliament. In that inner space he towered so high that the actual buildings seemed to be clustered about his feet.' She decided that she must speak of the experience to a saintly old mystic she knew. But this proved to be unnecessary: as soon as she arrived he began to speak spontaneously of the 'Angel' of the House of Commons . . . . A few years later, waiting for her son in the music school at Eton, 'I once more seemed to pass through the Singing into the ambience of a great Being. He appeared to have the school in his care and, like his fellow at Westminster, he created an atmosphere of brooding wisdom and calm.'

To ask whether such experiences are 'real' raises an interesting question. It implies that Rosalind Heywood may have been merely imagining the 'presences'. Yet if her description is accurate she became aware of them by 'letting the world fade out' and falling 'down the rabbit hole' into a state of trance-like awareness. What she 'saw' then may well have been merely the creation of her subconscious mind: that is to say her mind may have interpreted its perception symbolically, producing this impression of a gigantic being towering above the building. Yet our insight into the workings of clairvoyance suggests that the perception she was interpreting was of something real: the 'presences' were not poetic imagination, like the presences Wordsworth felt in the Lake District, but real 'Beings'. But if we can accept that possibility then it is hard to see why we should draw a line and describe Wordsworth's 'presences' as imaginary. The 'open' mind of the poet and artist can sense realities beyond the reach of our normal senses. The real problem is that our materialistic assumptions have a number of false premises built into them: it is only when we recognize this that we see that there is no sharp dividing line between the everyday world and the invisible world of the clairvoyant.

294

Rosalind Heywood was lucky. As an upper-class young English-woman whose father was in the Indian Civil Service (and whose mother could also 'see ghosts'), she experienced no conflict between the everyday world and the world of her clairvoyant insights. In due course she married an ex-army officer who worked in the War Office then became a diplomat, and who was also capable of flashes of clairvoyant perception. (Her younger son also developed odd 'powers': one day she asked him why he was looking at a London atlas and he told her that later in the day some stranger would ask him the way to a particular street. This happened within the hour.) In due course she was able to join the Society for Psychical Research and pursue her interest in the paranormal in a detached and scientific manner. There was never any temptation to develop mediumship since she had so many other things to do.

Eileen Garrett's career was altogether less smooth. Brought up by an aunt and uncle on a farm in County Meath, Ireland, she was an 'outsider' from the beginning. Her aunt was a strong-minded woman whose attitude towards the paranormal was one of total unbelief: she made the child's life a misery. One day, as Eileen was sitting on the porch, her favourite Aunt Leon walked towards her and told her, 'I must go away now and take the baby with me.' She ran indoors to fetch her aunt, but when they came out Aunt Leon had vanished. Eileen was whipped for telling lies and sent to bed. But the following day Aunt Leon died in childbirth. The aunt still refused to believe that the child had seen Aunt Leon and told her angrily that she must never speak of such things again, 'for they might come true'. Eileen withdrew into a world of her own and began to develop physical illnesses as a reaction against her rejection. A few days after the death of her uncle – whom she adored – the door opened and he walked into her room, looking cheerful and healthy, and had a long talk with her. He explained that she would have to put up with her aunt and do her best, and predicted that in two years' time she would go to London. Then he went out, closing the door behind him. 'It never occurred to me that I had seen a ghost, or that anything strange had taken place.' But when her cousin Ann died she saw a 'shadowy grey substance' rising above her body, gathering itself into a spiral before it disappeared.

Two years later, at the age of sixteen, Eileen Garrett found herself in London, and she soon married a pleasant young man whom she met at dinner in the house of her aunt's cousin. But when they came back from their honeymoon he told her seriously that she must abandon her tendency to 'visioning' and that it might lead to insanity. She felt more self-divided than ever. The birth of a son delighted her, until an unseen presence warned her that he would not be with her very long. A second child was born, but she felt a premonition that he would die young. Not long after this both children died of meningitis. Her marriage ended in divorce. During the First World War she met a young officer and married him. Not long after, in a crowded restaurant, she felt she had been caught in the midst of a violent explosion then 'saw' her husband blown to pieces. Two days later she was notified that he was missing.

She married again and had a daughter. The child developed pneumonia, and one day she overheard the doctor saying that he had given up hope. She took the child out of the cot and held her close. Suddenly she heard a voice say, 'She must have more air. Open the window.' When she had done this she became aware of a man standing beside the bed: her fear suddenly left her. 'The next thing I recall was a resounding noise in my ears, which turned out to be someone knocking at the door.' (This seems to indicate that she was in a condition of trance at the time.) It was her husband. When they looked at the child she was sleeping quietly, the crisis over.

Eileen Garrett then joined a spiritualist society and attended lectures on clairvoyance and psychometry. She also joined a group of women who held seances. At the third meeting she grew drowsy and fell asleep. When she woke up she was told that the dead had spoken through her and that she was a gifted medium. Someone advised her to consult a Swiss clairvoyant named Huhnli. In his presence she once again 'fell asleep'. When she woke up Huhnli told her that her 'control', a spirit named Uvani, had spoken to him, and that Uvani wanted to 'do serious work to prove the theory of survival'. When she went home and told her husband he was furious and told her she was going insane. She ignored him and continued to visit Mr Huhnli. Finally her conflicts caused a serious haemorrhage. As she lay recovering she at last began to understand what had been happening to her throughout her life. The passage in her autobiography in which she speaks of this makes it very clear how close her own experience had been to that of many of Ralph Allison's multiple personality patients:

I saw for the first time that the trance state might be part of a psychological pattern which had its inception in my early childhood. I began to understand how the pain and suffering of these early days had made me withdraw from the world of people into the world of light and colour and movement. I could now recall that the first time I had been successful in *escaping* the pain of the punishment inflicted on me by my aunt was when I so separated myself that I could see her lips moving as she scolded me, but not a word penetrated my ears. I now remember also that when the physical punishment became almost unbearable ... I learned to draw inside myself and would fall promptly to sleep, thereby banishing the painful after-effects of a beating .... I also recall the many episodes of amnesia which had taken place during the early and unsatisfactory years of my first marriage, and during the tragic episodes of my sons' deaths. I understood now more clearly that

296

these periods of so-called amnesia were also forms of escape from the too-painful conditions of living.

All this makes it clear that Eileen Garrett was lucky to escape becoming a multiple personality. A sceptic might argue that she *had* become a multiple personality and that Uvani was only another aspect of herself. Yet the incredible successes of her later mediumship argue strongly against this.

In fact her second important mentor, Hewat McKenzie, founder of the College of Psychic Science, startled her with his refreshingly sceptical attitude towards 'controls'. He explained that it was a mistake to regard the pronouncements of 'controls' as the word of some higher power – they were often limited personalities who needed just as much education and training as the medium. Lack of this, he thought, had allowed mediumship to deteriorate until it functioned mainly on the emotional and sentimental levels. This led Eileen Garrett herself to express doubts about whether Uvani was a real 'control' or merely a split-off fragment of her own mind – an attitude that shocked McKenzie.

Her third marriage having now broken up, Eileen Garrett became a full-time medium. As far as she was concerned it was rather frustrating. It simply meant that she became unconscious and was told what had happened when she woke up. It was only occasionally rewarding, as when Hewat McKenzie asked her to help him investigate a poltergeist disturbance. Uvani apparently talked to the 'disturbed spirit' and found out why it was causing so much trouble to its relatives: it turned out that the problem had to do with a lost will, which was found behind a picture frame. After this the disturbances ceased. But at most of her sittings she felt that the sitters were basically frivolous. They wanted to contact dead relatives for their own purely emotional reasons and had no real interest in the mysteries of life after death. It all struck her as irritatingly trivial and she began to feel revulsion at the part she was playing.

The level of the trance communications suddenly improved when a new 'control' called Abdul Latif began to appear. He claimed to have been a Persian physician at the time of the Crusades, and she was interested to discover later that she was not the first medium through whom he had manifested. Yet her sense of revulsion persisted, and she finally decided to give up mediumship and to accept a proposal of marriage from an old friend. Then once again she heard the voice that had announced the death of her child: it told her to make the best of her happiness since it would not last. On the day the marriage banns were published she developed a mastoid and he caught a chill: within a week he was dead. When she recovered from a serious illness she realized that her clairvoyant faculties were more highly developed than ever. At that point, sick of the vague sentimentality of English spiritualists, she decided to go to America. It was the autumn of 1931 and she was thirty-eight years old.

The United States proved at first to be an immense disappointment.

297

Once again she found herself expected to work with people whose only interest was in communicating with their dead loved ones. It was even worse when she reached Los Angeles and San Francisco. Then she discovered that there *were* a few more serious researchers, like Hereward Carrington, then working with Sylvan Muldoon, and the psychologist William McDougall and his assistant Professor J. B. Rhine. In New York she carried out a classic experiment in astral projection with a Newfound-land doctor who possessed the same ability. She 'projected' herself to a room of his house in Newfoundland while remaining fully conscious of the room in New York. The doctor came downstairs with a bandage around his head as she 'arrived': he sensed her presence and explained that he had had an accident. When she relayed this information in New York she heard someone say, 'That can't possibly be true – I had a letter a few days ago and he was quite well then.' The doctor asked her to look at the objects on the table; she described them to the stenographer in New York. Then he took down a book about Einstein from the shelf and read a paragraph to himself: in New York Eileen Garrett interpreted the sense of what he was reading. After this the doctor projected himself to the bedroom of a co-experimenter in New York and described it, mentioning that it had been redecorated since his last visit and that two photographs were no longer there. Then the experiment ended: it had taken fifteen minutes. The next day they received a telegram from the doctor mentioning the accident to his head; later his detailed notes were checked against the New York stenographer's record and found to be accurate.

As she became more absorbed in this kind of scientific work she abandoned mediumship in favour of clairvoyance. She summarizes the result of her years of experience thus: 'Now I believed I saw a certain principle at work behind all communication – *namely that the subconscious mind was a vehicle capable of expanding indefinitely and able to contact all possible realms of understanding which it might choose to reach*' – in short a recognition that we are living in an 'information universe' and that all this information is accessible to certain levels of the human mind.

Oddly enough her attempts to demonstrate her powers at Duke University with J. B. Rhine – the man who would become the father of scientific parapsychology – were unsuccessful: her score in reading Zena cards was no more than average. This, she was convinced, was because 'clairvoyance and telepathy depended upon an active radiation registering between two people or between an individual and an object', and since the Zena cards had no 'radiation' there was no link between them. (According to Max Freedom Long our vital force – *mana* – acts through an invisible substance called *aka* or 'shadowy body stuff'. This *aka* is 'sticky', according to the Kahunas, and can be drawn out into long, sticky threads, like spiders' webs; telepathy, clairvoyance and psychometry operate through these invisible telephone lines of *aka*. This would explain why Eileen Garrett found Zena cards impossible to work with but would not explain why other subjects obtained a high score.)

In 1934 she returned to England and entered into more scientific work with Dr William Brown in his laboratory at Oxford. Brown thought that she might be simply a multiple personality and wanted to question her under hypnosis. But although she was able to recall childhood memories in detail under hypnosis there was no sign of her 'controls'. It was only when she went into a mediumistic trance at the last session that Brown was finally able to talk to Uvani.

In her autobiography Eileen Garrett is so concerned with explaining the scientific investigations that she fails to make even a passing reference to one of the strangest cases she ever became involved in: the haunting of Ash Manor in Sussex. The house had been bought in June 1934 by an American named Keel, who had been surprised that the owner asked so little for it – he decided the drains must need extensive repairs. But one night in November Keel woke up to find an intruder – a little old man – in his bedroom. When he tried to grab him, his hand went straight through him, and Keel fainted. Then he rushed to his wife's bedroom, babbling incoherently, and she went to fetch brandy. Outside her husband's bedroom she saw the same old man – wearing old-fashioned clothes including leggings and a pudding-basin hat. When she tried to hit him her hands went through him and he vanished. After this the family saw him frequently: he would appear from a chimney and walk into a cupboard that had once been a priests' hole. He became such a frequent visitor that the family ceased to worry about him – particularly when Mrs Keel found she could make him vanish by reaching out to touch him.

The research officer for the International Institute for Psychical Research was Nandor Fodor, and he persuaded Mrs Garrett to accompany him to investigate Ash Manor. She went into a trance, and Uvani took over and explained that hauntings only occur when someone is in a bad emotional state. (It soon emerged that the Keel family had serious problems: Keel was homosexual and the daughter had a father-fixation and was jealous of her mother.) There had been a prison close to the house in the fifteenth century and many men and women had died there.

After this Uvani allowed the spirit of the old man to 'possess' Mrs Garrett. The old man seemed to mistake Fodor for his jailer and fell on his knees, seizing Fodor's hand so tightly that he howled with pain and was unable to free it. Finally the old man began to speak in an odd mediaeval English, talking about the Earl of Huntingdon and the Duke of Buckingham – who had apparently betrayed him – and begging Fodor to help him find his wife. The man said his name was Charles Edward Henley, son of Lord Henley, and referred to the nearby village under its mediaeval name of Esse. When he talked of revenge they tried to persuade him that the desire for revenge was binding him to the earth, and that he should make an effort to forgive. Finally, crying, 'Hold me, I cannot stay . . .' the spirit vanished. Mrs Keel, who was also

299

present, said that Eileen Garrett's face looked like that of the old man while he was 'possessing' her.

Several more sessions seemed to bring no further result although, oddly enough, Henley manifested himself through another medium at the College of Psychic Science. Uvani made the interesting statement that the Keels were responsible for preventing the ghost from escaping its earth-bound existence: he said that they were using it to get at one another. Confronted with this observation Keel admitted that it was true – and his admission had the effect of finally 'laying' the ghost.

It may be worth mentioning that more than thirty years later, Fodor remarked in his book *The Unaccountable* that not a single statement of the Ash Manor ghost had been verified by painstaking historical research, and that scholars had not found its mediaeval English authentic. So like most true ghost stories the tale of Ash Manor – which is authenticated by a number of scientific observers – fades into the realm of ambiguity demanded by James's Law.

Eileen Garrett returned to America, where she continued to work with scientists – among them Lawrence LeShan and Andrija Puharich – and gradually came to be accepted as the most remarkable 'psychic' of the century. Many other mediums, such as Mrs Piper and Mrs Leonard, had been extensively tested and found to be genuine, but only Eileen Garrett had been as determined as her investigators to understand the secret of her own powers.

In our Western culture such powers are regarded as abnormal or simply fraudulent. In other cultures they are taken for granted. In the late 1950s an anthropologist named Stiles spent some time studying the Montagnais Indians of eastern Canada. When he returned he described to his colleague Professor Clarence Weiant how the Indians could communicate with one another over a distance of hundreds of miles by 'clairaudience'. They would construct a small hut about the size of a telephone booth out in the woods, and stay in it until the power built up sufficiently for them to hold a two-way conversation with some distant relative. While this was going on the shelter would shake. Stephen Schwartz has recorded that a Roman Catholic missionary and a Canadian trapper who lived among the Montagnais also bore witness to the phenomenon.*

Another anthropologist, Doug Boyd, accompanied a team of scientists to observe an American Indian medicine man in action, and the results, recorded in *Rolling Thunder*, leave no possible doubt about his 'magical' powers. Boyd confirms the ability of the Indians to communicate with one another by means of telepathy, and their ability to control the weather. He watched as Rolling Thunder poked a stink bug with a stick and caused a violent storm. Each time Rolling Thunder flipped the bug over on to its back,

*Stephen Schwartz, *The Secret Vaults of Time, Psychic Archaeology and the Quest for Man's Beginnings*, p. 207.

300

. . . there was a loud, sharp crack: a bolt of lightning . . . . Again and again the act was repeated and again and again the lightning came . . . . It seemed to be synchronized precisely with the actions of the bug. I might have been watching someone scratching a screwdriver on a battery pole or touching two live wires together. It became apparent as it continued that this was an uncommon but natural phenomenon produced by a real cause-and-effect relationship.

After a few minutes of this there was a 'wild downpour'.

Rolling Thunder also demonstrated his powers in freeing an Indian who had been imprisoned for refusing to fight in Vietnam. Although Boyd did not witness this he confirmed the story through reliable witnesses. Another anthropologist, John Welsh, described how he had accompanied Rolling Thunder to Leavenworth prison and told the guards that he had come to collect the Indian to take him back home. A prison officer finally came out and told them that it would be impossible to visit the man. Rolling Thunder was persistent, and finally another officer came out and told them that the man had been transferred to another prison. Welsh and Rolling Thunder went to a nearby motel for the night. In the middle of the night Rolling Thunder became furiously angry: he told Welsh that he had been inside the prison and knew that the officers had lied. If they could use lies to get their own way, he could use fear.

The next morning Rolling Thunder insisted that Welsh join him in smoking a pipe and chanting on the river-bank. After a while the fire produced an intense black smoke that rose straight into the air. Then there was a crash of thunder and the clouds began to gather. One big black cloud, shaped like a funnel, seemed to follow them as they approached the prison again. There Rolling Thunder shouted so fiercely that the guards rushed in to fetch the prison officers. They told him to go away. Rolling Thunder pointed to the funnel and told them to watch it. As they did so it came towards them. Then sand and rocks started flying through the air and they were in the midst of a whirlwind. The prison gate was ripped off its hinges and went flying through the air. At this the prison officials were finally convinced: they brought out the prisoner and allowed him to leave with Rolling Thunder.

According to Boyd, Rolling Thunder's powers are the result of a special relationship with Nature based on his recognition that the earth is a living being. But such an attitude is not apparently essential to the practice of magic – as some of the guards at Leavenworth must have been aware at the time of Rolling Thunder's unwelcome visit. A quarter of a century earlier Leavenworth had housed a multiple murderer called Hadad. The psychologist Donald Powell Wilson first encountered him when he was taken to Hadad's cell and found his body hanging from the cell bars. It seemed that Hadad had used the belt of a warder whom he

301

had hypnotized on his rounds earlier in the day. The warder – who was also present when the body was discovered – was convinced that he was still wearing the belt around his waist, even when a colleague pointed out that it had disappeared. A few days later Hadad's corpse was carried into the autopsy room. As the surgeons were picking up their scalpels he slowly rose to a sitting position and said with an impeccable Oxford accent, 'Gentlemen, I would rather not, if you don't mind.' His later explanation was that he was able to enter a trance so deep that all his natural functions ceased.

The following day Hadad offered another demonstration of his powers. There were many epileptics on the psychopathic ward who had regular seizures. Hadad offered to stop all such attacks for three days. He did as he promised: the attacks started up again on the following Thursday afternoon. Wilson's own explanation was that Hadad had exercised his hypnotic powers when he was last in the ward, and that this was merely a demonstration of post-hypnotic suggestion.

Hadad offered Wilson another demonstration of his powers. He removed his clothes and lay across two desks, then went into a death-like state. Then, as he had predicted, the twelve signs of the zodiac appeared at different places on his body in the form of red welts – what Wilson calls an example of 'controlled dermographia'. When Hadad's vein was punctured there was almost no blood: Wilson confirmed that this was beyond the usual psychotic trance or catalepsy.

Wilson's investigations revealed that Hadad could enter and leave the prison at will. On one occasion he had vanished when in transit: the guards opened up the van to find it empty. Soon afterwards Hadad came knocking on the door of the prison, explaining that he had got lost on the way. On another occasion he was seen by the warden at a symphony concert in a nearby town and explained, 'It has been some time since I have been to a concert, and I felt it would be such a shame not to go. After all, I am only a short distance from the city.'

When Wilson asked him what he was doing in prison, Hadad declared that he was here on a mission. He was, he explained, destined to wander throughout the world seeking two 'excessively evil and malign spirits' – he meant human beings – 'and to relieve them of their corporeal anatomy' (i.e. kill them). He had already found one of them, 'and he is not'. But Wilson's enquiries revealed that Hadad had been a member of a notorious gang that was terrorizing the south-west. He had been the gang's 'finger man', using his occult skills to draw the gang's victims out of hiding so that they could be killed. When he was caught the police had riddled the car with machine-gun fire until it looked like a sieve, but Hadad had emerged unharmed. He claimed he had deflected the bullets.

Hadad told Wilson and a fellow medico that his mission on earth was almost completed and that he had selected them as the pupils on whom his mantle was to descend – they were to present themselves at his cell at 2 A.M. to take part in a 'blood rite'. They both declined the honour –

possibly to the loss of medical science. On the other hand Wilson's judgement may have been correct. He describes Hadad as a boaster who liked to claim he was greater than Mohammed or Christ (he even pointed out that he had risen after three days while Jesus had only been dead for two) – a kind of egoism that has been the Achilles' heel of many 'magicians', including the late Aleister Crowley. In spite of his obviously remarkable powers Hadad seems to have been rather a dubious human being, which may be why Wilson relegates his case to a mere few pages in a later chapter of his book *My Six Convicts*. On the other hand that could be the result of sheer embarrassment at having to admit to anything so preposterous.

Wilson's assumption that Hadad was a hypnotist may be incorrect. Another remarkable modern magus, Spyros Sathi (known as Daskalos) was questioned by an American academic, Kyriacos C. Markides, about some of the extraordinary feats of the Yacqui *shaman* Don Juan, as described by Carlos Castaneda: for example how Don Juan had given Castaneda a push and Castaneda had suddenly found himself two miles away. (The correct explanation is almost certainly that it never happened, but this was before Richard de Mille's analyses had revealed that the Don Juan books were probably a hoax.*) Daskalos replied by making a distinction between hypnosis and induced hallucination. Daskalos described a visit from an English scientist who had witnessed the Indian rope-trick – how the rope was thrown into the air and a boy then climbed up it. Later the scientist photographed the rope-trick and was disappointed to find that his photograph showed that both the boy and the rope remained on the ground. According to Daskalos 'the fakir spread his aura around and put the audience inside. Then he began to think intensely and he created with his mind all those images they were "seeing".' Markides asked if this was not a form of hypnosis. 'Hypnotism is a different phenomenon altogether. In hypnotism the hypnotist uses powerful suggestions through words or the help of some instrument [i.e. a pendulum] to an audience which is receptive and co-operative. The fakir uses the power of thought to influence his unaware audience telepathically and made them "see" things that did not exist on the gross material plane.' So what the fakir did – and probably what Hadad did – was 'magic' according to Crowley's definition: 'Magick is the science and art of causing change to occur in conformity with the will.' (Many stories confirm that Crowley himself possessed this power: for example he could make a perfectly sane and normal man drop on all fours and begin barking and whining like a dog.†)

Markides' remarkable book *The Magus of Strovolos* makes it clear that Daskalos is a magus in the most precise sense of the word. Daskalos, who lives in Nicosia, is widely known among Cypriots as a healer, and it was to learn more about his healing powers that Markides visited him in

*See Richard de Mille, *Castaneda's Journey* (1976) and *The Don Juan Papers* (1980).
†See my *Aleister Crowley, The Nature of the Beast*, p. 157.

1978. It soon became apparent that Daskalos is far more than a healer: that as a teacher, he deserves to be classified with Steiner and Gurdjieff. When Markides visited him Daskalos looked like what he was – a tall, mild civil servant in his mid-sixties. He explained to Markides that most of his healing was carried out in an 'out-of-the-body' state (which he calls exomatosis) with the aid of invisible helpers. Markides talked to a peasant whom Daskalos had just cured of a long-standing spinal injury and received from Daskalos permission to study him with the aim of writing a book about his powers.

One of Markides's first experiences of these powers was strikingly dramatic. A friend asked if Daskalos could see three Jewish women, two of whom had just come from Israel. The daughter of one of the women was suffering severe psychological problems. Daskalos lost no time in establishing his credentials as a psychic: he told the daughter that she was wearing a star of David over her heart, which was correct. The girl – who was called Hadas – then explained the problem: she was possessed by demons who would not allow her to rest. Her aunt declared this was sheer imagination. But after asking the girl to close her eyes and studying her for some time, Daskalos declared that she was possessed by the spirits of two Nazis, husband and wife, who had died in the bombardment of Hamburg and who hated Jews. They had already sent four other Jewish women into asylums and had succeeded in taking possession of the girl 'when their vibrations and yours were on the same frequency'.

Daskalos lit a candle and proceeded to perform a cabbalistic ritual using a six-pointed star and a white eagle. Markides noticed that when Daskalos concentrated on the candle flame it behaved in a peculiar way, becoming elongated and producing black smoke, then shrinking and guttering. As soon as Daskalos stopped staring at the flame – which was several feet away – it became still. The ritual went on for a long time, with Daskalos sternly addressing the flame. Finally, with an expression of relief, Daskalos told them that the spirits had been driven out and could no longer do anyone any harm. As always, he refused to accept money for his services.

A week later Markides talked to the girl, who had ceased to hear voices after the ritual of exorcism. She told him how the trouble had started after a quarrel with her boyfriend: as she lay in bed something seemed to enter her head. She became ill and nervous and vomited a great deal. A rabbi told her that on the fortieth day she would vomit more than usual, and that the problem would then go away. This proved to be true. But after a later quarrel with another boyfriend she felt something enter her stomach. After this she began to hear voices that told her they would torture her and make her go mad. Every night they tried to make her commit suicide. Then, through her aunt who lived in Cyprus, she had heard of Daskalos, who had now cured her.

Daskalos elaborated further. Possession, he said, could be of three types: by ill-disposed human spirits, by demons and by elementals. However possession can only take place if the vibration of the victim is identical with its own. 'In other words the person must himself have a predisposition to hurt.' He seemed to be hinting that it was the girl's vengeful thoughts about her boyfriend that had made her vulnerable to the attack.

'Elementals', Daskalos explained later, are thoughts and desires of human beings which come to have a life of their own. This may be either subconsciously or consciously. When human beings brood on any strong desire, 'psychic (or noetic) matter' is created, and this is the basic stuff of the universe. The 'elemental' is an inner mental picture. If the thought-desire is a negative emotion, like envy or hatred, it takes on a life of its own and moves towards the person at whom it is directed: but sooner or later it returns to its creator.

Daskalos describes an interesting experiment which throws some light on an incident in the life of Rolling Thunder. He told his students to close their eyes and imagine they were holding a snake. Their reaction told him that many of them found the idea horrifying, so he told them to change it to a golden snake. When they had carefully imagined it, Daskalos said, it would become an 'elemental'. They should then imagine releasing it on to the ground. 'I am telling you, you will have nothing to fear from snakes from now on. This elemental will enter inside any snake which may be ready to hurt you and will calm it down. This is a method you can use to tame animals around you.' One day when Doug Boyd was watching Rolling Thunder control ants by merely pointing his finger at them, a rattlesnake brushed his boot. Rolling Thunder knelt by the snake and held out his hands towards it. The snake coiled and raised its head to meet the hand but made no attempt to strike. When the hand went forward, the head went back; when the hand went back, the head went forward. Then Rolling Thunder raised both hands on either side of the snake's head and the snake swayed slowly between them, from one to the other. Finally, when Rolling Thunder stood up and dismissed it, the snake uncoiled and slid away. Markides spoke to an eye witness who had seen Daskalos place sugar in his mouth then invite a snake to help itself from it: the eye witness had almost fainted as the snake licked up the sugar. Rolling Thunder and Daskalos, it seems, had the same basic understanding of animals.

In 1981 Markides had a chance to observe an example of almost miraculous self control. He had heard that Daskalos was seriously ill with a foot wound that refused to heal. But Daskalos explained that he had deliberately taken on this illness in order to relieve his son-in-law of a heavy 'karmic debt'. His doctor had warned him to remain in bed; if he stood on the infected foot the wound would open up again. At this point in the conversation Daskalos offered to demonstrate what he was talking about with a 'phenomenon'. ('Normally I am not allowed to do phenomena but I'll make an exception.') Daskalos then went into a state of deep meditation for a few minutes and passed his hand over the infected right leg. Then he stepped lightly out of bed and proceeded to hop vigorously around the room on his right leg, in spite of Markides's remonstrances. When he climbed back into bed he went into meditation again and waved his hand over the leg. 'Now I must get the Karma back,' he told Markides cheerfully. He told Markides that the karma would take about another week before it was exhausted: in fact when Markides visited him six days later he was painting in his studio.

In spite of the ban on 'phenomena' Daskalos frequently gave proof of apparently paranormal powers. He was able to describe Markides's house in Maine in 'stunning detail', although he would have had no way of learning these details. One day Markides dreamed that Daskalos was talking to him, then he suddenly disappeared: he turned round and saw Daskalos approaching him from behind. The next day Markides mentioned to Daskalos that he had dreamed about him, and before he could say more Daskalos remarked casually, 'Oh yes, I was giving you a lesson on the nature of space in the fourth dimension.' On another occasion Markides and a friend were trying to find Daskalos, without success, and Markides remarked humorously that perhaps Daskalos was visiting a mistress. When they finally found him and asked where he had been he snapped, 'Visiting a mistress', then went on to say that he had overheard their 'silly conversation'.

It must be admitted that for the reader who is not a convinced 'occultist', *The Magus of Strovolos* is an extremely difficult book to swallow. When studied in isolation some of Daskalos's claims seem so extraordinary that the natural reaction is to regard him as either a charlatan or a practical joker. Yet when they are read in the context of his teachings and his remarkable healing powers they become altogether more credible. Markides himself confesses that his own original intention of studying Daskalos from the detached viewpoint of a sociologist gradually faded as he witnessed miraculous healing sessions and encountered 'coincidences' like the ones described in the last paragraph. It was events like these that convinced Markides that Daskalos was a genuine magus and not merely a healer with some peculiar beliefs and assumptions. He also noted that the longer he spent in the atmosphere of these beliefs and assumptions the more he himself became subject to unusual experiences. He describes how when he was struggling to translate a Byzantine hymn dedicated to St Spyridon (whom Daskalos claimed to be one of his past incarnations), he finally decided to give up and take a stroll to the library to read the newspapers. Having read the news that interested him in the *Hellenic Chronicle* he turned casually to another page and found an article about St Spyridon which ended with a translation of the hymn into English. 'Are these things', Markides asks, 'coincidences? Perhaps. But I cannot afford in all honesty not to raise questions in my mind whether perchance Daskalos and Iacovos [his chief follower] live in a world that, no matter how exotic and radically divergent from ours it seems, is nevertheless just as real if not more so.'

Soon after this Markides discovered that he 'felt as if I were a sociologist by day, transformed into a mystic by night'. On one occasion he dreamed that his son was being attacked by a whale: at that moment his son's screams woke him up. After this he began having 'lucid dreams' – dreams in which the dreamer knows he is asleep – in one of which he passed through the doorway into the psychic world. In each of these dreams he felt that the world he entered was more real than the waking state. In one of his dreams he was about to address a girl when she shrank back and said, 'You are not of our world.' Markides prefers not to speculate whether these were really dreams or whether he had gained a certain borderland access to the psychic world.

If the 'exotic and radically divergent' world of Daskalos is as real as our physical universe then it must be admitted that it sounds more like the world created by Bram Stoker or M. R. James than the universe Westerners take for granted. For example, Daskalos tells of a young girl he encountered on a visit to southern Greece who was suffering from psychological problems. Daskalos learned that her parents had refused to allow her to marry a shepherd many years her senior. Five years after the shepherd's death the girl claimed that she had seen him as she was looking after the goats. She fled and he followed her and hypnotized her. Three days later he came into her home and took her virginity. A doctor who examined her insisted that she had been deflowered by her own fingers but she denied it. Daskalos noticed red spots on her neck and she told him, 'He kisses me there, but his kisses are strange. They are like sucking, but I like them.'

So far it sounds like the fantasy of a frustrated virgin. But Daskalos went on to describe how, a few days later, he saw the shepherd – whose name was Loizo – coming into the house. He greeted him, and Loizo proceeded to explain that during his lifetime he had never had sexual relations with a woman – only with goats and donkeys. Now that he had a mistress he did not intend to let her go. Daskalos pointed out that he was no longer alive. 'What are you talking about? Here I am talking to you, I fuck, and you are telling me I'm not alive?' But Daskalos finally succeeded in convincing him that if he continued to draw energy from the girl he would 'remain in a narcotized state like a vampire', and he left, the dogs barking after him. When the local doctor asked Daskalos what had happened he explained that the girl had been suffering from illusions and that he had cured her by means of psychoanalysis. That night the doctor gave a lecture on psychoanalysis to the villagers while Daskalos listened, chuckling.

Daskalos went on to explain that many young men become 'possessed' by the masturbatory images of young women that they create, and that such elementals might begin to suck the etheric vitality of the individual. (According to Daskalos the succubi described by Stan Gooch would be such elementals.)

Daskalos explained there was an epidemic of black magic on Cyprus after the civil war in Lebanon had driven out many black sorcerers; they offered their services for money. One sorcerer agreed to kill a young couple for three hundred pounds, and to do it, trapped a demon inside a bottle which contained an image of a demon carved from an old tyre. He managed to place it under their bed, and they began to lose their energy and bleed from the nose and mouth. The young couple found the bottle and took it to Daskalos, who performed one of his rituals and cut off the connection between the demon and the young couple: their bleeding immediately ceased. Such a story would sound like the wildest absurdity were it not that Playfair witnessed so many similar cases in Brazil. The implication seems to be that in societies where there is a strong link with the primitive past, sorcery continues to be practised as a matter of course. But that is not the end of Daskalos's story. When he placed the bottle in his own private sanctum the demon struggled so hard that he escaped: there was a loud explosion that Iacovos also heard. But according to Daskalos the demon came back. 'He appeared to me like a mythological satyr. His colour was dark green. His eyes were red and he had protrusions on his forehead that looked like horns.' When Daskalos was holding a meeting of his inner circle the demon came in – presumably invisible to the others – and handed Daskalos an image of himself in baked clay which was still hot because of the change from one dimension to another. Daskalos and the demon became affectionate friends.

While Markides was listening to this story Daskalos assured him – to Markides's secret alarm – that the demon had just come into the room and sat next to him. It sounds as if Daskalos was indulging in a leg-pull. But the rest of the book makes it quite clear that although Daskalos has a sense of humour he does not indulge in leg-pulls. He is perfectly serious when he explains, 'Demons are archangelic emanations in the opposite side of existence in order to create the realms of separateness.'

Equally extraordinary was an incident concerning the American satellite Skylab. On the day Skylab was due to re-enter the earth's atmosphere Daskalos decided to go and take a look at it. In the presence of Markides and Iacovos he went into a trance, and when he returned said he had been trying to push Skylab into the southern hemisphere, where there was more sea for it to fall into. (At this point the Americans had lost control over it.) He did this by creating a moonlike disc in his mind and bouncing it off Skylab. The next time he went into a trance Daskalos declared that he had encountered intelligent beings in three flying saucers who were trying to divert Skylab by their own methods. 'These entities are really advanced. They live in the higher noetic world and have no form.' He went into another trance and when he emerged from this claimed that he and the flying saucer entities had changed the trajectory of Skylab. Daskalos explained that these 'superintelligences' are the guardians of the planet earth and that 'they truly love us'. In the event Skylab, which was expected to fall in the northern hemisphere, re-entered in the southern hemisphere; parts fell into the Indian Ocean and parts on Australia.

Obviously the individual reader must make up his own mind how far he can credit Daskalos's claims. It seems clear that Markides ended by accepting most of them: for example he had no doubt that when Daskalos claimed to be wrestling with Skylab *something* important and interesting had really occurred. Yet the most important parts of *The Magus of Strovolos* are not the stories of healing or exorcism but the exposition of cosmology and 'psychological teaching'. This, for example, might have been said by Gurdjieff or by some Zen master:

Let me ask you a question. How many things do you concentrate on with full awareness during your everyday life? Very few. When you train yourself to concentrate you will become aware of much more in your life. At first you devote a quarter of an hour every day. During that time you may take a walk and will fully notice everything around you. Nothing should escape your attention, nothing. You may feel tired at first because you are not accustomed to paying attention to everything around you, the ant walking, the flowers, the sounds, the voices. You perceive everything, you feel everything. When you start this exercise you learn that during that quarter of an hour you live much more fully, much more intensely, than at any other period of the day. You will discover that what is considered ordinarily as the awaking state is in reality a form of semihypnosis . . . .

Daskalos claims that his 'teaching' is not his own but comes to him from an entity called Father Yohannan – the biblical St John. It is Yohannan who takes over at the meeting of the 'Circle of the Research of Truth', delivers the lectures and answers the questions. And what Yohannan says is remarkably consistent with what has been said by other mystics and psychics. For example:

Can one communicate with a flower or a plant? Ordinary people, no matter how much they may love plants and flowers, cannot consciously communicate with them. They appear as objects to them, outside themselves. A poet may be inspired by the beauty of a flower, but can he incorporate into his consciousness the semi-consciousness of the flower? In the psychic world it is very different. When you advance you will be able to communicate with all forms of life. All things are alive and have their own language, vibrations and luminosity that you can feel in your psychic body.

This is a restatement of Eileen Garrett's comments on communication

309

with nature. Other remarks of Daskalos throw light on the process of psychometry: 'Within the psychic world there is no separation between us and an object outside us. When we co-ordinate ourselves and focus on something we are simultaneously one with that object. We are within it and around it.'

We may recall that when Maria de Zierold held an object and focused on it she became identified with the object so that if it was pricked with a pin she felt the prick, and if it was moistened with alcohol she could taste the alcohol. As Anne Bancroft looked at the branch of rhododendron she felt 'a sense of communication with it, as though it and I had become one'. Again and again it becomes clear that there is no basic distinction between the experience of the psychic and the experience of the mystic.

Again, students of Western occultism will be struck by the remarkable similarity between the basic ideas of Daskalos and those of Rudolf Steiner. This is obviously not because Daskalos has derived ideas from Steiner, for it is quite plain throughout the book that everything he says is the result of direct experience. It seems to be because there is a very close correspondence between Steiner's experience of the 'spirit world' and Daskalos's. Steiner, for example, is unique among Western mystics in insisting that the 'spiritual world' is man's *inner* world. Daskalos (or Yohannan) is on record as making the strange statement, 'When we leave our bodies, either through death or exomatosis, we actually enter within ourselves.' And a chapter dealing with the passage from death to rebirth might be inserted into one of Steiner's books without anyone noticing the difference.

According to Daskalos death is the separation of the physical body and the 'etheric double' (or 'aura'). The aura takes about forty days to dissolve away. At the moment of death there is an enormous sense of freedom and serenity. Then the individual enters the 'psychonoetic world, carrying with him his virtues and vices. In the psychic realms, feelings acquire far greater intensity, because they are no longer diluted by our physical bodies, so those who are subject to powerful negative feelings – like envy, rage, lust – will suffer from them with agonising intensity.' These are in effect the sufferings of hell – or rather of purgatory, for Daskalos denies the existence of Hell or retributory punishment. The purpose of these sufferings is 'so that we may find out who we really are.'

In the psychonoetic world the individual lives at once on the psychic plane and in his own subjective world. Even on earth human beings live inside their own heads as much as in the real world. On the psychic plane they can virtually ignore objective reality. So although, according to Daskalos, the psychic plane has trees, mountains, oceans and rivers (he says that our 'real world' is only a reflection of this psychic realm), 'most persons who live there perceive it through the elementals they themselves create'. Daskalos instances a gambler who died of tuberculosis

310

and who has created with others an environment like that he knew on earth: dirty windows and tables and the same fights and quarrels. Iacovos's dead grandfather still looks after an orchard, sells the fruit and worries about the rainfall. Sooner or later such people will realize that they could be doing far more interesting things, and move on to higher psychic planes. And finally the 'masters of Karma' will order the individual to return to earth to learn more lessons. Markides asked why all this was necessary: the reply was, 'to realize, perhaps, who one is and to acquire self-consciousness.'

All this is so like Steiner that there is virtually no difference. Steiner says that the aura takes three days to dissolve; Daskalos says forty. Steiner says that the spirit and the astral body enter the lower psychic worlds, and that the astral body dissolves when it is purged by its own suffering: Daskalos says only that an 'individual' enters the lower psychic worlds after death. But these differences – if they are differences – are trivial in comparison to the basic agreements. It may also be noted that Daskalos, like Steiner, attaches immense importance to the figure of Christ in universal history and even, like Steiner, speaks of arch-angelic hierarchies, including that of Michael and Gabriel. (According to Steiner, Gabriel was the *Zeitgeist* of the previous Rosicrucian epoch, which ended in 1879, and Michael is the guiding spirit of our own epoch.) Daskalos also insists on the reality of the Akashic Records or Universal Memory. He makes the interesting statement that,

... whatever exists, existed and will exist is imprinted in this pan-universal supercomputer. Furthermore, a single atom contains within it all the knowledge of the cosmos. It is, therefore, possible by concentrating on a single atom, to acquire information of something or some event that took place in the distant past. It is done by entering into the Akashic Records just as a scholar enters into a library to investigate a particular issue.

Daskalos, like Steiner, claimed to be able to see a person's past incarnations simply by using his capacity for psychic vision.

There is also basic agreement on the question of the 'planes of existence'. According to Daskalos man lives simultaneously on three planes: the material, the psychic and the noetic. All three are material universes, but at different levels of vibrations. (Lethbridge reached very similar conclusions with the use of the pendulum.) Our physical world of space and time is the lowest level. Next comes the psychic or four-dimensional world: 'Space here is neutralized and the individual can move over vast distances instantly.' (It is presumably in this dimension that the 'projection of the double' can take place.) Finally, in the noetic or fifth dimension, laws of space and time are transcended so that the individual can travel across time as well as space. Every individual has a 'corresponding body' for these three worlds, and all

311

three bodies make up the total personality. (The noetic body is divided into the higher and lower body, so the whole arrangement sounds oddly like the Huna conception of the three selves). There is nothing in the material universe that does not have its psychic and noetic counterpart (another notion that Lethbridge derived from his study of the pendulum). The earth too is a living being – nothing is actually 'dead'. But the noetic counterparts in the mineral and animal kingdom do not form bodies that can function independently of the material form: only man has this power. (Daskalos, like Steiner, denies that animals have 'souls', or individual egos.) Man's individual ego, or soul, is independent of his physical, psychic or noetic bodies, all of which can die: the soul is eternal. So again Daskalos's account of man corresponds closely with that of Steiner.

In fact one of the most fascinating things about Markides's account of Daskalos is that it so often reminds us of other exponents of 'the occult tradition'. When he speaks of the tides of vital energy that sustain the universe we are reminded of Mesmer and Reich. When he says that water is the dominant element on the psychic planes and that humidity is helpful to exomatosis we are reminded of Lethbridge. When he speaks of withdrawal into 'inward' states we are reminded of Eileen Garrett and Rudolf Steiner. When he speaks of the earth as a living being we are reminded of Rolling Thunder. When he compares everyday consciousness to a state of hypnosis we are reminded of Gurdjieff. Anyone who has even a nodding acquaintance with the 'occult tradition', from Hermes Trismegistos to Steiner and Ouspensky, can recognize that Daskalos is a living part of it. In a sense nothing he says is original. In another sense it is all original, for he is obviously speaking from direct personal knowledge and creating his own syntheses.

Daskalos, like Rolling Thunder, is one of those human beings who live with perfect comfort on the borderland between two worlds, the visible and the invisible. He seems to have been born with the capacity to experience the invisible. Others, like Eileen Garrett and Rosalind Heywood, had some difficulty in coming to terms with it but finally learned to accept the situation. Still others, like Albert Tucker, prefer to live this side of the borderland. But no one could accuse any of them of being 'sick sensitives', people with one foot already in the 'next world'. They are all quite obviously normal and sane human beings – if anything rather more balanced than the rest of us. The main difference is that they are aware when the 'invisible' impinges on the visible, while the rest of us remain oblivious to it. There can hardly be any doubt which has the wider and therefore the more rational view of life.

5

Completing the Picture

We must now face squarely the question that has become increasingly persistent during the second part of this book: how far does it *matter* whether there is a 'psychic world', whether spirits exist, whether reincarnation is a reality, whether mediums really contact the dead? We have seen, for example, that Eileen Garrett became increasingly bored and exasperated with spiritualism. Daskalos also warns against it, pointing out that trying to contact the dead can distract them from more important things. Steiner told an audience, 'The spiritualists are the worst materialists of all.' Adam Crabtree insists that it makes no difference whether he believes in the reality of the spirits he exorcizes or treats them as psychological fictions: all that matters is curing the patient. And this seems, on the whole, a sensible attitude. The world we live in is dangerous enough, with terrorists and muggers and serial killers, without spreading further alarm and despondency among the nervous by talking about ill-disposed spirits and devils.

This was my own attitude when I finished writing *Poltergeist*. The sheer weight of evidence left me in no doubt that there were such things as spirits. This in turn implied that life after death was a reality and that the spiritualists had been right all along. Yet I continued to feel that this is, in some basic sense, irrelevant. What is interesting about the paranormal is its suggestion that we possess 'hidden powers'. Human beings tend to suffer from the 'passive fallacy', the notion that we are mere products of the material world and that the material world is the ultimate reality. For a large proportion of our lives our consciousness is little more than a mirror that reflects this 'reality'. It is only in moments of concentration and excitement that we grasp that the real purpose of consciousness is to *change* the world. Synchronicities, flashes of clairvoyance or precognition or mystical insight, make us aware that our power to change the world is far greater than we imagine. This is the most important insight to arise from the study of the paranormal; this is the essence of 'the occult vision'. By comparison ghosts and spirits seem interesting but not particularly important.

I would now regard that view as an oversimplification. Dull states of everyday consciousness tell us that the material world is 'all there is'. States of more intense awareness reveal that this world is *not* 'all there is'. There are hidden realms of reality beyond the grasp of everyday

313

consciousness. And if 'spirits' are a part of these hidden realms then it would obviously be a mistake to dismiss them as unimportant. The problem is to try to discover precisely what part they play. Some important clues are offered in Ouspensky's chapter on experimental mysticism in *A New Model of the Universe*, and these must now be considered more fully.

Ouspensky explained that the first problem about the 'mystical realms' to which he gained access was that it was almost impossible to describe them because *everything was connected*. 'In order to describe the first impressions . . . it is necessary to describe *all* at once.' This is a vital clue. The more tired and dull I feel the more things appear to be 'separate'. If someone points to something and says, 'Don't you see what it *means?*' I shake my head: it 'means' nothing but itself. On the other hand when I am in a state of intensified vitality everything 'means' something apart from itself: everything seems to remind me of something else. I see that everything in the universe *implies* something else, and that that implies something else, and that that implies something else, so that a kind of network of relations seems to extend out to infinity. Consciousness is like a pool, and everything I look at makes ripples spread across its surface. When I am dull and tired it is exactly as if the surface has frozen solid.

We have all experienced these states that Ouspensky is trying to describe, for example when we see the solution to some problem 'in a flash', or when we experience that odd sense of joy as we smell the first odours of spring. It is the 'bird's-eye view'. But as we have seen, the 'everyday self' looks out from the left brain and operates with language and logic. So if the flood of intuition is too intense the left brain is left plodding hopelessly behind and the result is a sense of utter frustration.

I first noticed this as a child: too much happiness bored me. If I went for a walk on a sunny morning and began to experience an increasing sense of sheer joy, there came a point at which I grew tired of it and deliberately brought my mind back down to earth. Thinking about this later I always found it difficult to understand why I wanted that happiness to come to an end. Now the solution is obvious. When we experience a sudden insight we want to *grasp* it, to turn it into words. But the left brain is like an amanuensis who has to take everything down in longhand. If the intuitions come too fast he wants to shout, 'Slow down, slow down!' And if the speaker refuses to slow down he throws down his pen in disgust. As we saw in the section about Helen Keller (p. 88) our human task is to capture things in *words*, to become the masters of reality through the use of words and concepts. So too much intuitive insight is quite pointless.

Ouspensky goes on to remark that beyond this realm of marvellous insights (which he compares to a world of *very complicated mathematical relations*), he passed through a 'transitional state' that was not unlike the hypnagogic state on the edge of sleep. In this state he heard 'voices'.

'The voices spoke about every possible kind of thing. They warned me. They proved and explained to me everything in the world, but somehow they did it too simply.' He began wondering whether the voices came from his imagination, so he tried asking them questions. One of his questions concerned alchemy, and a voice which claimed to be a famous person told him that the answer would be found in a certain book. When he finally obtained the book he found that it contained 'certain hints very closely connected with my question, though they did not give a complete answer to it.' He concluded that the 'voices' were basically the same as those heard by mediums.

Yet oddly enough he was disappointed that in these mystical states he found nothing resembling the 'astral world' described by people like Steiner and Madame Blavatsky. He reached the conclusion that this is because such worlds do not exist. Yet his experiences of 'voices' seem to contradict this. So does his description of an episode already mentioned in which he tried to make contact with the dead. Ouspensky explains that he was thinking of a person about whom he felt some guilt for having let him down in the last years of his life. (It sounds from Ouspensky's comments as if he was talking about his father.) So during one of his mystical experiments Ouspensky expressed a wish to see this person and ask just one question. 'And suddenly, without any preparation, my wish was satisfied, and I *saw* him. It was not a visual sensation, and what I saw was not his external appearance, but *the whole of his life*, which flashed quickly before me. This life – this was he.' It sounds as if Ouspensky is saying that he merely experienced a sudden flash of insight, but this is not so. He goes on to say that although they held no conversation, 'nevertheless, I know that it was *he*, and that it was he who communicated to me much more about himself than I could have asked.'

But what the dead man communicated was as baffling as everything else in Ouspensky's mystical experiences. Ouspensky says:

> The man whom I had known and who had died had never existed. That which existed was something quite different, because his life was not simply a series of events, as we ordinarily picture the life of a man to ourselves, but a thinking and feeling *being* who did not change by the fact of his death. The man whom I had known was the *face*, as it were, of this being – the face which changed with the years, but behind which there stood the unchanging reality . . . . I saw quite clearly that the events of the last years of his life were as inseparably linked with him as the features of his face. . . . Nobody could have changed anything in them, just as nobody could have changed the colour of his hair or eyes, or the shape of his nose.

In other words Ouspensky saw the man as a 'four-dimensional continuum' – like Wilbur Wright's image of the sun as a four-dimensional golden tube – and recognized that in some respects this four-dimensional

315

totality was unchangeable, at least by *other* people. 'We are no more responsible for the events in one another's lives than we are for the features of one another's faces. Each has his own face . . . and each has his own fate, in which another man may occupy a certain place, but in which he can change nothing.'

This led Ouspensky to realize that 'we are far more closely bound to our past and to the people we come into contact with than we ordinarily think, and I understood quite clearly that death does not change anything in this. We remain bound with all with whom we have been bound. But for communication with them it is necessary to be in a special state.' These words are so close to Steiner's comments on death and life after death that it is hard not to feel that they are expressing precisely the same insight.

Ouspensky goes on to try to describe his insight using the image of a branch:

> If one takes the branch of a tree with the twigs, the cross-section of the branch will correspond to the man as we ordinarily see him; the branch itself will be the life of the man, and the twigs will be the lives of people with whom he comes into contact . . . . Each man is for himself such a branch, other people with whom he is connected are his offshoots. But each of these people is for himself a main branch and [other men are] the offshoots . . . . In this way the life of each man is connected with a number of other lives; one life enters, in a sense, into another, and all taken together forms a single whole, the nature of which we do not understand.

All this enables us to see that the simple notion that human beings survive death and continue to exist in 'another world' is somehow a gross oversimplification of the reality. Our physical universe, with its immensely high gravity which drags down our thoughts so that 'everything is separate', gives us a completely false picture of reality. This is why Steiner said, 'The spiritualists are the greatest materialists of all.' He meant that they are trying to reduce a four-dimensional reality to a simple three-dimensional image *which is fundamentally a falsification.* Even the question, 'Is there life after death?' is the wrong question, for all the misunderstandings are *inbuilt* into it. Ouspensky would obviously not reply, 'Yes, there is life after death.' Instead he would point out that our whole notion of what constitutes life – and therefore death – is fundamentally false, so that the question is very nearly meaningless. (The question, 'Is there a God?' has the same inbuilt misconceptions.)

All this enables us to see why the question, 'Do spirits exist?' is at once relevant and highly misleading. The evidence of poltergeist activity leaves no doubt that spirits exist and that to some extent these spirits are not subject to the laws of space and time that govern human beings. But to assume that such spirits offer a clue to the fundamental nature of the universe is a misunderstanding. Until we can begin to grasp the insights glimpsed by Ouspensky in his mystical experiments and to catch some kind of a glimpse of the 'total picture', questions about spirits are highly misleading and had better be left in abeyance.

The best way to begin to grasp this 'total picture' is to begin with the mystical glimpses of ordinary people. Consider for example the experience of an American scientist, C. Daly King, waiting on a New Jersey railway platform:

> On the platform there were several small housings for freight elevators, news-stands and so on, constructed of dun-coloured bricks. He was emotionally at ease, planning unhurriedly the schedule of his various calls in the city and simultaneously attempting to be aware, actively and impartially, of the movements of his body's walking and actively to be conscious at the same time of all the auditory sensations arising through his ears.

We can see that King was in a relaxed right-brain state and that he was also applying the discipline that Daskalos recommends, paying full attention to the external world.

> Suddenly the entire aspect of the surroundings changed. The whole atmosphere seemed strangely vitalized and abruptly the few other persons on the platform took on an appearance hardly more important or significant than that of the doorknobs at the entrance to the passengers' waiting-room. But the most extraordinary alteration was that of the dun-coloured bricks. They remained, naturally, dun-coloured bricks, for there was no concomitant sensory illusion in the experience. But all at once they appeared to be tremendously alive: without manifesting any exterior motion they seemed to be seething almost joyously inside and gave the distinct impression that in their own degree they were living and actively liking it. This impression so struck the writer that he remained staring at them for some minutes, until the train arrived and it was necessary for him to mount the steps and enter a car.*

On another occasion, when he was returning home from New York feeling rather tired, Daly King had a quite different kind of experience:

> Once more the scene altered unexpectedly and with a startling abruptness, as if one stage-set had been substituted instantly for another. But it was now chiefly the other people who held the focus of attention. They looked dead, really dead. One expected to see signs of decay but of course there were none. What one did see was

*C. Daly King, *The States of Human Consciousness* (1963), p. 120.

stark unconsciousness, scores of marionettes not self-propelled but moved by some force alien to themselves, proceeding along their automatic trails mechanically and without purpose. Some of the mouths were open and they looked like holes in cardboard boxes. The faces were blankly empty: even those upon which otherwise some expression would have been noticeable had been drained of any significance and one saw that those expressions were unrelated to the entities that wore them. For the first time the concept of the zombie became credible.

King says he experienced a curious mixture of compassion and contempt.

If we look more closely at these experiences we can see that the first was basically due to a surge of vitality: any sudden feeling of happiness brings the same experience in a lesser degree. In his autobiographical novel *Sinister Street* Compton Mackenzie describes his hero waiting at a street corner for a girl he has just fallen in love with, and says, ' . . . In his present mood of elation he could enjoy communication even with bricks and mortar.' But then Mackenzie's hero is waiting for his ladylove, and Daly King had no similar reason for delight. What happened in his case was slightly different. Everyday human consciousness is like a tyre with a slow puncture: we *leak*. Energy has to be continually created as it drains away. We observe this most when we are bored or suddenly discouraged: we actually feel the energy draining out of us like a deflating tyre. Concentration closes the leaks. Daly King had accidentally succeeded in closing all his leaks simultaneously, and the result was a sudden surge in the pressure of consciousness and an almost ecstatic sense of *control*.

On the second occasion he was tired, so the closing of the leaks brought no surge of inner pressure, only an awareness of his own freedom, by contrast with which the un-freedom of most other people became obvious. Ouspensky had once had a similar vision in which he saw that people were literally asleep, with their dreams hovering like clouds around their heads. In his heightened state of awareness Daly King was suddenly grasping the truth about human beings: that they are little more than machines that respond to stimuli from the environment. Such a vision also explains why the future may be regarded as more or less predetermined: because we do very little that is not purely mechanical.

Yet if we consider both experiences together the total insight is by no means depressing. What Daly King was grasping was that it is after all fairly easy to rise to this higher state of inner pressure. Our 'mechanicalness' prevents us from becoming aware of it, but the moment we become aware we can begin to do something about it. Hence the feeling of 'absurd good news'.

This is the essence of 'the occult vision'. The philosopher Fichte

318

once remarked, 'To be free is nothing: to *become* free is heavenly.' The reason should now be obvious. When we suddenly become free, when some crisis suddenly evaporates or new and fascinating prospects suddenly open before us, we respond with a *surge of energy*. This surge of energy lifts us up above our normal 'mechanicalness' and makes us aware of *connections*, and of the extent of our freedom. But since it is impossible to live without 'the robot' we soon sink back into our usual condition of 'unconnected' passivity.

I have described elsewhere the experience of a girl of my acquaintance who suddenly 'became free'. She was married to an American academic who was unfaithful to her and had finally decided to leave him – a hard decision since they had young children. Her brother had recently been offered an appointment in Ohio and suggested that she should come and keep house for him. Then her husband was offered another academic post in Oregon and begged her to go with him. For days she agonized about whether to go to Oregon with her husband or Ohio with her brother. Suddenly, as she was wrestling with the problem, it dawned upon her, 'I don't have to go to Oregon *or* Ohio. I'm *free*.' She said that the experience filled her with a sense of overwhelming joy and lightness, so that she felt as if she was walking on air. Even her tennis improved.

Here we can see that the freedom experience is basically a recognition that certain limits we took for granted were an illusion. But what precisely are these limits? For normal, healthy people they are not physical limitations. As I sit in this room I do not feel imprisoned by its four walls. The real limitation is my sense of *what is worth doing*. If I have just received some crushing disappointment every effort becomes a drain on my vitality. If I have just received some unexpectedly good news I have so much energy that I feel like turning cartwheels. I allow the things that happen to me to determine my sense of freedom. And because our lives are to a large extent repetitive, we begin to assume that we possess a certain precise degree of freedom, no more and no less. We might say that ordinary consciousness is a kind of 'habitual assessment' of our freedom, with a tendency to be on the low side.

We can also see that when Maslow's young mother had a peak experience as she watched her husband and children eating breakfast, this 'habitual assessment' was suddenly swept away by a surge of energy and she 'became free'. A moment before she *was* free but took it for granted: now she *became* free. She had *remembered* how much she had to feel delighted and relieved about. Our habitual feeling of unfreedom is a kind of forgetfulness.

Now this is in a sense one of our most cheering observations so far. After all nothing is easier to remedy than ordinary forgetfulness. I can tie a knot in my handkerchief, leave a note for myself, set the alarm on my watch . . . . We can understand, for example, that after Daly King had *seen* the bricks glowing with interior life, he would never again look

319

at those same bricks without remembering what he had seen and making an effort to regain the vision. And because he remembers, the vision becomes progressively easier to regain. This is why Maslow's students began having peak experiences all the time when they began talking and thinking about peak experiences. Here we have one of the most basic methods for recreating the peak experience or mystical experience: deliberately trying to remember, to conjure up that strange feeling of joy and serenity that lies at the heart of the peak experience. More often than not nothing seems to happen: the essence of the experience refuses to return. Then, perhaps five minutes later, it comes wandering into the head like a forgotten tune. And the more often we remember the tune the easier it becomes to recall it at will.

What has struck me again and again in discussing peak experiences and mystical experiences with those who have experienced them is that they happen so *easily*. We merely have to do something which breaks an old habit and the result is the peak experience. In other words our real problem is that we have a habit of *not* having peak experiences, of remaining preoccupied with the routines of everyday life. But the peak experience is a particular kind of insight, and once it has been experienced it tends to recur. Barbara Tucker, the wife of Albert Tucker, provided me with an interesting example. She described it quite casually as she was driving me to an outlying suburb of Melbourne, in response to some remarks I had made about Maslow. At the age of twenty she had suddenly become deeply interested in music. Her mystical experience came one day as she was listening to Beethoven's late quartet, Opus 132. 'I suddenly had the experience of seeing the entire universe.' She had taken no interest in mysticism and read nothing about it, so the experience came as something of a shock.

> And suddenly this vast horizon opened up to me. And suddenly I knew – or I saw – that time, past, present and future, were all one, and that I was God, and yet at the same time was only the minutest grain of sand. I can remember thinking, 'How incredible – how can you be two things at once?' And also I saw that the entire universe is on a grid system – I actually saw the grid stretching out into infinity – that every thought, every deed, every word, anything that happened, was not accidental. Everything in the universe was interconnected: every time you meet someone, it's not a chance meeting – there's a purpose for that meeting, and it all ties up with everything else in the universe. It was the most incredible thing to see – everything linking up, everything tying in. And that experience changed my life – it made me see things very differently.

Clearly she had 'seen' precisely what Ouspensky saw.

Barbara Tucker had three or four similar experiences within twelve months, all of them far less revelatory than the first yet each giving her a glimpse of the original vision. In a typical one she was at a party given by friends, feeling rather ambivalent about it. ('I tend to sit in a corner and not really enjoy them very much.')

> All the people round me were laughing and chatting and doing the things people do at parties – and then again, I suddenly saw all the connections between these people – how they all interconnected – how all this show that was going on was not, in fact, idle chatter. It was all interconnecting into their relationships with one another in the most extraordinary way. But what I thought was interesting was that I wasn't part of it. I was just a total outsider, a person looking in. I was not connected to them . . . .

It is of course very difficult to grasp exactly and precisely what she saw: as I listen to the tape she made for me, with its long pauses, I am conscious all the time of her attempt to force language to express the inexpressible. This is not because her experiences were ineffable but simply because language was made to express concrete facts and ideas: it is helpless to describe even the difference between the smells of an orange and of a lemon. What she saw obviously struck her as in some way self-evident, and the memory has remained with her quite clearly ever since.

What is also clear is that the capacity to grasp this type of experience can also lead to more straightforwardly 'psychic' experiences. Here again an event described by Albert Tucker provides a typical illustration. Partly as a result of the curious experiences already described he had become deeply interested in self-suggestion and self-hypnosis. He developed the habit of lying down for half an hour after lunch and inducing a state of deep relaxation, then giving himself all kinds of positive suggestions:

> In the course of doing this I'd had some rather odd little experiences, one of which was that the mattress and the bed would seem to convulse like a wave, and I'd feel this as a very distinct and unmistakable sensation, as if different waves of energy were coming through. I really felt that something was starting that I wasn't ready for. I didn't know where it was all leading, and I shied away from it.

During one of these sessions Tucker tried to envisage what might be happening to a friend who had taken some of his paintings to New York. 'All of a sudden an image flashed into my mind of a modern building with revolving glass doors. Through the doors I could see through into an art gallery. On the wall was a painting of mine – one of these paintings that my friend had taken with her.' This image continued to float into his mind at every 'relaxation session' for a week or

321

more. Some time later he went to New York, and on the first day set out full of enthusiasm to go and look at the Museum of Modern Art. From a distance it looked vaguely familiar. As he approached the revolving door he recognized it as the place he had seen so often in his after-lunch relaxation sessions. Facing him on the wall, exactly where he had 'seen' it, was the same painting.

It is interesting to speculate what might have happened if he had allowed the 'energy waves' to develop. It sounds like an experience of what the Hindus call the kundalini serpent, the spiritual energy that lies coiled at the base of the spine which can be released to flow upwards through the seven *chakras* – the points where man's physical body and the astral body are connected. It seems conceivable that he might have developed into a full-flown psychic, and it seems clear that even ordinary relaxation was enough to produce 'clairvoyant' perception. And so once again we become aware that there is no sharp dividing line between mystical experience and 'psychic' experience: one blends into the other.

But if mystical awareness is so 'close' then what prevents us from experiencing it every other day? This question goes to the very heart of the problem. The answer, in a single sentence, is that consciousness tends to focus upon what we lack rather than what we possess. From the moment we are born we struggle to achieve the things we lack, or think we lack: food and drink, possessions, the esteem of other people, security, personal fulfilment. It is only when we are faced with some threat or crisis that we grasp how lucky we are, how much we *already* possess. Then, suddenly, consciousness ceases to focus upon what we still want and focuses upon what we already have. This is what happened to Maslow's mother as she watched her husband and children eating breakfast.

When we are faced with a crisis we suddenly realize that we already possess the secret of happiness. Faced with the prospect of a concentration camp Hans Keller could say, 'If only I could escape from Germany, I swear that I would never be unhappy for the rest of my life,' and in that moment he could *see* that it would be perfectly easy to keep this promise. Standing in front of a firing squad Dostoevsky can see that all life is infinitely delightful, and that if he is fortunate enough to be reprieved it will be perfectly easy never to forget this insight. What has happened, of course, is that he has been plunged into the state we often experience in a warm bed on a freezing winter morning when we have to get up in five minutes: a state that might be called 'self-reflective awareness' in which we are intensely aware of ourselves *and* of our present situation, resting wholly *in the present moment* instead of straining our eyes into the future. This trick of inducing 'self-reflective awareness' is obviously the basic trick of the peak experience and of all human happiness.

This is the fundamental essence of Buddhism: to cease to be driven

322

by desire (i.e. consciousness of what we lack) and to recognize that we already possess the fullness of existence. Yet when the mystic tries to express this simple insight he finds himself wrestling with a kind of octopus of unsatisfactory language.

An American doctor, Franklin Merrell-Wolff, had his own experience of Nirvana in August 1936 and ten days later tried to express what happened in his journal:

I had been sitting in a porch swing, reading.... Ahead of the sequence in the book, I turned to the section devoted to 'Liberation', as I seemed to feel an especial hunger for this. I covered the material quickly and it all seemed very clear and satisfactory. Then, as I sat afterward dwelling in thought upon the subject just read, suddenly it dawned upon me that a common mistake made in the higher meditation, i.e. meditation for Liberation, is the seeking for a subtle object of Recognition, in other words, something that could be experienced. Of course, I had long known the falseness of this position theoretically, yet had failed to recognize it. (Here is a subtle but very important distinction.) At once, I dropped expectation of having anything happen. Then, with eyes open and no sense stopped in functioning – hence no trance – I abstracted the subjective moment – the 'I AM' or 'Atman' element – from the totality of the objective consciousness manifold. Upon this I focused. Naturally, I found what, from the relative point of view, is Darkness and Emptiness. *But I Realized It as Absolute Light and Fullness and that I was That.* Of course, I cannot tell what It was in Its own nature. The relative forms of consciousness inevitably distort non-relative Consciousness. Not only can I not tell this to others, I cannot even contain it within my own relative consciousness, whether of sensation, feeling or thought. Every metaphysical thinker will see this impossibility at once. I was even prepared not to have the personal consciousness share in this Recognition in any way. But in this I was happily disappointed. Presently I felt the Ambrosia-quality in the breath with the purifying benediction that it casts over the whole personality, even including the physical body. I found myself above the universe, not in the sense of leaving the physical body and being taken out in space, but in the sense of being above space, time and causality. My karma seemed to drop away from me as an individual responsibility. I felt intangibly, yet wonderfully, free. *I* sustained this universe and was not bound by it. Desires and ambitions grew perceptibly more and more shadowy. All worldly honours were without power to exalt me. Physical life seemed undesirable. Repeatedly, through the days that followed, I was in a state of deep brooding, thinking thoughts that were so abstract that there were no concepts to represent them. I seemed to comprehend a veritable library of

323

knowledge, all less concrete than the most abstract mathematics. The personality rested in a gentle glow of happiness, but while it was very gentle, yet it was so potent as to dull the keenest sensuous delight. Likewise the sense of world-pain was absorbed. I looked, as it were, over the world, asking, 'What is there of interest here? What is there worth doing?' I found but one interest: the desire that other souls should also realize this that I had realized, for in it lay the one effective key for solving of their problems. The little tragedies of men left me indifferent. I saw one great Tragedy, the cause of all the rest, the failure of man to realize his own Divinity. I saw but one solution, the Realization of this Divinity.*

This is a long and difficult passage. Yet Merrell-Wolff is obviously expressing the same insight that came to Barbara Tucker as she listened to the Beethoven quartet. 'I found myself above the universe . . . in the sense of being above space, time and causality.' 'I felt intangibly, yet wonderfully, free.' But the most difficult part is the description of how he arrived at this state of bliss – recognizing that the basic mistake is to look *outside* oneself for some kind of revelation. Suddenly we realize that what he did was to switch the beam of attention from what we lack to what we already possess, then on to his own essential being. This brought instant 'Nirvana'.

But the key to the whole experience obviously lies in the passage about the one great Tragedy – the failure of man to realize his own Divinity. To Western ears this almost has the ring of cliché – the kingdom of God is within you and so on. Yet Merrell-Wolff grasped it as an immediate truth. It reminds us that Beethoven told Elizabeth Brentano, 'Those who understand my music must be freed from all the miseries which others drag around with them . . . . Tell [Goethe] to hear my symphonies, and he will see that I am saying that music is the one incorporeal entrance into the higher worlds of knowledge which comprehends mankind, but which mankind cannot comprehend.' We may also recall that Beethoven told Court Secretary Von Zmeskall, 'The devil take you. I don't want to know anything about your whole system of ethics. *Power* is the morality of men who stand out from the rest, and it is also mine.' Beethoven obviously felt – as Merrell-Wolff did – that most of us take far too lowly a view of ourselves. Consequently we are too easily discouraged and are inclined to make mountains out of molehills. This inbuilt pessimism has become – as we saw in an earlier chapter – an integral part of our Western culture: 'Man is a useless passion,' 'Human life is solitary, poor, nasty, brutish and short,' 'Most men die like animals, not men.' We feel that this attitude is justified by the problems of modern civilization, the rat race, the rising crime rate, the atomic threat. For modern man, pessimism seems a *logical* response

*Franklin Merrell-Wolff, *Pathways Through to Space, An Experiential Journal*, pp. 4–5.

to human existence. Yet every peak experience, every flash of mystical intensity, reveals that this is nonsense. Why? Because they make us aware of ourselves as *active* forces, as 'movers', as beings who are capable of causing change in the universe. This was the essence of Beethoven's view of himself and the essence of Merrell-Wolff's Nirvana experience. 'We are gods,' says Daskalos, 'but we are not aware of it. We suffer from self-inflicted amnesia.'

Merrell-Wolff's method of achieving his Nirvana experience offers a vital insight. He did it by an extremely difficult method: looking inward, and then 'abstracting the subjective element' from the 'objective consciousness manifold'. That is he ignored everything that is 'not me' and thereby succeeded in focusing upon the 'me', the centre of consciousness. It was, as he tells us, a kind of darkness, and there was a time-lapse before he realized that it was 'absolute light and fullness'.

Quite instinctively most of us prefer a simpler method of focusing the 'me'. Anything that gives us a sudden powerful sensation illuminates the 'me' like a flash of lightning. 'God is fire in the head,' said Nijinsky, speaking about this sudden 'flash'. The same flash occurs 'when a man is fighting mad' and 'he completes his partial mind'. In Tantric yoga sex is deliberately used to produce this insight. But there is a disadvantage in these methods. The lightning flash is too brief to give us a chance to *grasp* what it is showing us. This is why Don Juan and Casanova and Frank Harris spend their lives trying to repeat the sexual experience a thousand times: they hope that with the thousandth illumination they might finally grasp what they are looking at. Yet the process tends to be self-defeating for the reason that Merrell-Wolff specified. They are seeking for 'a subtle object of Recognition', something they can grasp. In fact what Frank Harris grasps in the moment of sexual conquest is the absurd recognition that he is not Frank Harris. The actual truth is, 'I am God.' But a moment later he is again Frank Harris, and the insight is meaningless.

Daskalos explained the essence of the problem when one of his followers asked him about the meaning of personality. He explained that there are two personalities: the permanent personality and the present personality. The present personality is 'who I think I am at this moment'. The permanent personality is 'that part of ourselves upon which the incarnational experiences are recorded and are transferred from one incarnation to the next':

Let us assume [Daskalos said] that the permanent personality is a large circle. Imagine another circle outside without a periphery. We call that the soul, which is within God, within infinity and boundlessness . . . . There is also a small circle inside the other two which I call the present self-conscious personality. All three circles have the same centre. . . . The centre of the present and permanent personality, as well as the self-conscious soul, is the same.

325

The more the present self-conscious personality opens up as a circle, the more the permanent personality penetrates into the present personality. The higher you evolve on the spiritual path, the greater the influence and control of the inner self over the present personality. We habitually say, for example, that this man has conscience whereas another one does not. In reality there is no human being who does not have a centre.

So Frank Harris's problem, as he steps into this centre and recognizes that the circle spreads out to infinity, is that he momentarily ceases to be Frank Harris: a moment later he has no way of understanding what he has glimpsed. So what can he *do* about it? Daskalos would say that he must keep on maturing until he grasps the paradoxical fact that he is not his present personality. But this answer is bound to be disappointing for the rest of us, who feel that we would like some more specific recommendation. The alternative – trying to dive head first into mystical experience like Merrell-Wolff – is hardly more satisfying since as Merrell-Wolff himself admits, the experience evaporates and refuses to return when we want it.

In the course of this book I have tried to suggest that there *is* a more pragmatic and straightforward route to these insights. Ever since Plato Western man has realized that he has the power to put complex insights into clear and simple language. Many of the great philosophers expressed themselves with appalling obscurity, yet any intelligent commentator can explain their meaning in words that can be understood by a reasonably bright child. When the problems of mysticism are approached in the same spirit they begin to seem less bafflingly paradoxical.

The essential clue emerged in the third chapter of this book: the concept of 'upside-downness'. This, we saw, is the basic reason that our outlook tends to be negative. We have three sets of 'values': physical, emotional and intellectual. The intellect aims at a rational, objective view of the world but is continually being undermined by negative emotions. When we allow these emotions to overrule the intellect the result is a state of 'upside-downness'. And the world seen from a state of 'upside-downness' is a horribly futile and meaningless place. 'Upside-downness' produces 'the Ecclesiastes effect', the feeling that 'all is vanity'. It also produces what Sartre calls 'magical thinking', a tendency to allow our judgement to be completely distorted by emotion so that we cannot distinguish between illusion and reality.

Most murders are committed in a state of 'upside-downness', for 'upside-downness' involves loss of control. In *A Criminal History of Mankind* I pointed out that our energies operate on a counterweight system, like up-and-over garage doors. The forces involved could be referred to as Force T – standing for tension – and Force C, standing for control. When I become angry or impatient or tired, Force T clamours to be released, producing an uncomfortable sensation exactly like wanting to urinate badly. It attempts to destabilize me. On the other hand if I become deeply interested in something I deliberately 'damp down' these forces of destabilization to bring them under control. We can see that when Barbara Tucker went into a state of mystical insight as she listened to the Beethoven quartet she had achieved what might be called 'a condition of control'. All the forces of destabilization had been soothed into deep serenity.

All this seems so simple that it is hard to see why we cannot achieve conditions of control whenever we listen to music. The answer goes to the very heart of this problem. It is because our intellectual values are still 'upside-down'. Our underlying, instinctive feeling is that life is grim and difficult and something awful might happen at any moment. In other words, as absurd as it sounds, the basic problem is an intellectual one. It is not simply that our emotions are negative, but that our intellect *agrees with them*. Our judgement ratifies the 'upside-down' view of the world.

In fact the solution should be fairly straightforward. Whenever some minor crisis disappears I experience a sense of relief and a recognition of how delightful it is to be rid of the problem. If I have been suffering from toothache and then it stops, I deeply appreciate the condition of *not* being in pain. Absurdly enough, I am grateful for a negative state – not having toothache. If if could make proper use of my imagination I could be grateful for a hundred other negative conditions: not having a headache, not having earache, not having gout in my big toe . . . . Then why is it so difficult for me to make use of this simple method of enjoying life?

This brings me to the most important recognition so far. Our minds are inclined to accept the present moment as it is, without question. Of course we ask questions when we are unhappy or in pain. But in ordinary, everyday consciousness – what we might call 'neutral consciousness' – we accept the present moment *as if it were complete in itself.*

A little reflection reveals that this is a mistake of gargantuan proportions. Every dullard and stick-in-the-mud is a dullard because he makes this assumption. A few years ago, in a Cornish village not far from here, there died a man who boasted that he had never left the village during the entire course of his life. He had never even experienced the curiosity to go to the next village, less than a mile away. He was apparently a completely normal individual with no disabilities – except a complete lack of imagination. One imagines that he suffered from the same problem as Sartre's café proprietor in *Nausea*: 'When his café empties, his head empties too.' The present always struck him as self-complete.

Now the truth is that the present moment is always incomplete, and the most basic activity of my mind is 'completing' it. Imagine that a being from some distant galaxy suddenly finds himself, by some curious accident of space-time, travelling in a bus through Piccadilly Circus. For him the world appears to be a meaningless chaos, for he cannot understand a single thing he can see. When you and I see a man raising a match to his lips we know he is only going to light a cigarette, not set his hair on fire. When we see a woman place a handkerchief to her nose we know she is going to blow it, not tear it off. When we see a man climbing a ladder we know he is not hoping to reach the sky. When we see flashing lights advertising a toothpaste we know they are not announcing the end of the world. Our star dweller knows none of these things. His world is meaningless because he cannot 'complete' things. Anything he looks at might signify anything.

This makes us aware that the process of education is simply the process of 'completing' whatever we see. When my telephone rings I know that someone is ringing my number, but a baby has no idea of what is happening. When I look at a house I know that it has two or three sides that are invisible to me, but for all a baby knows it may be merely a façade. I 'complete' it in my mind without even realizing that I am doing so. This 'completing' is the most basic activity of all intelligent beings. And because we do it every waking moment of our lives we accept it as naturally as our heartbeat.

But our 'completing' activities tend to vary from moment to moment. When I am tired I may watch the television without taking it in: I cannot be bothered to 'complete' it. On the other hand when I set out on holiday the world seems to me an extraordinarily interesting place – I cannot understand why I ever thought it was dull. My mind is now doing its 'completing' work with enthusiasm and efficiency.

This is why we all crave experience. It is the only way of developing this all-important 'completing' faculty. Imagination helps, but it can never be a real substitute. Imagine two people watching a television programme about the pyramids of Egypt; one has visited the pyramids, the other has not. For the person who has visited the pyramids the programme has a whole extra dimension of meaning. He is able to 'complete' what he sees on the screen.

Of course we may 'complete' things quite wrongly. A paranoiac imagines that the whole world is engaged in a conspiracy against him: he believes that the window cleaner across the street is spying on him in order to report to the CIA. He is 'completing' the present moment but adding some quite unwarrantable assumptions. This example makes us aware that 'completing' is not as natural and instinctive as it looks. It is to some extent a precise intellectual activity. Even to 'complete' a detective novel, I have to use my powers of reason. But that kind of 'completing' is fairly obvious and presents no problems. It is the purely instinctive 'completing' that makes life so difficult, for we have a deeply ingrained habit of accepting the present moment as complete in itself and of consequently taking it for granted. Life is what it appears to be. If I am bored, that is because life is boring. If I am tired, that is because

328

life is tiring. If I am confused, that is because life is confusing. I gaze at the world as passively as a baby and wonder why, on the whole, it all seems so oddly meaningless. Kierkegaard expressed this confusion when he wrote:

> One sticks one's finger into the soil to tell what land one's in; I stick my finger into existence – it smells of nothing. Where am I? Who am I? How did I come to be here? What is this thing called the world? What does the word mean? Who is it that has lured me into the thing, and now leaves me there? . . . . How did I come into the world? Why was I not consulted . . . . And if I am compelled to take part in it, where is the director? I would like to see him.

These words were written in 1843. When Kierkegaard was 'discovered', almost a century later, critics found his attitude remarkably 'modern' and he became – together with Kafka – one of the culture-heroes of the existentialists. Yet we can see plainly that Kierkegaard's sense of bewilderment arose from a simple misunderstanding. He reminds us of a man who pushes frantically at a door, convinced he has been locked in and failing to realize that it opens inwards. His problem is a simple failure of 'completing'. This becomes obvious if we think of Dostoevsky in front of the firing squad, suddenly realizing that life is infinitely interesting and infinitely exciting – a feeling he expressed in *Crime and Punishment* when his hero says that he would prefer to stand on a narrow ledge for all eternity, in darkness and tempest, than die at once. In the urgency of the crisis his mind is galvanized into doing its proper work of 'completing'. And as soon as he does this, he sees that far from being meaningless, life consists of infinite vistas of meaning.

This, I repeat, is the central problem of human existence: we are inclined to accept the present moment as 'self-complete', like a painting on the wall of an art gallery. Of course, there are moments when fate presents us with such a delightful richness of experience that the moment *is* virtually self-complete. A child on Christmas day, a lover kissing the girl he adores, a mountaineer on the summit of Everest – these people experience such a breathtaking sense of the richness of life that the very thought of defeat or despair seems preposterous. But such glimpses of the 'bird's-eye view' are rare. For the most part we have to be content with a worm's-eye view *and 'complete' it from inside our own heads*. This is why all young people long to travel, to fall in love, to experience conquest: because they will then have the necessary materials for 'completing' stored in a lumber room behind the eyes. That at any rate is the theory. As I sit outside a Paris café on a sunny morning smelling the odour of Gauloises and roasting coffee beans and watching the passing crowds, it now seems to me that fate has handed me an insight that will always save me from despair – or even depression. I merely have to remember how wonderful life can be and I shall see that

329

temporary setbacks are unimportant. In such a state of mind even the worst miseries and humiliations are seen to be merely interesting challenges, like high waves to a surfer.

The artist has always seen it as his task to remind himself of these moments when he can see that the 'disasters of life are innocuous'. Wordsworth asked:

Whither is fled the visionary gleam?
Where is it now, the glory and the dream?

But he believed that the answer lay in 'recollection in tranquillity'. So did Proust. The problem is that recreating lost delight is more difficult than it looks: as Proust's Marcel remarks, 'It is a labour in vain to try to recapture it; all the efforts of our intellect must prove futile.'

There may be some truth in that, but once we understand the role of 'completing' we can see that it hardly matters. And now we can suddenly grasp the immense importance of the concept of 'upside-downness'. 'Upside-downness' is the feeling that the vicissitudes of life *are* important, that its disasters are anything but innocuous, that its brevity is all too real. In short it is a state in which short-sighted emotional values have imposed themselves on the intellect. This happens because in most of us emotional and intellectual values are roughly the same weight – like the two halves of an old-fashioned egg-timer. Our problem, as we see in every glimpse of optimism, is simply to add intellectual ballast until we can no longer turn 'upside-down' – or, at least, so that when we do turn 'upside-down' we can instantly right ourselves again. Beethoven's music reveals that he had achieved this state, which is why he told Elizabeth Brentano, 'Those who understand my music must be freed from all the miseries which others drag around with them.' When faced with problems that would make other romantics burst into tears Beethoven was strong enough to take hold of the egg-timer and turn it the right way up. But it was not simply a question of grim, bear-like strength: the real secret lay in his intellectual insight, an adult recognition that most of the problems that worry human beings are childish irrelevances. The power of Beethoven's music lies in its underlying optimism: not an emotional or temperamental optimism, but the insight of a philosopher who has balanced life in the scales of objectivity and decided that the good far outweighs the bad.

However, it is unnecessary to be a Beethoven or even a philosopher to grasp this insight. It comes with every peak experience: the recognition that most of our problems are due to 'upside-downness'. Whenever we experience delight we realize that the answer is simply to translate this delight into intellectual terms – words and ideas – *and then trust the intellect*. From then on we must learn to carry out the act of 'completing' with conscious deliberation, with the unshakeable certainty that it is providing us with the correct solution. When this truth is grasped the result is the insight the Buddha called Enlightenment. It is the recognition that most suffering is quite unnecessary and that we are fools to put up with it. We merely need to *grasp* this insight about 'completing' and 'upside-downness' to see that most human suffering is self-inflicted. The psychological mechanism involved is identical to that of religious conversion except that this conversion is a clear and objective perception with no overtones of 'faith' or belief in the unprovable.

The result of this insight is not a condition of non-stop euphoria but a calm recognition that life is *not* difficult, dangerous and treacherous, and that most of the problems that confront us can be dealt with by using what might be called 'constructive will-force'. This is based upon the certainty that if we behave sensibly and rationally we shall achieve what we want to achieve. Most of our problems are shadow-bogeys created by 'upside-downness'.

How is this insight connected to the 'occult vision' I have tried to outline in this book? To begin with it should be clear that it is completely consistent with the mystical experiences described by Anne Bancroft, Warner Allen, Arnold Toynbee, Merrell-Wolff, Daly King and the rest. The essence of their vision is always a sense of 'absurd good news' which springs from a sudden 'bird's-eye view' of life and history. This is often accompanied by a certain pity for human beings for their inability to recognize that most of their miseries and anxieties are self-inflicted, and for 'their failure to realize their own divinity'. On the other hand if they *are* divine then there is not much cause for pity, for they are bound to find out sooner or later.

An immense amount of vital energy is wasted in states of 'upside-downness', and 'enlightenment' frees this energy for more interesting uses. The result, as Anne Bancroft observes, is that 'everything is transformed'. 'I was in a different state of consciousness altogether ... there was a sense of clarity, of utterly beneficent, wonderful emptiness.' The emptiness is the emptiness around a man who stands on a mountain top. But because perception is suddenly vitalized with all this additional energy everything appears more alive. Daly King's feeling that the bricks were glowing with life is basically similar to Aldous Huxley's visions under mescalin.

This is of course perfectly understandable: it is merely an intensified version of Compton Mackenzie's feelings as he waits for his lady love. What is more difficult to understand is some of the other powers that seem to be activated by the insight: for example Derek Gibson's ability to see inside the trees and grass, as if everything was 'magnified beyond measure'. This is obviously another version of Albert Tucker's experience of being able to see every single thread in the man's tweed overcoat, or every hair on his wife's head as he looked at her 'astral form' on the bed. It seems clear that some *other* power of vision has been activated, some power of which we are normally unaware. Eileen Garrett described this as being a kind of clairvoyance. 'One sees the entire road completely ... and its further reaches are as meticulously discernible as the areas that lie close . . . .' But we have also seen, in the case of Toynbee, that the flood of insight seems to annihilate time so that he can actually see a battle that took place more than two thousand years earlier. Whether this 'seeing' is simply a case of heightened imagination is immaterial; we are still speaking of the sudden activation of 'hidden powers'. And as we saw in the chapter on 'time-slips', these seem to include an ability to wander back into the past. In short the powers that are activated are various powers enabling us to read the 'information' encoded in the universe around us. There is an obvious and direct link between 'enlightenment' and so-called clairvoyant powers. And these powers in turn *are simply an extension of our normal power of 'completing'.*

It seems then that Lawrence LeShan was correct: the universe seen by the clairvoyant has much in common with the universe seen by the mystic, and both are *bigger* and more complete than the universe seen by the rest of us. The view of the sceptic is based upon a misconception: that the mystic – or the clairvoyant – is offering an *alternative* to the ordinary reality that surrounds us. One of Daskalos's followers objected, 'Material reality is the only thing that I know exists. It is what I can feel, touch, see, smell.' And Daskalos replied, 'There is nothing more misleading than the five senses.' He means that our assumption that the five senses 'reveal' reality is mistaken. They only reveal the limited reality of the immediate present, *and this would be meaningless to us unless it was 'completed' by our minds.* The senses of the mystic and clairvoyant are like doors that will *open wider* than the doors of ordinary humanity. What they perceive is not an alternative reality but an extension of normal reality.

Few people would disagree that they would be better off if they could induce peak experiences and mystical illuminations at will and experience clairvoyance and precognition when necessary. What is rather more difficult to decide is whether we would be better off if we could see spirits and communicate with the dead. Here the essential link in the chain of argument is exomatosis or 'out-of-the-body experience'. Reports of this experience are so widespread that there seems to be little doubt that it should be included among our 'hidden powers'. Some writers even give reasonably detailed instructions about how it can be brought about. Here for example is a passage from John Heron's *Confessions of a Janus-Brain*:

> Years ago I lived in a remote cottage alone in the Isle of Man, and through the use of dietary control, ritual and meditation, I obtained for a period a measure of command over the process of going out of the physical body in the ka body. [Heron uses this term for the 'astral body'.] I will describe the experience in the present tense, as if it is happening now.
>
> I lie in bed, it does not matter in what position as long as I am

332

very deeply relaxed both mentally and physically. I then imagine all the energy in my body being drawn to a central point around the area of the solar plexus: I consciously 'withdraw' energy from all the extremities and focus it, condense it, in this one place – which is really, of course, a ka space within the physical body.

I must hold this conscious force of energy in the ka region of the solar plexus, without any distraction of attention to, or any 'leaking' back of energy to, the extremities. The challenge is to sustain the focus for a sufficient time, in a state that combines intense alertness with deep relaxation. The activity of consciousness is contracted to a central point, without drifting back to the limbs – which remain totally inert, dispossessed. Then, after a certain period of charging up, the process of going out begins.

Going out is a dramatic experience. There is a very powerful and very rapid spiral thrust of energy, an intense vortex of motion in ka space, that hurtles my consciousness from the solar plexus region up to and out through my head. It is like being carried off in a rushing whirlwind.

There is no way this process can be confused with phantasy or delusion or anything of the sort. It is a vertiginous encounter with the profound reality of inner space. The potent vortex or subtle energy ruthlessly detaches me from the safe moorings of my physical body, and I surge into the world beyond.

Heron goes on to say:

Once I have transcended fear and surrendered to the powerful energy of the process, I am out of the physical body and start to travel. My experience of travelling to ka domains has always been that of moving at very high speed, in something like a rushing energy wind, with all my ka senses occluded so that I have no awareness of what sort of spaces I am travelling through. I only feel the presence, but have no perception, of those who are conducting me on the journey . . . .

And here, as in the case of Arthur Ellison, we encounter the notion of the involvement of some kind of 'protective entities'. (Ellison, we may recall, felt hands grasping his head and firmly guiding him back to his body.) These are not invariably encountered in descriptions of 'out-of-the-body' travel, but often enough to suggest that they are a normal part of this 'astral world'.

But do they *really* exist? 'Astral travel' undoubtedly involves an element of imagination: for example Daskalos explains that in order to get to some place on the other side of the world the 'astral traveller' merely has to imagine it and he is transported there. So it is arguable that 'out-of-the-body experiences' are simply a version of Jung's 'active

333

imagination', and that the entities who may be encountered are really 'archetypes of the collective unconscious', like Philemon and Salome. There is no reason why we should not take this view and refuse to go any further: that is, we could – figuratively – draw a line under 'astral travel' and ignore all the evidence for spirits, poltergeists and communication with the dead. In that case we could define paranormal research simply as the study of the 'hidden powers' of the unconscious mind – a view that might be labelled the 'anthropic' theory of the paranormal. And if we are prepared to admit the existence of Jung's 'collective unconscious' then it must be admitted that the arguments in favour of the anthropic theory are very powerful indeed. Spirits, according to this theory, are the creation of the human imagination, a response to man's deep instinctive fear of death.

The anthropic theory strikes me, on the whole, as reasonable and satisfying, and the majority of paranormal researchers appear to agree. All the same I am not happy with it, for most of them, if asked privately, will admit that they are inclined to accept the reality of 'survival'. Not long before her death from lung cancer I asked Anita Gregory – known as one of the most sceptical of modern researchers – if she believed in life after death. She replied:

> You quite rightly say that I am considered one of the most tough-minded investigators of the SPR. Let me try and explain what I mean by that. To me, being tough-minded means being careful and conscientious about evidence, scrupulous about methodology and searching as regards possible failings both of my own and those of other people. This type of hard-nosedness is for me a matter of principle and it often, much to my regret, brings me into conflict with people I like and with whom I see eye to eye on larger matters.
>
> There is however quite another sense of 'tough' and in that sense I do not qualify at all. That is the sense of being a reductive positivist, entertaining a belief about the world as a very bare and spare concatenation of accidents and causal pushes and pulls. So far as I'm concerned, this is a mean and meagre philosophy to which I do not subscribe. I think the world is a very mysterious and wonderful place and we only know a small fraction of its properties.
>
> I ought to say that I have never made a very special study of survival but I am very impressed by the evidence for it. I mean not only the traditional SPR-type mediumistic evidence (excellent though much of this is) but also the more recent near-death experience type of evidence. There are also some of the reincarnation data that are not at all easily dismissed; although in their case the evidence seems to point more to an occasional accident rather than a systematic happening.

334

So all in all, I am inclined to go a bit further than Alan Gauld and say I do tend to believe in the personal survival of death. Admittedly it hasn't been *proved* but then hardly anything ever has or could be that is at all at the edges of knowledge.*

In my own experience most researchers would be willing to make some such cautious admission, although few of them would be happy to be quoted. The reason is obvious. The evidence for 'hidden powers' – telepathy, clairvoyance, even precognition – is very strong indeed, and most reasonable people would be willing to concede that a belief in them is not incompatible with a scientific attitude. But a man who admits to a belief in communication with the dead is in danger of being labelled a spiritualist and dismissed as a credulous sentimentalist. This happened in the 1920s to Sir Oliver Lodge and Sir Arthur Conan Doyle: there was a general feeling – which still persists – that they had gone soft-minded. What is not generally realized is that both of them were finally convinced only after many years of scepticism. Lodge had been interested in telepathy since 1884; it was only in 1908 that he finally admitted that he accepted survival. His friend Conan Doyle remained unconvinced; it was not until 1915 that he received overwhelming evidence for the survival of his brother-in-law Malcolm Leckie, killed at Mons, and admitted his conversion to a belief in life after death.

This is undoubtedly the reason that Jung spent most of his life insisting that all 'occult' phenomena can be explained in terms of the unconscious mind and that he had never had any direct experience that convinced him otherwise. It was only after an accidental fall in 1943, when he was sixty-eight, brought him close to death that he decided to burn his boats and admit to a lifelong interest in the paranormal and a belief in life after death. His earlier attitude was plainly a matter of caution.

Surprisingly enough even T. S. Eliot abandoned an attitude of rigid orthodoxy a few years before his death (in 1965) and admitted to an admiration for Rudolf Steiner:

I think that the present time will spontaneously lead to something like the separation of individual human beings from time's events. They will stand on their own feet, and from their innermost being they will seek new paths, spiritual paths.

It seems to me that Goethe, for example, had a compass of consciousness which far surpassed that of his nineteenth-century contemporaries. Rudolf Steiner expressly upheld this, and I do too.

In a certain connection, atomic science has a meaning, namely inasmuch as it is in the hands of men who are in no way able to cope with it. It has no importance whatever for the progress of

*Letter to the author.

335

mankind. I see the path of progress for modern man in his occupation with his own self, with his inner being, as indicated by Rudolf Steiner.

But these remarkable words were uttered in a broadcast on Nordwestdeutscher Rundfunk on 26 September 1959 and remained unreported in England or America.

Eliot would certainly have been startled if he could have foreseen that the atomic science he regarded with such suspicion would, within a quarter of a century, give birth to a theory that was in fundamental agreement with Steiner. This was the 'anthropic principle' that we have already considered briefly. In the final chapter of this book it deserves to be examined in more detail.

6

Towards the Unknown Region

As soon as man began to study the heavens he reached the conclusion that our earth is the centre of the universe. And since man is obviously the most intelligent creature on earth, it followed that he must also be the most important creature in creation.

In 1512 a canon of the Church named Nicholas Copernicus realized that many of the riddles of astronomy could be cleared up by assuming that the sun, not the earth, is the centre of the universe. Being a timid soul he preferred not to publish the idea, even though the Pope's right-hand man, the Cardinal of Capua, urged him to do so. His book *On the Revolutions of the Heavenly Bodies* finally appeared when he was on his death-bed.

On the whole his misgivings were well-founded. As the new theory slowly gained acceptance science came to recognize that man is less important than he assumed. By the mid-nineteenth century most scientists had come to accept that man is an accidental creature who was born on an unimportant planet of a second-rate star. Religious men were inclined to challenge this view. But it was not until 1974 that science began to raise its own mild objections.

It was in this year that an astronomer named Brandon Carter, of the Paris Observatory, formulated what he called 'the weak anthropic principle'. This stated, in effect, 'Well, there's one thing about the universe – no one would be here to observe it if it hadn't created the observers in the first place. So in that respect, at least, we are privileged.' In other words it may have done it accidentally, but it *did* it. So we needn't regard ourselves as total nonentities.

But when we speak of 'accidentally' we are using a word that has no place in science. If the universe is a machine then there is no accident: everything *had* to happen the way it has. And this in itself is something of a puzzle. If we imagine two gods sitting in a 'dimensionless hyperspace' and discussing the idea of creating a universe, we can see that they would have an infinite number of choices: 'What about the weight of the electron – what shall we make that? How about the speed of light? What about the force of gravity? And electromagnetic forces. . . .' If any of these had been different the universe as we know it would never have come into existence. But these 'constants' were not different and our universe *did* come into existence. And in due course it

337

brought *us* into existence. If even one of those constants had been changed we wouldn't be here either.

Considerations like this led Carter to formulate what he called 'the strong anthropic principle', which says that the universe is such that life *had* to develop. That sounds, at first, a controversial statement, almost religious in its implications. But anyone who reads the foregoing sentences again will see that it is a strictly logical consequence of our scientific argument.

Long before Carter thought of the anthropic principle scientists had been aware of certain interesting oddities about the relation between man and the universe. For example our planet just happens to be perfectly suited to the incubation of life. The sun had to be exactly at the right temperature: a few degrees higher or lower and there would have been no life. Gravity had to be exactly the right strength: slightly lower and there would have been no atmosphere; slightly higher and the struggle to move would have been too great for living things. Life on earth is balanced on a knife edge, and if Victorian divines had known about this they would undoubtedly have used it as a proof that God created the earth especially for man. This has been called 'the fine-tuning effect' and it applies to the whole universe: in short the universe itself seems singularly suited to the existence of life. The eighteenth-century theologian William Paley pointed to his watch as a proof of the existence of God, arguing that even a savage would recognize that such a complicated instrument must have a maker, and that this applies even more to man. The fine-tuning argument is in some ways similar, except that a better comparison would be a vast jigsaw puzzle, every part of which fits exactly into the next part. The physical constants of the universe interlock in precisely that way. And one *inevitable* result has been the creation of life.

So far the argument has remained within the bounds of the most rigidly materialistic science: we are merely saying that life is one of the inevitable side-effects of a universe such as ours. But some scientists – such as Fred Hoyle and the chemist Lawrence Henderson – took it a stage further and argued that the universe seems almost unreasonably suited to the existence of life. In the 1950s Hoyle was working out how the elements are created in the heart of the stars. He noted that in order to make carbon – the essential element for life – two helium nuclei have to collide, a contingency as unlikely as two billiard balls colliding on a billiard table the size of the Sahara desert. But when this has happened the new atom seems to attract a third helium atom to make carbon: no other element behaves in this way. Moreover if another helium atom hits the carbon it produces oxygen, another element essential for life. Then why has not all the carbon in the universe been converted to oxygen? Because the forces involved are so subtly out of tune that only about half the carbon gets converted to oxygen – a highly convenient accident for the creation of life. Hoyle came to the extraordinary conclusion that:

338

A commonsense interpretation of the facts suggests that a 'super-intendent' has monkeyed with the physics – as well as chemistry and biology – and that there are no 'blind forces' worth speaking about in Nature. I do not believe that any physicist who examined the evidence could fail to draw the inference that the laws of nuclear physics have been deliberately designed with regard to the consequences they produce inside stars.

This is only one step away from saying that these laws have been designed to produce life. This is a startling conclusion, but not quite so anthropomorphic as Paley's watch argument. When we add to it the impressive body of evidence about the fine-tuning of the universe, it seems a justifiable assumption – if only an assumption.

As we saw earlier (p. 177) Professor John Wheeler has taken this argument an astonishing step further. Wheeler's argument is based upon Heisenberg's uncertainty principle. The simplest interpretation of this principle is that we cannot know both the position and speed of an electron (or photon) because in order to observe them we have to 'interfere' with them. It is a little like trying to observe the development of a piece of film by shining a powerful light on it: the exposure destroys the photograph. However Wheeler and many other quantum physicists insist that the Heisenberg principle means far more than this. It means – according to Bohr and Wheeler – that the electron *has* no position until we 'expose' it by observing it. This means in turn that we 'create' it by observing it, for until we observe it, it is nowhere in particular. This interpretation of the Heisenberg principle led Wheeler to the strange position – reminiscent of Bishop Berkeley – that we may be creating the whole universe by observing it: after all, the universe is made of electrons.

Wheeler explained his view by describing a game of twenty ques-tions he had once played at a dinner party. Someone is sent out of the room: an object is chosen, then the victim is re-admitted and has to ask twenty questions to try to determine the nature of the object. Wheeler noticed that his friends were smiling as he came in, and guessed they had decided to play a joke on him. What puzzled him was that when he asked the questions there was a perceptible pause before he received an answer, and the pauses got longer as the game went on. Finally Wheeler asked, 'Is it cloud?' His friends thought for a long time then said yes, and everyone burst out laughing. It turned out that they had decided not to choose a word: anyone could answer as he pleased, but all the answers had to be consistent. This, Wheeler says, is a good simile for describing Bohr's view of the electron. Everyone assumes it has position and velocity before it is observed, just as Wheeler assumed that a word had been chosen before he came into the room. But there was no word: he created it by asking questions. And according to Wheeler there is no electron before the scientist creates it by trying to observe it.

339

We also noted in the earlier chapter the experiment in which, in some baffling way, a single photon appears to 'interfere' with itself. Wheeler has devised a slightly more complicated version of this experiment which he believes to be crucial to the participatory anthropic principle. A beam of light is split into two beams – at right angles to one another – by a half-silvered mirror, then these two beams are made to cross by reflecting them off two more mirrors. Now another optical device is introduced at their crossing point, so that both beams become a mixture of the two. This device can be so adjusted that one of the double-beams cancels itself out. (Imagine two lots of waves on a pond superimposed on one another so that they vanish and the surface becomes flat.)

What is so astonishing is that if the beam is dimmed until it becomes only one photon at a time, this 'interference' effect still takes place. That seems absurd: one photon has nothing to interfere with, so it should be able to choose either of the two paths. Why it does not do so is baffling. If a photon-counter is introduced into the system to find out just what is happening, this mysterious effect promptly vanishes and the photons behave just as one might expect them to, choosing either path. Wheeler argues that this proves that the photon does not exist until it is observed. And the same thing, he suggests, applies to our universe.

There is one obvious objection. We know the universe existed for billions of years before life came along. Is Wheeler telling us that it did not exist before there were observers?

He is indeed. He argues that if you use the light from a distant star for the same experiment, that light set out millions of years ago. Yet the same argument applies: the light does not exist until it is observed. So, says Wheeler, we are actually creating the past. His view is summarized by John Barrow and Frank Tipler as follows:

> Wheeler points out that according to the Copenhagen interpretation, we can regard some restricted properties of distant galaxies, which we now see as they were billions of years ago, as brought into existence now. Perhaps *all* properties – and hence the entire universe – are brought into existence by observations made at some point in time by conscious beings. However, we ourselves can bring into existence only very small-scale properties like the spin of the electron. Might it require intelligent beings 'more conscious' than ourselves to bring into existence the electrons and other particles?*

In fact Wheeler's participatory anthropic principle is simply an updated version of Berkeley's suggestion that we bring things into existence by seeing them, a position that we all instinctively reject as absurd. Most of us will take the view that if the Copenhagen interpretation leads to this preposterous view then the Copenhagen interpretation must be wrong. It

*John Barrow and Frank Tipler, *The Anthropic Cosmological Principle* (1986), p. 470.

seems far more likely that Einstein was correct and that the electron *does* have both position and velocity, even though science has no way of determining them.

But even if we reject Wheeler's participatory anthropic principle, the two earlier versions remain unshaken. And, as Barrow and Tipler point out, they suggest one more logical step to a Final Anthropic Principle:

> Suppose that for some unknown reason the strong anthropic principle is true and that intelligent life must come into existence at some stage in the Universe's history. But if it dies out at our stage of development, long before it has had any measurable non-quantum influence on the Universe in the large, it is hard to see why it *must* have come into existence in the first place. This motivates the following the generalization of the strong anthropic principle.
>
> *Final Anthropic Principle: Intelligent information-processing must come into existence in the Universe, and, once it comes into existence, it will never die out.*

In other words, according to the anthropic principle the existence of life in the universe seems to argue that the universe was somehow designed to create life and that life is finally destined to colonize the furthest corners of the universe. It is not even necessary to subscribe to Hoyle's view that some 'superintendent' has been monkeying with the physics to arrive at this conclusion. We merely have to recognize that a lifeless universe is a great machine in which there is no such thing as chance: everything *has* to happen as it does. And since it brought life into existence it follows that it *had* to do so. But until it reached the stage of intelligent self-reflection life had virtually no freedom: it was driven by blind biological urges. Once it developed intelligence it also developed some degree of freedom – and as far as life is concerned, freedom means freedom to expand and evolve. It seems possible of course that the mechanical forces of the universe will again squash it into extinction, but logically speaking that seems unlikely. Life is the power to defy mere brute force, to struggle for survival. If it can emerge into a mechanical universe and survive for half a billion years there seems to be no logical reason why its higher intelligent forms should be doomed to extinction.

At which point it must be admitted that in a sense, this whole argument is irrelevant. We are assuming, as modern biologists do, that life was somehow created out of dead matter by some kind of chemical reaction. This book has rejected such a position from the very beginning. If paranormal research seems to demonstrate anything at all it is that life is, in some fundamental sense, independent of matter. It belongs to another order of reality. In the universe of the modern biologist there is no room for clairvoyance, precognition, out-of-the-body experiences, poltergeists,

341

time-slips or synchronicities, and there is certainly no room for life after death. Since – to anyone who examines it with an open mind – the evidence for all these things is convincing, the notion that our universe 'brought life into existence' must be rejected.

The only alternative is that life somehow entered the universe of matter from 'outside'. This is known as vitalism. The vitalist view is that life is trying to insert itself into matter and to enlarge the 'leak' of freedom, its ultimate aim being total control over matter. So the vitalist version of the anthropic principle is that at a certain point in its evolution, the universe created the *conditions* that were suitable for the invasion of life and that life immediately took advantage of it.

However, the view expressed by vitalists like Henri Bergson and Bernard Shaw is that life was simply a blind force that gradually struggled its way – on earth – into self-consciousness. But again the evidence of the paranormal throws doubt on this view. If man possesses 'hidden powers', when did they evolve? Even the curious ability of mathematical prodigies to work out whether some eight-figure number is a prime defies what might be called the 'simple vitalist' view of evolution. If it has taken man so long to evolve to the present stage then it ought to take another million years or so to evolve an ability that surpasses that of our best computers. Synchronicities also seem to argue that that mind has some odd power of causing coincidences which is equally unexplainable in straightforward evolutionary terms. And if we accept the evidence for clairvoyance, precognition, 'spirits' and life after death, then it becomes clear that simple vitalism is hopelessly inadequate to explain our universe.

What have the mystics to tell us of the nature of the universe? Without exception they insist that there *is* a meaning and purpose which is invisible to our earth-bound intelligences. Even the simplest mystical experience seems to contradict our basic human experience of being in one place at one time. 'My consciousness passed out across the ocean and the land in all directions, through the sky and out into space.' 'The boundary between my physical self and my surroundings seemed to dissolve and my feeling of separation vanished.' 'I understood that the scheme of the universe was good, not evil . . . .' 'I saw that the universe is not composed of dead matter, but is, on the contrary, a living Presence. . . . I saw that all men are immortal.' 'We alone are responsible for our sufferings and problems in consequence of the misuse of our free will.' 'In an instant of time I suddenly knew, without any doubts, that I was a part of a "Whole".'

Such experiences seem to make so little sense that we are tempted to dismiss them as some form of drunkenness, or perhaps some variety of 'dream consciousness'. But in the aftermath of dreaming or drunkenness we can see quite clearly that we were out of touch with reality. The mystics assert again and again that they felt their experience to be *more real* than our 'ordinary reality', and that this absolute certainty persisted when they were once again trapped in the normal world of human consciousness. If that is true then there ought to be at least a reasonable chance of learning to grasp their experience by means of our limited human awareness.

One 'experimental mystic', R. H. Ward, devoted a book to his own experiences with dental gas and the drug LSD, and this affords us some interesting insights.* The first thing that strikes us is the remarkable similarities between Ward's experiences and those described by Ouspensky. Describing his experience of nitrous oxide gas, Ward says, '... I passed, after the first few inhalations of the gas, directly into a state of consciousness already far more complete than the fullest degree of ordinary waking consciousness. ...' Here again we have that basic assertion that the reason we cannot comprehend our universe is that our consciousness is so dull and dim. It seems capable of very little but focusing on what is under our noses.

Ward again emphasizes the unreality of our idea of time. 'In one sense it lasted far longer than the short period between inhaling the gas and "coming round", lasted indeed for an eternity, and in another sense it took no time at all.'

Ward was surprised that far from being rendered unconscious, he was suddenly far *more* conscious than usual. 'For already I knew, I understood, I actually was, far more than I normally knew, understood and was ....' He adds that he felt he was *rediscovering* those things 'which had once been mine, but which I had lost many years before. While it was altogether strange, this new condition was also familiar; it was even in some sense my rightful condition. Meanwhile, what was becoming unreal, slow and clumsy was the ordinary world I was leaving behind.'

The meaning of these words is quite clear. Man has *descended into* matter – into this 'outer Siberia' of the universe – from some far more desirable condition. This also seems to be confirmed again and again by people who have been on the point of death. Raymond Moody's book *Life After Life*, a study of dozens of 'near-death experiences', is full of phrases like, 'For a second I knew all the secrets of the ages, all the meaning of the universe.' There is a sense of knowledge, of release, of exaltation, which seems to suggest that the experience of dying is an experience of ascending *out* of matter, out of 'Siberia', and back into our natural condition. And this raises, obviously, the interesting question of why human beings should descend into 'Siberia' in the first place – particularly if, as Steiner suggests, it is our own choice.

Ward seems to have passed quickly into the realm that Ouspensky called a world of mathematical relations. Ward prefers to call it 'a region of ideas'. But ideas, in the form of concepts, were quite unnecessary, 'since one could manage perfectly well without them: this was a condition of complete and spontaneous lucidity, where there was

*R. H. Ward, *A Drug Taker's Notes.*

343

not the slightest need to "think". One simply knew; and one knew not merely one thing here and another thing there . . . one knew everything there was to know. Thus one knew that everything was one thing, and that *real knowledge* was simultaneous knowledge of the universe and all it contains, oneself included.' In other words 'separateness' had disappeared; everything was *seen* to be connected. In this realm, he says, there was a marvellous feeling of 'rightness'. Images and symbols had become unnecessary. 'All was idea, and form did not exist. (And it seems to me very interesting that one should thus, in a dentist's chair and the twentieth century, receive practical confirmation of the theories of Plato.)' In this region of ideas, 'everything lived and moved; everything "breathed", but breathed with the "one breath" which is the universal inspiration and expiration expressed in the cardinal opposites of day and night, male and female, summer and winter. Indeed the wonderful and awe-inspiring livingness of everything seemed to be part of the interrelatedness of everything.'

Like Ouspensky, Ward realized that our human notions about subject and object are quite wrong. He grasped 'a new realization of the relationship between subject and object . . . . One knew and understood this different world as a spectator of it, recognizing it as the object of one's apprehension, but at the same time knew and understood that it existed within oneself; thus one was at once the least significant atom in the universal whole and that universal whole.' (Barbara Tucker expressed it, 'And suddenly I knew – or saw – that time past, present and future were all one, and that I was God, and yet at the same time was only the minutest grain of sand.') Ward explains that it is necessary to *'think inside out'* in order to understand this baffling new relationship beween subject and object.

Ward's 'upward flight' ended in 'a perfection of light', a state of 'indescribable purity' and perfect unity. Again he experienced the odd feeling of familiarity, as if this was something he *remembered*. After this began the 'downward flight' back to earth, back through the region of ideas, then, 'as consciousness diminished towards the consciousness of everyday life', the region of ideas began to take on forms:

On its nether fringes the symbols we need in the waking state if we are to comprehend 'intuition' were supplied. In a flash . . . I *saw the meaning*; the meaning, that is, of the universe, of life on earth, and of man. As the darkness of what we flatter ourselves is consciousness closed in upon me, and even as I was dimly to be aware that I was 'coming to', the sum of things appeared before my inward eyes as *a living geometrical figure*, an infinitely complicated and infinitely simple arrangement of continually moving, continually changing golden lines on a background of darkness . . . . This living geometrical figure seemed to be telling me that *everything is in order*, that everything works according to an

344

ineluctable pattern, and that... nothing ever need be wholly meaningless, even on earth.... Provided we bear the pattern's existence in mind, even pain... can have meaning; so can death; so can the worst that we may have to endure; while the possibility of discerning this meaning is itself the meaning of divine mercy.

And as he came out of the gas he tried to recapture this vision of meaning in the words 'Within and within and within and...' repeated like an endlessly recurring decimal.

Ouspensky had also seemed to see the 'meaning' in the form of a geometrical figure,

> ... in the semblance of some big flower, like a rose or a lotus, the petals of which were continually unfolding from the middle, growing, increasing in size, reaching the outside of the flower and then in some way again returning to the middle and starting again from the beginning.... In this flower there was an incredible quantity of light, movement, colour, music, emotion, agitation, knowledge, intelligence, mathematics, and continuous unceasing growth. And while I was looking at this flower *someone* seemed to explain to me that this was the 'World' or 'Brahma' in its clearest aspect and in the nearest approximation to what it is in reality – 'If the approximation were made still nearer, it would be Brahma himself, as he is,' said the voice.

This image of a flower unfolding then returning continually to its own centre also seems to explain Ward's 'within and within and within....'

Here again perhaps the most easily understandable part of Ward's vision is his recognition of the 'connectedness' of everything, the realization that 'nothing is separate'. He says, 'Things were related to one another which to ordinary thinking would have no connexion whatever, and related to one another in ways which we cannot normally conceive. Things which we should call far apart, whether in space or time or by their nature, here interpenetrated; things which we should call wholly different from one another became one another.' The moment we begin to experience a feeling of rising vitality we have an odd sense of the *meaningfulness* of everything – as if everything we looked at were communicating with us – and the feeling that everything *reminds* us of something else.

In his essay on mysticism and logic, Bertrand Russell dismisses such 'glimpses' as mere feelings, as if they could be compared with drunkenness. Ward and Ouspensky have no doubt that they amount to a wider glimpse of reality. And modern brain research indicates that they are probably correct. In his book *Megabrain*, Michael Hutchison describes a machine called the 'Transcutaneous Electro-Neural Stimulator', invented by brain physiologist Joseph Light, which can send an electric current into the brain. Light chose a frequency of 7.83 Hz, the frequency of the electrical field resonating between the earth and the ionosphere, which appears to be capable of harmonizing the body and brain with the earth's electromagnetic energy. Hutchison was attached to the machine, but was unaware that it was switched on:

Yes, yes, I cried. I felt as if I were bursting at the seams. Full of wonder and excitement, I told Light some of my feelings about brain research. I told him about an article I was in the process of rewriting about the brain. I told him how I had become interested in the brain. At that moment a series of studies I had read about a variety of subjects, including the relation between protein syn-thesis and memory and the biochemical basis of addiction all flew together in my skull and I understood something new. Gesturing wildly and scribbling on a paper napkin, I began to explain my new insight . . . Suddenly I stopped, with my mouth hanging open in wild surmise. People seated in nearby booths were peering at me with great interest. 'Listen to me talk!' I said to Light. 'Jabbering like a wired-up monkey!'

Light gave me a demonic grin and pointed his finger at the black gizmo on the table, and I realized that all this while subtle little electrical waves had been insinuating their way into my brain. I burst out laughing, filled with immense pleasure. I felt that my brain was working faster and more efficiently than ever before – ideas were tumbling into place so fast that I could hardly capture them.

Clearly, Hutchison is describing an experience that is fundamentally the same as Ouspensky's sensations in his mystical states: connect-edness – 'a man could go mad from one ashtray.' We could hardly demand a better proof that our brains are usually subnormal, and that when we begin to experience fascination and excitement we are coming closer to our normal capacities. Hutchison is also describing what Koestler calls 'the Eureka experience', when insights suddenly lock together, like a jigsaw puzzle, forming a pattern. 'At that moment a series of studies I had read about a variety of subjects . . . all flew together in my skull and I understood something new.'

What Light had done was to cause his machine to release large quantities of the brain's natural opiates, the painkilling and euphoria-causing endorphins. He told Hutchison how he had once driven six hundred miles to a conference hooked up to his brain machine, had spent the whole journey doing useful mental work, then, after the conference, had driven straight back. 'When I got back I wasn't even tired.'

It is significant that Ward calls the chapter in which he describes his own experience 'Consciousness is not a constant'. For this obviously

346

lies at the root of the problem: our assumption that ordinary consciousness tells us the truth about the external world. Yet every time we have a peak experience we see once again that ordinary consciousness deserves to be regarded with mistrust. Because it is so dim and dull it virtually tells us lies. Once we begin to see this we can also grasp that there are a number of distinct levels of consciousness that every one of us experiences during the course of a lifetime.

Let us, simply as an exercise, see if we can recognize the most fundamental of these levels. Let us start off with the basic state of non-consciousness that we experience in very deep sleep, and call this Level O. In that case Level 1 is the level we experience as we dream, and which persists in hypnagogic experiences.

Level 2 is the most basic level of waking consciousness: that is *mere awareness*. A child experiences this when he is too tired to take any interest in anything. He may be on his way home from a party but he gazes blankly at the passing world. If you were to ask, 'What have you just seen?' he would reply, 'I don't know.' His consciousness is merely a mirror reflecting the outside world. Nietzsche once said that we envy the cows their placidity, but it would be no use asking them the secret of their happiness for they would have forgotten the question before they could give the answer. This is Level 2.

At Level 3 consciousness has become self-aware but it is still dull and heavy – so heavy that we are only aware of one thing at a time: everything seems to be 'merely itself', utterly without meaning, and your own reflection in a mirror seems to be a stranger. This is the level that Sartre calls nausea.

Level 4 is the normal consciousness we experience every day. It is no longer too heavy to move: it has learned how to cope with existence yet it tends to think of life as a grim battle – possibly a losing battle. Consequently it tends to sink back easily towards Level 3 and to find experience meaningless and boring.

So far the one thing the levels all have in common is a basically *passive* attitude towards life and experience. At Level 5 this ceases to be so. This is a level that I have labelled provisionally 'spring morning consciousness' or 'holiday consciousness'. It is characterized by that bubbling feeling of happiness we experience when life suddenly becomes more interesting and exciting and all kinds of prospects seem to be opening up in front of us. Quite suddenly caution and doubt disappear; life becomes *self-evidently* fascinating and delightful. This is the feeling that Hesse's Steppenwolf experiences as he tastes a glass of wine and is reminded of 'Mozart and the stars'.

Level 6 could be labelled the 'magical level'. It is what happens to a child on Christmas Day, when everything combines to make life seem wonderful. Or imagine the consciousness of two honeymooners on their wedding night looking down from a balcony on to a moonlit lake, with the dark shapes of mountains in the distance. In such states we feel a total reconciliation with our lives. 'For moments together my heart stood still between delight and sorrow to find how rich was the gallery of my life,' says Steppenwolf. Problems seem trivial; we see that the one real virtue is courage. Consciousness has become a continuous mild peak experience, what J. B. Priestley calls 'delight'.

Level 7 is Faculty X – Toynbee's experience on Pharsalus, Proust's experience as he tastes the madeleine dipped in tea. There is an almost godlike sensation: 'I had ceased to feel mediocre, accidental, mortal. . . .' This is more than a peak experience: it is an odd sense of *mastery over time*, as if every moment of your life could be recalled as clearly as the last ten minutes. We suddenly realize that time is a manifestation of the heaviness of the body and the feebleness of the spirit. We can also see that if we could learn to achieve this condition of control permanently, time would become, in a basic sense, non-existent.

The most interesting thing about the levels beyond Level 7 – the levels explored by Ouspensky and other mystics – is that they seem to *contradict* the evidence of our senses and of everyday consciousness. The inner becomes the outer, the outer becomes the inner, man is the whole universe and a mere atom, space and time are seen to be illusions and so on. Yet we can see that these contradictions are already inherent in everyday consciousness. At Level 2 consciousness has no kind of 'connectedness'; it is merely a flow of meaningless impressions. Level 3 – nausea – starts to arrest this flow, to connect things together, but it keeps collapsing into a sudden perception that the world is after all quite meaningless and futile. Level 4 – ordinary consciousness – 'connects' things to a far higher degree, yet it still takes it for granted that life is an endless uphill struggle and that we have to make a continuous effort to see any meaning in it. At Level 5 – 'holiday consciousness' – all this changes: there is a sense of being able to see to distant horizons, of becoming aware of 'Mozart and the stars'. We suddenly realize that the world around us is so fascinating in itself that no effort is required. Everything makes us think of something else and so we are kept in a continuous state of interest and excitement.

At Level 6 – 'magic consciousness' – we seem to be floating in a sea of meaning and find it hard to understand how we could ever have been unhappy, or how anyone else could be. Even the worst experiences of the past now seem deeply interesting attempts to teach us something, essential steps on the upward path to this sense of optimism and control. The only tragedy in the universe seems to be that so many people lack the courage and sheer dogged stubborness to *keep going* and so miss this literally 'heavenly' sense of wonder and reconciliation.

Level 7, with its sense of freedom, of mastery over time, is only a short step from the mystical level, just as Level 6 – 'magic' – is only a short step from Faculty X. A sudden additional effort can carry the mind over the threshold into that strange realm where 'separateness' is seen to be a delusion caused by fatigue and everything is *seen* to be connected. One of the most encouraging things about this insight into the levels is that each level is only a short and easy step away from the previous one.

All mystical experience leaves us confronted by the same fundamental question: *What are we doing here? And what are we supposed to do now we are here?* If the mystical experience gives us an odd experience of 'returning home' to our proper state of being, then what are we doing here in the first place? Why have we descended into this 'outer Siberia'?

One assumption seems obvious: that we are here for a purpose. Like the pioneers who went to the Yukon we are driven by some powerful compulsion. *The stakes are obviously higher than we think.* The obvious explanation is that we are a colonizing expedition, and that our purpose is to colonize the realm of matter. According to this view life – or spirit – is attempting to establish a bridgehead in matter, just as man might attempt to establish a space-station on the moon. The trouble is that the supply lines are too long so that contact with base is irregular and uncertain. Even radio contact is intermittent. And after years in these difficult surroundings the explorers tend to become obsessed with the mere problem of survival and to forget why they came there. This is why for millions of years life on earth was little more than a story of murderous conflict, with one species gobbling up another. And that is still why some of the ablest men on our planet devote their lives to the futile pursuit of money and power – unable to see any logically-appealing alternative.

The basic problem, quite clearly, is that we waste so much time on the first four levels of consciousness, whose dullness makes them virtually useless. Mere survival is all very well, but it is not until we achieve Level 5 that we begin to live to some purpose. It is only then that we cease to be undermined by the suspicion that life is an endless uphill struggle, a battle that cannot be won, and recognize that even in 'outer Siberia', the world is endlessly fascinating. It is worth noting that all healthy human beings achieve regular glimpses of 'spring morning consciousness', when they rise like a cork from Level 4 to Level 5, for these glimpses are what Maslow meant by the peak experience. And in such moments we can see clearly that the major problem is the number of *mistakes* we make when we are confined to the lower levels.

We can also see that the fundamental cause of all human problems is the entity I have called the robot, the automatic part of us that takes over when we are tired and does our living for us. The robot is absolutely essential to life on earth; we could not survive for ten seconds without him. When mystics descend from their realms of pure enlightenment into this 'unreal, slow and clumsy' world of human reality, the robot is waiting for them at the door. He is even more important than symbols and language, for very simple organisms can survive without symbols and language but no creature can survive without his robot.

349

It is the sheer weight of the robot that makes us feel we are living in a 'wooden world'. We can see for example that the moment Ouspensky or Ward returned from the mystical realm of perfect freedom and found themselves 'back in the body' they once again found themselves saddled with all their boring old habits and worries and neuroses, all their old sense of identity built up from the reactions of other people, and above all the dreary old *heaviness*, as if consciousness has turned into a leaden weight. This is the sensation that made the romantics feel that life is a kind of hell – or at the very least, purgatory.

Yet we know enough about the robot to know that this feeling is as untrustworthy as the depression induced by a hangover. The trouble with living 'on the robot' is that he is a dead weight. He takes over only when our energies are low. So when I do something robotically I get no feedback of sudden delight. This in turn makes me feel that it was not worth doing. 'Stan' reacts by failing to send up energy and 'Ollie' experiences a sinking feeling. Living becomes even more robotic and the vicious circle effect is reinforced. Beyond a certain point we feel as if we are cut off from reality by a kind of glass wall: suddenly it seems self-evident that there is nothing new under the sun, that all human effort is vanity, that man is a useless passion and that life is a horrible joke devised by some demonic creator. This is the state I have decribed as 'upside-downness', the tendency to allow negative emotional judgements to usurp the place of objective rational judgements. Moreover this depressing state masquerades as the 'voice of experience', since it seems obvious that you 'know' more about an experience when you've had it a hundred times. This is the real cause of death in most human beings: they mistake the vicious circle effects of 'upside-downness' for the wisdom of age, and give up the struggle.

On the other hand it takes only a flash of non-robotic consciousness – the delight of a spring morning, the sudden relief when a crisis disappears – to make us aware that 'upside-downness' is an appalling mistake. Here it is *we* who are in control, instead of being controlled by the robot, and non-robotic states are characterized by this sense of being in control. In these 'conditions of control' our vitality is so high that everything looks fresh and interesting; the result is the overwhelmingly authentic sense of 'absurd good news'. If you asked someone who is experiencing this state to define exactly what he 'sees', he would reply that it is a clear and objective recognition that the universe really *is* infinitely exciting and beautiful. It also brings a dazzling vision of how human life might be *transformed*. For we can see, instantly and intuitively, that the 'Ecclesiastes effect' is a confidence trickster who makes life seem dull and boring by assuring us that it *is* dull and boring – the process is closely akin to hypnosis. In 'conditions of control' we can see through the lie, and the effect is a kind of revelation. Suddenly everything is clear. Now we are free of the robot we can see that the world is full of infinite and fascinating variety; it is the robot who irons

350

out our perceptions and makes everything look alike – makes every house look like every other house, every tree look like every other tree. More importantly we can see the way that the mechanisms of the robot produce 'upside-downness' and that it is our unconscious conviction of the truth of 'upside-downness' – the feeling that life is not worth *too much* effort – that really obstructs us from spending far more time in the non-robotic states. (If you wish to measure your own unconscious level of 'upside-downness', observe your feelings next time you do something 'pointless' like picking up something you have dropped or closing a door that should not have been left open: in moods of 'upside-downness' it causes a sinking of the heart and costs a real effort.) In conditions of control we suddenly recognize that 'upside-downness' is a *logical* error, and that if we could once grasp this with the conscious mind, as we can grasp the trick of doing long division or extracting a square root, a tremendous load would be lifted from the mind and the peak experience would become an everyday occurrence.

In fact this load *is* lifted from the mind every time some crisis disappears and we see the world without 'upside-downness'. This explains why Maslow's students found it so easy to have peak experiences once they began thinking and talking about them. The peak experience enabled them, in a flash of insight, to see through the mechanisms of 'upside-downness' and to recognize that there is no earthly reason why we should not live on a far higher level of optimism. The peak experience is not a trick but a *perception*. This is why it always produces a feeling that could be interpreted 'Of *course*.'

Understanding the robot also enables us to grasp the mechanism of depression and neurosis. In non-robotic consciousness – freedom consciousness – we experience a continual feedback of interest from all our activities and this recharges our vital batteries. When we are 'on the robot' there is no feedback and our batteries become flat. So people who spend too much time living robotically find themselves engaged in a continual struggle against discouragement, the suspicion that life is a losing battle. A few extra problems and the vicious circle effect can lead to nervous breakdown. Yet once we can grasp that this is a logical error, one of the nastier tricks of 'upside-downness', we can see that it is an almost laughable absurdity on the level of a schoolboy howler. Goethe's Mephistopheles describes himself as 'the spirit that negates', and it is almost as if most of us had a tiny Mephistopheles living inside our heads waiting to turn our certainties upside down and whisper, 'It isn't really worth the effort . . . .' Yet it should now be possible to see that 'upside-downness' involves a simple mistake, analogous to the mistake of a man who walks into a dimly-lit room and suspects that he is going blind. The moment he realizes there is nothing wrong with his sight he heaves a sigh of relief and the anxieties vanish like hobgoblins. If we could once grasp that nausea and depression are simple forms of 'upside-downness', they would immediately cease to be dangerous.

My own panic attacks, described in chapter 1 of Part Two, reveal how dangerous they can be: I felt that I was slipping down a slope that led to insanity. At its worst 'upside-downness' produces a feeling of standing on the edge of an abyss. I have cited elsewhere* an interesting case in point concerning the novelist Margaret Lane. In 1945 a prolonged and difficult labour had left her in a condition of total exhaustion. She was delighted to be a mother but found herself in a dangerous state of emotional oversensitivity: when the cat caught its paw in the door she felt it was a major tragedy. At this point a copy of the *New Yorker* arrived containing John Hersey's famous account of the dropping of the atom bomb on Hiroshima. She said that it seemed so terrible that it blew all her emotional fuses. Suddenly she ceased to be capable of feeling; life became completely grey and uninteresting. She continued to be a good wife and mother by behaving as she 'ought' to behave; but she felt drained of all emotional response. One of the symptoms of this inner 'deadness' was that grass looked like blue paper and leaves looked like green tin. (These are well-known symptoms of schizophrenia.)

This state continued for a long time. Every time some pleasant circumstance started to arouse a response in her she became aware of what was happening and the feeling promptly disappeared. Living became a kind of ritual, without any love or hatred. But one day she and her husband were tempted to buy a cottage in Hampshire and went to view it. Naturally she was feeling more cheerful than usual, but as she walked alone in the field behind the cottage, the grass still looked like blue paper and the leaves looked like green tin. Suddenly she noticed some blue flowers: their blue was so intense that she stared at them with a flash of pleasure. As she did so the 'emotional freeze-up' vanished. The grass and leaves suddenly looked normal again. She burst into tears as she realized that the 'thaw' had started. And over the next few days the capacity to feel and respond slowly came back again.

Here the problem of 'upside-downness' can be studied in detail. The physical fatigue of a difficult birth had left her drained; Hersey's account of Hiroshima had the effect of plunging her into 'nausea', the feeling that human life is meaningless, brutish and short. When human beings are in a healthy state of mind their natural response to evil is a sensible desire to prevent it happening again, but 'nausea' brings a feeling of helplessness and passivity. So Margaret Lane found herself trapped in a vicious circle of negativity and 'upside-downness', which she was unable to escape because it seemed to her to be based upon a *logical* recognition. As her vitality fought back, her resistance increased. The pleasure of seeing the blue flowers produced a peak experience that lifted her clear of 'nausea' and freed her from the vicious circle of negativity, the 'Mephisophelean point of view'.

Beyond the Outsider: Appendix 1.

352

In Margaret Lane's experience we can see on a magnified scale something that happens to most of us a dozen times a day – that sudden feeling of 'let down', that life is, after all, rather an uphill struggle, and that perhaps we are fools to put so much effort into it. This feeling is accompanied by a mini-version of the collapse experienced by Margaret Lane. Because it is a mini-version, a mini-peak experience is enough to bring about a quick recovery – a dry martini, a favourite programme on television, the sound of a child laughing. But recognizing the mechanisms of the mini-collapse would be enough to prevent them from happening.

In Grace Metalious's *Return to Peyton Place* the heroine has a serious car accident because the accelerator of her car jams. The author comments that if she had been a more experienced driver she would have realized that she only had to put her toe underneath it and unjam it. The same applies to the 'vicious circles' that produce so many nervous breakdowns and suicides.

It now becomes possible to attempt an answer to the earlier question, What are we *doing* in this 'wooden world'? In states of visionary ecstasy mystics like Ouspensky *see* the answer to the basic problems of human existence, but it all happens so quickly that they cannot even begin to pin it down in language. And that is the problem: *to pin it down*. It could be compared to a traveller who is lost in a forest and who is suddenly whisked up into the air by an angel and shown the way to the nearest main road. But as soon as he is back on the ground he forgets what he saw. His problem is how to retain enough of it to draw a map.

When R. H. Ward was returning to waking consciousness, he remarks, 'the symbols we need if we are to comprehend "intuition"' were supplied.' In our 'wooden world' we need words and symbols to pin down meanings because we cannot *see* the meanings all the time: we keep losing them, like a man who goes into a room to get something then forgets what he went in for. Robert Graves's friend Smilley was unusual in this respect: he could 'see' the answer to a complex mathematical problem in one 'bird's-eye view' and did not need the mathematical symbols and formulae that enable the rest of us to grope our way to a solution. Symbols – and words and concepts – are our way of struggling towards the meanings we cannot grasp 'in a flash'. (Of course every one of us has sudden flashes of insight: the trouble is that we cannot connect them up to other insights.) Which explains, incidentally, why Ouspensky compared the 'mystical realm' to a world of complicated mathematical relations: mathematics is a model of the way we struggle from smaller to greater meanings.

So what we are doing with our slow and clumsy logic is advancing step by step into the realm of pure intuition, the mystical realm glimpsed by Ward and Ouspensky. It is of course very pleasant to have mystical glimpses of the meaning of life, but what gives human beings really deep satisfaction is to *pin them down* in words so that they cannot escape.

Please note that although most of us feel that life is painful and difficult – so that poets like to refer to it as a 'dim vast vale of tears' and to suggest that we are here to improve our characters – we all realize, in states of 'spring morning consciousness', that it *can* be a perpetual delight. Ouspensky is not being quite accurate when he talks about the 'wooden world'. In all states of consciousness above Level 4 the 'resistance' of the 'wooden world' is a source of delight: think of the pleasure of a skier who feels the wind whistling past his ears, of a racing driver travelling at top speed, of a strong swimmer forging his way against the current, and it is obvious that life experiences itself most intensely in the face of resistance. And this may explain why the force of life decided to undertake the hazardous venture of invading the realm of matter.

There its problems began. Before it could establish a foothold in matter it had to create the robot, and the robot soon became a Frankenstein's monster that came close to destroying its master. Its immense complexity robs life of spontaneity and undermines it with discouragement. Yet it should also be plain that human beings are now close to a turning-point in their evolution. It is at the lower levels of consciousness that life is most enslaved by the robot: at higher levels its influence becomes progressively less powerful until, at the mystical level, it vanishes entirely. At Level 4 human beings already catch repeated glimpses of Level 5 – 'holiday consciousness' and the peak experience. What prevents us from establishing a secure foothold on this higher level is the problem of 'upside-downness', and the peak experience makes us aware that *this is not a real problem*. Once we have grasped this insight and pinned it down in language, the problem will evaporate.

The basic weapon in this evolutionary struggle is language. Consider the following sobering reflection: if Voltaire could read the last dozen pages of this book he would not have the slightest idea of what we are talking about. He thought in cruder categories (atheism versus superstition, etc.), and for all his intelligence he would be as baffled as if I were talking Chinese. Yet most fairly intelligent modern readers can understand what we are saying without any difficulty. This is because language has succeeded in pushing so far into the realms of the unknown since the late eighteenth century. Every new concept – the fourth dimension, intentionality, the peak experience, Faculty X – is a bridgehead thrown out into that region of the inexpressible – Ouspensky's mystical level where everything is 'seen'. The business of language is to make these connections that Ward and Ouspensky *saw* as soon as they passed beyond the level of ordinary physical consciousness. And once these connections have been pinned down in language they become, so to speak, permanent revelations of meaning, like Margaret Lane's blue flowers.

This was an insight that suddenly struck me in the early 1970s when a friend came to see me to ask if I had any research he could do for me: he felt

354

he was on the verge of a nervous breakdown and wanted something to occupy his mind. I had to explain apologetically that I had nothing to offer. But as he left I gave him a copy of my book on Maslow, *New Pathways in Psychology*. A few days later he rang me. 'You knew what you were doing when you gave me that book, didn't you?' He told me that the first chapter, describing Maslow's concept of the peak experience, had lifted him straight out of his depression. Maslow's ideas had enabled him to *get to grips* with his problem, which until then had seemed a dangerous and invisible enemy. As he read the book the depression had simply evaporated.

The story underlines a point of central importance: it is surprisingly easy to move from one level to another; the chief obstacle is doubt – that moment-to-moment feeling that the efforts demanded by life are not really worth it. And, as Blake says:

If the sun and moon should doubt
They'd immediately go out.

Yet it is doubt that offers us the essential key to this problem. Consider what happens when you experience that sinking feeling, or when you force yourself to do some task that strikes you as a waste of time. You 'leak', and your energies drain away. Most of us spend a great deal of our lives trying to cope with leakage, with an underlying lack of enthusiasm for everyday tasks. Doubt causes our energies to become *scattered and diffused*. They could be compared to billiard balls scattered over a table-top. The moment we pay attention we draw the balls towards the centre of the table. If we become absorbed in something the balls press together into a tight cluster. If I am galvanized into intense concentration the pressure causes some of the balls to climb on top of the rest. But this is as far as most of us can get: the effort exhausts us, or some doubt intervenes, and we allow the balls to scatter once again. But occasionally, if some crisis or sense of purpose causes us to make some desperate effort of will – like a man standing before a firing squad – we can cause the balls to form a second tier and then even begin to form a third. As this happens the sense of meanings, of 'connections', becomes so exciting that we momentarily grasp the real purpose of our powers of concentration: to 'concentrate' the billiard balls into a pyramid. If we could actually achieve the 'pyramid' our minds would be fed by such a powerful sense of meaning from the 'ranges of distant fact' that 'doubt' would become an impossibility: there would be no temptation to allow the balls to scatter, any more than a child might be tempted to fall asleep in the middle of his birthday party. This is Faculty X, the level of concentration that precedes the mystical experience. It is a recognition of what human consciousness is one day destined to achieve, what Shaw's Captain Shotover called 'the seventh degree of concentration'. It

355

would be a state in which man would be totally in control of his 'hidden powers', and in which the evolutionary struggle would be conducted in the full conscious daylight of awareness. At that stage the negative forces that at present obstruct us would have been left far behind.

The history of human evolution reveals that such a development is inevitable. We have already noted that for its first half billion years, life on earth was little more than a ruthless struggle for survival, an endless record of brutality. This was hardly a recipe for Utopia, so the next step was a drive towards the development of intelligence. This was an astonishingly successful venture, and as recently as two-and-a-half thousand years ago a remarkable number of human beings began to grasp that the major aim of human existence is the development of intelligence and the creation of circumstances that will foster it. The invention of the drama in ancient Greece was one of the most important steps in this development. It taught men that they possess a theatre inside their own heads, and in this theatre Socrates and Plato taught their pupils to stage dramas of ideas. The evolution of man over the next two thousand years was the evolution of this inner theatre. Another name for it is imagination, for what it actually means is that man is playing out the dramas of the external world on an internal stage. And the development of imagination made man realize that this inner world is independent of the accidents and contingencies of matter. It was this recognition that transformed him from a remarkably intelligent ape into a being who recognized – no matter how dimly – that he was potentially a god.

What is imagination? It is the power to make connections. An uncle of mine once sat on the branch of a tree as he sawed it off at the trunk and was surprised when he landed on the ground: he had failed to make the necessary 'connections' in advance. That sounds absurd, but I have just done something almost equally absurd. I broke off work to make myself a cup of tea and absent-mindedly filled the kettle to the top, failing to 'see' that it would take much longer to boil. Imagination is the power to anticipate reality by conjuring up mental connections.

Now when imagination is working well it spreads like a forest fire and I 'see' all kinds of connections. (I am emphasizing the word 'see' because Ouspensky and Ward insist that they literally *saw* that everything in the universe is connected.) When I feel tired or dull, it is as if the forest is soaked in rain, and the fire fails to spread. But when I am feeling full of energy on a spring morning, my mind and my senses seem to combine to make dozens of connections – with past spring mornings, with childhood, with memories of the countryside, with water sparkling in the sunlight.... C. S. Lewis once said that the very *idea* of autumn filled him with deep longing, and again we can see that this longing is compounded of yellow leaves, the smell of bonfires, soft grey skies and the thought of toasted muffins, and a thousand other things. Our minds obviously have this power to 'spread sideways' into a thousand connections, but the wood is usually too damp to burn. Or to put it another way, our brains are too dull, so that the great treasury of memory hidden inside us is inaccessible to ordinary consciousness.

Sex is a particularly potent releaser of connections. It is easy to imagine that as Anthony made love to Cleopatra for the first time, or Paris to Helen, they experienced an almost mystical sense of total reconciliation, a sense that everything in the universe is good. This explains the perennial popularity of love stories: we only have to read about a boy falling in love with a girl to experience that warm surge of interest that means that the imagination is touched. It also explains the popularity of pornography – and here we encounter one of the most remarkable of human evolutionary developments. Man is the only creature on earth who can imagine a sexual act in such realistic detail that he can carry it through to a physical climax. As absurd as it sounds, masturbation is one of humankind's most remarkable evolutionary advances. But we can also see that the invention of the drama, and later of the novel, were remarkable extensions of the human power of imagination. With a novel in her hands the daughter of some nineteenth-century country vicar could live as richly as Helen of Troy – in a sense more richly, for the real Helen spent her days carding flax and trying to stave off boredom.

It was this development of imagination that gave rise to what we call the romantic movement, every one of whose poets and artists and musicians glimpsed this vision of the sheer variety of the universe. The vision always filled them with courage and pure affirmation, so that Shelley wrote:

I vowed that I would dedicate my powers
To thee and thine – have I not kept that vow?
With beating heart and streaming eyes, even now
I call the phantoms of a thousand hours
Each from his voiceless grave . . .

We can also see that Shelley is speaking of the same 'glimpse' that overwhelmed Proust as he tasted the madeleine.

These poets recognized that we should not blame the universe – or God – for the problems of human existence, but the narrowness of our senses. Blake wrote, 'Man has closed himself up, till he sees all things through the narrow chinks of his cavern,' while Goethe declared:

The spirit world is never closed
Your heart is dead, your senses shut . . .

Yet what made the romantics so miserable – sometimes to the point of suicide – was the feeling that there was nothing they could *do* about this narrowness: that man is trapped in a kind of prison and sentenced to life. It was true that the world of imagination permitted a certain freedom, yet indulgence in its delights only seemed to make them less capable of coping with the problems of the physical world. After a trip to the 'land of dreams' they usually felt completely debilitated. It seemed obvious that imagination was merely an *escape* from the harshness of 'real' reality and that it only made things worse when you had to cope with the dreariness of a cold Monday morning. Now a person who regards the world of the mind as unreal yet who feels he still prefers it to the stupidity and coarseness of reality is an 'Outsider', and the human race is still in the 'Outsider' phase of its evolution.

The 'Outsider' problem was perfectly defined by Carlyle when he talked about the conflict between Everlasting Yes and Everlasting No. In other words it was the problem of *which is true*: those moments of sheer affirmation when it is self-evident that life is infinitely fascinating, or the depressing sense of ordinariness that fills most of our waking lives. Some of Van Gogh's paintings are the most powerful expression of the affirmation experience ever made, yet he left a suicide note that read, 'Misery will never end.' Nietzsche's philosophy is the most penetrating and wholesale rejection of romantic pessimism ever made, yet he died insane. All the romantics were dragged down by this suspicion that their moments of vision were illusions and that optimism is only another name for whistling in the dark. Every one of us experiences a smaller version of the same problem a dozen times a day: a beam of sunlight brings a glow of happiness that is immediately succeeded by a 'sinking feeling' at the thought of the electricity bill. With these continual swoops from optimism to pessimism and back again it is not surprising that Shakespeare's Macbeth thought life a tale told by an idiot.

The solution to this ancient problem bursts upon us as soon as we understand the mechanisms of the robot. What tormented the romantics was the suspicion that the moments of vision and peak experiences were pleasant illusions caused by an overflow of vital energy, and that they had no more significance than the euphoria induced by alcohol. In that case the truth is that life is dull, boring and *ordinary*, and the artists who want to turn it into something mysterious and exciting are self-deceiving escapists. As soon as we understand the mechanisms of the robot we can see that this is simply untrue. The robot is rather like the damper on a piano which stops the strings from vibrating. But it is *natural* for a string to vibrate and to cause other strings to vibrate. Non-robotic consciousness is natural consciousness. This means that it is natural for consciousness to grasp the *connectedness* of things. When Maslow's marine saw a nurse for the first time in years he had a peak experience because he suddenly realized that women are different from men. She was not merely *a* woman, she was all women – the Eternal Feminine. And when human beings are in a state of intellectual excitement they suddenly glimpse the *implications* of

358

an idea: they seem to stretch out like the strands of an immense spider's web. The robot produces the sense of 'separateness' by damping our mental strings, but this is an interruption of the natural vibration.

In short it is the robot who dulls our senses so that they seem to be covered with a thin layer of some insulating material that prevents us from feeling anything; it is the robot who makes our experience seem dull and repetitive; it is the robot who reduces the infinitely complex world of reality to 'ordinariness'. *So robotic perception is false, and non-robotic perception is true.* If the romantics had understood this it would have removed the deep underlying cause of their misery and despair by making them aware that the moments of vision are a genuine perception, not some pleasant delusion. For *until* we can make up our minds about this basic question, life is bound to be a series of pendulum-swings between optimism and pessimism, determination and discouragement. We are in the position of a financier who is asked to invest in an enterprise that at one moment appears to be sound and prosperous and the next on the verge of bankruptcy: while he is unable to make up his mind his capital lies idle. The moment he knows the enterprise to be sound he can get on with the business of financing it. The moment we grasp that the apparent 'ordinariness' of the world is a delusion created by the robot and that 'absurd good news' is a glimpse of the underlying reality, we can get on with the business of transforming our lives.

How can we learn to escape the delusions of the robot? How can we transform robotic consciousness into non-robotic consciousness? This was the problem to which Gurdjieff devoted his life, and his solution consisted of what he called 'alarm clocks', a series of shocks and stimuli that would galvanize people out of their 'mechanicalness' into a higher level of effort – for, like James, he recognized that it is efforts and excitements that carry us over the dam. For example, Gurdjieff made a habit of entering the dormitory where his pupils were asleep and snapping his fingers, and everyone had to be out of bed and in some complicated position within seconds. Obviously such a technique would have the effect of encouraging alertness: the trouble with such methods is that they can easily become mechanical. But the real danger is that this strenuous approach tends to induce a sense of grim determination that easily slides into pessimism: it is sad to record that Ouspensky spent his last days drinking too much and daydreaming gloomily about the good old days in Russia. Even Gurdjieff conveyed a curious impression of sadness in his final years. It makes us aware that the 'freedom feeling' is essentially a sense of optimism, a feeling that life is full of marvellous possibilities. This happens when the subconscious mind is in a positive mood – in which state it is as if we had switched on a kind of rose-coloured underfloor lighting. This is what Maslow's students did when they began to think and talk about peak experiences, and it explains why they then continued to have peak experiences. The peak experience is a perception that all is well and that the 'upside-downness' which usually fills us with mistrust is a misunderstanding, a childish delusion.

This also enables us to see why Maslow was mistaken when he said that the peak experience cannot be induced at will. We *do* induce peak experiences, but the mechanism is so subtle that we fail to grasp how we do it. Goethe revealed that he understood the mechanism when he made the spirit tell Faust, 'Your heart is dead, your senses shut.' The heart, oddly enough, seems to be the essential organ concerned. When we are in a hurry or doing something we dislike, we *clench* the heart, exactly like clenching a fist, and nothing can get in. When we are filled with a sense of multiplicity and excitement we somehow 'open' the heart and allow reality to flow in. But in that state we only need to entertain the shadow of some unpleasant thought for it to close again. And human beings are so naturally prone to mistrust that it is hard to maintain the openness for very long. Children on the other hand find it easy to slip into states of wonder and delight when the heart finally opens so wide that the whole world seems magical. The 'trick' of the peak experience lies in this ability to relax out of our usual defensive posture and to 'open the heart'. Maslow's students quickly learned the trick, and then did it repeatedly.

We can now begin to understand the future direction of human evolution. Socrates once said that since the philosopher spends his life trying to separate his body from his spirit, death should be regarded as a consummation. That comment sounds like a piece of sophistry: yet if we can accept the evidence of the mystics and of the near-death experience, it may be less absurd than it sounds. In which case we are still left confronting the central question: if that is so, what are we doing here? And more importantly, what are we supposed to do now we are here? We can glimpse the answer in the peak experience and in what Ouspensky and Ward said about the mystical experience. If the 'all is well' feeling is a valid insight and not some absurd oversimplification, then human beings create most of their own problems through their confused and negative attitudes. They then compound the problem through mistrust and a kind of self-belittlement. Peak experiences bring the insight that if these attitudes could be eliminated we could live on a far higher level of affirmation and of freedom, a level – as Shaw put it in *Back to Methuselah* – on which all life would be akin to sexual ecstasy. H. G. Wells glimpsed the same vision in books like *A Modern Utopia* and *Men Like Gods*, but his scientific materialism made him see the problem in purely social terms so that he failed to grasp that the 'new age' could only be founded upon a new *psychological* insight: as a consequence his future Utopias seem oddly disappointing and unreal. The freedom insight, Maslow's recognition of 'higher ceilings of human nature', means that human beings are mistaken to assume that this world is, in its fundamental nature, a 'dim, vast vale of tears'. We are not trapped in some kind of original sin; only original stupidity. And stupidity can be overcome by a determined effort of intelligence.

At the present stage our problem is to grasp the mechanisms of the peak experience and to understand that the sinking feeling is not a glimpse of the basic meaninglessness of life but merely a 'leak' which reduces our inner pressure. It would then be self-evident, for example, that Sartre's nausea is merely a state in which the billiard balls are scattered all over the table-top: that is why meaning has collapsed – it is impossible to grasp meaning with scattered attention. The depression that made Graham Greene play Russian roulette was also a scattering of the billiard balls: the click of the hammer caused them to sweep together into the middle of the table, bringing a vision of meaning. The same applies to Proust's 'glimpse' as he tasted the madeleine: which means in turn that his sensation of ceasing to feel 'mediocre, accidental, mortal' was a *genuine perception*, a glimpse of 'hidden powers', not some vagary of the nervous system.

This book has been an attempt to show that these 'hidden powers' are a sign of our evolutionary potential. For anyone who is willing to consider it with an open mind, the evidence is overwhelming. When Alfred Russel Wallace found that a hypnotized schoolboy was 'sharing' his own sensations he had stumbled on an undiscovered human potential. So had William Denton when he realized that his wife and sister-in-law could 'read' the history of ancient stones. So had Arnold Toynbee when he 'saw' the battle of Pharsalus re-enacted. So had Jane O'Neill when she spent an hour in Fortheringhay church as it had existed five hundred years ago. So had Wilbur Wright when he dreamed winners of future horse-races. So had Susie Bauer when an intense longing somehow 'transported' her more than seven hundred miles. So had Ouspensky when he foresaw that he would not be making his intended trip to Moscow. All these cases, and hundreds more, make it clear that our assessment of human capabilities is absurdly limited and inaccurate. The mistake comes about through the limitations of our bodies and the dullness of our senses – *not* through our powers of reason. There is no contradiction between our powers of reason and the glimpses we achieve in moments of vision and flashes of 'intensity consciousness'. Our chief problem is to interpret these glimpses in terms of reason and logic. As we do so we become aware that there is a vital link between mystical experience, paranormal experience and the unexplored powers of imagination.

Let me try to state briefly what is at issue. Man is the first animal on earth to possess a sense of long-term purpose. The absurdity is that he applies this purpose to his physical life but not to his mental life. The result is that physically speaking he has become the lord of civilization, while mentally speaking he is still living in the days of

Ecclesiastes. He has climbed the world's highest mountains and explored its most inhospitable wildernesses, yet where consciousness is concerned he has hardly ventured beyond his own backyard. If he feels like a change of consciousness he pours himself a whisky or buys a ticket for the cup final. The result is that he accepts peak experiences as a pleasant kind of bonus instead of recognizing their implications: that all life could be a kind of continual peak experience. And so every time he climbs to the top of some foothill, he admires the view and then turns round and goes back to the bottom again, instead of recognizing that his real business is to scale the mountain that lies beyond. He does this because he takes it for granted that the natural state of the billiard balls that constitute his awareness is to remain scattered over the table-top, and that what he experiences when they are gathered in a tight cluster was never meant to be a permanent state of affairs. So he accepts mental stagnation as a norm (for that is what ordinary consciousness amounts to) and makes no attempt to build his insights into a pyramid.

As long as this remains true man will continue to mark time at his present stage of evolution. The moment it ceases to be true, the next stage of human evolution will commence.

Bibliography

Allen, Warner. *The Timeless Moment*. Faber & Faber, London.

Allison, M.D., Ralph with Schwarz, Ted. *Minds in Many Pieces*. Library of Congress, U.S.A., 1980.

Arkle, William. *The Hologram and Mind*. Acorn Publishing, Gloucester.

Baker, Dr Robin. *The Mystery of Migration*. Macdonald Futura Books, London, 1980.

Bancroft, Anne. *The Luminous Vision*. George Allen & Unwin, London, 1982. Allen & Unwin, U.S.A., 1982.

Barrett, Sir William. *Death-Bed Visions*. The Aquarian Press, Northamptonshire, 1986. First published 1926.

Barrow, John D. and Tipler, Frank J. *The Anthropic Cosmological Principle*. Clarendon Press, Oxford, 1986.

Bentov, Itzhak. *Stalking the Wild Pendulum*. E.P. Dutton, New York, 1977.

Bird, Christopher. *The Divining Hand*. E.P. Dutton, New York, 1979.

Blackmore, Susan J. *Beyond the Body*. Granada Publishing, 1983.

Blakeslee, Thomas R. *The Right Brain*. Macmillan Press, London, 1980.

Boyd, Doug. *Rolling Thunder*. Random House, New York, 1974.

Briggs John and Peat, F. David. *Looking Glass Universe*. Simon & Schuster, New York, 1984.

Buchanan, M.D., Joseph Rodes. *Manual of Psychometry: The Dawn of a New Civilization*. Holman Brothers, Boston. 1885.

Bucke, M.D., Richard Maurice *Cosmic Consciousness*. University Books, New York. 1961.

Capra, Fritjof. *The Tao of Physics*. Shambhala, California, U.S.A., 1975.

Carlson, Rick J. *The Frontiers of Science & Medicine*. Wildwood House, London, 1975.

Corliss, William R. *The Unfathomed Mind: A Handbook of Unusual Mental Phenomena*. The Sourcebook Project, Glen Arm. U.S.A., 1982.

Coxhead, Nona. *The Relevance of Bliss*. Wildwood House, London, 1985.

Crabtree, Adam. *Multiple Man: Explorations in Possession and Multiple Personality*. Collins, Ontario, Canada, 1985.

Cracknell, Robert. *Clues to the Unknown*. Hamlyn Paperbacks, Middlesex, 1981.

Crookall, Robert. *The Mechanisms of Astral Projection*. Darshana International, India, 1968.

Crowe, Catherine. *The Night-Side of Nature*. The Aquarian Press, Northamptonshire, 1986. First published 1848.

Denton, William. *The Soul of Things.* The Aquarian Press, Northamptonshire, 1988. First published 1863.

Dunne, J.W. *An Experiment with Time.* Faber and Faber, London, 1927.

Dunne, J.W. *The New Immortality.* Faber and Faber, London, 1927.

Ebon, Martin. *Exorcism: Fact Not Fiction.* New American Library, New York, 1974.

Flammarion, Camille. *The Unknown.* Harper & Brothers, London & New York, 1900.

Flammarion, Camille. *Death and Its Mystery: Before Death.* T. Fisher Unwin, London, 1921.

Flammarion, Camille. *Death and Its Mystery: At the Moment of Death.* T. Fisher Unwin, London, 1922.

Flammarion, Camille. *Death and Its Mystery: After Death.* T. Fisher Unwin, London, 1923.

Fodor, Nandor. *The Haunted Mind.* Garrett Publications, New York, 1959.

Forman, Joan. *The Mask of Time.* Macdonald and Jane's Publishers, London, 1978.

Gabbard, Glen O., and Twemlow, Stuart W. *With the Eyes of the Mind.* Praeger Publishers, U.S.A., 1984.

Garrett, Eileen J. *My Life.* Psychic Book Club, London, 1939.

Garrett, Eileen J. *Adventures in the Supernormal: A Personal Memoir.* Creative Age Press, New York, 1949.

Gooch, Stan. *Creatures from Inner Space.* Rider & Co., London, 1984.

Goss, Michael. *Poltergeists: An Annotated Bibliography of Works in English, circa 1880–1975.* The Scarecrow Press, Metuchen, N.J, U.S.A., London, 1979.

Green, Celia and McCreery, Charles. *Apparitions.* Hamish Hamilton, London, 1975.

Greene, Graham. *A Sort of Life.* The Bodley Head, London, 1971.

Greenhouse, Herbert B. *Premonitions: A Leap Into the Future.* Turnstone Press, London, 1972.

Grey, Margot. *Return From Death.* Arkana, London, 1985.

Gurney, E., Myers, F.W.H. and Podmore, F. *Phantasms of the Living, Vols. 1 & II* Trubner & Co., London, 1886.

Hardy, Sir Alister. *The Spiritual Nature of Man.* Oxford University Press, Oxford, 1979.

Heron, John. *Confessions of a Janus-Brain.* Tondymion Press, London, 1987.

Heywood, Rosalind. *The Infinite Hive.* Pan Books Ltd, London, 1966.

Hofstadter, Douglas R. and Dennett, Daniel C. *The Mind's I.* Penguin Books Ltd, Middlesex, 1982.

Hudson, Thomson Jay. *The Law of Psychic Phenomena.* G.P. Putnam's Sons, London 1902.

Hurley, J. Finley. *Sorcery.* Routledge & Kegan Paul, London and U.S.A. 1985.

Hutchison, Michael. *Megabrain*. Beech Tree Books, 1986.

Inglis, Brian. *Science and Parascience*. Hodder & Stoughton, London and U.S.A., 1984.

Inglis, Brian. *Natural and Supernatural*. Hodder & Stoughton, London and U.S.A., 1977.

Jaynes, Julian. *The Origin of Consciousness in the Breakdown of the Bicameral Mind*. Houghton Mifflin, U.S.A., 1976.

Jenkins, Stephen. *The Undiscovered Country*. Neville Spearman, Suffolk, 1977.

Jinarajadasa, C. *Occult Investigations: A Description of the Work of Annie Besant and C.W. Leadbeater*. The Theosophical Publishing House, India, 1938.

Johnson, Raynor C. *Watcher on the Hills*. Hodder & Stoughton, London, 1959.

Jung, C.G. *Memories, Dreams, Reflections*. Recorded and edited by Aniela Jaffe. Collins and Routledge & Kegan Paul, London, 1963.

Kardec, Allan. *The Spirits' Book*. Lake-Livraria Allan Kardec Editora Ltd, Brazil, 1972.

Keller, Helen. *The Story of My Life*. Doubleday, New York, 1954.

Keyes, Daniel. *The Minds of Billy Milligan*. Random House, New York 1981.

King, C. Daly. *The States of Human Consciousness*. University Books, New York, 1963.

Knight, David C. *The E.S.P. Reader*. Castle Books, U.S.A., 1969.

Koestler, Arthur. *The Invisible Writing: Being the Second Volume of Arrow in the Blue*. Collins with Hamish Hamilton, London, 1954.

Krippner, Ph.D., Stanley. *Human Possibilities*. Anchor Press/Doubleday, New York, 1980.

Krippner, Ph.D., Stanley and/Villoldo, Alberto. *The Realms of Healing*. Celestial Arts, California, 1986.

LeShan, Lawrence. *Toward a General Theory of the Paranormal*. Parapsychological Monographs No. 9. Parapsychology Foundation, Inc., New York, 1969.

LeShan, Lawrence. *The Medium, the Mystic and the Physicist*. Turnstone Press, London & U.S.A., 1974.

Lethbridge, T.C. *Ghost and Ghoul*. Routledge & Kegan Paul, London, 1961.

Lethbridge, T.C. *The Power of the Pendulum*. Routledge & Kegan Paul, London, 1976.

Lewis, C.S. *The Screwtape Letters*. Fontana Books, London, 1955.

Lewis, I.M. *Ecstatic Religion*. Penguin Books, Middlesex and U.S.A., 1971.

Long, Max Freedom. *The Secret Science Behind Miracles*. DeVorss, California, 1981.

Lorimer, David. *Survival? Body, Mind and Death in the Light of Psychic Experience*. Routledge & Kegan Paul, London and U.S.A., 1984.

Lyttelton, Edith. *Our Superconscious Mind*. Philip Allan, 1931.

McDermott, John J. *The Writings of William James*. Random House, New York, 1967.

McKellar, Peter. *Mindsplit*. J. M. Dent, London, 1979.

MacKenzie, Andrew. *Riddle of the Future*. Arthur Barker Ltd, London, 1974.

MacKenzie, Andrew. *The Seen and the Unseen*. Weidenfeld and Nicolson, London, 1987.

Maeterlinck, Maurice. *The Unknown Guest*. Methuen, London, 1914.

Markides, Kyriacos C. *The Magus of Strovolos*. Routledge & Kegan Paul, London and U.S.A., 1985.

Martensen, Hans L., *Jacob Boehme: Studies in his Life and Teaching*. Rockliff, London, 1949.

Mavromatis, Andreas. *Hypnagogia*. Routledge & Kegan Paul, London and New York, 1987.

Merrell-Wolff, Franklin. *Pathways Through to Space*. Julian Press, New York, 1983.

Merrell-Wolff, Franklin. *The Philosophy of Consciousness Without an Object*. Julian Press, New York, 1983.

Michell, John and Rickard, J.M. *Phenomena: A Book of Wonders*. Thames & Hudson, London, 1977.

Monroe, Robert A. *Journeys Out of the Body*. Doubleday, U.S.A., and Souvenir Press Ltd, London, 1972.

Moody, Jr., Raymond A. *Life After Life*. Bantam Books, U.S.A. 1975.

Moody, Jr., Raymond A. *Reflections On Life After Life*. Corgi Books, London, 1978.

Muldoon, Sylvan J. and Carrington, Hereward. *The Projection of the Astral Body*. Rider & Co. London, 1968.

Muldoon, Sylvan J. and Carrington, Hereward. *The Phenomena of Astral Projection*. Rider & Co., London, 1969.

Murray, Muz. *Sharing the Quest*. Element Books, Dorset, 1986.

Myers, F.W.H. *Human Personality and its Survival of Bodily Death*. University Books, New York, 1961.

Noakes, Ben. Ed. *Saw a Ghost*. Weidenfeld & Nicolson, London, 1986.

Oesterreich, T.K. *Possession, Demoniacal and Other*. Kegan Paul, Trench, Trubner, London, 1930.

Ornstein, Robert E. *The Nature of Human Consciousness*. W. H. Freeman, San Francisco, 1973.

Osborn, Arthur W. *The Future is Now*. University Books, New York, 1961.

Osty, Eugene. *Supernormal Faculties in Man*. Methuen, London, 1923.

Ouspensky, P.D. *A New Model of the Universe*. Routledge & Kegan Paul, London, 1931.

Penfield, Wilder. *The Mystery of the Mind*. Princeton University Press, Surrey and New Jersey, 1975.

Platt, Charles. *Dream Makers*. Xanadu Publications, London, 1987.

Playfair, Guy. *The Flying Cow*. Souvenir Press, London, 1975.

Playfair, Guy. *The Indefinite Boundary*. Souvenir Press, London, 1976.

Playfair, Guy. *This House is Haunted*. Souvenir Press, London, 1980.

Playfair, Guy. *If This is Magic*. Jonathan Cape, London, 1985.

Priestley, J. B. *Man and Time*. Aldus Books, London, 1964.

Priestley, J. B. *Over the Long High Wall*. Heinemann, London, 1972.

Prince, Morton. *The Dissociation of a Personality*. Longmans, Green. New York, London, Bombay & Calcutta, 1913.

Prince, Morton (and others). *The Doris Case of Quintuple Personality: Contributions to Psychology*. Richard G. Badger, Gorham Press, Boston, 1916.

Prince, Walter Franklin. *Noted Witnesses for Psychic Occurrences*. University Books, New York, 1963.

Rhine, J. B. *The Reach of the Mind*. Penguin Books, Middlesex and U.S.A. 1954.

Richet, Ph.D., Charles. *Thirty Years of Psychical Research*. W. Collins Sons, London, 1923.

Rogo, D. Scott. *Phantoms: Experiences and Investigations*. David & Charles, Devon, 1976.

Rogo, D. Scott. *The Infinite Boundary*. Dodd, Mead & Co. Inc. New York, 1987.

Russell, Peter. *The Brain Book*. Hawthorn Books, New York, 1979.

St Clair, David. *Drum and Candle*. Macdonald, London, 1971.

Sanderson, Ivan T. *'Things' and More 'Things'*. Pyramid Books, New York, 1967.

Schatzman, M.D., Morton. *The Story of Ruth*. Zebra Books, New York.

Shallis, Michael. *On Time*. Burnett Books, London, 1982.

Sinclair, Upton. *Mental Radio. Does it work, and how?* Werner Laurie, London, 1930.

Staal, Frits. *Exploring Mysticism*. Penguin Books, Middlesex, 1975.

Stevenson, M.D., Ian. *Twenty Cases Suggestive of Reincarnation*. American Society for Psychical Research, New York, 1966.

Tart, Charles T. *Altered States of Consciousness*. Anchor Books, New York, 1969.

Taylor, John. *The Shape of Minds to Come*. Michael Joseph, London, 1971.

Thurston, S. J., Herbert. *Ghosts and Poltergeists*. Burns Oates and Washbourne, London, 1953.

Toynbee, Arnold T. *A Study of History*. Oxford University Press, New York, 1963.

Tyrrell, G.N.M. *The Personality of Man*. Penguin Books, Middlesex, 1947.

Vallee, Jacques. *Messengers of Deception*. And/Or Press, U.S.A., 1979.

Van Dusen, Wilson. *The Natural Depth In Man*. Harper & Row, New York, 1972.

Van Dusen, Wilson. *The Presence of Other Worlds*. Harper & Row, New York, 1974.

Vaughan, Alan. *Incredible Coincidence: The Baffling World of Synchronicity*. Signet Books, New York, 1980.

Volgyesi, Ferenc Andras. *Hypnosis of Man and Animals*. Bailliere, Tindall & Cassell, London, 1966.

Ward, R. H. *A Drug Taker's Notes*. Gollancz, London, 1957.

Watson, Peter. *Twins*. Sphere Books, London, 1984.

Watts, Alan W. *The Way of Zen*. Penguin Books, Middlesex and U.S.A., 1957.

Webb, James. *The Harmonious Circle*. Thames & Hudson, London, 1980.

Wilbur, Ken. *The Holographic Paradigm and Other Paradoxes*. Shambhala Publications, Colorado, 1982.

Wilson, Colin. *The Occult*. Hodder & Stoughton, London, and Random House, New York, 1971.

Wilson, Colin. *Mysteries*. Hodder & Stoughton, London, 1978.

Wilson, Colin. *New Pathways in Psychology*. Victor Gollancz, London, 1979.

Wilson, Colin. *Poltergeist!* New English Library, London, 1981.

Wilson, Colin. *Afterlife*. Harrap, London, 1985.

Wilson, Colin. *Rudolf Steiner: The Man and His Vision*. The Aquarian Press, Northamptonshire, 1985.

Wilson, Colin. *The Essential Colin Wilson*. Harrap, London, 1985.

Wilson, Colin. *The Psychic Detectives*. Pan Books, London. (Paperback) 1984, Mercury House, California, 1985.

Wilson, Colin with Wilson, Damon. *The Encyclopedia of Unsolved Mysteries*. Harrap, London, 1987.

Wilson, Donald Powell. *My Six Convicts*. Panther, London, 1956.

Zdenek, Marilee. *The Right Brain Experience*. Corgi Books, London, 1985.

Zohar, Danah. *Through the Time Barrier*. Granada Publishing Ltd, London, 1983.

Index

93, 94–6, 97, 327, 361; negative vision, 73, 100; 'useless passion', 71
Sathi, Spyros, *see* Daskalos
Schaberl, Anne-Marie, 234
Schatzman, Morton: *Story of Ruth*, 255
schizophrenia, 74, 75
Schmidt, Helmut, 151–2
Scholz, Wilhelm von: *Chance*, 146
Schopenhauer, Arthur, 169; *World as Will and Idea*, 71
Schreiber, Flora Rheta: *Sybil*, 224
Schumann waves, 106–7
Schwartz, Stephen, 300; *Secret Vaults of Time*, 300 n
Science, 167
Scotsman, The, 80
Scott-Elliott, W., 137
Screwtape Letters, The (Lewis), 97, 213
Seale, Jack, 194–5, 208–9
Seaton, David, 249–50
second sight, 30
Secret Science behind Miracles, The (Long), 224–7, 244
Secret Vaults of Time, The (Schwartz), 300 n
Seen and the Unseen, The (MacKenzie), 178 n
Séguier, 199
Seifert, 200
Self and Its Brain, The (Popper/Eccles), 228
self-hypnosis, 34, 268, 321
self-suggestion, 321
Selleny, Josef, 267–8
serial universe, 172
Seven Sermons to the Dead (Jung), 144
sex instinct, 71–2, 73, 96–7, 189–90, 233, 248, 249, 254, 256, 325, 357
Shackleton, Basil, 147
Shakespeare, William, 59, 65, 224, 358
Shallis, Michael: *On Time*, 161
shamans, see witch-doctors
Shanti Devi, 228–30
Sharing the Quest (Murray), 22
Shaw, G. B., 342, 355; *Back to Methuselah*, 360
Shelley, P. B., 357
Sherman, William, 29, 114, 122
Showery, Allan, 261–2
Sidgwick, Henry, 247
Siegfried, 140
Silberer, Herbert: *Chance*, 146
Silva, Edivaldo, 241, 242
Silverman, J., 74–5
Sinclair, May, 132–3, 139, 141, 142, 143, 157, 162
Sinclair, Upton: *Mental Radio*, 132–3, 139

Sinister Street (Mackenzie), 318, 331
Sizemore, Christine, 217–18, 219, 221, 224, 231, 279; *Eve*, 217–18
Skylab, 308–9
Slater, Bill, 269–70
Smilley, F. F., 54–5, 171, 353
Smythe, Frank L., 82; *Mountain Vision*, 79–80
Soal, S. G., 147, 151
Society for Psychical Research, 28, 62
Socrates, 57, 130, 231, 232, 256, 356, 360
somnambulism, 198
Sophia, 283
Sorcery (Hurley), 273 n
Sort of Life, A (Greene), 73, 74, 86, 91, 98
Soul of Things, The (Denton), 29 n, 108–9, 137
space–time continuum, 174
Spencer, Herbert, 44
Sperry, Roger, 64–5
Spirits' Book, The (Kardec), 240–1, 265
Spiritual Diary (Swedenborg), 138–9
Spiritual Nature of Man, The (Hardy), 38 n
spiritualism, 135–6, 229–30, 231–2, 239, 258, 259, 313
Springer, Jim, 167, 168–9
Stalking the Wild Pendulum (Bentov), 112–13
States of Human Consciousness, The (King), 317
Stead, W. T., 165
Steiner, Rudolf, 138, 139, 315, 343; Akashic Records, 136, 137, 143; *Cosmic Memory*, 137; Daskalos, 310, 311, 312, 313; 'Dead Are With Us', 138; Eliot on, 335–6; 'intellectual soul', 253; 'Never complain', 240; self-awareness, 172; spiritualism, 135–6, 137–8, 316
Steppenwolf (Hesse), 43, 132, 347, 348
Stevens, W. W., 229–30
Stevenson, Ian: *Twenty cases*, 228
Stewart, Gloria, 151
Stiles, Mr, 300
Stohr, Oscar, 167
Stoker, Bram, 307
Stoker, Leading Aircraftsman, 259–60, 261
Story of My Life, The (Keller), 88–9
Story of Ruth, The (Schatzman), 255
Strange Life of Ivan Osokin, The (Ouspensky), 160
Strange Powers (Wilson), 251
Strength to Dream, The (Wilson), 352
Stroud, John, 166
Study of History, A (Toynbee), 80, 81, 83–4
'Suggestion about Mysticism, A' (James), 53

suicide: tendency towards, 69, 73, 74, 87, 91, 96, 98, 361

Sulla, 109

Sullivan, Mrs, 88–9

Summers, Rev. Montague, 253, 254; *History of Witchcraft*, 251

Sunday Express, The, 251

Sunday Times, The 148

Sungma, 272–3

superconscious, 36

Surin, Fr Jean-Joseph, 264–5

Swedenborg, Emanuel, 270–1; *Spiritual Diary*, 138–9

Sybil (Schreiber), 224

synchronicity, 59, 145–53, 156, 165–6, 177, 179, 210, 313, 342

Tanous, Alex, 193

Tart, Charles, 185, 192

Taylor, John, 227

telepathy, 30, 121, 133, 199, 202–4, 280; and astral projection, 62; *doppelgängers*, 186–7; Gooch, 134; Playfair, 133–4, Sinclair, 139, 141; word coined, 61, 109

terreiros, 244, 252

Tesla, Nicola, 60

Theosophical Society, 136, 137

Thigpen: *Three Faces of Eve*, 217, 278

This House Is Haunted (Playfair), 256

Thomas, Dylan, 95; 'Lament', 71

Thompson, Frederick, 266–7

thought transference, 109

Three Faces of Eve (Thigpen/Cleckley), 217, 278

Through the Time Barrier (Zahar), 177

Thus Spake Zarathustra (Nietzsche), 102

Tidman, Graham, 158

time: Dunne, 157–8, 172, 173, 174; extended, 112–14; Garrett, 104–5, 125; Moore, 35; Shallis, 161; 'time-pockets', 79–85, 104, 112, 113, 136, 331, 332; 'time-slips', 210, 332; Wright, 173, 174, 180

Time and the Conways (Priestley), 160

Timeless Moment, The (Allen), 35

Tipler, Frank: *Anthropic Cosmological Principle* 340–1

Titanic, 165

Toldoth Jeschu, 136

Tombe Eric, 262–3

Total Man (Gooch), 254

Toward a General Theory of the Paranormal (LeShan), 31, 35, 83 n

Toynbee, Arnold: Crete, 80; Ephesus, 80–1; Mistra, 81, 83, 91, 94, 99–100, 112;

Monemvasia, 81; Mutilus, 83–4; Pharsalus, 79–80, 81, 83, 99–100, 104, 105, 112, 113, 137, 348, 361; *Study of History*, 80, 81, 83–4, 214; 'time-pockets', 79–85, 104, 112, 113, 136, 331, 332

trabalho, 252, 253

Tranquille, Fr, 264, 273

transcendental meditation, 89–91, 204

Transcutaneous Electro-Neural Stimulator, 345

Tremlow, Stuart W.: *With the Eyes of the Mind*, 186

trivial values, 99–100

Trollope, Anthony, 75

Tucker, Albert and Barbara, 288–92, 320–1, 324, 327, 331, 344

Twenty Cases Suggestive of Reincarnation (Stevenson), 228

twins, 166–9

Tyrrell, G. N. M.: *Personality of Man*, 208

umbanda, 245, 252

Unaccountable, The (Fodor), 300

unconscious, 225; collective, 139–41, 143, 334

'Under Ben Bulben' (Yeats), 209

Undiscovered Country, The (Jenkins), 114

Unfathomed Mind, The (Corliss), 206

universal memory, 311

Unknown, The (Flammarion), 149

'Unknown, The' (Maupassant), 96–7, 100

upside-downness, 99–102, 326–7, 330–1, 350, 351, 352, 360

Valis (Dick), 272

Vallee, Jacques, 148

Van Buuren, Clarence, 142

Van Dusen, Wilson, 128–30, 131; *Natural Depth in Man*, 138 n; *Presence of Other Worlds*, 138 n, 270–1

Van Eeden, Frederik, 195–6

Van Gogh, Vincent, 358

Vennum, Lurancy, 229–30

Verity, L. S., 61–2, 182, 206

Veronica, 175, 284

Verrall, Margaret, 33–4

Versailles, 103–4, 179

vision, 213, 287–312; moments of vision, 22, 25, 27

vitalism, 342

Viv, Louis, 263–4

Vogel, Marcel, 134

Volgyesi, F. A.: *Hypnosis of Man and Animals*, 202

380